The Digital Filmmaking Handbook

Fourth Edition

The Digital Filmmaking Handbook

Fourth Edition

Sonja Schenk
Ben Long

COURSE TECHNOLOGY
CENGAGE Learning™

Australia, Brazil, Japan, Korea, Mexico, Singapore, Spain, United Kingdom, United States

COURSE TECHNOLOGY
CENGAGE Learning™

The Digital Filmmaking Handbook
Fourth Edition
Sonja Schenk and Ben Long

Publisher and General Manager,
Course Technology PTR: Stacy L. Hiquet

Associate Director of Marketing:
Sarah Panella

Manager of Editorial Services:
Heather Talbot

Marketing Manager: Jordan Castellani

Acquisitions Editor: Megan Belanger

Project Editor and Copy Editor: Marta Justak

Technical Reviewer: Ben Nilsson

Interior Layout Tech: Judy Littlefield

Cover Designer: Mike Tanamachi

Indexer: Valerie Haynes Perry

Proofreader: Sue Boshers

For product information and technology assistance, contact us at
Cengage Learning Customer & Sales Support, 1-800-354-9706.

For permission to use material from this text or product, submit all requests online at **cengage.com/permissions.**
Further permissions questions can be emailed to
permissionrequest@cengage.com.

All trademarks are the property of their respective owners.

All images © Cengage Learning unless otherwise noted.

Library of Congress Control Number: 2011926543

ISBN-13: 978-1-4354-5911-3

ISBN-10: 1-4354-5911-3

Course Technology, a part of Cengage Learning
20 Channel Center Street
Boston, MA 02210
USA

Cengage Learning is a leading provider of customized learning solutions with office locations around the globe, including Singapore, the United Kingdom, Australia, Mexico, Brazil, and Japan. Locate your local office at: **international.cengage.com/region.**

Cengage Learning products are represented in Canada by Nelson Education, Ltd.

For your lifelong learning solutions, visit **courseptr.com.**

Visit our corporate Web site at **cengage.com.**

Printed in the United States of America
2 3 4 5 6 7 13 12

ACKNOWLEDGMENTS

Many thanks to our editor, Marta Justak, for having the vision to take this book to the next level and to Judy Littlefield for making it a reality. Thank you to our technical editor, Ben Nilsson, for offering exceptional expertise and sharing his passion for filmmaking. And a special thank you to our publisher, Stacy Hiquet, without whom this book would not exist.

Last, but not least, we'd like to thank the filmmakers who gave us their photos, their video clips and, most importantly, their stories: Alexandra Komisaruk, Regina Saisi, William MacCollum, Paquita Parks, and Jason Hampton.

ABOUT THE AUTHORS

Sonja Schenk is a Los Angeles-based writer, director, and producer. As a filmmaker, she directed the feature-length comedy, *The Olivia Experiment,* and has written several screenplays. Her short films have been shown in film festivals and galleries across the country. Her producing credits include several prominent television series, including *The Bachelor, High School Reunion,* and others. She has edited scripted feature films shown at film festivals such as Sundance and documentaries for European and American television. She is also the author of an editing handbook, *Digital Nonlinear Desktop Editing,* and has contributed many articles on filmmaking and technology to various publications.

Ben Long is a San Francisco-based photographer, videographer, and writer. The author of over a dozen books on digital photography and digital video, he has been a long-time contributor to many magazines, including *MacWeek, MacUser, MacWorld UK,* and more. He is currently a senior contributing editor for *Macworld* magazine, a senior editor at CreativePro.com, and has created several photography instruction courses for Lynda.com. With experience in every aspect of video production, Long's video clients have included Global Business Network, Blue Note Records, and 20th Century Fox. His videos have played around the world, on Broadway, and up and down the Hudson River accompanied by acclaimed musician Don Byron. He also dabbles in computer programming, and has written image editing utilities that are in use in the Smithsonian, the British Museum, and the White House.

CONTENTS

INTRODUCTION . . . .**xxiii**

1 **Getting Started** **2**

Better, Cheaper, Easier 3
Who This Book Is For 8
What Kind of Digital Film Should You Make? 8

2 **Writing and Scheduling** **12**

Screenwriting 13
  Finding a Story 14
  Structure 14
  Writing Visually 16
  Formatting Your Script 18
  Writing for Television 23
  Writing for "Unscripted" 24
  Writing for Corporate Projects 25
Scheduling 26
Breaking Down a Script. 27
  Choosing a Shooting Order 29
  How Much Can You Shoot in a Day? 29
  Production Boards 30
  Scheduling for Unscripted Projects 32

3

Digital Video Primer 34

What Is HD? 35
Components of Digital Video 36
   Tracks. 36
   Frames. 36
   Scan Lines 37
   Pixels 38
   Audio Tracks. 41
   Audio Sampling 42
Working with Analog or SD Video. 43
Digital Image Quality 46
   Color Sampling 47
   Bit Depth 48
   Compression Ratios 49
   Data Rate 49
Understanding Digital Media Files 49
   Digital Video Container Files 50
   Codecs. 50
   Audio Container Files and Codecs 55
Transcoding 55
Acquisition Formats 57
Unscientific Answers to Highly Technical Questions. 58

4

Choosing a Camera 60

Evaluating a Camera 61
Image Quality 62
   Sensors 62
   Compression. 65
   Sharpening. 66
   White Balance 68
   Image Tweaking 68
Lenses 69
   Lens Quality 69
   Lens Features. 70
   Interchangeable Lenses 71

Never Mind the Reasons, How Does It Look?. 72
Camera Features. 73
    Camera Body Types 73
    Manual Controls 76
    Focus 76
    Shutter Speed. 77
    Aperture Control 79
    Image Stabilization 81
    Viewfinder. 82
    Interface. 83
    Audio 84
    Media Type. 85
    Wireless 86
    Batteries and AC Adaptors 86
DSLRs 87
Use Your Director of Photography 88
Accessorizing 89
    Tripods 89
    Field Monitors. 90
    Remote Controls 90
    Microphones. 90
    Filters 90
    All That Other Stuff 91
What You Should Choose 91

5 Planning Your Shoot .92

Storyboarding 93
    Shots and Coverage 95
    Camera Angles 97
    Computer-Generated Storyboards 101
    Less Is More. 104
Camera Diagrams and Shot Lists. 104
Location Scouting 108

Production Design. 112
    Art Directing Basics 113
    Building a Set. 113
    Set Dressing and Props. 114
    DIY Art Direction. 114
Visual Planning for Documentaries 116
Effects Planning 117
    Creating Rough Effects Shots 119

6 Lighting 120

Film-Style Lighting. 121
The Art of Lighting. 122
    Three-Point Lighting 122
Types of Light 125
    Color Temperature 125
    Types of Lights 126
    Wattage 126
Controlling the Quality of Light. 129
    Lighting Gels. 131
    Diffusion. 131
Lighting Your Actors 132
    Tutorial: Three-Point Lighting 132
Interior Lighting. 135
    Power Supply 135
    Mixing Daylight and Interior Light 135
    Using Household Lights 136
Exterior Lighting 136
    Enhancing Existing Daylight 137
Video Lighting. 138
Low-Light Shooting 139
Special Lighting Situations. 139
    Lighting for Video-to-Film Transfers 140
    Lighting for Blue and Green Screen. 140

7 **Using the Camera** **142**

Setting Focus 143
Using the Zoom Lens 147
    Controlling the Zoom. 151
Exposure. 152
    Aperture 153
    Shutter Speed. 154
    Gain 156
    Which One to Adjust? 157
    Exposure and Depth of Field 157
White Balancing 158
Composition 162
    Headroom 164
    Lead Your Subject. 164
    Following Versus Anticipating 167
    Don't Be Afraid to Get Too Close 167
    Listen 168
    Eyelines 168
    Clearing Frame. 169
    Beware of the Stage Line. 169
    TV Framing. 169
    Breaking the Rules 170
Camera Movement 170
    Panning and Tilting. 170
    Zooms and Dolly Shots 171
    Tracking Shots 171
    Handholding. 171
    Deciding When to Move 173
Shooting Checklist. 174

8 Production Sound 176

What You Want to Record 177
Microphones. 178
    What a Mic Hears 179
    How a Mic Hears 182
    Types of Mics 183
    Mixing 185
    Connecting It All Up 186
    Wireless Mics 187
Setting Up. 188
    Placing Your Mics 188
    Getting the Right Sound for the Picture 194
    Testing Sound. 195
    Reference Tone 196
    Managing Your Set 196
Recording Your Sound 197
    Room Tone. 198
    Run-and-Gun Audio 198
Gear Checklist. 199

9 Shooting and Directing .200

The Shooting Script. 201
    Updating the Shooting Script. 202
Directing. 202
Rehearsals 203
Managing the Set 204
Putting Plans into Action 205
    Double-Check Your Camera Settings 206
    The Protocol of Shooting. 206
    Respect for Acting 206
Organization on the Set. 208
    Script Supervising for Scripted Projects 208
    Documentary Field Notes 209

10   DSLRs and Other Advanced Shooting Situations 210

What's Different with a DSLR? 211
DSLR Camera Settings for HD Video 214
Working with Interchangeable Lenses 216
    What Lenses Do I Need? 216
How to Get a Shallow Depth of Field 218
Measuring and Pulling Focus 219
    Measuring Focus 220
    Pulling Focus 220
Advanced Camera Rigging and Supports. 221
Viewing Video on the Set 224
Double-System Audio Recording. 227
    How to Record Double-System Audio 229
Multi-Cam Shooting. 230
    Multi-Cam Basics 231
    Challenges of Multi-Cam Shoots 232
Going Tapeless 233
    On-set Media Workstations 234
    Media Cards and Workflow 234
    Organizing Media on the Set 235
    Audio Media Workflow 237
Shooting Blue-Screen Effects 237

11   Editing Gear 240

Setting Up a Workstation. 241
    CPU 242
    RAM. 242
    Storage. 242
    Monitors 243
    Videotape Interface. 244
    Custom Keyboards and Controllers 246
    Backing Up 246
Networked Systems. 247
    Storage Area Networks (SANs) and Network-Attached
        Storage (NAS) 247
    Cloud Storage. 248
    Render Farms. 248

Audio Equipment 249
Digital Video Cables and Connectors 250
    FireWire 250
    HDMI 250
    SDI and HD-SDI 250
    Fibre Channel 251
    Thunderbolt 251
    RS-422 251
    Audio Interfaces 251
Know What You Need 252

12   Editing Software 254

The Interface 255
Editing Tools 256
    Drag-and-Drop Editing 256
    Three-Point Editing 256
    JKL Editing 257
    Insert and Overwrite Editing 257
    Trimming 258
    Ripple and Roll, Slip and Slide 258
    Multi-Camera Editing 259
    Advanced Features 260
Organizational Tools 261
Importing Media 262
Effects and Titles 264
    Types of Effects 264
    Titles 266
Audio Tools 266
    Equalization 267
    Audio Effects and Filters 267
    Audio Plug-In Formats 267
    Mixing 267
    OMF Export 268
Finishing Tools 268
Our Software Recommendations 268
Know What You Need 269

13

Preparing to Edit 270

Organizing Your Media 272
    Create a Naming System. 273
    Setting Up Your Project. 274
Importing and Transcoding 276
Capturing Tape-based Media. 280
    Logging. 280
    Capturing 282
Importing Audio 282
Importing Still Images 283
Moving Media. 284
Sorting Media After Ingest. 285
    How to Sort by Content 286
Synchronizing Double-System Sound and Picture 286
Preparing Multi-Camera Media 288
Troubleshooting 288

14

Editing 290

Editing Basics. 291
    Applied Three-Act Structure 293
Building a Rough Cut 293
    Watch Everything 294
    Radio Cuts 294
    Master Shot—Style Coverage 294
        Tutorial: Creating a First Cut 295
Editing Techniques 305
    Cutaways and Reaction Shots 305
    Matching Action 306
    Matching Screen Position 307
    Overlapping Edits 307
    Matching Emotion and Tone 308
    Pauses and Pull-Ups 308
    Hard Sound Effects and Music 309
        Tutorial: Refining Your Cut 309

Transitions Between Scenes 311
  Hard Cuts. 311
  Dissolves, Fades, and Wipes 311
  Establishing Shots. 311
  Clearing Frame and Natural "Wipes". 312
Solving Technical Problems. 312
  Missing Elements 312
  Temporary Elements 312
Multi-Cam Editing 313
Fine Cutting 314
  Editing for Style. 314
  Duration 315
  The Big Picture. 315

15 Sound Editing 316

Sounding Off. 317
Setting Up. 318
Temp Mixes 319
Audio Levels Metering. 320
  Clipping and Distortion 321
Using Your Editing App for Sound 321
Dedicated Sound Editing Apps 325
Moving Your Audio 327
Editing Sound 328
  Unintelligible Dialogue 328
  Changes in Tone. 329
  Is There Extraneous Noise in the Shot? 329
  Are There Bad Video Edits That Can Be Reinforced with
    Audio? 330
  Is There Bad Audio? 330
  Are There Vocal Problems You Need to Correct? 330
Dialogue Editing 331
  ADR. 332
  Non-Dialogue Voice Recordings 332
EQ Is Your Friend 333
Sound Effects 336
  Sound Effect Sources 337

Music 337
    Editing Music 338
    License to Play 339
    Finding a Composer 340
    Do It Yourself 341
Fix It in the Mix 342

16 Color Correction 344

Color Correction 346
    Advanced Color Controls. 349
Seeing Color 350
    A Less Scientific Approach 353
    Too Much of a Good Thing 354
Brightening Dark Video 355
Compensating for Overexposure 358
Correcting Bad White Balance. 360
Matching Footage from Different Cameras and Shoots. 361
    Using Tracks and Layers to Adjust Color 362
Black-and-White Effects 362
Correcting Color for Film 363
Making Your Video Look Like Film 363
One More Thing 365

17 Titles and Effects 366

Titles. 367
    Choosing Your Typeface and Size 368
    Ordering Your Titles. 369
    Coloring Your Titles 370
    Placing Your Titles. 370
    Safe Titles. 371
    Tutorial: Create Your Main Title 372
Motion Effects. 377
    Keyframes and Interpolating 377
    Slow-Mo and Speed Ramps 379

Integrating Still Images and Video 379
Special Effects Workflow 380
Compositing 101 383
    Keys 384
        Tutorial: Creating a Luminance Key 385
        Tutorial: Using a Chroma Key 390
    Keying Tips 394
    Mattes 396
    Mixing SD and HD Footage 398
        Tutorial: Adding Camera Shake 401
Using Effects to Fix Problems 404
    Eliminating Camera Shake 404
    Getting Rid of Things 405
Moving On 409

18 Finishing 410

What Do You Need? 412
    Start Early 412
    What Is Mastering? 413
    What to Do Now 414
Preparing for Film Festivals 414
DIY File-Based Masters 415
    Preparing Your Sequence 415
    Color Grading 418
    Create a Mix 419
Make a Textless Master 420
    Export Your Masters 420
    Watch Your Export 421
Web Video and Video-on-Demand 422
    Streaming or Download? 422
    Compressing for the Web 423
    Choosing a Data Rate 425
    Choosing a Keyframe Interval 425

DVD and Blu-Ray Discs. 426
   DVD and Blu-Ray Compression. 428
   DVD and Blu-Ray Disc Authoring 430
High-End Finishing 432
   Reel Changes 432
   Preparing for a Professional Audio Mix 433
   Preparing for Professional Color Grading 434
   Putting Audio and Video Back Together. 435
Digital Videotape Masters 435
35mm Film Prints. 437
   The Film Printing Process 438
   Printing from a Negative 438
   Direct-to-Print. 439
   Optical Soundtracks 439
Digital Cinema Masters 440
Archiving Your Project. 441

GLOSSARY 443

INDEX 471

INTRODUCTION

Once upon a time, the world of filmmaking was very small and most of it was contained in one place: Hollywood. In those days before the advent of digital technology, through trial and error, the studios developed an exceptional workflow designed to track a massive amount of data without using computers.

Today, thanks to modern technology, there are myriad digital tools available to filmmakers in the form of hardware and software. And the old studio workflow, while still potentially valuable, is in need of an upgrade.

In this book, we'll guide you through the modern digital filmmaking workflow and show you the tools (and toys) that will make your life easier. We'll help you navigate the ever-changing developments of new technology while keeping the big picture in mind: storytelling. Because despite all the changes since the heyday of Hollywood, the heart of filmmaking remains unchanged.

What You'll Find in This Book

This book is organized into three parts, just like a film shoot: preproduction, production, and postproduction.

Part I: Preproduction Chapters 2 through 5 cover the traditional stage of "preproduction," the part of the process during which you make all the decisions necessary to start shooting: writing, technology basics, planning, scheduling, storyboarding, set design, and choosing a camera.

Part II: Production Chapters 6 through 10 cover the traditional stage of "production," the principal shoot of your project: lighting, using the camera, shooting, and recording production sound, including a special new chapter on shooting with DSLR cameras.

Part III: Postproduction Chapters 11 through 18 cover the traditional stage of "postproduction": workstations and equipment, organizing and media management, editing, sound design, color correction, titles, special effects, and delivery of the finished product—everything from streaming video to a digital cinema screening in a theater.

Finally, although we assume no formal training in video or film production, we might—on occasion—use film and video production-related terms. You'll find definitions for these terms in the glossary. You might be surprised to learn how much you already know about video production. Watching movies is the best way to learn the visual literacy required of a good filmmaker, and most people have seen plenty of movies.

Look for the "What to Watch" tips for suggested movies and TV shows to watch along the way.

Filmmaking is a challenging, exciting, and always instructive process. We wish you the best of luck in your filmmaking endeavors. Now, it's time to get started!

WHAT TO WATCH

Rewatch a film you saw recently. Pick a film you saw recently and watch it again. Instead of paying attention to the story, pay attention to how the film was made. This time, look at how it is shot, where the camera is, and why. Listen to how music is used (or not used), if there are any graphics or special effects, and if there are any unusual editing choices. Try to imagine the creative choices the director made during each phase of filmmaking: preproduction, production, and post. Now start thinking about your own film in these ways. Remember, when a film is well made, you won't see "the strings." So, to learn from the work of a good filmmaker, you have to actively observe how the film was constructed.

Companion Web Site Downloads

The tutorial media for this book can be found at the companion Web site: *www.thedigital filmmakinghandbook.com.*

The Web site also features blog postings, product reviews, and articles about new digital filmmaking developments.

In addition, sections of previous editions that feature older technology, such as analog video-tape, are now available on the Web site.

1

Getting Started

Photo credit: Jason Hampton

This year marks the 10-year anniversary of the first edition of *The Digital Filmmaking Handbook*. Looking back, it's rather shocking to see that 10 years ago the way films were made was very different. It's an exciting time to be updating this book because filmmaking technology has improved so dramatically. Video image quality has become so good that 35mm motion picture film, at least for indie filmmakers, has gone the way of 35mm still photography film: no one is shooting on it anymore. Digital is easier, cheaper, and although some will argue that it lacks a quality that film has, no one can say that it doesn't look good in its own way.

Large crisp images with tons of detail, amazing low-light capabilities, a greatly simplified post-production workflow, and prices that keep dropping make digital video the most popular choice for everyone from indie filmmakers to hobbyists. And, in addition to overall improvements in quality, working with digital video is much easier than it was 10 years ago.

Better, Cheaper, Easier

Why are things so much better for filmmakers today than they were in 2000? First, image quality is better. Ten years ago, DV was the norm for lower budget filmmakers. Nowadays, it's HD. A quick comparison of a DV image and an HD image says it all (see Figure 1.1)

DV (640x480 px)   **HD (1920x1080 px)**

Figure 1.1

Video image quality 10 years ago (left) and today (right).

But it's not just image quality that's improved, computers are better, too. Faster data processing and digital connectivity mean that you don't have to build and outfit a computer with specialized hardware upgrades to ensure that it can handle digital video editing. Yes, you'll still need to make sure you have a computer with certain baseline characteristics, but you'll most likely be able to use it straight out of the box, and it will probably cost less than a video-capable rig of 10 years ago (see Figure 1.2).

Storage drives are bigger and cheaper. Everyone's got lots of media these days, so even non-filmmakers commonly use storage drives that hold one terabyte (Tb) or more. That means HD-capable drives are easy to find at local retailers or online.

Monitors are better, cheaper, and more compatible across the board. Oh, yeah, and they're wider. In the old days, you had to have a separate special video monitor in addition to your computer monitor, and those old-school monitors were square. Nowadays, you can use flat panel HD monitors for everything, and they are widescreen, just like your HD video (see Figure 1.3).

But the biggest improvement of the last few years is in the price and quality level of HD video cameras. You can get a DSLR camera that shoots full-quality HD video like the Canon T2i (see Figure 1.4) for about $700 (not including lenses and accessories), or you can get a very good HD camera that is considered comparable to 35mm film cameras, like the fully-customizable RED One (shown in Figure 1.5). The $20,000 price tag of the RED One might sound expensive, and it is, but the RED One is designed to go head-to-head with high-end digital cinema cameras, which start at around $65,000.

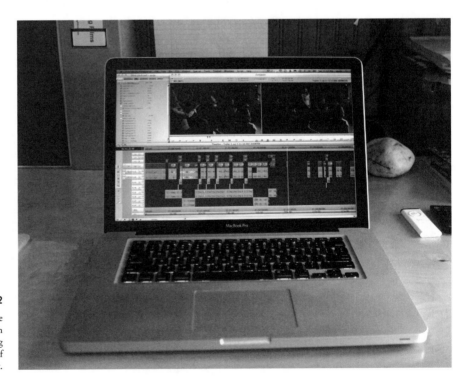

Figure 1.2

Top-of-the-line computers, like this Apple MacBook Pro, can serve as a digital video editing workstation straight out of the box.

Figure 1.3

Add about $500 in accessories (2Tb RAID storage, Bluetooth keyboard and mouse, 24" HD monitor), and a laptop becomes a very comfortable video editing workstation.

Figure 1.4

The Canon Rebel T2i DSLR camera can shoot full-quality HD video at a fraction of the cost of standard HD video cameras.

DSLRs and HD

Everyone's talking about shooting HD with DSLRs—including us! In fact, we've added an entire chapter on it. In Chapter 10, "DSLRs and Other Advanced Shooting Situations," we cover everything you need to know about shooting with DSLR cameras.

Figure 1.5

The RED One is a special full-customizable digital cinema camera aimed at indie filmmakers.

If you're shooting on tape, you'll still need some sort of video interface to get media off the videotape and into your computer, but as file-based media becomes the norm, you are much more likely to simply remove a disc from your camera, put it into your computer, and drag the files across (see Figure 1.6).

Figure 1.6

In a typical tapeless editing workflow, video is digitized inside the camera, stored on a disc, such as SD cards, and the resulting digital files are copied to the computer's storage drive.

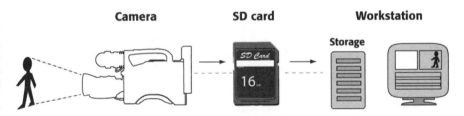

And there's more. Lighting technology continues to improve: smaller HMIs, LED panels, and professional fluorescents use less power so that you don't need a generator, give off less heat making the set more comfortable for everyone, and are professionally calibrated so that you can ensure that your project looks great (see Figure 1.7).

In fact, perhaps the biggest challenge is keeping up with all the new technology that's available out there. One of the best ways to stay up-to-date is to attend trade shows like DV Expo in California (see Figure 1.8). You can see all the latest gear in person and speak to product reps who will fill you in on the latest developments, and it's also a great way to meet other filmmakers.

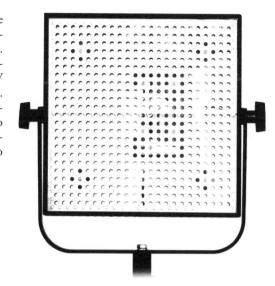

Figure 1.7

New and improved lighting solutions, like these LED lights from LitePanels, mean that it's easier to shoot with standard household power.

Figure 1.8

Attending trade shows, like DV Expo in Pasadena, California, is a good way to stay up-to-date with the latest technology.

To sum up, over the last 10 years, digital video prices fell through the floor at the same time that the quality flew through the ceiling, and technology that practically required an engineering degree 10 years ago is now significantly easier to use. So what are you waiting for?

Who This Book Is For

Digital video is everywhere these days—on your television, your computer, your game console, and your smart phone. And the ways to acquire it abound too: camcorders, cell phones, built-in cameras on your computer, and point-and-shoot cameras that just happen to record HD. What used to be the rarified territory of "film geeks" is now the norm.

There's a reason for that. The fact is that the collaboration, imagination, and work involved in crafting even a short film are extremely enjoyable. Digital video technology makes it possible to make films for fun. And with Web-based distribution, you no longer have to be a hobbyist filmmaker with no audience. You can actually present your finished work to the world for practically zero cost.

This book will teach you everything you need to know, whether your aim is to create a feature-length movie with the hope of screening in a theater, an industrial or corporate production, or a short film or music video simply for your own enjoyment.

This book is meant to be both a start-to-finish production guide and a reference for learning more about particular tasks. For more experienced users, we've included details on the latest technologies and strategies for refining a digital workflow to reduce your production costs and to enhance creativity. From sophisticated shot design to cutting-edge graphics, *The Digital Filmmaking Handbook, 4th Edition* will show you how to create images and effects that are rarely associated with low-budget productions. For serious beginning filmmakers, this book provides a wide overview of the entire process of making a movie from the very first steps of writing a screenplay to shooting to the final screening.

Full-blown video production is a huge affair that involves many different arts, crafts, and sciences. No single volume can address the tremendous amount of training and expertise that is required to master all of these disciplines. However, we have tried to fill you in on the questions you need to ask, and the major problems and issues you will have to solve at each stage of your production. So even though this book doesn't cover, for example, 3D animation, our postproduction chapters should at least bring you up to speed on the issues you can expect to face when trying to create visual effects. These questions should help you better interface with the artisans and craftspeople who *do* have the skills for these various disciplines and point you in the direction of further self-education if that's your intention.

Whether your goal is an industrial project, a short subject for your Web site, or a feature-length movie for a film festival, *The Digital Filmmaking Handbook, 4th Edition*, contains everything you need to know to get your project in the can.

What Kind of Digital Film Should You Make?

Every project, no matter what it is, will have its own unique set of challenges. That's part of the thrill of filmmaking. Every film is a different learning experience, with a different set of variables. No matter how experienced you are, you have an opportunity to learn something new from every project.

If you are reading this book and trying to figure out what type of project you should start, here are some of your options:

■ **Video shorts for the Web.** Thanks to Web sites like YouTube, everyone has the opportunity to create and distribute short videos for potentially millions of viewers. And there are many other Web sites that seek more specialized content: travel videos, sketch comedy, music performances, to name only a few. Even the big studios create shorts for the Web, in the form of trailers and film clips, to promote their high-budget feature films. On some level, every filmmaker who reads this book will find he or she needs to create at least one video short for the Web related to their project, whether that's a trailer, a promotional clip, segments broken down into "webisodes," or the whole thing. For that reason, we've added an expanded section in Chapter 18, "Finishing," to walk you through the process of getting your video on the Web.

■ **Short films.** For many, a short film is the ideal first film project. It has all the elements of a full-length feature film, but on a much smaller scale. You'll learn about every stage of the process, from screenwriting to shooting to editing and finishing, but the task won't be quite so overwhelming, and it definitely won't be as time-consuming and expensive. If you've never made a scripted film of any kind before, this is the way to start. But do your homework first. There is an audience for short films in festivals, on the Web, and occasionally on cable TV networks or as a package of shorts on Blu-ray or DVD. Typically, short films are under 30 minutes in length, but many believe they are best when they range from 5–10 minutes. After all, the average half-hour sitcom only has about 20 minutes of actual content, so if your "short" is longer than that, it starts to not feel like a "short." Making a great short film is like writing a great short story, it's a different animal than full-length movies and creating a great short has its own unique challenges. For those who decide to make a short, every chapter of this book will be relevant to your project.

■ **Corporate and industrial projects.** These types of projects may not be what you dreamed of when you decided to become a filmmaker, but let's face it, they are plentiful and they almost always involve receiving a paycheck for your work—something that sadly you can't count on with the other types of projects listed here. What's more, they'll require the same skill set and problem-solving challenges of any of the other personal filmmaking projects you may be working on. Corporate videos are driven by an agenda that is usually given to you by your boss(es). They have a narrative, but it's usually about a product or a business or an event, rather than a character. Every chapter of this book is relevant to corporate and industrial videos but take a special look at Chapter 2, "Writing and Scheduling," where we discuss the nuts and bolts of these types of projects.

■ **Webisodes.** This is the newest item on the list, and it's one that is definitely still evolving. Webisodes are usually an ongoing story that unfolds in segments that are under 10 minutes in length. Sometimes, these segments add up to a longer story, such as "Dr. Horrible's Singalong Blog," and sometime they are more like a sitcom, such as "The Guild." As of this writing, there many "webisodic" video projects out there, but the form has yet to be truly defined. This is an exciting opportunity for new filmmakers. Every time a new type of storytelling evolves, the door opens to create a new crop of success stories. There are no real rules yet, but writing, shooting, and finishing webisodes involves all of the elements discussed in this book. In addition, we feature a special section on finishing for Web distribution in Chapter 18 that's of crucial interest to webisodic filmmakers.

- **Television pilots.** In a perfect world, all television pilots would be pitched, ordered in advance, and paid for by a network. But that's not always the case, especially for innovative or non-scripted TV series. Instead, producers (that's TV-speak for "director") take a gamble and shoot their own pilot episode. Then they present that material in the form of a *pitch reel* or a finished cut of the first episode of the series, aka the *pilot*. It's called a pilot because it flies out ahead and leads the series—unless it crashes and burns. If you consider the range of shows on TV—from daytime talk shows to reality TV shows to sit-coms to hour-long dramas—and that's just the tip of the iceberg—then you know that the choices and options are almost limitless. But whatever the genre, your TV pilot will need all the resources covered in this book. When TV production differs greatly from film production, this book tries to address those differences.

- **Documentaries.** The filmmaking equivalent of "non-fiction" or "journalistic" writing, documentaries today have a strong and growing audience. If you think of some of the most exciting and controversial films of the last decade, they are often documentaries. Films like *Fahrenheit 9/11*, *Supersize Me*, and *An Inconvenient Truth* have had a demonstrable effect on our perception of the world around us. This is the power of documentary filmmaking. Documentaries are shot in a way that is very different from scripted films, but they share many of the creative challenges—structuring a story, crafting a style in terms of how the film is shot, refining the structure in the editing room, designing the sound, intensifying emotions with music, and enhancing the film with graphics. All of these things are as necessary for documentaries as they are for scripted films. Like a good biography, just because it's "real" doesn't mean it's not art. In this edition, we've added some special sections for documentarians. In Chapter 9, "Shooting and Directing," you'll find a section on the unique concerns of shooting for documentaries and also a special section in Chapter 14, "Editing," on editing documentaries because these are both areas where making a documentary is significantly different than making a scripted film.

- **Scripted feature films.** Whether you agree with it or not, or like it or not, at the time of this writing, scripted feature films are still the top of the pyramid in the entertainment industry. Frankly, they may not hold that status for long, but at least for the time being, the feature film is still king. What does that mean for you? It means that if you are a director and you have directed a live action feature film, you are now eligible to direct any project lower on the Hollywood pyramid, which is everything else. (We didn't say you had to like this or agree with it!) And the same goes for writers, cinematographers, actors, editors, composers, graphic designers, visual effects artists, the list goes on. Having that feature film credit will open doors, guaranteed. After that, it's your talent that will keep your career going. So that's one big reason to do a feature film. But there are others. The scripted feature film is the filmmaking equivalent of the novel. If that long format of storytelling is your true love, then the feature film is the way to go. Making a feature will require great resources, especially if you are going to do it independently. But there's no question that it will be a rewarding experience.

Questions to Ask Yourself

If you're seriously thinking of embarking on a digital filmmaking production, you're about to begin a very complicated process. The more you know before you start, the more smoothly things will go for you. Before you dive in, you should know the answers to these questions:

- What is your final product? Projected theatrical release? Home video? Broadcast television? Blu-ray? Webisodes? Corporate/educational use? (Chapters 3, "Digital Video Primer," and 18 can help you understand the technical specifications for these different formats.)

- What peripheral products will you be creating? Work-in-progress DVD copies? Email-able trailers? Press kits? Outputting different formats requires more planning than a project that sticks to one type of output does.

- What equipment do you already own or have access to that you can use to produce your project? Consider this question carefully, as some older equipment—both computer and video equipment—might be more of a hindrance than a help.

- How much time and money do you want to spend? Remember that postproduction can often cost as much or more than production.

If you take the time to make some hard decisions before you shoot, you'll save time and money throughout the process. Even if you can't find all the answers up-front, you should at least know all the questions.

What Equipment Do I Need?

This book assumes you will be using a Macintosh or Windows-compatible computer. Some familiarity with your operating system of choice is required, as well as a video camera of some kind. Guidelines for selecting equipment are provided throughout the book. We also assume that you are familiar with some basic computer terms, such as RAM, kilobytes, megabytes, clock speeds, and so forth. A glossary is included in the back of the book.

Filmmaking is a challenging, exciting, and always instructive process. We wish you the best of luck in your filmmaking endeavors. Now it's time to get started!

2

Writing and Scheduling

Photo credit: Sonja Schenk

All successful video productions begin, of course, with a well-written script and a lot of planning. Planning can involve everything from budgeting and scheduling to previsualizing your shots using storyboards or animation software. Because preproduction is where you'll determine much of the look and quality of your project, good planning weighs heavily on your production and postproduction success.

If you're eager to start shooting, then it can be tempting to skimp on planning, but foregoing any part of the planning stage can lead directly to increased expenses and headaches. Bear in mind that planning is probably the *last* time in your production cycle where your project is still truly under your control, so you might as well enjoy it! Once production starts, you'll have to start facing the reality of things going differently than you expected, so revel in the joy of imagining and planning for how you'd *like* things to go.

In this chapter, we're going to thoroughly discuss the writing and scheduling of your project. Due to space limitations, we won't be covering budgeting or financing in this book. However, there are voluminous budgeting and scheduling articles that you can download for free from *www.thedigitalfilmmakinghandbook.com/chapter2*.

Preproduction is a very dynamic process. For example, your schedule is often affected by the size of your budget, and troubles with scheduling can often impact your finances, which might shrink your budget, which could result in the need for rescheduling. Both schedule and budget are guided by the nature of your script. Because these processes all affect each other, it's important to realize that preproduction is not necessarily a linear, step-by-step process. Keep that in mind while reading this chapter. But first, you need a script.

Screenwriting

No doubt, at some point in your life you've read a book that's been made into a movie. And, no doubt, you've probably walked out of the movie adaptation thinking "why did they change that part?" or "why did they leave that other part out?" It's easy to simply think that the screenwriter did a bad job, and certainly moviemakers don't always share your own take on the emotional tone of a particular book.

More often than not, though, movie adaptations are very different from their source books because cinema and prose are simply very different art forms. To think that a book can be directly translated into a movie shows an ignorance of the particular narrative, pacing, and content differences that exist between these two forms. Someone once said, "Trying to talk about music is like trying to dance about architecture." Trying to make a straight translation from written text to moving images is almost as difficult.

The point is that screenwriting is a very particular type of writing, and as such, it demands a good amount of study and practice. No amount of production can save a poorly written script, so it's important to spend the time building a sturdy screenplay.

No matter what type of project you're shooting—feature film, TV show, documentary, or corporate video—you still need to understand the basic concepts of good storytelling and strong screenwriting.

Finding a Story

We're going to spend a lot of time talking about "story," so let's get some basic concepts out of the way. Consider the following:

> Mary had decided to go for a walk, so she called her dog, Spot, got his leash, and went outside. She walked down the sidewalk and crossed the street in front of the small, neighborhood grocery store. She liked the store and was always happy to see the "regulars" buying their food. She kept walking until she got to the park. As always, the park was filled with dogs that were running, and jumping, and catching Frisbees. Both she and Spot really liked it in the park.

Not much of a story, huh? In fact, Mary's story isn't really a "story" at all; it's just a series of events. That series of events could continue for pages and pages, covering all of the events that happened during Mary's day. In the end, we would simply have a much longer, boring description of a bunch of events.

"Maybe Mary is just a boring person," you might be thinking. Certainly, subject matter has a lot to do with making a story interesting. If Mary was an international super-spy instead of a woman walking her dog, the story might automatically be more interesting. However, even with the seemingly boring events of Mary's life, it is possible to tell a more compelling story:

> Mary was going stir crazy. She'd been stuck in the house all day long. and it was starting to get to her. She called her dog, Spot, put on his leash, and went outside. She crossed the street in front of her neighborhood grocery store. She liked the store and always felt comfortable there. But now, when she looked in and saw the lines of people loaded down with heaps of cans and boxes, she just felt more stir crazy. She walked on until she finally reached the park, and there, at last, she was able to relax.

This story might not be Shakespeare, but it does feel more like a story than a simple chain of events. However, both stories contain exactly the same series of events. Nothing new happens in the second story—it's still just a tale of a woman going for a walk with her dog—but in the second story Mary has a goal: she's stir crazy, and she needs to relax. This goal is stated in the very first sentence.

The simple addition of a goal provides a structure and direction to the tale, transforming it from a chain of events into a story. Why does this difference matter? Because the goal we created is not just for Mary. By stating it, we've also given the reader a goal—something to find out, and a reason to continue listening.

Story First

No matter what type of production you're planning, your first writing task is to decide what your story is about. Industrial and corporate presentations, music videos, documentaries, marketing or advertising pieces—they all need to have clear, well-defined stories even if the story is as simple as the one about Mary and her dog.

Structure

In the preceding example, we took a pretty boring chain of events and turned them into a story by giving our main character a goal. However, we did something else as well: we gave the story a structure. If you look at the second story, you'll see that it has a very definite beginning, middle, and end.

In the beginning, we learn that Mary has a problem: she's stir crazy. In the middle, we see her go to a store, which is normally comforting, but this doesn't solve her problem. Perhaps her problem is worse than she realized. In the end, she finally finds a comfortable place to be and is no longer stir crazy.

Learning this simple structure will do more than anything else to help you tell better stories and make better movies. Not only will you be able to create movies that are more interesting to your audience, but by following this structure, you'll also have an easier time finding your way through the writing, shooting, and editing of your movie.

This beginning/middle/end structure is commonly referred to as the *three-act structure,* and it is the basis for all Hollywood movies. If "beginning, middle, and end" is too abstract, think of the three sections as *setup, complication,* and *payoff.* In our story about Mary, the setup was that she was stir crazy, the complication was that her usual way of calming down didn't work, and the payoff was that she finally found peace.

Failure to deliver on any of these parts results in very predictable audience reactions. Projects that have a weak first act (the setup) are usually perceived as boring; projects with a weak second act (the complication) are usually seen to be lacking in substance; and projects with a weak third act (the payoff) are typically regarded as pointless.

This beginning/middle/end structure can be applied to any type of production. Even if you're doing a simple corporate training video that is nothing more than a talking head, what that head says should have a discernible structure. Remember, a three-act structure is designed to keep your audience engaged and compelled.

Treatments

If you've worked out the details and structure of your story, you might want to consider writing a "treatment" before you begin writing the script. A treatment is the telling of your story in prose. Sometimes, your treatment will have some dialogue; at other times it will simply be a description of what's happening in the story. Treatments help you organize your thoughts, get any initial images and dialogue down on paper, and serve as a way to present your story to other people. If you have a producer or investor who's interested in your story idea, showing him a treatment might help you secure some funding.

Three-Act Structure

Hollywood movies use a very well defined, three-act structure. In fact, it's so well defined, you can usually set your watch to it.

- **Act I: The beginning.** Wherein the main character is introduced, along with his or her nemesis, and the supporting cast. The main character's "problem" is also introduced. This section usually takes 20 to 30 minutes.

- **Act II: The middle.** The main thing that happens in Act II is that the character's problem is complicated. This is the bulk of the movie, and any subplots are usually introduced and solved here. Very rarely are new characters introduced in this act. Halfway through the act—that is, in the exact middle of the movie—the main character's luck will change, and things will start working out in his or her favor. By the end of the second act, the solution to the problem will be clear. This act is usually 40 to 50 minutes long.

- **Act III: The end.** In this act, the main character's problem is solved. This usually takes about 20 minutes.

Yet another way to define this structure is: Act I: Introduce the hero; Act II: Torture the hero; Act III: Save the hero.

Unlike a stage play, there is never a clear separation of acts presented in a movie. The actual change might be a simple cut from one scene to another, or the scene might just barrel on ahead into the new act. It's not important that the audience *knows* where the act breaks are, but that doesn't mean that they aren't there.

You don't have to follow this structure, and many movies don't. However, it is a fairly simple, effective way of ensuring a compelling story that "moves."

Raiders of the Lost Ark

Raiders of the Lost Ark follows the typical Hollywood structure very closely, so it provides a good example of how the three-act structure works. (If you haven't seen the movie, you'll need to see it in order for this explanation to work.)

Act I ends right after the fight in Marion's bar. We have all of our main characters, and we have our problem—find the Ark before the Nazis do.

Act II ends when the Nazis show up to take the Ark off the ship. More specifically, it ends when Indy swims to the Nazi sub and climbs aboard. With Indy, the Nazis, the girl, and the Ark all on board, we're ready for the final confrontation.

Act III ends with the end of the movie. He got the Ark. (Never mind that it was taken away from him by the good guys, he still did what he was supposed to do.)

More About Structure

For more about feature film structure, check out the article on structure at *www.thedigitalfilmmakinghandbook.com/chapter2/structure.pdf*. This essay provides a much more detailed analysis of the structure of *Raiders*.

WHAT TO WATCH

Baghead is a hilarious film with a solid three-act structure, but thanks to the unique twists and turns of the plot, and the original characters, it is far from formulaic.

Writing Visually

Most beginning screenwriters make a very simple mistake: they forget that movies are made up of *pictures*. Yes, there's dialogue and talking and music and all that other stuff, but first and foremost: movies are a *visual* form of storytelling.

Let's go back to *Raiders of the Lost Ark* for a moment. Consider the beginning of the movie. In *Raiders*, you have to go two minutes into the movie before you encounter the first line of dialogue, the line "The Hovitos are near." In other words, the first two minutes are told completely in pictures. Sure, there's music and sound effects, but you can turn the sound down, and the scene still makes sense.

In screenwriting, "show, don't tell" should be your constant mantra. To understand more about writing visually, check out the essay WritingVisually.pdf located at *www.thedigitalfilmmakinghandbook.com/chapter2*.

Write Silents

One of the best ways to practice writing visually is to deny yourself dialogue. Writing silent shorts and scenes is a great way to learn how to explain things without talking. An example of a silent short script entitled *Consumer Electronics* can be found at *www.thedigitalfilmmakinghandbook.com/chapter2/tutorials2*.

Creative Writing Exercises

- If you're finding yourself a little short on ideas for scripts and stories, why not give yourself a predefined structure of some kind. That's what we did for the *Consumer Electronics* script that's included at *www.thedigitalfilmmakinghandbook.com/chapter2/tutorials2*. We wanted to write a short, and we wanted it to be something we could shoot easily, so we decided to try to think of a story that could be shot in a house, and that featured a single item that one might find in a typical home. To make the exercise a good lesson in visual storytelling, we also decided that it had to be a dialogue-free scene. We'll be using this script throughout our production examples. If you'd like to follow along with your own project, try writing a simple story using the same guidelines.

- One of the hardest tasks that a writer faces is cutting his script, but it's very easy to write things that are too long. Usually, any "fat" in your script becomes obvious once you start shooting. Sometimes, though, you might have a good, tight script, but still be bound by time or money. That was our problem when we decided to shoot a scene from *Richard III*. Take a look at the Richard III.pdf file in *www.thedigitalfilmmakinghandbook.com/chapter2/tutorials2*. This is the complete Shakespeare scene, and it runs over 10 minutes when read by the actors. We wanted it to come in around 5 minutes. See if you can cut it down to that length. (To see our cutting, with some explanations of why we chose the cuts we did, check out the Richard.pdf file we use in the Chapter 14 tutorials folder on *www.thedigitalfilmmakinghandbook.com*.)

- A simple writing warm-up. Although it might not always feel like it, your brain constantly makes things up and tells stories. Very often, though, this storytelling part of your brain is tripped up by the rational, sensical part of your brain. Try this simple yet difficult exercise: Get a piece of paper and a pen and start writing a story while counting backward, out loud, from 100. Count at a consistent, regular pace and don't stop writing. The idea is that the counting will tie up that sense-obsessed part of your brain, freeing the content-creating part to write. Lean too far in either direction, and you'll stop counting or stop writing. When you do it right, you'll usually find that you get stories that are very dream-like. Just as you need to warm up before exercising or playing a musical instrument, performing writing warm-ups before you start can often greatly ease your real writing work.

Creative Writing Exercises (continued)

- Because it's a rhythm, the three-act structure is something you can actually start to feel after a while, once you start learning to pay attention to it. Being able to recognize the rhythms in the movies you watch will help you better understand and control the structure and rhythmic beats in your own script. Start watching movies with an eye toward picking out the act breaks and other rhythmic elements. Can you feel where Act I is? Where the midpoint is? When Act III begins? See if you agree. Be warned, though: once you start watching movies with an eye or feeling toward these structural devices, it can change the way you experience some stories. Suspense stories, in particular, become much less suspenseful when you're able to realize things like "this must be a false ending, because they haven't actually solved the problem yet." However, such a reading also makes you realize that the enjoyment of these types of movies usually derives much more from the telling, than from the actual narrative points.

Other Structures

The dominance of a rigid three-act structure is something that has only come to cinema in the last 30–40 years. Before that, movies did not all adhere so tightly to the rigid rhythms and practices of a modern three-act structure. Watch *Casablanca*—a masterpiece by any measure—and note that it doesn't spell out all of the problems at the very beginning. It's difficult to tell where the Act I break actually occurs. Similarly, Earnest Lehman, the screenwriter of *North By Northwest*, said that he considers that to be an *11*-act script!

- Feeling stuck on a script? Though you can follow all sorts of structural guidelines, and pound your head against your desk, often the answer to your script problems lies not with you, but with your characters. They're often the ones that have the information you need to figure out what happens next. The problem is that you usually only hear what your characters have to say from the scenes they're in. If you're stuck, and not writing scenes, then you'll quickly get out of touch with your characters. In these instances, it's often a good idea to find *other* ways of getting your characters to talk to you. Try conducting interviews with them for various publications. See what they say to the editor of your local newspaper, to a tabloid magazine, to a news weekly, or an entertainment news program. Or write a scene where they're all on a daytime talk show arguing about their issues. Sure, they might start throwing chairs at each other, but this kind of unbridled talk just might give you some insights into their wants and desires that will feed you lots of ideas.

Formatting Your Script

Traditional movie screenplays have a very specific format that has been designed and refined to convey much more than just dialogue and scene descriptions. Screenplay format makes it easy to quickly judge budget and scheduling concerns in a script. No matter what type of project you're working on, writing screenplays in this format will make your production job much easier.

Screenplay Format

One of the biggest advantages of screenplay format is that it makes it easier to determine the length and pacing of your script. If you follow standard screenplay margins and layouts, your script will average one minute of screen time per page. In reality, there is a lot of variation, of course. A one-page description of an epic sea battle might actually take five minutes of screen time, while a page of witty banter might fly by in 20 seconds. On average, the one-page-per-minute rule is a good guideline to follow because over the entire length of the screenplay, it will be about right.

If you follow traditional screenplay format, your script will be divided into scenes delineated by *sluglines*. A slug tells whether the following scene is INTerior or EXTerior, the location of the scene, and whether the scene takes place during the day or night. For example:

```
INT. MAD SCIENTIST'S PANTRY — NIGHT
```

Sluglines make it easy to count and reorder your scenes, and make it simple for a producer to quickly arrive at an approximation of cost. If your script has a lot of EXT scenes at NIGHT, then it's going to be more expensive (lights, location shots, and overtime add up quickly). Similarly, if your slugs all run along the lines of:

```
EXT. UPPER ATMOSPHERE OF MARS — NIGHT
```

then it's pretty obvious that your script is effects-heavy and, therefore, expensive.

Standard screenplays are always typed in 12-point Courier with the margins shown in Figure 2.1.

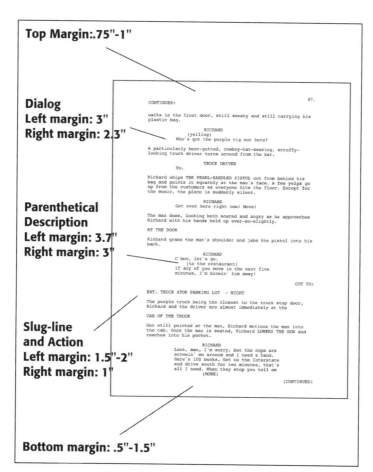

Figure 2.1

Although measurements can vary, if you use the margins shown here, you'll have a script formatted in "standard" screenplay format.

Standard screenplay format has a number of other conventions as well. For example, if a scene continues from one page to the next, then "CONTINUED" is placed at the bottom of the first page. Similarly, if a character's dialogue jumps to another page, then "MORE" is placed below the flowing dialogue. Through the years, screenplay conventions have been refined and standardized as a way of making script breakdown, budgeting, and scheduling much simpler. It's safe to say that if your screenplay is not formatted according to standard conventions, no one in the film industry will read it. A poorly formatted screenplay is an instant indication of a very "green" screenwriter.

A Sample Screenplay

On the Chapter 2>Tutorials page of the companion Web site there is a copy of a scene from *Richard III* (Richard III.pdf) presented in standard screenplay format. This document will let you see what a normal screenplay should look like. We'll be using this script for many examples later in the book. The Richard III Cut.pdf is an alternate version of the scene that we'll be looking at later.

Multi-Column Formats

If you're writing a script for a news, industrial, educational, corporate presentation, or advertising production, then you'll most likely want to use a multi-column, A/V script format. (*A/V* is short for audio/video). Much simpler than screenplay format, A/V formats are ideal for planning and scripting live broadcasts, short subjects, and other multi-camera, multi-source shoots (see Figure 2.2).

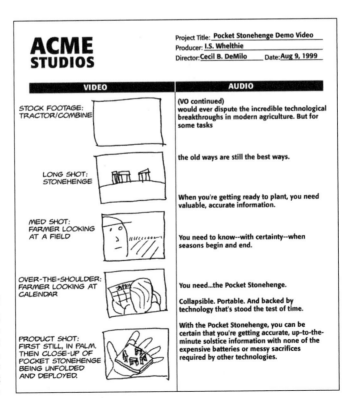

Figure 2.2

A/V format scripts are divided into multiple columns. Shown here: one for the spoken text (either live talent or voice-over), and another showing simple sketches of any accompanying visuals.

Sides

Sometimes it is useful to create "sides" for your talent, especially when recording dialogue or voice-over narration. "Sides" usually consist of one or two relevant pages pulled out of your script. Often, they only contain the actors' lines, making it easier to read and giving the actor(s) more freedom to uniquely interpret the dialogue by removing stage directions that would otherwise dictate the performance.

Screenwriting Software

A whole range of writing software exists that not only makes it easy to render your scripts in standard screenplay format, but also provides some valuable tools for editing and restructuring your script.

Programs such as Final Draft, Celtz, and Final Draft A/V format your scripts as you write (Figure 2.3). Anyone who has tried to add all the MOREs and CONTINUEDs manually will find this one feature worth the investment.

In addition to formatting, Final Draft provides a lot of automation. Character names can be entered by simply typing the first few letters of a name, and the program does a very good job of anticipating what the next character's name will be, making it simple to type back-and-forth dialogue. Final Draft provides other utilities, including a Scene Navigator that lets you see your scenes as a series of index cards that can be easily rearranged (Figure 2.4).

Celtz is free and includes storyboarding and other movie project management tools. It is also possible to create your own template in Microsoft Word.

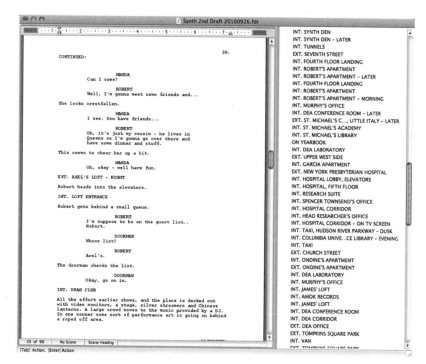

Figure 2.3

Final Draft provides a complete, automated screenplay-writing environment. Character names, scene locations, and other repeating elements can be automatically entered by the program. The Navigator (on the right) lets you jump from scene to scene within the script.

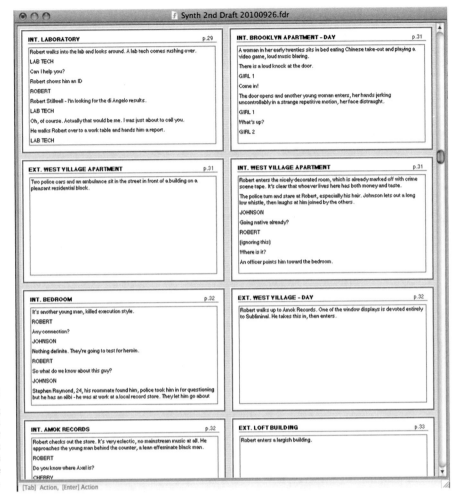

Figure 2.4

Like many screenwriting programs, Final Draft includes a special mode that lets you view your script as a series of index cards, one per scene. In this mode, you can simply rearrange cards to restructure your script.

The Pitch

Unfortunately, you can't expect your script to speak for itself. Most potential backers and crew members won't have the time or patience to read an entire script, so you'll have to win them over with a good pitch. The classic *elevator pitch* is a good guideline: pretend you get in an elevator with Steven Spielberg and have to pitch your movie in the time it takes for the elevator to reach his floor. For more on pitches, check out *www.thedigitalfilmmakinghandbook.com/chapter2/pitching.pdf*.

Writing for Television

Television has come into its own in the past decade. Thanks to smart, creative shows like *The Sopranos, Lost,* and *Mad Men,* to name only a few, TV is no longer the poor stepchild of feature filmmaking. TV series can have a depth and breadth that is impossible to achieve in a feature-length film. They have room to explore many characters and to develop multiple storylines to create the "arc" of a season so that there is a story that occurs within each episode, and then a greater story that occurs over the season, and then, with longer running shows, a narrative that occurs over the entire run of the series.

Scripted teleplays in the United States fall into two basic categories: hour-long and half-hour. It used to be that hour-long television shows were always dramas and half-hour shows were always sitcoms, but today those strict delimitations are increasingly blurred. *Nurse Jackie* is a half-hour show that contains as much drama as comedy, while *True Blood* is an hour-long show that offers much comedy in addition to its gothic thriller elements.

Formats for TV shows can vary a lot, even within the same genre. The following short list is a good place to start, but if you are writing for a show that already exists, you should do some research and make sure that you are using the right format.

- **Hour-long dramas** usually have four acts, not including *teases*, the montages of clips from the previous or upcoming episode(s) that usually open and close a TV show. Assuming a minute per page, the script should be about 40 pages long.

- **Half-hour comedies** usually have three acts, not including teases, and are about 20 pages long.

Other than varying lengths, teleplays use formatting and rules similar to movie screenplays.

A Word About Teases

Writing *teases* is definitely part of the writing of a TV show, but no one writes them until they are in the middle of a season that is actually airing. In other words, leave them out of your original *spec* teleplay.

WHAT TO WATCH

Friday Night Lights, **season 1** is an excellent example of how a TV series can successfully develop a story arc across the entire season without sacrificing character development.

Writing for "Unscripted"

Unscripted projects, such as documentaries, reality television, and the news still require some "writing." Documentary writing is a little different from the other forms of script writing that we've discussed because it's usually more of a journalistic type of writing. There are two approaches to documentary production:

- **Inductive**, where you spend as much time as you need (or can afford) shooting your subject, and then cut that source footage into a finished product.

- **Deductive**, where you write a scripted piece and then go out and shoot the footage you need to support that script.

In an inductive documentary, the shooting and editing is, in a sense, the writing process. During shooting, you'll capture all of the raw material that you will then pare down and organize into a finished edited piece. In a deductive documentary, the production process is more akin to that of scripted projects.

There's no right or wrong way to work, although there are advantages and pitfalls to each approach. An inductive process is usually better for covering an event, person, or place. You'll want to keep an open mind and not have any preconceived notions about your subject, lest you blind yourself to good footage or important events. But even if you're committed to being open-minded, you'll still benefit from planning and anticipating the problems and challenges of your shoot by creating a shot list or simply having an idea of what you need to capture in your head. (For example, "Joe admits to Jenna that he is moving to Las Vegas.") Then ask yourself before you wrap that day if you feel you achieved what you wanted. Later, when you get back to the editing room, you'll look at your footage and try to see what kind of story is there. Often, you'll be surprised to find out that the final story is very different than what you thought it was going to be.

In the deductive process, you'll do your research and learning at your writing desk. Once you've finished writing, you'll then try to find footage that illustrates your text. Though shooting will occasionally lead you to revise your script and make changes on the fly, in general your final project will probably end up fairly close to what you scripted.

WHAT TO WATCH

Catfish is a riveting documentary that was shot with the inductive process. The filmmakers followed their subject and were rewarded with some stunning twists and turns.

Outlines

Outlining is an excellent way to "script" or previsualize a documentary project. It helps ensure that your project has a beginning, middle, and end, and it also can serve as a quick checklist on the set.

Reality TV is a blend of traditional documentaries and game shows. "Competition" reality TV shows like *Survivor* and *Project Runway* feature a strong game element, whereas "follow" shows such as *Little People, Big World* are much closer to traditional documentaries. Soft-scripted reality shows like *Keeping Up with the Kardashians* or *The Hills* use real people in situations that are often dreamt up or enhanced by "writers" (aka producers). The issue of "writing" in reality TV is a hot button topic, and some people define writing very broadly (creating ideas or soft-scripting), while others define it very narrowly (writing text in a document). Controversy aside, reality TV typically does involve writing scripted texts such as voice-over, dialogue for the host(s), teases, recaps, and so on. Soft-scripting typically looks more like an outline or a bulleted list or maybe just an idea someone has on the fly.

The Writers Guild Foundation

A non-profit offshoot of the Writers Guild, the Writers Guild Foundation offers valuable resources for screenwriters of any level. Lectures, workshops, and writers' commentaries after screenings are often available as streaming video on their Web site.

WHAT TO WATCH

Project Runway, **season 8** introduced us to an HIV-positive designer at the beginning, but didn't reveal his health issues until a very moving episode half-way through the season, a great example of how in reality TV strong choices can be made even though there is no "writing" involved.

Writing for Corporate Projects

For the most part, when you write for any type of "industrial" project—be it a training video, marketing piece, or presentation video—you face the same issues and concerns as when you write a fictional short or feature. You still have a story to tell, that story needs to have a structure, and you must tell that story visually. So, just as you need to apply a goal and a structure to a fictional script, corporate and industrial scripts also need to have the same type of beginning/middle/end narrative drive to them. Corporate and industrial scripts are usually heavily based on interviews, or on voice-over narration with additional video footage or graphics to illustrate concepts. Even though these types of video do not always have "dramatic" real-world scenes in them, they still benefit from a sturdy three-act structure.

Before you commit any words to paper, try to get a clear idea of the "problem" that will be solved. Introducing and explaining the problem will constitute your first act. Next, you'll want to explain why this problem is difficult or worthwhile to solve. This will serve as your second act, the complication. Then you present the solution to the problem.

In a fictional project, the second act is usually the longest. In a corporate production, however, the third act is usually the longest, because you'll want to spend a long time dealing with the details of the solution you're proposing.

Corporate productions have a big wrinkle, though. Before you begin writing, you need to give thought to who you believe the audience is for your particular production. A production aimed at a management team will probably have a very different message from one aimed at a board of directors. If your audience already has a deep understanding of the problem you're going to present, then you'll want to make a shorter first act, and devote the time to beefing up the areas that they'll be less familiar with. You don't want to bore your audience with information they already have, so an understanding of who your intended audience is, what they already know, and what they need to know, is essential.

Know Your Audience

No matter what type of project you are writing, it is always invaluable to have a sense of who your desired audience is and to tailor your story to that audience.

Corporate script writing often involves several levels of approval, and this type of writing by committee can quickly become a frustrating "too many cooks in the kitchen" kind of situation. Because you don't want to invest a lot of time writing a detailed script, only to have it ripped asunder by your boss or client, it's often best to write your first few script passes in the form of simple *treatments*, or short synopses of the intended project. Treatments are easier to write, and allow you to quickly present a concept that can then be reworked and adjusted before you start writing the actual shooting script.

Scheduling

Eventually, after many rewrites, you'll have a "finished" script. (The script won't really be finished because you'll make loads of changes in production and postproduction, but you'll at least have something you can use to start shooting.) Now you're ready to start preparing for your shoot.

The first step in taking a story from the page to the screen is to create a schedule for the production. To make a realistic shooting schedule, you'll need to determine the resources you need for each scene, the number of script pages you'll try to shoot each day, and the order in which you want to shoot the scenes. There are many variables involved in every production—actors, crew members, props, locations, available daylight and weather conditions, equipment rental limitations, and so on. The organization of these elements can be complicated and difficult, and variables can change at any time. In addition to managing resources, a good schedule also helps you conform to a specified budget while allowing for the creative needs of the production.

As you might have guessed, scheduling is intimately tied to budgeting. Often, the same person who creates the schedule also creates the budget. You can create a realistic schedule without a budget, but you do need to have a general idea about how much money you can afford to spend on the principal shoot, whether it's $5,000 or $500,000. A $2,000 budget for a feature-length project will be dependent on getting most things for free—especially locations, props, and talent—so scheduling a day of shooting in the ballroom of the most expensive hotel downtown is probably not going to be an option. With $200,000, however, the ballroom is something you can realistically consider. Keeping your budgetary limitations in mind is the key to creating a realistic schedule.

Producing

"Producer" is probably the most confusing job title in the entertainment industry. First of all, there are many different types of producers. So what exactly is a producer? Some producers are financiers. They either invest personally in films or they raise money from other investors. Other producers deal with the "business" of making a film. They manage the budget, the schedule, and the staff. Other producers are creative producers. They make decisions about everything from story to casting to marketing. In television, the term "producer" can be someone who takes on the role that most people traditionally consider to be the director's job, and it can also be the writer. The TV series equivalent of writer-director is known as the "showrunner" and that person usually has a title of "executive producer." There can be upward of five executive producers on a TV show, but typically only one or two of them are actually running the show. The upshot is that a producer can wear many hats, especially when the project is lower budget and has a smaller staff as a result.

Just as producers wear many hats, there are many software-based tools that producers find useful:

- Spreadsheet software, such as Microsoft Excel

- Task management software, such as Omni Focus

- Calendars

- Project management software, such as Microsoft Project, Movie Magic Scheduling, Gorilla, or Celtz

- Document organization or paperless office software, such as DevonThink Pro

- Outline creation software, such as Omni Outliner

- Online document sharing, such as Google Docs (although some prefer a private network solution)

- Accounting software, such as Intuit QuickBooks and Movie Magic Budgeting

- Film-oriented document templates, such as those available at subscription-based Web sites like *www.filmproposals.com*.

Breaking Down a Script

The first step in creating a shooting schedule is to analyze your script to determine exactly what you'll need in terms of cast, crew, locations, props, and other resources. Fill out a breakdown sheet for every scene in your movie, using a form like the one shown in Figure 2.5. Script breakdown marks the first time that you'll need to translate your vision of each scene into a list of tangible things. Be meticulous as you make these lists, so that you don't leave out anything important. It's also a good idea to consult with your director of photography, art director, costume designer, and so forth during this process.

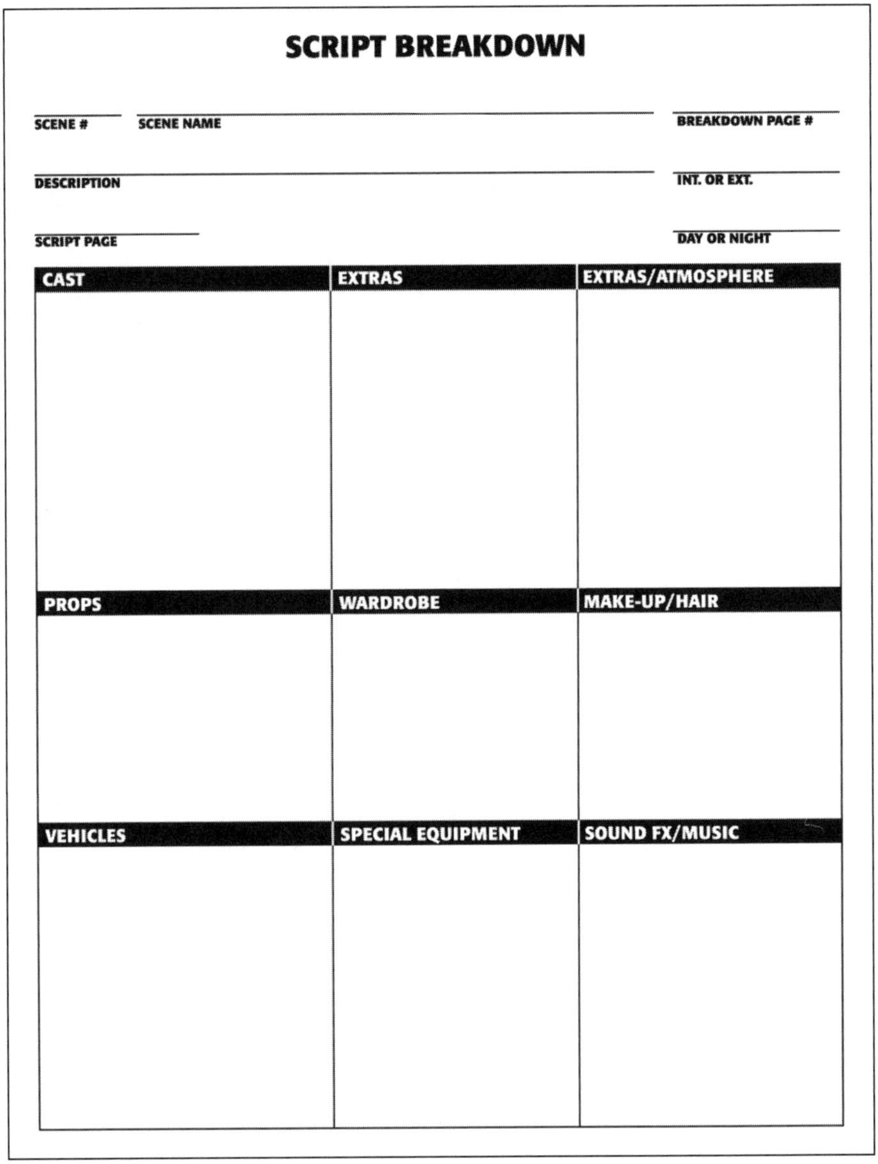

SCRIPT BREAKDOWN

SCENE #   SCENE NAME   BREAKDOWN PAGE #

DESCRIPTION   INT. OR EXT.

SCRIPT PAGE   DAY OR NIGHT

CAST	EXTRAS	EXTRAS/ATMOSPHERE

PROPS	WARDROBE	MAKE-UP/HAIR

VEHICLES	SPECIAL EQUIPMENT	SOUND FX/MUSIC

Figure 2.5

A sample breakdown sheet. To begin scheduling, you need to fill out such a sheet for each scene in your script. (A template for this breakdown sheet, Breakdown Sheet.pdf, is included on the Chapter 2 page of the companion Web site.)

Now a breakdown exercise. Read the text of the scene from Shakespeare's *Richard III*, which is on the *www.thedigitalfilmmakinghandbook.com* Web site in standard screenplay format (Richard III.pdf on the Chapter 2 page), and determine how you want to interpret the scene. Will you create a period piece set during the actual reign of Richard III? Will you transpose the scene to the modern-day White House? Or maybe an inner-city gangster drama? Use your creativity and come up with something you'd enjoy directing. Then print out the script breakdown sheet, also on the Chapter 2 page of the Web site (Breakdown Sheet.pdf) and start filling it out. Who are the cast members? Will there be extras? What props do you need? Where is the location?

Choosing a Shooting Order

Once you've determined the resources you'll need for each scene, you can start to organize your shoot accordingly. You might organize the shoot in terms of your locations, shooting all of the scenes in the main character's house first, then all of the scenes at his job, and so on. Or you might organize the shoot based on the availability of cast members, or the need for special shooting conditions, such as a blue-screen stage or a rainstorm. Or you might want to schedule the biggest, most expensive, most complicated scene first to guarantee that it gets shot before you run out of money, or last to make sure that you don't blow your entire budget on a single expensive scene.

If you organize the shoot in one of these ways, you'll be shooting *out of sequence*. It's very common to shoot out of sequence, but many people prefer to shoot as close to the script order as is reasonably possible to get better performances from the actors. Just imagine if you were an actor and had to shoot a scene where you celebrated your first wedding anniversary one day, and then shot the scene where you first met your wife on the next day. On the other hand, if your movie includes a subplot about a terrorist who never interacts with the main characters until the final scene, you can easily shoot all those subplot scenes out of order without making things difficult for the actors.

Scheduling Preproduction

A rule of thumb is that you need the same number of days for production prep time (securing locations, props, wardrobe, permits, travel plans, and so on) as you need for the shoot itself. So if you are planning a 15-day shoot, you'll need 15 days of prep time to set it up properly.

How Much Can You Shoot in a Day?

Traditionally, most film productions aim to shoot a certain number of pages each day. Studio films often shoot about two pages per day, whereas many independent filmmakers must opt for a less luxurious schedule, often shooting upward of eight pages per day. Of course, this all depends on what you are shooting. Typically, a page of dialogue requires much less time to shoot than a page of action does. A page that includes special effects or complicated camera moves will require even more time.

To plan your day's shoot, you can use these basic rules of thumb:

- One script page takes an hour to shoot (not including setting up the lighting, and so on) so most productions can count on shooting 5–8 pages per day.

- Changing the lighting setup, or moving all the lights around so that you can shoot from another angle, usually takes an hour.

- Changing locations, sometimes called a *company move*, takes about three hours, assuming the next location is nearby.

Chaos Theory

Why is good scheduling important? Consider the following production schedule scenario for a medium-budget production with a union cast and crew:

You're shooting a Western on location in Arizona. Everything's good to go, you have a bunch of extras, four actors, and a union crew. After getting everyone from the airport to the location—which counts as a day of paid labor plus per diem money for cast and crew—you awaken at your desert location the next day to a giant thunderstorm. It's short-lived, but now the dusty town isn't very dusty. Luckily, you've prepared for just such an event by scheduling alternate "cover sets" throughout your shoot. Therefore, you move everyone into the saloon to shoot the gambling scene. Unfortunately, you don't need your lead actress for this scene, but you'll have to pay her anyway, since anything less than a 10-day break is considered a "holding" day in a SAG (Screen Actor's Guild) agreement. To "hold" her, you'll have to pay her.

Because of the delays due to changing locations, you're only going to shoot one page of script instead of the three that you were aiming for that day. Moreover, you have a very early, 3:00 A.M. call tomorrow for some crew members, and you have to give them 12 hours of "turnaround"—the time between the "wrap" of one day's shoot and the "call" of the next day's shoot. This means that your lighting crew and art department must leave the set at 3:00 P.M., to have enough turnaround time before you need them at 3:00 A.M. the next morning.

It's hectic, and you're patting yourself on the back for having it all under control, when your lead actor takes you aside and explains that shooting the gambling scene out of sequence is a big problem for him, motivation-wise, so he'd prefer to shoot the scene in the barn where he has a heart-to-heart talk with his horse. Unfortunately, the horses don't arrive until tomorrow.

WHAT TO WATCH

Lost in La Mancha is a documentary about the attempted making of a feature film based on "Don Quixote" by director Terry Gilliam. It is probably the most extreme example of what can go wrong during the filming of a movie, and it was all captured on videotape by a secondary crew. Also good are *Burden of Dreams* and *Hearts of Darkness*.

Production Boards

Shooting schedules for feature films use a tool developed long before the advent of computers: the production board. Production boards provide a method for tracking a very large amount of information in a way that's modifiable and portable. Using the information that's entered in the breakdown sheets (refer back to Figure 2.5), you create a production strip for each scene in the film. Each production strip contains the duration of the scene (in script pages), the slugline of the scene, and a one-line description of the scene. The production strips are placed in a set of production boards. The result is a spreadsheet with rows of cast member names and other important elements, and columns for each scene in the movie (Figure 2.6).

At the intersections of the rows and columns, you can see which cast members are involved in a scene, and when those scenes will be shot. In addition to cast members, you can list special props and equipment. The final set of production boards is a hard-backed folder that is taken onto the set for easy reference. Because each scene is on a separate, removable strip, you can easily rearrange the scene order on the fly if, for example, an actor gets sick or the location is rained out. Production boards allow for the type of thinking on your feet that's always necessary during a shoot. Old-school production boards can still be purchased at stationers who specialize in serving the entertainment industry.

Film Scheduling Software

No matter what your project, film production scheduling software such as Movie Magic Scheduling, Gorilla, or Celtz can be invaluable. These apps can import properly formatted screenplays and automatically create breakdown sheets (refer to Figure 2.5) and production boards (Figure 2.6).

Rush		Sheet 1 — EXT - Intersection - Cole/Carl - Night — Scs. 1, 2 — Leo Arrives in town and gets off the MUNI	Sheet 2 — EXT - Top of stairs outside X's building - Ni — Scs. 6 — Leo arrives at his front door for the first time	Sheet 3 — INT - Leo's apartment building - Night — Scs. 4 — Leo arrives inside his apartment for the first time	Sheet 4 — INT - Leo's Room - Night — Scs. 5 — Leo sees his room for the first time	End Of Day 1 – 7/22/99 – 12 7/8 pgs.	Sheet 13 — INT - Leo's Room - Day — Scs. 15 — Leo wakes up for his first day on the job	Sheet 39 — INT - Leo's Room - Day — Scs. 39 — Leo shows Annie his project for the first time	Sheet 16 — INT - Leo's Room - Day — Scs. 44 — Leo calls Annie for the first time	Sheet 11 — INT - Leo's Room - Night — Scs. 12 — Leo sits by his window and sketches	Sheet 12 — INT - Bathroom in Leo's apartment - Night — Scs. 14 — Leo brushes his teeth and finds his mail	Sheet 14 — INT - Leo's Room - Night — Scs. 24 — Leo arrives home after his first day on the job	End Of Day 2 – 7/23/99 – 138 3/8 pgs.	Sheet 5 — INT - Leo's Room - Day — Scs. — Leo wakes up and calls Dan Tuttle on the phone
Sheet Number:		1	2	3	4		13	39	16	11	12	14		5
Page Count:		2 3/8	2 5/8	3 1/8	4 6/8		14 4/8	37 6/8	38 3/8	10 5/8	13 5/8	23 4/8		6 3/8
Shoot Day:		1	1	1	1		2	2	2	2	2	2		3
Character	**No.**													
Leo	1	1		1	1		1	1	1	1	1	1		1
Annie	2							2	2					
Grandfather	3													
John	4													
Satij	5													
Wayne Houston	6													
Dan Tuttle	7													7
Vince	8			8	8									
Bill	9													
Bus Dev 1	10													
Bus Dev 2	11													
Extras:														

Director: B Long
Producer: B Baker
Asst. Director:
Script Dated: July 1, 1999

Figure 2.6

Production boards organize the details of your shoot in a simple-to-read spreadsheet format.

Planning for Pickups

After you're done with your principal shoot, you might find that you need to reshoot or add new scenes. These pickups are usually shot after a first rough cut has been finished. Maybe there was a lighting problem in the only good take of a key scene, or maybe you decided that the way an actor played a scene doesn't work. Most projects schedule a day or two for pickups in advance to reduce the likelihood of cast and crew availability problems.

Scheduling for Unscripted Projects

While scheduling for a feature film can be complicated, thanks to the script, you at least know what your end product is going to be, so you can account for all of the shots that you might need to get. With a documentary project, or any form of "journalistic" project, where you're covering a person or event with no set goal or list of particular shots or scenes, your scheduling tasks will be a little different.

They're called *documentaries* for a reason; your goal when shooting one is to document your subject as thoroughly as possible so that you'll have plenty of footage to work with once you're back in the editing room. In general, you'll probably shoot 20 to 30 times more footage than a scripted movie, and in some cases, this ratio may go even higher.

Obviously, if you're covering a particular event, your scheduling chores center on the duration of that event. If it's a complex event that involves several crews of shooters, then you'll need to map out a shooting strategy and schedule ahead of time. Similarly, if you only have one camera rig, but it's a very long event, then you'll need to schedule your crew in shifts for continuous shooting.

Most of your other shooting tasks will probably involve interviews or trips to other locations to gather supporting material. Scheduling these is usually just a simple process of sorting out which interview subjects or locations are available at particular times and scheduling accordingly.

Documentaries often have the advantage of not having such a tight shooting schedule as scripted features, but they also need to be able to "run and gun" when something unexpected happens. Planning for documentaries should always include the assumption that some sort of "surprise" will happen on every day of shooting. If there aren't any unexpected events, you might want to consider whether or not you are capturing interesting material.

Photo credit: Paquita Parks

3

Digital Video Primer

Photo credit: Sonja Schenk

W hat is the best way to shoot my project? Should I shoot 24p? What is the difference between 1080 and 720 HD? What type of digital video will look most like film? What are codecs? What do I need to know about audio? Should I worry about transcoding? What do all those other acronyms and numbers mean?

In this chapter, we're going to introduce you to the fundamentals of digital video technology. Consider this chapter a reference for the terms and concepts you will encounter on a day-to-day basis during your production process, as well as throughout the rest of this book.

What Is HD?

By now, you should have a script and have started to work out what your budget and your shooting schedule will be. And you should have started to make decisions about the way you want to shoot your project. At this point, you probably have lots of questions but one thing should be certain: you are shooting in high definition (HD). Why? Because all digital formats with a resolution greater than standard definition (SD) video are considered HD. In other words, unless you are using old equipment, HD is almost impossible to avoid these days.

HD is a tricky thing to discuss because the term itself does not actually refer to any one particular type of digital video. Rather, it's a "set" of digital video formats and specifications.

However, when digital filmmakers talk about shooting HD, they're almost always talking about one of the three primary subsets: 720, 1080, and digital cinema.

- **720** has a resolution of 1280×720 and is always scanned progressively. It supports the following frame rates: 23.976p, 24p, 25p, 29.97p, 30p, 59.94p, and 60p. It has a native aspect ratio of 16:9.

- **1080** has a resolution of 1920×1080 and can be scanned progressively or be interlaced. It supports the following frame rates: 23.976p, 24p, 29.97p, 30p, 50i, 59.94i, and 60i. It has a native aspect ratio of 16:9.

- **Digital cinema** is a very high-resolution digital format that aims to be comparable to 35mm film. It has a resolution of 2000 horizontal pixels (usually referred to as 2K) or greater, is progressively scanned, and usually has a frame rate of 24, but some cameras can shoot at variable frame rates.

If the previous descriptions of 720, 1080, and digital cinema leave you cross-eyed, don't worry. We'll explain what all that means in the next few pages.

All of these formats are of very high quality. Each frame of 1080 is almost double the size of a frame of 720. However, 720 offers the option of 60 frames per second, which doubles the information of the highest 1080 frame rate (see Figure 3.1) and 2K digital cinema is only a little bigger than 1080 HD. So it can be hard to say exactly which one is a better format.

Digital cinema cameras that record 2K video come with a heck of a lot more than just an extra hundred lines of scan resolution. Their extremely good latitude and dynamic range is what makes them so incredible, in comparison to, let's say, standard HD cameras like the Panasonic HPX-170 or the Sony EX3. Furthermore, 720p can be described as useful for certain kinds of video production that require long record times, like weddings or corporate industrial videos. On that level, it can sometimes be more about logistics than anything else.

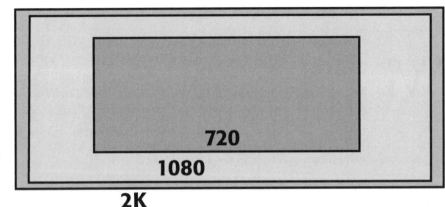

WHAT TO WATCH

Broadcast network TV—ABC broadcasts 720p and all the other networks broadcast 1080i. Be sure to look at network original programming, such as the news and not the commercials.

Components of Digital Video

At the simplest level, all digital video is a collection of electronic signals recorded by a camera onto a piece of media: videotape, optical disk, hard drive, or flash memory. No matter how the signals are stored, all digital video consists of tracks, frames, scan lines, pixels, and audio samples.

Tracks

During a shoot, your video camera captures video and audio information, converts it into electronic data, and stores it onto its recording medium. All of this data is laid down in separate tracks (sometimes called *channels* or *streams*), typically one video track and two audio tracks. (Some cameras and audio recorders can record four or more tracks of audio.) In addition, most digital cameras record some form of data track that includes information such as the time of day, timecode, camera settings, and so on.

Frames

The video track consists of a series of still images, or frames, that, when played in sequence, appear to be moving. Frames of video are similar to frames of film, except that you can't see them by holding them up to the light. Instead, you need a computer to decode the electronic information that constitutes each frame and display it on a monitor.

Each second of video contains a specific number of still images in order to give the illusion of motion. The number of still images, or frames, per second is called the *frame rate*. When motion picture film was invented, it originally ran at a frame rate of 18 frames per second (fps). With the advent of sound, the frame rate had to be increased to 24fps to get audio that was in sync with the picture.

There are many different frame rates associated with HD. The reason is that when HD was developed, it needed to be compatible with a variety of existing media: film, American analog broadcast video, and European analog broadcast video. Each of these three potential sources for HD defines a subset of HD frame rates:

- **24p and 23.976p.** Frame rates based on film.

- **29.97p, 30p, 59.94i, 60i, 59.94p, and 60p.** Frame rates based on American television.

- **25p and 50i.** Frame rates based on European television.

As you're trying to decide which frame rate to use when you shoot, you can narrow down your options by using this list. For example, if you are doing a project in the United States, there is no reason to shoot 25p or 50i.

24P

24p is used when shooting video footage that will eventually be transferred to film. It is also used when transferring projects shot on film to HD for broadcast. Some argue that shooting 24p results in more film-like footage even if it is never transferred to film. 24p can be either 720 or 1080, so be sure to specify!

Scan Lines

Each individual frame of video is composed of a series of horizontal lines that are scanned across the screen starting at the top. With some types of video, these scan lines start at the top and work their way down to the bottom, filling the screen entirely, a process called *progressive scanning* (p).

With other types of video, the scan lines start at the top but only draw the even-numbered lines until they get to the bottom; then the odd-numbered lines are filled in from top to bottom (see Figure 3.2), a process called *interlaced scanning* (i). Each pass across the monitor is called a *field,* and each frame of interlaced video consists of two fields. The order in which the fields are drawn can change, depending on how the video is recorded.

If you are wondering which one is better, there's no clear answer, but progressive scanning is definitely simpler and more intuitive, so given the choice, most filmmakers these days opt for progressive scanning. However, if your project is destined for broadcast television, the network may require that you use a form of HD with interlaced scanning.

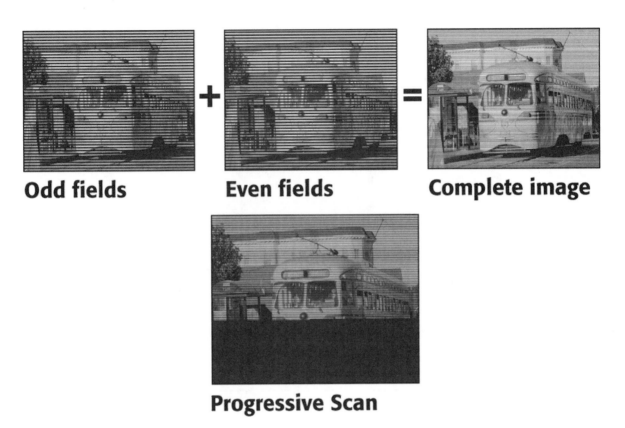

Odd fields   **Even fields**   **Complete image**

Progressive Scan

Figure 3.2
Interlaced video uses two fields to make up a complete frame of video; progressive scan video does not have fields.

Pixels

A pixel, short for "picture element," is the smallest component of a video image. A frame of 720 HD video consists of a grid of 1280 pixels in width and 720 pixels in height. A frame of 1080 HD video contains a grid that's 1920 pixels wide and 1080 pixels tall. These pixel dimensions are one way that people describe the resolution of a frame of video.

Vertical Resolution

The number of horizontal lines that fit on the screen is known as the *vertical resolution*. Some of the horizontal lines in each video frame are used to convey information that isn't part of the visible image, something you don't really need to worry about. For example, the vertical resolution of 1080 HD actually consists of 1125 vertical lines, of which 1080 are visible.

Horizontal Resolution

When it comes to image quality, you hear a lot of talk about "resolution," especially when discussing video cameras. When speaking of resolution, people are usually referring to the horizontal resolution—that is, how many individual pixels (or dots) there are in each one of those horizontal lines. The vertical resolution mentioned earlier is fixed, but the horizontal resolution is variable.

Due to the way in which the human eye works, a set of alternating black-and-white lines, like those in Figure 3.3, will look like gray mush if the lines are small enough. Horizontal line resolution measures how many alternating black-and-white lines can fit in a video image before turning into an indistinct gray mass. Due to its subjective nature, horizontal line resolution is not a hard-and-fast figure. It varies according to such factors as the monitor, the camera hardware, how bright the room where the monitor is, how far you are from the monitor, and how good your vision is. Some cameras, lenses, and monitors have a greater capacity for displaying distinct vertical lines, and these devices are considered to have better "resolution."

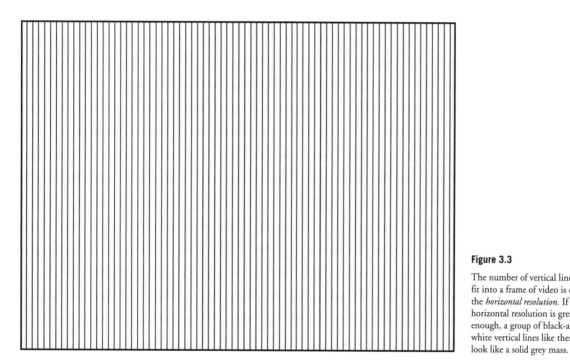

Figure 3.3

The number of vertical lines that fit into a frame of video is called the *horizontal resolution*. If the horizontal resolution is great enough, a group of black-and-white vertical lines like these will look like a solid grey mass.

Film Resolution

The resolution of 35mm film is higher than the resolution of 1080 or 720 HD video. Film is an analog medium so it doesn't have pixels, but nevertheless it is considered to have a minimum resolution of 2048 × 1080 pixels, or 2K. In other words, in order for a digital video format to approximate the resolution of 35mm film, it must have a resolution of 2048 × 1080 pixels or higher. Digital video formats that have this resolution are often referred to as *digital cinema formats*, rather than HD. The resolution of digital cinema formats range from 2K to 4K (or 4096 × 2160). The RED One is a digital video camera that acquires footage in the digital cinema range, which is why it is often used for shooting feature films.

WHAT TO WATCH

Slumdog Millionaire won the Academy Award for best cinematography and was mostly shot in a digital cinema format.

Aspect Ratio

The ratio of the width of an image to its height is called the *aspect ratio* (see Figure 3.4). HD video (both 1080 and 720) and 35mm film formats have a widescreen native aspect ratio, 1.78:1 (aka. 16:9) for HD video and 1.85:1 for most 35mm film. Typically, wider is considered more "cinematic." Shooting in a wider format lets you put more information across the screen and is a truer representation of the way our field of vision works. Older SD and analog television displays and older computer monitors have a native aspect ratio of 4:3, or 1.33:1. In addition, 16mm, 8mm, and Super8 film all have a native aspect ratio of 4:3.

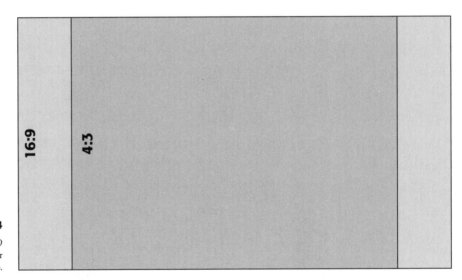

Figure 3.4

The larger rectangle has a 16:9 aspect ratio, while the smaller rectangle has a 4:3 aspect ratio.

Pixel Shape

Most newer digital video formats use square pixels but some older formats, like DV and HDV use non-square pixels. If your video uses non-square pixels, you might have to go through some extra steps in postproduction. For a more in-depth information, look at the pixel aspect ratios document at *www.thedigitalfilmmakinghandbook.com*.

WHAT TO WATCH

Lawrence of Arabia is known for its stunning widescreen photography. Also worth checking out: *2001 A Space Odyssey* and *Dr. Strangelove* (just in case you thought widescreen was invented recently).

Describing HD

Because "HD" isn't one specific thing, the various types of HD video are usually described by three things: the pixel dimensions (or resolution), the number of frames or fields per second, and the scanning method (interlaced or progressive).

720/24p is HD video with a resolution of 1280 × 720 and a frame rate of 24 progressively scanned frames per second. 1080/60i is HD with a resolution of 1920 × 1080 and a frame rate of 60 interlaced fields per second. Because 1080/60i is one of the most popular HD configurations for television, it is often simply called *1080i*. Similarly, 720/60p is often referred to as *720p*. In this book, we use the full description (1080/60i) in order to avoid confusion. We use 720 and 1080 to refer to the entire range of frame rates that share those resolutions.

There's one more thing to be aware of: interlaced HD video is described by the number of fields instead of frames. 1080/60i has 60 *fields* per second. Since two interlaced fields of video add up to one frame of video, the frame rate is still 30 frames per second—60i is just a different way of describing the same thing and letting you know that it's interlaced. Progressively scanned HD video, on the other hand, is described by the number of frames. 720/60p has 60 frames per second.

Audio Tracks

There's a saying that sound is 50 percent of a movie. Luckily, it's not quite as complicated as video. Earlier, we said that each HD video file consists of a video track and two (or more) audio tracks. Because an HD file can have multiple audio tracks, they can be configured to work together, or mix, in different ways.

Stereo Sound

Stereo sound consists of two channels of audio mixed together in a special way: one channel is balanced somewhat to the left, and the other is balanced somewhat to the right. When played back, a "stereo" field is created that creates a more three-dimensional perception of where the sounds are coming from.

The only type of production sound that is typically recorded in stereo is music. Stereo sound is usually reserved for the final mix of a soundtrack for a film or TV show. The built-in microphones on most camcorders are stereo, but these mics are usually not suitable for serious production work. You can, of course, buy or rent stereo mics to attach to your camera, and these will record separate left and right channels directly to tape; however, this is not necessary if you are primarily recording dialogue.

Mono Sound

Mono sound consists of one track (or channel) of audio. *Almost all of the sound that you record during your production is mono.* If you record a line from a microphone into a digital audio recorder, you are probably recording mono sound because most microphones are not stereo microphones—that is, they don't record separate left and right channels that create a full stereo field. Even if you record onto both channels of the digital audio recorder with a mono microphone, you're still recording mono: you're simply recording the same mono signal on the recorder's two channels.

If you patch a lavalier mic into channel one and let the camera's built-in mic record to channel two, you are still recording in mono. Granted, you are creating two different mono recordings of the same thing, but the two different channels will sound very different due to the quality of the microphones and their positioning. In no way do they add up to a stereo recording.

There's nothing wrong with recording mono production sound; in fact, it's usually considered ideal. You'll record many different tracks of mono sound and later you (or a sound editor) will mix them together in different ways to get a stereo mix and a surround sound mix.

Recordings Versus Mixes

When you record sound on a movie, typically you record as many mono tracks as you need. Later, when you edit the scene, you typically put several audio tracks together to create a mix.

Surround Sound

For theatrical projection, Blu-ray Discs, DVDs, and HDTV, surround sound is the norm. Surround sound mixes generally consist of 5.1 or 7.1 channels of sound that correspond to the position of speakers in a room or theater. They give an even more intense three-dimensional feeling to the environment than do stereo mixes. (Those .1 channels refer to a subwoofer that provides extra bass.) Mixes and surround sound are discussed more thoroughly in Chapter 15, "Sound Editing" and also in Chapter 18, "Finishing."

Audio Sampling

Just as a frame of video is broken down into pixels, waves of sound are broken down into samples to create digital audio (see Figure 3.5). The rate at which the audio is sampled can vary, and, as with a video or still image, the higher the sampling rate, the better the quality will be. Professional digital audio is usually sampled at 48kHz (DAT quality) or less commonly at 44.1kHz (CD quality). As a rule, never record at less than 48kHz unless you have a very specific reason to record lower quality sound. Some digital cinema formats can handle 96kHz sampling.

See the section on codecs later in this chapter for a discussion of the different types of digital audio formats.

Analog sound wave

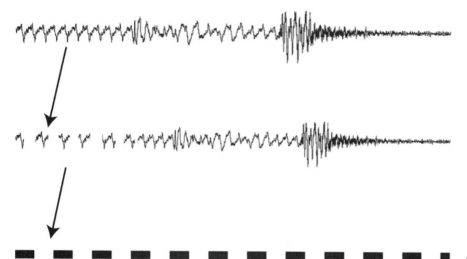

Digitally sampled sound

Figure 3.5

An analog sound wave (top) is broken into small samples, resulting in a digital audio file (bottom).

Working with Analog or SD Video

It's hard to believe that analog and SD video were a common part of the filmmaking process until as recently as five years ago. Technology has improved so quickly that it's now pretty easy to move forward with HD and never look back.

Unfortunately, not everyone has this luxury. If you work on a TV show that's been around for a while, you'll have to deal with SD clips from old seasons from time to time, or perhaps you're doing a documentary on Martin Luther King, so all your archival media is in SD format. That means you're going to have a project that mixes both HD and SD media. Or maybe you invested in high-quality SD equipment and aren't quite ready to make the leap to HD. Whatever the reason, there are some things to be aware of when dealing with analog/SD footage:

- The aspect ratio of analog/SD footage is 4:3 (or 1.33:1).

- The resolution of analog video is 640 × 480 pixels and each pixel has a rectangular shape. Most forms of digital video have square pixels. This is why analog video sometimes looks stretched on your HDTV.

- The resolution of SD video is 720 × 480. This digital format is much more easily compatible with HD formats.

- The frame rate of analog video (in the United States) is 29.97fps.

- Analog video is interlaced, which means it has two fields for every frame.

- If you transfer analog video to an HD format, you will have to decide whether or not to have it blown up to fill the width of the entire frame, which will mean that you must crop off the top and bottom of the image, or to have it fill the height of the frame, which means there will be two black areas on either side of the frame (see Figure 3.6). Some people choose to fill these areas with graphics or a background of some sort. (More about integrating HD and SD footage in Chapter 17, "Titles and Effects.")

For those of you who must continue to work with analog footage, we've saved the discussion of how analog video works from the previous edition and put it on the Web site for this book at *www.thedigitalfilmmakinghandbook.com.*

Figure 3.6

When transferring analog or SD video to HD, you must choose between a cropped image (bottom) or an image that does not fit the entire frame (top).

Why 29.97?

When broadcast video in America was first standardized, all television was black and white (or more correctly, monochrome) and had a frame rate of 30fps. When color technology was added, broadcasters and the FCC needed to figure out a way to differentiate color video from black and white. The solution? Slow the frame rate of color video down by 1/1000th of a percent (.001). That way, existing monochrome TV sets could continue to pick up the monochrome 30fps signal and new color TV sets could pick up the 29.97fps color signal. Unfortunately, in America we are now stuck with the legacy of obsolete monochrome media and have all sorts of strange frame rates that are a bit difficult to remember. When transferring 24fps media to NTSC video, the 24fps footage is also slowed down .1% to 23.976fps in order to maintain audio sync with 29.97fps media.

WHAT TO WATCH

Paranormal Activity is a great example of how any type of image-quality can work if it suits the story. This movie feels so real precisely because it was shot with the kind of camcorder almost everybody owns.

Stick with the New

Using older video gear can introduce a world of pain to your project. Older, analog, or SD video is very different, technically speaking, from HD video. They have different frame rates, different aspect ratios, different pixel shapes and most importantly, don't look as good. Trust us, it's not worth it!

Timecode

When you shoot digital video, your camera keeps track of the time and assigns a number to every single frame that you record. This is extremely useful in postproduction if you have to move your media from one system to another, if you are working with low-res proxies and plan to upgrade your media later on, or if you need to reconstruct your project at a later date. It can also make synchronizing multi-cam footage much easier.

Some cameras automatically use their internal clock to record timecode that corresponds to the actual time of day, known as time-of-day timecode. A shot that has a starting timecode of 11:07:40:15 was shot at about seven minutes after 11 A.M.

SMTPE timecode is a standardized type of timecode that doesn't reflect the time of day. Rather, the user can set the starting time however they want. Typically, the first tape or disk is set to 01:00:00:00 and then next one is set to hour 2 and so on.

Because the frame rate of analog NTSC video is an odd 29.97 frames per second, drop frame timecode was developed to help round off the fractional frames to less awkward whole numbers. Drop frame timecode is the standard for analog and digital 29.97fps video for broadcast television in America.

Timecode (continued)

If you're shooting with a camera that doesn't have timecode, such as a DSLR, then each shot will start at zero. But luckily, your camera will still record metadata in each video file that includes timestamp information that your computer can use in postproduction.

Time-of-day timecode and correct time stamps in the metadata can be very useful in post-production, so make sure your camera's internal clock is set to the correct time and date.

For a more detailed discussion of timecode and also key code for film, check out the timecode document in the Chapter 3 folder at *www.thedigitalfilmmakinghandbook.com*.

Digital Image Quality

Let's face it, the primary reason most of us care about all this techno stuff is because we care about image quality. All of us want our projects to look as good as possible. And even though all types of HD video have the potential for a very high quality of image, in practice, it doesn't always work out that way.

That's because as you work to create your film, the image you first record will go through a series of processes, all of which affect image quality (see Figure 3.7).

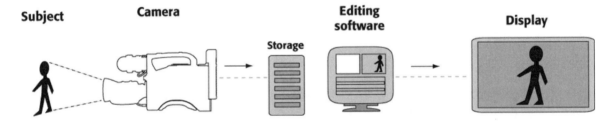

Figure 3.7

The image quality food chain: subject (includes lighting, location and production design), camera (lens, sensor, digitization, acquisition format), editing (intermediate format[s] and delivery format) and display.

That brings us to a very simple question: why is there a difference between shooting 1080/24p with an HDV camera and shooting 1080/24p with a Sony XDCAM? After all, they share the same image size and frame rate. Lens quality and image sensors in the camera are part of the reason, but the more significant reason is compression. If you have an HDTV, you've probably already noticed how much difference in quality there can be from one show to another. Sports broadcasts typically look significantly better than the HD commercials that air alongside them, and often much better than dramatic shows, local newscasts, or documentaries. This is due in large part to the different formats used, each of which uses a different type of compression.

Full-resolution digital video files are very large. A single frame of 1080p HD video contains over 2 million pixels. Multiply that by 24 frames in a second, and suddenly you have a *lot* of data to store and manipulate. Computers today are very powerful, but dealing with images of this size is still a challenge. That's where compression steps in. The software that handles this task is called a *codec*, short for COmpressor/DECompressor. Codecs discard or diminish unnecessary (mostly) visual information to reduce the total amount of video data, which helps ensure that your video files can be captured and viewed in real time.

As you create your project, you'll encounter various types of compression along the way. Compression happens in the camera, as video is captured, or acquired, It can also happen if you import, or transcode media, into your editing application. It happens again when you output or master your final project to various digital formats such as videos for the Web, Blu-ray Discs, and uncompressed HD for digital projection, to name only a few of the many options.

Earlier, we talked about the various components of digital video (tracks, frames, scan lines, pixels, and audio samples), but digital video is more than just the sum of these parts. That's because every digital video compression scheme, or algorithm, determines how color is handled (color sampling and bit-depth), exactly how much compression is used (compression ratios), and how quickly the information captured is moved around (data rate).

Color Sampling

In grade school, you might have learned about the primary colors that can be mixed together to create all other colors. What they probably never explained in school was that those are the primary subtractive colors, or the primary colors of ink. When you talk about the color of light, things work a bit differently.

Red, green, and blue are the three primary colors of light; you can create any other color of light by mixing those primaries together. However, whereas mixing primary colors of ink together results in a darker color, mixing light creates a lighter color. Mix enough ink, and you eventually get black, but if you mix enough light, you eventually get white. (See Color Plates 1 and 2.)

Video cameras and televisions create color by mixing the three primary colors of light. In addition to red (R), green (G), and blue (B), the video signal has another element, which is lightness, or luminance (Y). The lens on your camera sees each of these four elements as separate, continuous analog waves, and digital cameras must first convert the waves into numbers, through a process called *sampling*. Each wave is broken into a series of bits that can be stored on the digital tape as 0s and 1s. The denser the samples, the better the perceived quality of the image will be (see Figure 3.8).

Very few samples ⎯⎯⎯⎯⎯⎯→ **Millions of samples**

Figure 3.8

As the number of samples increases from left to right, the image becomes clearer.

When a digital camera samples an image, the degree to which it samples each primary color is called the *color sampling ratio*. A fully uncompressed video signal (also known as *RGB color*) has a color sampling ratio of 4:4:4. The first number stands for the luminance, or luma, signal (abbreviated y'), and the next two numbers stand for the color difference components (Cb and Cr), which together add up to the full chroma signal. 4:4:4 means that for every pixel, four samples each are taken for the luma signal and the two chroma signals.

To make the resulting data smaller, and therefore more manageable, usually about half of the color information is discarded. Uncompressed digital cinema formats can have a color sampling ratio of 4:4:4, but many very high-quality digital video formats actually throw out half of the color information. These formats have a color sampling ratio of 4:2:2, which means that for every four luma samples, there are two of each type of color samples. The human eye is more sensitive to differences in light and dark (luminance) than to differences in color (chrominance). In theory, the discarded color information is detail that the human eye cannot perceive, so it's worth throwing it out for the sake of saving storage space. (See Color Plate 3.)

The color sampling ratio of most HD formats is 4:2:2. Some HD formats, like HDV, use 4:2:0 color sampling, which reduces the color information of 4:2:2 by 25 percent, which is an amount of color reduction that is considered visible to the viewer. For more about light and color, see Chapter 6, "Lighting," and Chapter 16, "Color Correction."

Bit Depth

Digital video usually has a bit depth of 8, 10, or 12 bits. Digital devices speak in ones and zeros (two "digits," hence the term *digital*). A single one or zero is called a *bit*, and a group of bits can be grouped together to represent a single number. When it comes time to assign a numeric value to the color of a particular pixel, then the number of bits that are used to make up that number becomes something of an issue. With more bits, you can record a greater range of numbers, which means you can represent more colors. This bit depth of a particular format refers to how many bits are used to represent the color of each pixel and is also sometimes referred to as quantization.

Basically, it's just the same as boxes of crayons. If you only have eight crayons, the pictures you draw don't have nearly as much color detail and variation as if you have a box of 64 crayons. Similarly, if you only have 8 bits available for representing the color of each pixel, you don't have nearly as much color detail and variation to work with as if you have 10 bits per pixel.

Higher-end cameras capture three streams of video, one for each color: red, green, and blue (see Color Plate 4), and each channel usually has 8 bits per pixel, for a total of 24 bits or 10 bits per pixel for a total of 30 bits, which is partly why cameras with 3 chips are touted above those with only one. (In Chapter 4, "Choosing a Camera," there is in-depth information about cameras and image quality.) For blue-screen work, or other compositing tasks, or for projects where you really want to be able to manipulate the color of your final image, a format that uses a higher bit depth will allow higher-quality, cleaner adjustments.

Compression Ratios

To fit more data onto a tape and to better facilitate digital postproduction, most digital video formats use some type of data compression. This compression process can greatly affect the quality of your image. Uncompressed video has a compression ratio of 1:1, while compressed video can range anywhere from 1.6:1 to 10:1. Video compressed at a 10:1 ratio has 10 percent of its original data. Although throwing out 90 percent of your image data might sound a little scary, rest assured that modern compression schemes can deliver excellent results, even with very high compression ratios. In fact, video DVDs use a fairly extreme level of MPEG-2 compression, showing that heavily compressed video can still be commercially viable.

As explained earlier, a video format with a 4:2:2 color sampling ratio compresses the video signal by discarding half of the color information. However, this discarded information is not visible to the human eye, so this compression is considered lossless.

When the color sampling rate dips to 4:1:1 or 4:2:0, the information that has been discarded *is* visible to the eye, so this compression is considered lossy. However, the image quality of 4:1:1 and 4:2:0 video, such as HDV, is still considered excellent.

Data Rate

When a digital video camera records an image, the amount of information that is stored for each second of video is determined by the video format's data rate, or bit rate. For example, HDV has a data rate of 25 megabits per second (Mbps). This means that 25Mbps of information are stored for each second of video. (If you factor in audio, timecode information, and the other "housekeeping" data that needs to be stored, HDV actually takes up about 36Mbps.) DVCPRO HD, on the other hand, ranges from 40 to 100Mbps of information for each second of video. As one would expect, more information means a better picture, and the data rate is one of the reasons that DVCPRO HD has higher quality than HDV. Uncompressed 4:4:4 HD video has a data rate of over 800Mbps, while video that is compressed for streaming over the Internet usually has a low data rate of 10Mbps or less.

Understanding Digital Media Files

As digital video cameras move toward file-based acquisition, the clarity of the various digital video formats gets murkier. It used to be that you simply looked at the type of videotape itself to identify the format: a Beta SP tape meant the format was Betacam, a VHS tape was VHS. The physical size and structure of the tape itself determined the quality of the images and audio that it could record.

Nowadays, file-based acquisition means that the format of the recording media itself matters less and less because tapeless media, like SD cards or flash drives, are simply neutral storage devices that can store any type of file that fits.

The good news is that digital video now works in a way that is intuitive to anyone who uses a computer: files are stored on discs or drives. The not-so-good news is that it's pretty hard to look at a list of files and figure out what the quality or format of that file is.

There's another big change in regard to media and file formats. With a traditional videotape-based workflow, you would pick a format and stick with it throughout the shooting and editing process. If you did decide to introduce another videotape format into your workflow, typically it would be at the end when you mastered to a higher-quality format.

With tapeless formats, it doesn't work that way anymore. In fact, you will be likely to use at least three different file formats as you shoot, edit, and finish your film. You'll start with an acquisition format, which is the format, usually proprietary, that your camera uses to capture video. Then you'll transcode your media to an intermediate format, often also proprietary, during the editing process. And finally you'll use several different delivery formats to finish your project and distribute across various media.

We'll go over formats a little later in this chapter, but first, let's talk about how exactly those tapeless digital video and audio files work.

Digital Video Container Files

When you pull digital video media off a piece of videotape or disk and onto your computer, the media is stored in a file on your hard drive. These files are called *container* files. QuickTime movies (.MOV), MP4 (.MP4), Material Exchange Format (.MXF), Flash video (.F4V), Windows Media Video (.WMV), and Audio Video Interleaved (.AVI) are some popular digital media container file types for video.

Each of these container files can hold a video stream, two or more audio streams, and some sort of data stream. The data stream can hold additional information, such as subtitles, chapter information, tags, and digital rights management (DRM) data. The type of container file doesn't necessarily affect the image or sound quality. Instead, the container file supports a selection of different codecs that it works with to determine exactly how the media is stored (see Figure 3.9). That means that the image quality can range from 4:4:4 uncompressed to highly compressed HDV, but the file type (.MOV, .AVI, and so on) remains the same. The video stream will use one codec, and the audio streams will use special audio codecs. Because they hold all these different types of files in one package, container files are also known as *wrappers*.

Codecs

Earlier, we mentioned that video and audio data must be compressed before they can be played and stored by your computer (unless you have special hardware for playing uncompressed video), and the software that handles this task is called a *codec*. Codecs are built into the hardware in a digital video camera or video card. In your computer, they are usually software-based and managed either by the video architecture of your operating system, by the digital video editing application that you are using, or by your Web browser.

If you have ever created a Web video on your computer, you have probably been presented with a choice of different codecs. Likewise, if you have made the choice between viewing HD or SD footage using a streaming video on-demand service like Zune, you have been presented with a choice of codecs. Sometimes, decisions about codecs are disguised in "user friendly" language (see Figure 3.10), and sometimes, they are displayed in their full, complicated glory (see Figure 3.11). But regardless of how they are presented, codecs are always a part of interacting with digital video.

Figure 3.9

When you export video from the QuickTime Player, it will display information about codec used in that container file.

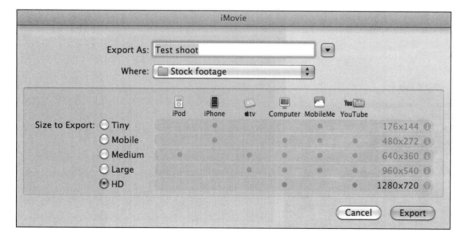

Figure 3.10

Some applications dumb it down for you, which isn't always a bad thing.

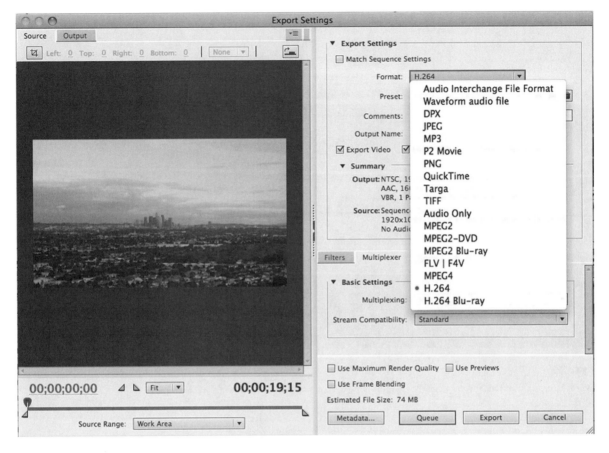

Figure 3.11

Adobe Premiere lets you choose from many different codecs when you export video.

Codecs can be either lossy or lossless; that is, they either degrade the image quality or leave it unaffected. Most compression is lossy, but that doesn't mean the loss is necessarily visible to the human eye, in fact most digital video codecs are lossy and yet the image quality is fantastic. (See the earlier explanation of color sampling.) The more complicated a shot, the more likely that you will see compression artifacts. A wide shot with lots of small detail, such as the leaves in the upper shot in Figure 3.12, is much harder to compress than a simple close-up of a person like the lower shot in Figure 3.12. Also, many video codecs are a little biased toward human facial features and skin tones so they do a better job compressing shots of faces.

Digital video codecs fall into two categories: intraframe and interframe compression. Intraframe compression treats each frame of video as a still and compresses it separately. Interframe uses keyframes to compress a video clip section by section. The MJPEG and DV codecs use intraframe compression, whereas the various MPEG-based codecs use interframe compression. Interframe compression is more sophisticated than intraframe compression, and it is therefore more able to deliver highly compressed files with less visible loss of image quality. However, codecs that use interframe compression are not well suited to editing, because you can only make edits at the keyframes. Interframe codecs, such as H.264, are great for acquisition in the camera, but then it is recommended to transcode these camera original files to another codec such as Apple ProRes or Avid DNxHD for postproduction.

Figure 3.12

Complicated images such as wide shots and moving camera shots (top) are more prone to compression artifacts than simple shots such as close-ups (bottom).

Many codecs take longer to compress than they do to decompress. (These are called *asymmetrical*.) Most of the codecs that you'll eventually use to output a finished movie are asymmetrical. For example, although it might take hours to compress a movie using the Sorenson or MPEG codecs, the computer can decompress it and play it back in real time.

Uncompressed digital video still involves a codec, even though it's technically not compressed. That's because all digital video requires quantization to take an analog image and render it into digital 0s and 1s; however, since this compression is invisible to the human eye, or "lossless," it's considered "uncompressed." Uncompressed video has a color sampling ratio of 4:4:4 and is primarily used for visual effects, 3D, and blue/green screen shooting because the additional color information that isn't visual to the human eye is helpful when doing refined computer-generated imagery. As high-quality digital cinema formats grow in popularity, the use of 4:4:4 codecs, such as the R3D codec, become more common, but the large file sizes do tend to require extra computer hardware.

Different codecs are used for different purposes. You'll use high-compression/lower-quality codecs for Web or mobile delivery (.mp4, .3gp, and so on) and low-compression/higher-quality codecs for higher-quality digital television or digital cinema delivery (h.264, .f4v, .wmv, .xmf, and so on).

There are many different video codecs out there, but they tend to fall into a few broad categories:

- **MPEG-4** based codecs were originally developed for highly compressed Web video, such as MP4, Sorenson, and DivX (all a subset called *MPEG-4 part 2*), but they have been expanded to include very high-quality codecs, such as H.264, AVC HD, AVC Intra, and others used by many higher-end HD cameras such as Sony's HDCAM SR, Panasonic's AVCCAM line, and most DSLRs (a subset known as *MPEG-4 part 10*). MPEG-4 uses interframe compression and is also used for certain Blu-ray Discs and DVDs. It is easily the most commonly used family of codecs at the time of this writing.

- **MPEG-2** based codecs were originally developed for full-frame broadcast-quality video, and they use interframe compression. MPEG-2 is used for some Blu-ray Discs, DVDs, and digital video formats, such as XDCAM, MPEG-IMX, and HDV.

- **DCT-based** compression is used in some high-end digital video cameras, such as Sony's HDCAM and high-quality intermediate codecs, such as Apple ProRes.

- **VC-3 based** compression is software-only and allows for 8- or 10-bit 4:2:2 1080 and 720 HD video. Avid's high-quality DNxHD intermediate codecs use VC-3 based compression.

- **MJPEG** (Motion-JPEG) is an older codec family based on the still image compression algorithm of JPEG that uses intraframe compression. Older editing hardware, such as the Avid Meridien board, uses MJPEG.

- **JPEG 2000** is a newer codec developed in 2000 and intended to replace the older MJPEG codec. It is known for maintaining very high image quality at high bit rates and is primarily used for file-based digital cinema projection.

- **MPEG-1** is an older delivery codec originally developed to compress video to fit onto CDs. It uses interframe compression, is not used in editing applications, and there are no cameras that shoot MPEG-1. The popular MP3 audio format is derived from the MPEG-1 standard.

- **DV** is an SD codec that was the high-end consumer video format of choice until a few years ago. It uses intraframe compression and is limited to a 4:3 aspect ratio and an image resolution of 720 $\times$ 480 pixels.

Audio Container Files and Codecs

When audio is stored in a separate file without video, it is usually stored in one of several standard PCM formats: WAV, AIFF, or SDII. These are all uncompressed formats, and all fall under the category of PCM audio.

As long as you maintain the same sampling rate, conversions between different PCM audio file types are lossless. MP3 is a highly compressed audio format that offers very small file sizes and good sound quality, despite the compression. Typically, MP3 is not considered a great file format for editing audio in films. MP4 (sometimes called *MPEG-4* because both MP3 and MP4 are part of the MPEG video specification) is a successor to MP3 that offers better compression without degrading quality. A 128K MP4 file delivers 160K MP3 quality in a much smaller space. AAC format (which you might have encountered in downloads from the iTunes Music Store) is just an MP4 audio file with a special digital-rights-management (DRM) "wrapper."

Dolby AC-3 audio consists of 5.1 channels of Dolby Digital Surround Sound. Typically, the 5.1 channels are designed to create a surround environment in a movie theater, so the channels are laid out as left, center, right, left surround, right surround, and the .1 channel is an optional subwoofer track for low-frequency sounds. HD video formats offer AC-3 5.1 sound. DTS and SDDS audio are other forms of surround sound used for feature films. (You'll find more about surround sound formats in Chapter 18.)

Transcoding

The process of converting a piece of media from one codec to another is called *transcoding*. Most video container file formats can support a wide range of different codecs. So, for example, you can have a .MOV file that uses the H.264 codec, and you can also have a .MOV file that uses the Avid DNxHD codec. If you shoot footage with a camera using H.264, drag it to your desktop, and then convert it to DNxHD to work with Avid Media Composer, you are transcoding your original media (see Figure 3.13). The file itself will still be a .MOV file, but you will have fundamentally changed your media.

Transcoding can be a hardware-based or a software-based process and whenever you move digital video around, you run the chance of transcoding your media. Transcoding isn't necessarily bad; in fact, it's often necessary and beneficial, but you should make sure you are not unintentionally transcoding your media to a lower quality codec.

So how and when does transcoding happen? The first way has to do with how you move media from your camera to your computer. If you are dragging and dropping files from a disc or hard drive to your computer's hard drive, you are not transcoding. But if you are using a cable running from your camera or videotape deck to a video input on your computer or video card, then you need to be careful. If you shoot HD, then you need to make sure that the chain of connectors and cables between your camera and your computer is all digital. If your camera has an analog video-out connector, such as S-video, then simply by sending your video out through this connector you are transcoding it into an analog signal. Then when it gets to your video card or connector on the computer, it is being transcoded back into a digital signal. It's true that you may not see a huge difference in the resulting image, but it's better to avoid transcoding your media more often than is necessary for your workflow.

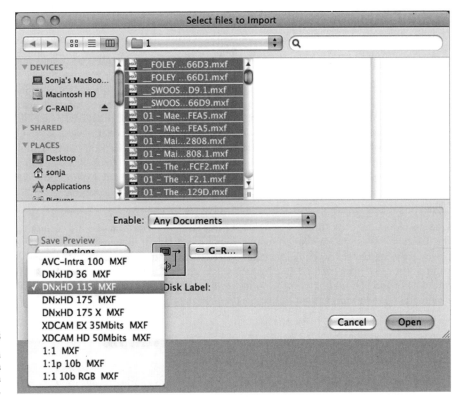

Figure 3.13

The Import Files window in Media Composer 5 offers a selection of codecs to choose from as you transcode your media.

The second way that transcoding happens is when you bring your video files into your editing software. Typically, if you use the Import command to bring video into an editing app, you are basically telling the editing software to transcode your footage into a codec that the application prefers. Higher-end applications make you aware of this process, but more consumer-oriented apps, such as Apple iMovie, will do this automatically (see Figure 3.14). Basically, if you try to bring media into your editing software, and it takes a while to do so, you can probably assume the app is transcoding your media.

Figure 3.14

Some apps like Apple iMovie automatically transcode your media when you bring it into the application.

The third way that transcoding happens is when you export media from your editing application to a file for viewing. Typically, you'll create several different masters at the end of your editing process: a high-resolution master for screenings, a low-res master for Web streaming, and several other options in-between. We'll discuss how to transcode your final cut for various delivery formats in Chapter 18.

Going Native

When editing applications offer "native support" for various types of media, that means you will be able to edit those formats without the need for transcoding.

Acquisition Formats

Video footage is almost always acquired by a camera (unless it is computer-generated), and every video camera records to a specific, usually proprietary, format. Because video cameras are constantly being updated and developed, acquisition formats change frequently. Also, be aware that some higher-end cameras can record more than one format.

Here is a list of what's out there for digital video acquisition at the time of this writing:

- **DV** is still out there, but fading fast. This 25Mbps SD format was designed to work with FireWire-based DV video (Digital8, DV, DVCAM, or DVCPro), and it uses the hardware DV codec in the camera or video deck to compress and decompress the video on DV tape stock.

- **HDV** is the "consumer" HD format and is much more compressed than the other HD formats, resulting in a lower quality image. As a result, it also has a low bit rate (about 25Mbps), which means it can be transferred or captured via FireWire. HDV camcorders use the MPEG-2 codec to record 4:2:0, 8-bit color images on either DV tape or SD cards.

- **DVCPRO-HD** is technically part of the DV family but employs a more complex DV encoding algorithm and higher bit rates (40–100Mbps) resulting in high-quality 4:2:2, 8-bit HD video.

- **MPEG-IMX** is a 4:2:2, 8-bit format that uses intraframe compression and records to optical discs or digital videotape. It is a popular ENG (electronic news gathering) format for TV, news, and so on.

- **XDCAM HD** from Sony is a 4:2:2, 8-bit direct-to-disc professional HD format that uses MPEG-2 compression to record to optical discs or memory cards.

- **AVCHD** is a tapeless MPEG-4–based HD format developed by Panasonic and Sony and aimed at consumer-grade HD cameras. It offers 4:2:0 8-bit color sampling, and it is used by several different types of cameras, including the Panasonic AVCCAM line and most DSLR cameras that shoot HD.

- **AVC-Intra** is a 4:2:0, 10-bit MPEG-4–based HD codec that comes in either a 100Mbps or 50Mbps format. Developed by Panasonic, this format is often used in conjunction with proprietary P2 cards.

- **HDCAM** is a 4:4:4, 10-bit HD codec used by the Sony professional family of camcorders that uses proprietary DCT-based compression.

- **Red R3D** is a high-quality digital video format that seeks to compete with 35mm film, offering 2K, 3K, and 4K resolutions and using the proprietary R3D codec.

- **Apple Pro Res** started out as an intermediate codec used for editing, but with the introduction of the Arri Alexa digital cinema camera, it is now also an acquisition format.

- **ArriRAW** is a digital cinema codec used by the Arri line of cameras.

Intermediate Formats

After you acquire your HD video, you'll bring it into your computer in order to edit it. Some editing applications use intermediate formats for optimized playback during editing. Most intermediate formats are proprietary, and although you are not always required to transcode your camera-original media into an intermediate format, usually the editing process works better if you do. The **Apple ProRes** family of intermediate codecs is designed to work with Final Cut Pro, and the **Avid DNxHD** family of intermediate codecs are designed to work with Avid's line of editing applications, including Media Composer 5. Both offer several quality levels available, including an "uncompressed" codec. More about intermediate formats in Chapter 13, "Preparing to Edit."

What If I'm Shooting with My Smart Phone?

Sometimes, it's impossible to resist the instant gratification of shooting with a consumer device such as an iPhone or a point-and-shoot camera. Bear in mind that at the time of this writing only the newest devices can shoot full HD video. Here are some strategies for dealing with "low-end" media.

- **Stay low.** If you shoot low-quality consumer video and your goal is to create a video for the Web, then you might want to consider sticking with lower-end consumer technology throughout your project. Rather than upgrading (transcoding) this footage into high-res HD, it's easier and cheaper to just use a lower-end editing application like iMovie and finish with a Web-oriented codec such as Sorenson.

- **Mix it up.** If most of your project is HD, but you have a few shots that you want to incorporate that were shot on a low-quality consumer camera, the best strategy is to transcode this media into the intermediate format that you are using to edit. (Your editing app should be able to do this easily for you.) Then use the FX capabilities of your editing software to integrate this footage with your HD footage. For more about how to use basic special effects to mix HD and SD footage, take a look at Chapter 17.

Unscientific Answers to Highly Technical Questions

So back to those questions in the beginning: What is the best way to shoot my project? Should I shoot 24P? What is the difference between 1080 and 720 HD? What type of digital video will look most like film?

Here are some unscientific answers:

- **Shoot the best quality you can.** Why? Because it will look better. Have you ever watched a tiny thumbnail-sized trailer of the latest Hollywood blockbuster? It looks pretty good, even though it's highly compressed. Most likely, it was shot on film or a digital cinema format. For whatever reasons, higher-quality acquisition formats hold up better even when they are transcoded into a low-quality delivery format.

- **Don't let production values stop your production.** Why not? Because if your story is strong, no one will care what it looks like. Most people stop noticing things like compression artifacts a minute or two into the story. Yes, a beautiful-looking film is compelling and some may disagree, but we feel that story is more important than beauty. Great shots are the icing on the cake, but the story is the cake. In a dream world, you have both, but a great story can stand alone. If you don't believe this, watch some documentaries. Documentary subject matter very rarely allows for ideal shooting. But with a subject with a compelling story, this simply doesn't matter.

- **720 or 1080?** Extreme video nerds are going to put a price on our head for saying this, but it doesn't really matter whether you choose 720 or 1080. They're both excellent. If you work for a TV network that requires 720, then you should shoot 720. Or if the camera you love only shoots 720, then shoot 720. If not, you will probably shoot 1080 because it sounds better, and that's what most people are choosing if they have a choice.

- **24p?** If you are making a film-like project, whether it's a feature length or a short, you might as well shoot 24p. The things that made it difficult to deal with in the past have faded away. Plus, the whole film world is set up to expect and work with 24fps. And even if you can't see a difference between 24fps and 30fps, you'll at least be saving about 20 percent in terms of storage space on your hard drives thanks to the lower frame rate.

- **Go with the flow.** If you are making a TV project in the U.S., you might as well stick to standard 29.97fps because the American TV world is set up to expect and work with that frame rate. If you are making a project destined for computers or the Web, choose 30fps because that's what is expected for the Internet. If you are making a video project outside the U.S., you should use the standard European frame rate of 25fps. If you are shooting a feature film, shoot 24fps. If you want your TV/Web project to look like film, you can do more with some well-chosen postproduction processes like color grading than a lower frame rate will ever come close to, in terms of creating a "film look."

- **Digital cinema?** If you can afford it, yes! But just remember that every step of the postproduction pipeline is going to cost more, not just the camera. Choosing a digital cinema format that records to SD cards could help you save a few bucks, though.

- **What looks most like film?** A film look is based on more than high image resolution and low frame rates. It's also the lens, the camera itself, shot design, production design, lighting, locations, quality of acting, and many other variables. And that's exactly what we're going to talk about in the upcoming chapters.

4

Choosing a Camera

Photo credit: William MacCollum

The most exciting developments in the digital filmmaking world today center around the camera. From DSLRs that can cost under $1,000 and offer an image quality to rival $20,000 video cameras to digital cinema camcorders like the RED One that shoots film-quality 4K video to specialty cameras like Panasonic's consumer-grade 3D camcorder, the options for digital filmmakers continue to grow.

But with so many different cameras on the market, how do you figure out what's right for you?

Evaluating a Camera

The most important thing to know when evaluating a camera is that there's no one single spec that defines overall quality. A good camera is dependent on many different components and specifications.

For example, that tiny HD camcorder that offers 720p seems like a steal when compared to a larger, more complicated camera like the JVC model shown in Figure 4.14, which also offers 720p. You might think "This is great! I can shoot with the camcorder, and it will look the same as that big fancy camera—after all they are both 720p." We hate to burst your bubble, but it will not look the same, because image quality depends on much more than just pixel count.

All cameras are not created equal and understanding the features and trade-offs of different cameras is essential to selecting a camera and using it to its full potential.

In this chapter, we'll explain the various features and functions of digital video cameras, with details of how these features work, and guidelines for evaluating and selecting the right camera for your project. Be aware that this chapter goes hand in hand with Chapter 7, "Using the Camera," and Chapter 10, "DSLRs and Other Advanced Shooting Situations." Here we cover the "what" and "why," and in those chapters, we cover the "how."

Choosing a camera is a process of weighing three factors: image quality, price, and features. Some feature filmmakers will be most concerned about image quality and the ability to record 24p, particularly if they are planning on digital projection. Other filmmakers might value portability and a low profile over image quality. And others might have special needs, like the ability to shoot underwater or record at high frame rates for true slow motion.

As a rule, the more consumer-oriented the camera, the less control you'll have over how it shoots because consumer-grade cameras are designed for the casual shooter and most manufacturers sacrifice control for ease of use. And there's a good reason for that—shooting with a full-featured camera can be pretty complicated. Professional-grade cameras offer total control, but there is a much steeper learning curve before you will be comfortable using these cameras.

Although we will mention a few cameras by name in this chapter, the goal of this section is to give you the information and techniques you need to evaluate a camera on your own.

Whether you're buying or renting, if you consider the questions raised here, you should be well prepared to make a shrewd camera choice.

Image Quality

Film shooters have an advantage over video shooters in that image quality is heavily dependent on lenses and the film stock they stick in their camera. It's not so simple with digital video. In addition to the usual concerns about lens quality and camera features, you also have to worry about how good a job the camera does at actually capturing, processing, and storing an image.

Two factors contribute the most to your camera's image quality (or lack thereof): the camera's lens and the chips the camera uses to create an image.

Sensors

In the old days, video cameras used vacuum tubes for capturing images. Today, video cameras use special imaging sensors called *CCDs* (charge-coupled devices) or *CMOS* (complementary metal-oxide semiconductors). Just as their tube-based predecessors used either one or three tubes to capture an image, chip-based cameras use either a single sensor to capture a full-color image, or three separate sensors to capture separate red, green, and blue data, which is then assembled into a color image

An image sensor looks like a normal computer chip, but with a sort of light-sensitive "window" on the top (see Figure 4.1). The imaging window is divided into a grid, and the finer the grid, the higher the resolution of the sensor will be. The circuitry controlling the sensor can determine the amount of light striking each cell of the grid, and that data is used by the camera to build an image.

Figure 4.1

An Olympus CCD image sensor.

Single-chip cameras have red, green, and blue filters arranged over clusters of cells in the sensor. These filter the light coming through the lens and allow the camera to record color images. In a three-chip camera, a series of prisms split the incoming light into separate red, green, and blue components, and directs each of these components onto a separate sensor. Because the camera dedicates an entire sensor to each color, color fidelity and image detail are much improved over single-chip cameras (see Figures 4.2 and 4.3).

The image data gathered by the sensor(s) is passed to an onboard computer that processes the data and writes it to digital storage media. How the computer processes the data can have a lot to do with how images differ from camera to camera. Some cameras tend to produce warmer images, with stronger reds and magentas, while others might produce cooler, less-saturated images with stronger blues. One approach is not better than the other, but you may find that you have a personal preference, or that one is better suited to the tone of your project.

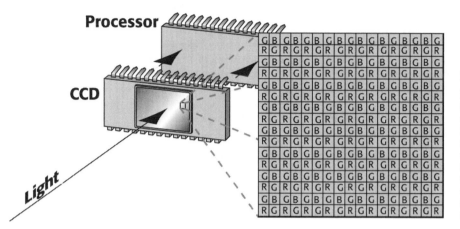

Figure 4.2

In a single-chip camera, light is focused by the lens onto the sensor. Red, green, and blue filters placed over alternating cells of the sensor enable the camera to calculate color. The resulting data is passed on to the camera's processor. (Notice that there are far more green cells to accommodate your eyes' high sensitivity to green.)

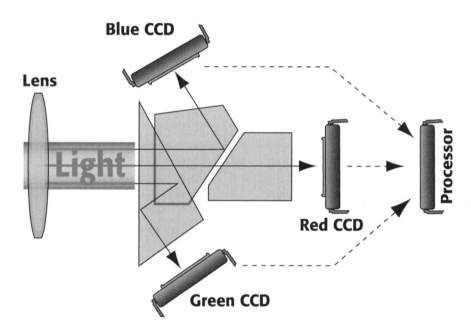

Figure 4.3

In a three-chip camera, light is focused by the lens onto a series of prisms that split the light into red, green, and blue. Each component is directed toward its own sensor.

Evaluating a Sensor

When evaluating a camera, first look at its color reproduction. If you're a stickler for accuracy, you'll want to see if the camera can create an image with colors that are true to their originals. Even if you're not concerned with color accuracy, look for color casts or odd shifts in color.

It's also important to pay attention to video noise. Noise comes in two flavors: luminance noise, which appears as monochromatic speckly patterns in your image (see Color Plate 5), and chrominance noise, which shows up as colored blotches, usually red, green, or magenta (see Color Plate 6). Although you ideally want an image without noise, this isn't always possible, especially when shooting in low light. However, when evaluating noise response, you'll find luminance noise less annoying, since it tends to look a lot like film grain and it's easier to remove later on in postproduction. Chrominance noise, however, is never attractive, and is extremely difficult to minimize in postproduction.

You'll also want to check the camera's response to different lighting situations. Unfortunately, your average electronics store is not the best place for testing a camera. However, if you can manage to point the camera out a window or into the dark recesses of a shelf or cabinet, you should be able to get an idea of the sensor's dynamic range, or latitude, which is the range from dark to bright that the camera can record in the same shot. In addition to the dynamic range, look for color consistency, casts or shifts in color, and keep an eye out for noise.

CCD-based cameras can have a tendency to create vertical white bands when exposed to bright elements in a scene. Different cameras employ different techniques to deal with this problem, and some are better than others. When evaluating a camera, point it at a bright light (but never at the sun!) and then quickly tilt the camera down. Look for vertical banding and smearing during the camera move. Vertical banding is not a reason to reject a camera, since you can always work around it, but it is important to know if your camera has this tendency.

CMOS-based cameras are immune to the above, but can be prone to visual distortion, known as the rolling shutter effect, which happens when the shutter is slower than the physical movement of the camera. The result is a "Jell-o" effect during pans. Tops of objects might move across the screen more slowly than their bottoms.

Sensor Size

Thanks to DSLRs that shoot HD, there's a lot of talk about image sensor size floating around these days. That's because DSLRs are small, relatively inexpensive cameras, but they boast large image sensors that help them record a very high-quality image.

The current gold standard for image sensor size is based on 35mm still photography. With 35mm still film, the image is exposed directly onto the negative, which is approximately 35mm wide and 24mm tall (see Figure 4.4). Higher-end DSLR still cameras try to replicate the image quality of 35mm film by using similarly-sized image sensors, also known as full-frame sensors.

Micro four-thirds sensors are smaller than full-frame sensors, but they use special technology to make up for the size difference. The Panasonic AG-AF100 and the Sony NEX-VG10 are recently developed camcorders that have micro four-thirds sensors. By contrast, most HD video cameras have smaller sensors, ranging from 1/8 to 2/3 of a full-frame.

Bigger image sensors make better-looking images. They have a greater dynamic range, a lower tendency toward noise, and they are more capable of capturing a shallow depth of field.

Micro 4/3 sensor

2/3" sensor   **1/2" sensor**

Full frame sensor (35mm)

Figure 4.4

A full 35mm still film frame compared to 4/3-, 2/3-, and 1/2-image sensors.

Why Is Shallow Depth of Field So Important?

One of the defining trends in modern still and motion photography is the prevalence of shallow depth of field. When shooting with shallow depth of field, things in the background will be out of focus, which helps bring more attention to the subject in the foreground. To achieve shallow depth of field, you need a camera with a larger image sensor and the right lens with the right lighting conditions. We'll talk more about how to achieve this look in Chapters 7 and 10.

Compression

The first place that your digital video gets compressed is in the camera. Every camera uses a compression algorithm, or codec, to turn the analog subject into a digital signal, and that process affects image quality greatly. In Chapter 3, "Digital Video Primer," we discussed compression in great detail and provided a list of acquisition formats.

Most lower-budget indie filmmakers will find that 8-bit, 4:2:2 compression is acceptable for their needs. Less than that (such as HDV's 4:2:0 color), and the image quality will be too low; more than that, and it will look fantastic but be very expensive. Be aware that some high-end cameras can record in more than one codec (see Figure 4.5).

Figure 4.5

The Arri Alexa digital cinema camera can record in the ARRIRAW format and also in two variations of the Apple ProRes codec.

Sharpening

Many cameras try to improve image detail by applying sharpening filters to each frame of video, just as you might apply a sharpen filter to an image in Photoshop. While these features are great for improving fine detail in a shot, they are often too much of a good thing. Apply too much sharpening, and diagonal or curved lines will appear jagged or aliased.

Oversharpening is easiest to spot on moving objects or during camera movements. Areas of high-contrast—a car in front of a brightly lit wall, for example—are also prone to oversharpening artifacts. When testing a camera, pan it about and look at objects that have very high-contrast edges. Look for "moving," jagged edges. Next, point the camera at an object with a thin, high-contrast horizontal line across it. Look to see if the line is stable, or if it flashes on and off. Tilt the camera off-axis and watch how much the edge of the horizontal line changes and whether or not aliasing increases (see Figure 4.6).

Sharpening can also be a *good* thing, so as you are watching for aliasing, also pay attention to how sharp the camera renders fine detail. If you are testing in an electronics store, objects with buttons, switches, and LEDs make great subjects for camera tests.

Higher-end cameras often have a sharpening control. If the camera in question has such a control, play with it and see if you can use it to resolve oversharpening problems. Pay attention to how fine detail changes as you adjust the sharpening. Also, look for any color shifts or changes as you adjust sharpening controls (see Figure 4.7).

Figure 4.6

Oversharpening can create annoying artifacts that jump and slide around your image. In the upper image, notice the strong aliasing around the top of the glasses. The bottom image lacks the aliasing around the glasses.

Figure 4.7

If your camera has a manual sharpness control, you can decide how much sharpening is appropriate for your image.

White Balance

To accurately represent color, your camera needs to know what objects in your image are white. Once the camera is calibrated for white, it can more accurately reproduce other colors. Most cameras can automatically adjust their white balance once they've been told what kind of light is being used to light the location. We'll discuss how to white balance in Chapter 9, "Shooting and Directing" and also in Chapter 16, "Color Correction."

When evaluating a camera, see what white-balance options are included. At the very least, a camera should provide separate settings for indoor or outdoor shooting. Better cameras provide presets for specific kinds of lights. The ideal white-balance control is a fully manual control that takes a white-balance reading off a white object that you hold in front of the camera and lets you save it as a custom preset.

Image Tweaking

While most cameras offer simple color balance controls, experienced shooters will want more advanced controls that allow them to perform exacting adjustments to the camera's image quality. High-end digital cinema cameras are typically accompanied by a special on-set video technician whose job it is to make sure that the video signal is properly recorded using special instruments. Video engineering is way beyond the scope of this book, and if you're not going to be running the camera yourself, it's not something you need to concern yourself with. However, if you're planning on using an experienced director of photography, and you want the best image quality possible, you'll want a camera that can afford corrections such as custom gamma, pedestal (or black level), and knee (or white level) settings.

Lenses

Just as a film camera works by using a lens to focus light onto a piece of film, a digital video camera uses a lens to focus light onto the imaging window of a sensor (or group of sensors). Moreover, just as the quality of lens on a film camera can mean the difference between good or bad footage, the quality of the lens on your video camera can mean the difference between sharp images with good color and soft images with muddy color.

At the high-end consumer level, most digital video cameras have fixed, zoom lenses; that is, you can't change the camera's lens as you might on your DSLR camera. At the professional level, digital video cameras have interchangeable lenses that let you select from a variety of zoom ranges, wide angles, and telephoto options. Thanks to the popularity of shooting HD video with DSLR cameras, video camera manufacturers are starting to offer less pricey camcorders with interchangeable lenses such as the Panasonic AG-AF100 (see Figure 4.8).

Figure 4.8

The Panasonic AG-AF100 is an HD camcorder under $5,000 that supports interchangeable lenses.

Lens Quality

When evaluating lens quality, look for changes in brightness across the image. Does the lens produce images that are brighter in the middle than at the edges, also known as *vignetting?* As you zoom the lens in and out, does the image get darker as the lens goes more telephoto?

Look for distortion around the edge of the image, particularly at wide angles. Does the image bow in or out as you zoom the lens back and forth? Similarly, look for changes in sharpness and detail throughout the lens's zoom range.

Chromatic aberration occurs when the lens does not equally focus all wavelengths of light. This problem is usually worse in single-chip cameras, though three-chip cameras with lower-quality lenses can also suffer from chromatic aberration. You can spot chromatic aberration by looking for fringes of red or green in high-contrast areas or around dark lines. (See Color Plate 7.)

Lens flares are those weird circles that appear when the lens is pointed into a bright light. Although lens flares have their uses—you'll see them a lot in "hot burning desert" scenes, or around flying titles—you want to be sure that flares only happen when you *want* them to happen. A lower-quality lens will flare very easily, and most lenses will have trouble with flares when shooting bright light sources at very wide angles. When evaluating a camera, zoom the lens to its widest angle outside during the day and see how easily it flares when you pan it around.

F-stops Versus T-stops

Still cameras and most video cameras rate their lenses in f-stops, but motion picture film cameras and high-end digital cinema cameras rate their lenses in t-stops. T-stops are highly calibrated to account for any absorption of light by the lens itself (for example, light that won't make it to the image sensor). In practical terms, this means you can swap lenses and keep the same t-stop setting.

Lens Features

Depending on the quality of their controls, some lenses are easier to use than others. To make sure your lens provides controls that let you get the kind of camera movements and effects that you want, consider the following:

- **Zoom control.** Is the zoom control well positioned? How long does it take to zoom from full wide to full telephoto at the slowest speed? Ideally, this should be about 30 seconds. How quickly can it zoom its full length? You'll want this to be fairly quick to allow for quick framing of shots. How well does the zoom control work? Can you zoom at a constant speed? Can you make smooth zooming accelerations and decelerations? Is there a knob that allows for very fast zooms, or snap zooms?

- **Manual focus.** If your camera has manual focus, where is the control? Whether electronic or mechanical, test the camera's manual focus for ease of use and reliability. Also be sure it holds focus when set. If the lens in question has a focusing ring (like what you'd find on a 35mm SLR camera), check to see if it has distances marked on it.

- **Aperture control.** As with focus rings, some higher-end lenses have manual rings for controlling the lens aperture. (Apertures are discussed later in this chapter.) Check for f-stop markings, ease-of-use, and accuracy.

- **F-stop rating.** All lenses have a widest possible f-stop that they can achieve. This determines both low-light capabilities and the ability to shoot shallow depth of field. A lens with a low f-stop rating, such as f1.2, can shoot in very low-light situations and achieve extremely shallow depth of field. A lens with a higher f-stop rating, such as f4, will not do as well in low-light situations. Lower numbers mean better low light/shallow depth of field. A lens with a lower number is considered a "faster" lens.

- **Minimum objective distance.** How closely can the lens focus? For shooting small objects or getting extreme close-ups for cutaways, this can be important.

Lower-end cameras tend to have lenses built right into the camera's body, but this doesn't mean that they're necessarily bad lenses. In fact, many professional cameras offer high-quality, built-in Zeiss lenses.

Interchangeable Lenses

Interchangeable lenses are one of the more exciting trends for digital camcorders. They offer an extra level of control over how your camera records images, and they can give you the flexibility to shoot successfully in all sorts of situations. However, if you are tending toward a camera that features interchangeable lenses, you have some extra research and expenses headed your way. High-quality lenses are not cheap, and having the right selection on hand is a matter of personal taste, affordability, and the requirements of your shooting situation.

- **Zoom lenses.** Lenses with variable focal lengths, or zoom lenses, are often the first purchase for camera owners looking to build a collection of lenses. They offer the flexibility that we've all become used to, thanks to camcorders with built-in zoom lenses. If you're shooting under hectic circumstances where changing lenses isn't an option, or just hoping to travel light, having a good basic zoom lens is important.

- **Prime lenses.** Fixed focal length lenses are called *prime lenses*. Prime lenses typically offer a shaper image than zoom lenses, and they can also have very low f-stop ratings, which means they can be great for low-light photography. A basic set of primes usually includes a wide angle, a "normal" angle, and a telephoto lens (see Figure 4.9).

Figure 4.9

Zeiss Prime lenses for SLRs.

- **Cinema lenses.** High-end motion picture lenses are a little different than still photography lenses. They are designed with the specific needs of motion photography in mind and have very accurate focus marks to facilitate manually pulling focus. They measure light in t-stops rather than f-stops, and cinema zoom lenses try to keep the same t-stop rating across the range of the zoom lens. All this accuracy comes at a price, and a set of cinema primes from Zeiss or Schneider can run upward of $20,000 (see Figure 4.10).

- **Lens accessories.** All lenses are not alike, and you may find that you need an adaptor to fit the lens you want to the camera you prefer. Be sure to look into this before you make any big purchases.

Figure 4.10

A Zeiss Compact Prime cinema lens.

Never Mind the Reasons, How Does It Look?

At some point, you need to take a step back and look at the images produced by the cameras you are considering. You may find that you like one image better than another, and you may have no idea why. That's okay. If you prefer one image over another, but can't find a technical reason for your preference, don't worry about it. In the end, your subjective opinion is more important than any technical benchmarks or specifications.

Digital Zoom

Most consumer video cameras include a digital zoom feature. When digital zoom is activated, the camera will begin to digitally enlarge the image after you have zoomed to the optical limit of the lens. The results of these "fake zooms" have improved, thanks to the higher resolution of HD video, but they still leave something to be desired when compared to a "real" lens-based zoom. At extreme zooms, shapes become blobby mosaics of muddy color, and even a minor amount of digital zoom can introduce noise and ugly artifacts. Unless you are intentionally going for a grungy look, digital zoom is a useless feature—turn it off and leave it off! (If you are going for a grungy look, shoot non-grungy footage and grunge it up in postproduction. You'll have much more flexibility, and can always repurpose the footage for non-grungy uses if you need to.)

Camera Manufacturer's Web Sites

Camera manufacturers offer detailed specs and data sheets on their Web sites. Because camera technology changes quickly, consider these the most reliable resources for information on cameras.

Camera Features

Once you've narrowed down your choices to a few camera models that offer the quality and lens features that you want, you can begin assessing other camera features to try to narrow your choice further. As a filmmaker, your requirements are different from the casual home user (see Figure 4.11), so examine each camera's features carefully.

Camera Body Types

Digital video cameras range in size from portable pocket cameras all the way up to large, shoulder-mounted units. Choosing a particular camera body involves balancing features and shooting style with cost.

Figure 4.11

Pocket-sized cameras are portable and easy to use, but they lack the features and image quality of higher-end cameras.

Smaller cameras typically lack connectors, such as HDMI video output or audio jacks (more about audio jacks in Chapter 8, "Production Sound.") They usually don't have as many manual features, and they practically never include such niceties as lenses with aperture and focus markings, sharpening controls, and refined image-quality adjustments.

On the other hand, small size makes a camera easier to carry and ideal for surreptitious shooting. For documentaries, a low-profile camera might help you to get candid footage (nothing shuts up a timid interview subject faster than sticking a big lens in his or her face), or to shoot clandestinely in locations that wouldn't normally allow a camera.

On the other hand, you simply won't be able to get the beautiful shots that you see in great-looking feature films with a consumer-level camera.

As you look at cameras, don't ignore the camera's physical feel. To get the footage you need, you must be able to move the camera with great precision. If a camera is too heavy (or light) or too bulky for you to pan and tilt comfortably, you may not be able to get the shots you want. The camera's weight can also have budgetary consequences, as a heavier camera will require a sturdier—and therefore more expensive—tripod.

- **Pocket cameras.** Tiny point-and-shoot cameras, like the one in Figure 4.11, sacrifice quality for size, but are convenient and simple to use. They typically cost $200 or less.

- **Consumer-grade camcorders.** Handheld camcorder models are a little bigger than pocket cameras and are designed to fit comfortably in your hand. They usually have a single chip and offer flip-out LCD displays, but lack manual override, external microphone connectors, and other advanced features. Prices range from $200–1,000 (see Figure 4.23).

- **Professional camcorders.** Entry-level pro cameras feature a relatively light-weight camera body (1–2 lbs), usually have three chips, external connectors, and offer lots of manual control. They typically range from $2,000–5,000 (refer to Figure 4.12).

Figure 4.12

The JVC GY-HM100 is
an entry-level professional
handheld camcorder.

- **Professional shoulder-mount cameras.** Larger shoulder-mount cameras sport three chips for better image quality, and they can weigh 10 lbs or more. The heavier weight makes for easier handheld shooting and smooth, steady camera moves. They are more comfortable to hold for a long period of time because the weight is distributed to your shoulder. They start at around $5,000 and go up as high as $30,000 (see Figure 4.14).

- **Digital cinema cameras.** Digital cinema cameras like the RED One and the Arri Alexa are built to handle lots of added-on hardware and to support big lenses. They can shoot raw, uncompressed video with a resolution of 2K or higher. Prices range from $20,000 for the RED and over $50,000 for most other models (shown in Figure 4.5).

- **DSLR cameras.** The main reason that people are so excited about DSLR cameras that shoot full HD is that they are relatively cheap (under $3,000), and yet they offer high image quality and are relatively full-featured, at least in terms of image control. They are also harder to use than a video camera because the DSLR camera body is not designed for shooting motion video. So, while the initial price tag is low, you might find yourself spending a lot of extra money to make up for deficiencies in the SLR design (see Figure 4.24). More on this later in this chapter and in Chapter 10.

- **Specialty cameras.** Whether you need to shoot underwater, shoot at high frame rates, or shoot with a tiny Bluetooth cam mounted on a remote control helicopter drone, there are lots of unique consumer-level cameras out on the market that offer special capabilities that you can't get anywhere else.

- **3D cameras.** The newest item on this list, 3D cameras use two lenses to record two separate images that work together to create a single image that looks more like what we see in real life (see Figure 4.13).

Figure 4.13

3D cameras like the Panasonic HDC-SDT750 use two lenses to create an image that looks more like what we see in real life.

WHAT TO WATCH

Cave of Forgotten Dreams is a documentary by Werner Herzog about the 30,000-year-old artwork found in a the Chauvet cave in France. The film begins with an amazing aerial shot over a vineyard, rising up to the face of a cliff where the cave is located. Later in the movie, the specialty camera and rig are revealed. Also, due to the tight spaces in the cave, you can see a lot of how the movie crew had to work under extraordinary circumstances.

Rent or Buy?

When it comes to cameras, there is always the possibility of renting a higher-end camera if you can't afford to buy one. After all, you may be only planning to shoot for a couple weeks and then not again for several months. If so, renting may make more sense for you. Be aware that to rent higher-end cameras and other gear, you'll probably need liability insurance.

WHAT TO WATCH

Tiny Furniture was shot entirely with a Canon 5d DSLR camera.

WHAT TO WATCH

The Social Network was shot entirely with the RED One camera.

Manual Controls

The most important feature for the serious videographer is the ability to manually override the camera's default factory settings. Controls for manually setting the camera's focus, aperture, shutter speed, audio levels, and white balance are essential for flexible shooting.

The problem with automatic mechanisms is that they're not too smart, and they have no artistic flair. Rather, they are designed to produce a good picture under common, ideal shooting situations. In other words, if you are shooting something like your family on vacation in Hawaii in bright daylight, it will look great, but if you're trying to get a moody shot of a woman standing in the shadows in front of a bright window, you're probably not going to be able to get the look you want unless you use a camera that allows you to manually override the camera's default settings and control the iris yourself, like the one shown in Figure 4.14.

Figure 4.14

Higher-end shoulder-mount cameras like the JVC GY-HM790U provide a full set of manual controls, pro-level audio inputs, high-quality progressive scan modes, and more.

Focus

With manual focus controls, you can choose what to focus on and compose your shots the way you choose (see Figure 4.15). Similarly, manual aperture controls (sometimes referred to as *iris* or *exposure*) let you compensate for difficult lighting situations such as harsh backlighting.

Lower-end cameras typically provide electronic manual focus controls that are accessed through a menu system or from buttons on the camera's control panel. Higher-end cameras will have lens-mounted rings just like the rings on a 35mm still camera.

Lower-end cameras usually don't have values marked on their focus or aperture controls; instead, they display simple slider graphics in the camera's viewfinder. While this is effective, the lack of quantifiable settings can make it difficult to get the same settings from shot to shot. Such electronic controls are not necessarily suited to changing aperture or focus on the fly, making it difficult to do rack focus or pull focus shots. (See Chapter 7 and Chapter 10 for more information on focus and depth of field.)

Figure 4.15

Manual controls give you more freedom for composition. In this example, we used manual focus and aperture controls to go from an image with a sharp, focused background to one with a soft, blurry background.

Manual What?

We'll discuss the theory and use of manual iris and shutter speed in Chapter 7.

A good auto focus mechanism is also important. It used to be that serious camera operators avoided auto focus, but a well-designed auto focus mechanism can be a boon if you are running and gunning, shooting in a situation where it's hard to see the LCD to determine focus, or if you simply aren't comfortable with focusing manually. How responsive is the auto focus? How fast is it? Does the camera offer the capability to adjust the point of focus to areas other than the center of the frame?

Focusing Is Part of the Lens

If your camera has interchangeable lenses, the ability to auto focus and manual focus may change, depending on the lens' capabilities.

Shutter Speed

Most cameras automatically select a shutter speed based on the aperture setting, a process called *shutter priority*. Many cameras also provide manual shutter speed control, which gives you an extra degree of creative control. By switching to a higher shutter speed—1/200th to 1/4000th—you can stop fast-moving action, such as sporting events. A faster shutter is great for picking out fine detail, but faster speeds eliminate most motion blur, which can result in an image with very strobic, stuttery motion (see Figure 4.16).

Unfortunately, lower-end digital video camera manufacturers frequently provide fast shutter speeds, but they often skimp on slow ones. If you are ultimately planning to transfer your finished video to film, it's a good idea to look for a camera that can shoot at 1/60th of a second. At this speed, you'll tend to get a better film transfer.

Figure 4.16

(Top) At a somewhat "normal" shutter speed of 1/60th of a second, the moving car has a pronounced motion blur. (Bottom) At 1/4000th of a second, moving objects in each individual frame are frozen. When played back, the video can have a somewhat "stroboscopic" look.

Frame Rates

Most HD cameras record a variety of frame rates, starting at 24fps and going as high as 60fps. (See Chapter 3 for the lowdown on all the possible frame rates of HD.) However, pocket-sized video cameras, point-and-shoot still cameras that record video, and cell phone cameras do not always offer a full selection of frame rates, especially when recording full-sized HD. Be sure to check the camera's specifications before you buy.

True Slow Motion

Many cameras offer a "slow-mo" setting, but they don't offer true slow motion. True slow motion requires the ability to shoot at a higher frame rate—at least 60fps. Digital cinema cameras can often shoot up to 100fps, and there are some special consumer-grade camcorders that shoot at high frame rates as well. If your camera doesn't offer true slow motion, avoid the in-camera slow-mo and save the motion effects for postproduction.

Aperture Control

Like the iris in your eye, the iris in your camera's lens lets you control how much light passes through the lens to the image sensor. Being able to control the size of the iris, or aperture, manually is a crucial camera feature. Shooting video is all about movement. Even if you have the camera locked down on a tripod, odds are something within the frame is moving and when things move, the light changes. A camera set to auto iris will try to correct for these changes, and the result is often an image that gets brighter and darker as things move around.

A classic example of auto iris is when a person holding a camera enters a house. For a few seconds, the image is very dark and then it suddenly brightens up. An experienced shooter with a camera set to manual iris control can walk into the house and quickly change the iris as the threshold is crossed, making the transition feel seamless. The auto iris feature has no aesthetics; it simply aims for always having an image that is bright and easy to see. So, if you are shooting a crime thriller and want a shot of a dark figure in a dark room silhouetted against a bright window, an auto iris control is going to mess up your shot (see Figure 4.17).

Test Your Camera

Be sure to do a test shoot before you begin your main shoot.

Faux Progressive Scan

On some cameras, the progressive scan mode doesn't shoot a true 30 full frames per second. Instead, it shoots a single field and duplicates it to create a full frame. Very often, it does this at a much slower frame rate of 15 frames per second. Although this can look a lot like a regular progressive scan, you're only getting half the vertical resolution. Stay away from these faux progressive modes.

Figure 4.17

Sometimes, artistic choices, like this blurry silhouette, are technically wrong, so you'll need to disable auto focus and auto iris to get this effect.

Faux Widescreen

If you need a widescreen image (and most of us do these days), be sure to get a camera that offers a native aspect ratio of 16:9. Some lower-end cameras include a non-native "widescreen" mode that lets you shoot in a 16:9 aspect ratio, but they achieve this by cropping the top and bottom of the frame to letterbox the image down to 16:9. The downside to this "hacked" 16:9 effect is that you lose a lot of vertical resolution. If your CCD only has 360,000 pixels and you're using a third of them for black areas above and below your image, you're effectively shooting with much lower resolution than your camera is capable of (see Figure 4.18).

Figure 4.18

The widescreen feature on some cameras simply masks the top and bottom of your image, effectively wasting a third of your vertical resolution!

Image Stabilization

Because it's difficult to hold a one- or two-pound camcorder steady, most cameras now provide some sort of image stabilization feature to smooth out bumpy, jittery camera movement. Image stabilization technology—though no substitute for a tripod—is very effective and (usually) has no ill side effects.

There are two kinds of image stabilization: electronic and optical. Digital image stabilization (DIS, sometimes called *electronic image stabilization*) requires an image sensor with a larger imaging size than the actual image size that is displayed. DIS works by detecting camera motion, analyzing it to see if it's intentional or not, and then digitally moving the image to compensate for unwanted motion. Because the camera is overscanning the actual field of view, there are enough extra pixels around the edges to allow for this kind of movement (see Figure 4.19).

Figure 4.19

In digital image stabilization, the camera scans an area that is slightly larger than the recording video and then adjusts the frame to compensate for shake.

Since the camera is constantly moving the image about the screen to compensate for shake, electronic stabilization can often result in softer, slightly blurred images. We've also seen some cameras show a slight color shift when using DIS. However, most DIS functions in use today do an excellent job of stabilizing the image without noticeably degrading the quality.

Optical image stabilization (OIS) doesn't alter your image, but instead changes the internal optics of the camera to compensate for motion. In an OIS system, the lens can reshape some of its optical elements to redirected light onto the correct part of the image sensor(s) to compensate for camera shake (see Figure 4.20).

Since OIS doesn't ever touch your image data, there's no chance that it will corrupt your image. On the downside, because it's more complicated, optical stabilization costs more than electronic stabilizing. Also, because the stabilization is tailored to a particular lens, if you add wide angle or other attachments that change the focal length of your lens, OIS will stop working.

When evaluating a camera, try some motion tests—both slow and smooth, and fast and jittery—to see how each camera's stabilization feature affects overall image quality.

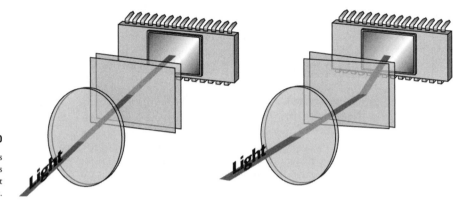

Figure 4.20

Optical image stabilization works
by reshaping one of the lens
elements on the fly to correct
for camera movement.

Image Stabilizing in Post

Thanks to the high-resolution of HD video, stabilizing shaky footage in postproduction is a viable option. Check out Chapter 17, "Titles and Effects," for more on this subject.

Viewfinder

Most video cameras have two viewfinders: an eyepiece viewfinder and a flip-out LCD viewfinder. Because you can tilt an LCD into different viewing angles, flip-out LCDs afford you a wider range of shooting options. However, because an LCD drains your battery quickly and can be difficult to see in bright light, you might not be able to use it all the time. Yes, you want a high-quality LCD, but don't let LCD quality weigh too heavily when choosing a camera.

Some higher-end cameras include a feature called *zebra stripes* that displays diagonal black-and-white lines in areas of your image that are overexposed. These lines are not recorded to tape; they only appear in the viewfinder. If you're manually setting your shutter and iris, zebra stripes are a must-have for situations when you don't have an external monitor to look at (see Figure 4.21). Top-of-the-line cameras let you set the brightness level at which the zebra stripes appear. This is useful if you are trying to shoot with a low-contrast ratio, as is sometimes recommended for video-to-film transfers.

Many professional shoulder-mount video cameras and digital cinema cameras do not have LCD displays, but in some cases, there are special separate LCD viewfinders that can be added onto the camera. Often, a field monitor is used to see what the camera is shooting on a larger display. If you are shooting HD, this field monitor needs to be HD as well, or else you won't really be seeing the image that is actually being recorded. To send true HD video out to a field monitor, you'll need a camera that has an HDMI or HD-SDI cable output.

Figure 4. 21

The diagonal lines in this viewfinder are the "zebra stripes" that indicate overexposure.

Interface

All cameras today are small computers, and even consumer cameras have complicated menus and settings. At the lowest end, you'll find the menus written in plain English; at the high-end, unless you're an experienced camera operator, you'll need the manual to make sense of the menu items.

Typically, the menu interface offers control over the following:

- Formatting media.
- Setting date and time. This is important if you are using time of day to synchronize multiple cameras together.
- Video recording format. Most cameras offer a selection of image sizes and frame rates.
- White balance and color presets.
- Ability to turn off automated features, such as auto focus, auto iris, and so on.
- Preview and playback features.
- In-camera special effects.

In addition to the menu options, most video cameras offer status displays in the viewfinder or on the LCD screen. A good camera warns you when your battery is running low or when you are running out of space to record media. Some cameras are definitely better at this than others.

Avoid In-Camera Special Effects

Most video cameras, especially lower-cost cameras, include a number of special effects ranging from sepia tinting to "arty" posterizing looks. We don't recommend using any of these features. It's better to shoot unprocessed video so as to have the greatest flexibility during postproduction.

Audio

It's pretty safe to say that the microphones included on almost all camcorders are lousy. Low-quality to begin with, their usefulness is further degraded by the fact that they often pick up camera motor noise, as well as the sound of your hands on the camera itself. Consequently, an external microphone jack and a headphone jack are essential for quality audio recording. In addition to replacing the lousy onboard mic on your camera, an external mic jack lets you mix audio from a number of mics and feed the results into your camera. We'll discuss audio hardware more in Chapter 8.

Ideally, you want a camera that has XLR mic connectors that can be switched between mic and line-level inputs. Many lower-end cameras offer a small TRS mic jack instead of XLR, which is okay if it suits the type of mic you plan to use. Make sure the connectors are positioned so that mic cables and connectors won't get in the way of moving the camera and shooting (see Figure 4.22).

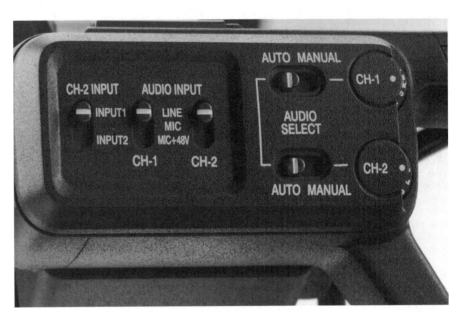

Figure 4.22

This JVC GY-HM100 is an entry-level professional camcorder that provides excellent audio controls.

A headphone jack is a must-have to ensure that you're actually recording audio. (You'll be surprised at how easy it is to forget to turn on a microphone.)

Manual audio gain controls let you adjust, or attenuate, the audio signal coming into the camera, making it easy to boost quiet voices, or lower the level on a roaring car engine. At the lower end, very few cameras have audio meters and manual adjustments although some can display level meters on the LCD screen. This isn't a deal breaker, but they're nice to have if you can get them.

Many cameras have an auto gain control or auto limiter, which will automatically try to limit loud noises. Unfortunately, like many automatic features, since you have no control of an auto gain feature, you can't always be sure that it's not limiting your sound more than you'd like or perhaps worse, boosting the audio unnecessarily. Again, these features aren't deal breakers, but if your camera is outfitted with such a limiter, you'll need to experiment with it to learn how sensitive it is. Ideally, your camera will allow you to disable this feature if you want.

Recording Sound to a Separate Device

You've probably heard that most DSLR shooters opt to record audio on a separate device, aka dual system sound. Having a camera with limited audio features isn't the only reason to use a separate audio recording device. It also frees the camera from lots of unwieldy cables and can work well for multi-cam shooting. See Chapters 8 and 10 for more information.

Media Type

Cameras today record to a variety of media: SD cards, flash memory, optical discs, and digital videotape. SD cards and flash memory use solid state technology, which is more stable than hard discs that spin, because there are no moving parts. Also, damage to one part of the drive doesn't necessarily result in failure of the whole drive (see Figure 4.23).

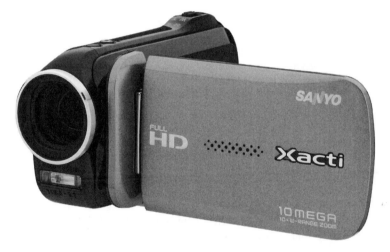

Figure 4.23

This typical handheld consumer-grade HD camcorder from Sanyo records HD video onto SD cards.

Digital videotape is relatively stable, too, but it isn't non-linear so it simply is not as convenient to use as tapeless storage. Instead of instant access to any file or piece of media, you'll have to wait for the tape to fast-forward or rewind.

Optical discs are the least stable and have not proven especially popular, but Sony does offer a line of higher-end cameras that use the Professional Disc format, and there are still some consumer-grade camcorders that record to DVD or Blu-ray out there (all are types of optical disc).

Cameras with Hard Drives

If you are using a pocket camera or cell phone to record to a built-in hard drive, your camera will be occupied while you download the files to your computer. Plan for down time if you're shooting lots of footage.

There is a lot of talk these days about tapeless or file-based workflow. We talk about working with file-based media at length in the shooting Chapters 7–10, Chapter 13, "Preparing to Edit," and also Chapter 18, "Finishing." But here are the basics: file-based workflow is the same for digital video as it is for digital still photography or any other type of file. You have to be extra careful not to accidentally erase or copy over your media, and you have to be very careful about making backup copies of everything.

Working with SD Cards

Not all SD cards are created equal. Rather, there are several classes of SD cards available, and for shooting HD, the top of the line class 10 is recommended. Since SD cards can work in a wide variety of devices (cameras, audio recorders, laptops), and they are too small to write on, it can be easy to lose or confuse SD cards on the set, so extra care is required. A standard 16GB class 10 card will hold about 12 minutes of 1080/24p HD video. At present, the largest size for SD cards is 32GB.

Wireless

Wireless video transmission is available at the very low end and the very high end, although neither can handle streaming full-quality HD. There are several small camcorders that can stream video wirelessly via Bluetooth. And at the high end, some professional cameras can accept special add-on microwave hardware that can transmit a signal wirelessly to a field monitor. Look for expanded wireless options in the future.

Batteries and AC Adaptors

Having a battery die mid-shot is more than just an inconvenience, it's a waste of time and money. Unfortunately, most cameras ship with batteries that won't last over a long shoot day. When purchasing, find out what other batteries are available, and how long they will last.

Ideally, you'll want enough battery life for several hours of shooting. Battery cost should be factored into your assessment of final camera cost. Note that using an LCD viewfinder will consume your batteries faster. If you know you'll be using the LCD a lot, you'll need more batteries. This is also true for any other energy-intensive operations, such as lens-based image stabilization and mechanical zooming.

Professional cameras tend to use standardized batteries made by Anton Bauer. These batteries can power cameras, walkie talkies, lights, and many other types of gear. In fact, they can now even power Apple laptops for long-term use on the set.

Some cameras can accept AC adaptors that let you plug them into wall outlets. Naturally, this affects ease of movement, but it can be worth having an AC adaptor on hand just in case.

Third-Party Batteries

For extra-long life, consider a battery belt such as those made by NRG Research. With enough juice to power a camera and light for several hours, a battery belt is a great—though bulky and costly—solution to short battery life.

DSLRs

The hottest topic when it comes to cameras these days is shooting HD video with DSLRs.

If you're new to the dialogue, here are the basics: DSLRs, or *digital single lens reflex* cameras, are digital still photography cameras and some of them are equipped to shoot full-sized HD video (see Figure 4.24). Not every digital still camera is a DSLR and not every DSLR can shoot full-sized HD video, but the handful that are capable of it produce amazingly high-quality images that rival those of high-end digital video cameras.

Figure 4.24

A DSLR camera fully outfitted with a Zeiss cinema lens, matte box, follow focus mechanism and baseplate with rods.

In fact, one could say that they offer the best image quality among all HD cameras, except for digital cinema cameras. And that's a big deal because top of the line DSLRs cost around $2,500 and some of them cost as low as $700–800 for the camera body. So when you're talking about a $700 camera whose next competitor, image-wise, is a $20,000 digital cinema camera, suddenly it's clear what all the fuss is about.

Because they are designed to be still photography cameras first and video cameras second, there are some trade-offs. DSLRs have two features that give them the capability to record better images than most other video cameras: large image sensors and the ability to use interchangeable lenses. But there are two other features that DSLRs are clearly not as good at handling as the average handheld camcorder: movement and sound.

First, on almost all DSLRs, you'll have no auto focus when shooting video. At the time of this writing, a few models get around this problem, but all other DSLRs were limited by the nature of DSLR viewfinders and design. So you'll be using all manual focus, all the time. This can require a camera assistant, and because you can only use the LCD screen when shooting video, you might need an extra monitor or LCD shade if you're shooting in bright light.

Second, the body style of DSLRs is not designed for movement, and many of the working parts are difficult or awkward to use while shooting. Some still photography lenses have manual focus rings that are very small because the assumption is that you'll either use auto focus, or that it won't be difficult for you to look at the lens to find the focus ring. The placement of buttons and controls on the camera body isn't always that ergonomic either.

To get around these issues, there are all sorts of accessories out there, from follow-focus mechanisms to add-on viewfinders to specialized camera rigs. (More about special DSLR gear in Chapter 10.) Lastly, the CMOS sensors in DSLRs are particularly prone to the rolling shutter problems we described earlier. Although there are postproduction solutions (see Chapter 17), sudden camera movement and very fast subject matter is going to be something to avoid.

In addition, DSLRs were not designed with much attention to audio recording so although they do record audio, they often do not record audio well. Most people who shoot with DSLRs opt to record their audio separately, using handheld audio recorders and other devices. Others use special audio accessories attached to the camera to allow for better audio recording.

And that's not all, since part of the reason for a DSLR's high image quality is due to the ability to accept interchangeable lenses, it doesn't make much sense to decide to shoot with a DSLR and then not equip it with great lenses. Lenses can be a big investment. and if you decided to go with digital cinema lenses, you'll be looking at an investment of $20,000 or more for a full set. In addition to that, you'll also need additional hardware for your small camera to be able to hold such big lenses.

Is it worth it? It depends on your project. For a run-and-gun shoot, probably not. For a documentary with carefully-composed, locked-down shots, it could be great. Since the basic camera body isn't expensive, you have the option of starting small and upgrading. And, of course, there is always the option of renting cameras, lenses, and accessories as needed.

Camera manufacturers have started to take the inner workings of DSLRs and put them in camcorder bodies like the Panasonic AG-AF100 (refer to Figure 4.8). These cameras start in the $5,000–6,000 range and remove the need for the crazy accessorizing. Look for more cameras like this in the near future.

Use Your Director of Photography

If you have already chosen a director of photography (DP), talk to him (or her) about your camera needs. Your DP may have ideas about how to shoot your project that will not only make for better-looking video, but also help enhance the emotional impact of your scenes. Depending on what sort of effects you want to achieve, some cameras might be better than others. If you'll be shooting your feature yourself, then consider the same questions you would ask a DP:

- Is there a particular "look" that you are striving for? Grungy old film? Supersaturated and glossy? Muted and subtle?

- Are you planning on certain camera movements? If so, you'll need to make sure that the camera you choose can support the accessories needed to get these shots.

- Do you have special postproduction needs? If you know, for example, that you will be shooting blue-screen footage, then you'll want the best image quality you can afford.

- Does your shoot require more than one camera? If so, you may need to consider going with cheaper cameras.

- Are you going to rent a high-end, professional camera? If so, you may need to hire a professional operator. Consider this in your budget.

Accessorizing

As with any piece of gear, there are loads of accessories available for your camera. And while many are fun frivolities, others are necessary for a serious production. Pick out your camera before you start shopping for any of the following items, though. Different cameras have different needs, and you don't want to buy an expensive accessory only to find it has the wrong type of connector, or is the wrong shape for your camera.

Tripods

There is absolutely *no* substitute for a good tripod. A tripod is also essential for some complex camera motions, such as smooth pans with simultaneous zooms. Camera movement is part of your visual vocabulary, and most camera movements require a tripod. Shooting without one limits your vocabulary.

The ideal video tripod has a fluid head for smooth movement and easy-to-find handles for locking and unlocking each axis of the tripod's motion: pan, tilt, and pedestal (see Figure 4.25). Check for stability and sturdiness and make sure the tripod can support the weight of your camera, along with anything else you may need to have onboard (audio mixer, microphones, small lights, and so on).

Figure 4.25

A fluid head tripod designed especially for DSLRs by Sachtler.

Advanced Camera Rigging

Getting the shot you want can require more than a tripod. Check out the "Advanced Camera Rigging and Supports" section in Chapter 10.

Field Monitors

Back in the old days, the only person who got to see what was being shot was the camera operator. Nowadays, it's not uncommon to find half the set gathered around a monitor, or group of monitors. Higher-end cameras send full-HD video out through HDMI cables, while lower-end cameras use analog outputs. For more about monitoring video on the set, check out Chapter 10.

Remote Controls

Many cameras can be controlled remotely with a USB cable connected to a computer. At the high-end, special proprietary remote controllers are available from camera manufacturers as well.

Microphones

All video cameras—even at the higher end—have marginal microphones, so you'll need to replace these with professional units designed for the type of shooting you'll be doing. We'll discuss mics in Chapter 8.

Filters

You can use filters to change the color or optical properties of the light in your scene. Most filters screw directly onto the threads on the end of your lens, although some have special mounting brackets and some are built into the camcorder itself.

In general, using filters to create special effects should be avoided, since those same effects can usually be done in post. However, there are a few types of filters that are useful during production:

- UV haze filters
- Polarizing filter
- Diffusion filters
- Neutral Density or ND filters

We'll discuss filters more in Chapter 7.

DSLR Accessories

There are many accessories designed specifically for DSLR cameras that shoot HD video and we go over them in detail in Chapter 10.

All That Other Stuff

There are any number of other cool and useful accessories ranging from bags and trunks for protecting and transporting your camera to housings for shooting underwater. Depending on the nature of your shoot, you might very well need to budget for extra pieces of gear.

What You Should Choose

When it comes down to it, most digital features are shot on one of a few different higher-end cameras. Entry-level professional cameras in the $2,000–5,000 range, such as the Panasonic HVX200, have been workhorses for documentarians, corporate producers, and students learning to shoot because they offer professional features, very good image quality, and a reasonable price.

For filmmakers with a bit more of a budget, the RED One digital cinema camera has been the camera of choice. Recently, however, many independent filmmakers are opting to shoot on DSLRs, particularly the Canon 5d and 7d, because the image quality is impressive and the price tag is low (at least until you add those lenses and accessories).

If a consumer-grade camera is all you can afford, don't worry, because there are plenty of good single-chip units out there. After all, *Catfish*, a theatrically-released documentary by Henry Joost and Ariel Schulmann, was partially shot with the Canon PowerShot TX1, a pocket-sized single chip camera.

It can be easy to get caught up on the bells and whistles, but the bottom line is that if the camera can get the shots you want, then it's the right camera for the job.

5

Planning Your Shoot

Photo credit: Sonja Schenk

It's been said that making a movie is a lot like going to war, and while you most likely won't be risking life and limb during your production, as a producer or director, you will be managing a large group of people, all with diverse talents and goals. In addition, you'll be trying to balance these talents and goals against budgetary constraints, scheduling problems, inclement weather, temperamental actors, and any number of impossible-to-predict problems. Each one of these problems and issues will end up slowing down your shoot and that will translate directly into a financial impact. The best way to steel yourself against these problems is with meticulous, thoughtful planning.

There's no correct way to plan, and different types of shoots require different degrees of planning. In Alfred Hitchcock's *Vertigo*, there is a scene in which Jimmy Stewart spies on Kim Novak as she shops in a San Francisco flower store. Observers of the shoot reported seeing Hitchcock meticulously plan and arrange all of the cars that were passing by the window in the background of the shot. Color, shape, speed, order—he planned and calculated it all. Hitchcock was also an avid storyboarder, utilizing his accomplished draftsman skills to create detailed illustrations of exactly what shots he would get.

At the other end of the extreme are directors like Woody Allen, who don't storyboard at all, but choose to plan and block their shots on-set, with the actors. However, even if they don't storyboard, these directors still do meticulous planning by working with their camera and production crews to prepare sets and costumes, determine a "look" for their work, and much more.

As a director, you're responsible for everything the viewer sees on-screen, whether it's good or bad. With a little preparation, you can improve your odds that the viewer is seeing something good.

Your main tool for preparing for your shoot is the storyboard. Because storyboarding requires you to perform the first serious visualization of your project, the storyboarding process forces you to answer some questions that you might not have dealt with during the writing of your script. From choosing locations, to the look of your production, to how your project will be edited, storyboarding is where you'll make many practical decisions about how you'll shoot your script.

Storyboarding

Storyboards are comic-book-like representations of the images in your production (see Figure 5.1). How well they're drawn and what they look like doesn't matter, just as long as they convey to you and your crew a reasonable approximation of how the composition, framings, and edits in your production will play out. The amount of detail in your storyboards will depend on the type of scene you are creating. For a scene of three people talking around a dinner table, your storyboards will probably be less detailed, and will serve more to help you plan framing and cutting. For a special effects–heavy shot of a spaceship flying into a space-port on an alien planet, your storyboards will include more detail to help your art department and visual effects crews plan and prepare for their work, and to help you make sure that what you shoot on location can be accurately merged with effects that will be created months later after your sets are long dismantled.

Figure 5.1

A picture can be worth a thousand words when drawn by a great storyboard artist.

It doesn't necessarily matter if you shoot exactly what you planned in your storyboards. More important is the information that you will learn while storyboarding. Until you meticulously start to plan things on paper, you might not know how much coverage you will need for a particular scene, or that you're going to need a particular set piece or prop.

Whether or not you choose to draw storyboards, you still need to go through a "storyboarding" process. That is, you need to methodically plan the visual images and details that you will use to create your final product. This planning ranges from deciding how to frame and shoot a scene, to choosing a location, cast, set, and props for your shoot.

You don't have to storyboard, and many great directors don't. However, if you decide not to storyboard, you should at least create a list of shots for each scene. The last thing you want to do when you get to a location is to keep your cast and crew waiting because you haven't spent any time thinking about how to shoot. In addition, storyboards and shot lists provide a way to quickly and effectively communicate your vision to your director of photography, art director, and anyone else who needs to understand your goals.

You'll often start storyboarding before you've chosen any locations or built any sets. Obviously, if you already know the location of a scene—the Golden Gate Bridge, for example—then you can storyboard somewhat accurately. Generally, though, you'll first create somewhat abstract, non-location specific storyboards. Later, if the shot calls for it, you can go back and refine your storyboards after you've chosen locations, built sets, created props, and so on.

In addition to visualizing the movement of your camera, you'll also use storyboards to explore the motion of elements within your scene. For complicated effects or action shots, your storyboards will be your first opportunity to choreograph your scenes.

Shots and Coverage

Once you start shooting, your main concern will be to get all of the coverage that you will need when you're in the editing room. The term *coverage* refers to the number and types of shots you need to shoot to "cover" a particular scene. How much coverage is necessary? That all depends on your tastes, the needs of your script, and how much shooting you can reasonably manage to do.

It's important to realize that, although you might have written a very "visual" script, you probably didn't write out specific shots. (In fact, you shouldn't have written out specific shots; it makes your script much less readable.)

WHAT TO WATCH

There's nothing more meticulously planned than the action sequences in James Bond movies, such as **Tomorrow Never Dies**. Check out the shot list and diagram we created below. There are many other James Bond films out there if you want to try it yourself.

How many shots does it take to make a scene? When a scene is well shot and expertly edited, you won't even be aware of one shot turning into the next. In fact, unless you actually choose to look at the number of shots, you might not ever have any idea of just how many shots it takes to create a scene.

Let's take a look at a real-world example. Perhaps you've seen the James Bond movie *Tomorrow Never Dies*. Like all James Bond movies, this one begins with an action sequence that takes place before the main credits. One could describe this sequence as follows:

> On top of a snow-covered mountain, a group of terrorists have met to sell weapons. Having snuck in to the location, James Bond has set up a small video camera, which is relaying images back to headquarters where M and a number of generals are watching. After a lot of fighting and a daring air battle, Bond manages to escape with a nuke-laden airplane before a missile launched by the generals strikes the mountain.

As you can see, it's your basic "excuse me, I have to save the world" type of James Bond scene, and the entire thing lasts about nine minutes. However, take a look at this list of the first 19 shots in the scene:

1. Wide-shot: Terrorist arms bazaar. Pan down to reveal a video camera.

2. Reverse-angle of the video camera.

3. Shot of what the camera sees (called a "point-of-view" or POV shot).

4. Shot of the camera lens zooming.

5. Another POV shot. We zoom in to a group of terrorists.

6. Another shot of the video camera panning and zooming.

7. Another POV shot. This time, we see a fat, bearded man.

8. Another shot of the video camera.

9. Another POV shot. This time, some trucks.

10. Yet another shot of the video camera.

11. And yet another POV shot. Two terrorists making a deal.

12. Again, a shot of the video camera.

13. A POV shot of some guns.

14. Now, we see three big-screen monitors showing the videos we've just seen. The camera pans down to reveal a man speaking.

15. Medium shot of two men in military uniforms. They watch the screens.

16. The speaking man again.

17. Reverse shot showing the whole room, including the men and the big screens.

18. Close-up of a woman.

19. 2-shot of the woman and the speaking man.

There you have it, 19 shots, each completely different, and almost every one of them requiring a different camera setup—that is, the camera and lighting had to be moved and rearranged for *each* of these 19 shots. What's really amazing, though, is that these 19 shots account for only *one minute* of screen time! And this is a two-hour movie!

If we imagine what the terrorist arms bazaar set looked like, we can get a good idea of all of the different locations where they would have to put the camera to get the first 13 of those shots (see Figure 5.2).

Two things are interesting about this scene: first, you can see that it can take a *lot* of different angles and setups to get the coverage you need to make the scene you want. Second, when you watch this scene, you don't ever think "Man, there sure are a lot of different camera angles here." In other words, if you shoot and edit well, your audience won't necessarily even realize how many different shots they're seeing.

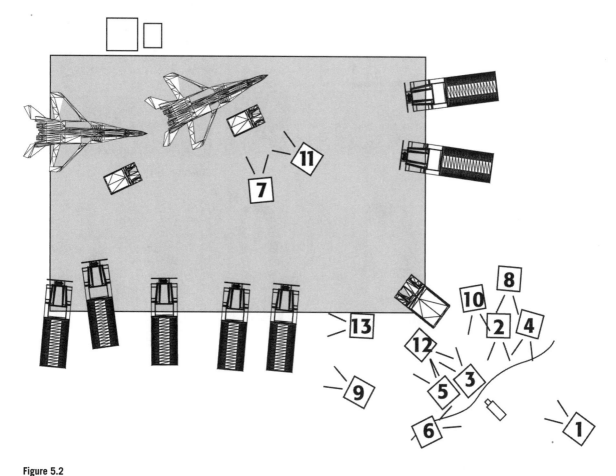

Figure 5.2

This map shows a rough approximation of the set for the first scene of the James Bond movie *Tomorrow Never Dies*, including camera positions and orientations for the first 13 shots. Note that these 13 shots take up only 40 seconds in the first scene! That's a lot of work for 40 seconds of finished film.

Camera Angles

Here's a list of the types of shots or camera angles you can use to compose a scene. Figure 5.3 shows samples of each type of shot and how you might represent such shots, framings, and cuts within your storyboards.

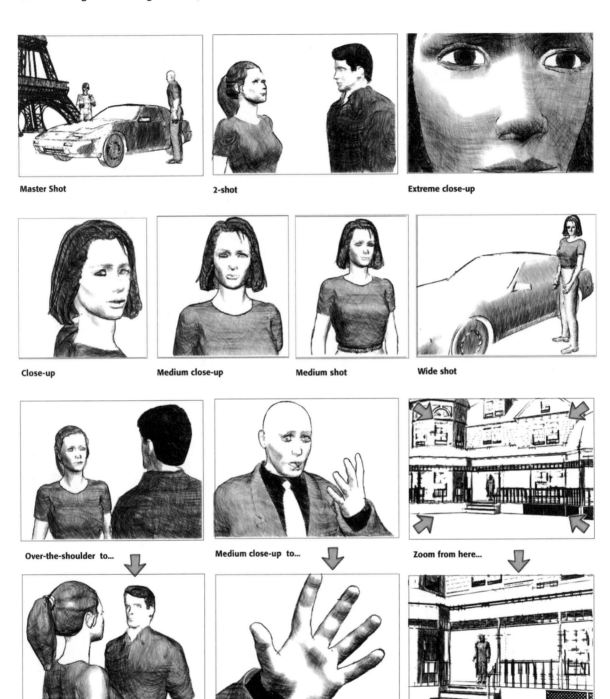

Master Shot

2-shot

Extreme close-up

Close-up

Medium close-up

Medium shot

Wide shot

Over-the-shoulder to...

Medium close-up to...

Zoom from here...

...Reverse

...Point-of-view

...to here

Figure 5.3

Camera angles.

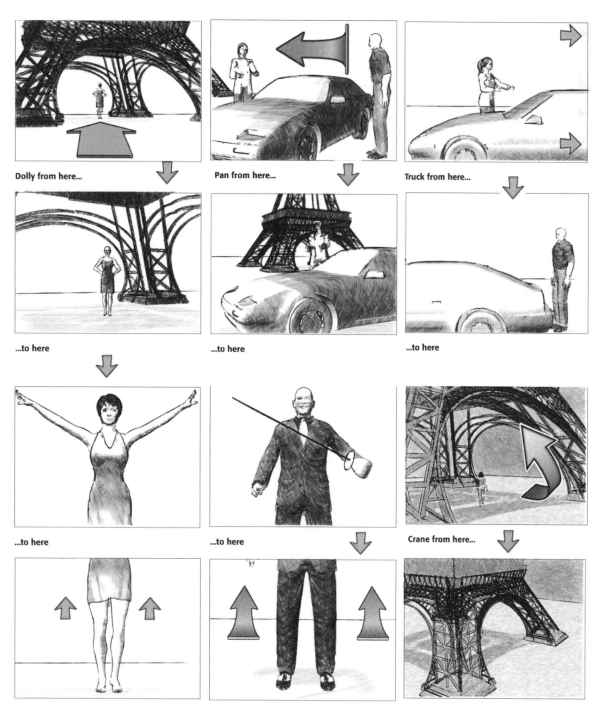

Dolly from here...

Pan from here...

Truck from here...

...to here

...to here

...to here

...to here

...to here

Crane from here...

Pedestal from here...

Tilt from here...

...to here

Master shot: A master shot is usually a wide, often static shot that covers all the action in a scene. Master shots "establish" the scene—its location, geography, participants, and tone. They give the viewers their first, big hit of information in a scene. Sometimes, master shots are used more as a "safety" shot or a backup in case the planned coverage doesn't work. However, a great master shot can provide coverage for simple scenes in a single shot and save time and money on the set.

2-shot: A shot used to cover a dialogue scene between two actors. Both actors are visible, usually from mid-torso up. Two shots can be "clean," meaning that no part of the second person is visible in the shot, or "dirty" meaning that you can see a bit of the other character.

Over-the-shoulder (OS): Also used to cover dialogue scenes between two actors. The shot focuses on one actor, but contains the silhouette or partial view of the second actor in the foreground. If over-the-shoulder shots are not composed to frame out the second character's mouth, they can make it difficult to change or rearrange dialogue in the editing room.

Reverse: A view 180 degrees from the previous shot. Usually used in combination with a POV shot or an OS shot.

Point of view (POV): A shot where the camera shows the point of view of one of the characters. Often a dolly move or handheld.

Extreme close-up (ECU): A very tight close-up, such as a shot of someone's eyes or a bug on his or her nose.

Close-up (CU): A tight shot where the subject fills the entire frame. If the subject is a person, a shot of his or her head.

Medium close-up (MCU): A slightly wider shot than a close-up. Usually like a sculptured "bust"—head, neck, shoulder, upper torso.

Medium shot (MS): On a person, usually a view from the waist up.

Wide shot (WS): A shot that shows a whole area, usually full-figure in the case of people.

Tracking (or dolly): A moving shot that uses a camera dolly (a wheeled cart that travels along special tracks) to push the camera through the scene. Often an opening shot or a POV. Depending on how they're designed, dolly shots can travel from side to side or forward and back.

Crane: A moving shot that uses a camera crane to move the camera through the air, allowing movement on an X-Y-Z axis.

Pan: A side-to-side movement of the camera, where the camera rotates around its base. The resulting motion is what you would see if you stood in one place and turned your head from side to side. Often used to follow a figure across a frame.

Tilt: Similar to a pan, but the camera tilts up and down. Analogous to tilting your head up or down. Usually used to reveal something, like a character who just ripped his pants.

Pedestal: Raising or lowering the camera, usually by adjusting the tripod on which the camera is mounted. Creates a "rising periscope" point of view. Very rarely used in features.

Zoom: A lens movement from a tight to a wide shot (zoom out), or a wide to a tight shot (zoom in). Good for that "caught-on-tape" look.

Dolly counter zoom: A shot where a dolly and a zoom are performed at the same time. In the resulting shot, the framing of the image stays the same, but the depth of field changes dramatically. Objects in the background foreshorten and appear to float backward. The most famous example is in *Jaws*, when Roy Scheider sees the shark in the water on the crowded beach. His POV of the shark is a dramatic dolly counter zoom.

Slow reveal: Usually a pan, tilt, or dolly that reveals something that at first wasn't apparent. A woman laughs at a table, pan over to reveal that her husband just spilled his wine.

Computer-Generated Storyboards

There are a good number of computer-based previsualization tools that can make your storyboarding work much easier. Hand drawing storyboards can take forever, so even if you have great drawing skills, these programs let you create professional-quality storyboards with detailed sets, characters, and symbols in a fraction of the time it would take to make them from scratch. Even if you're an experienced illustrator, the convenience and speed of CG storyboards can be a real time and money saver. You can draw some key frames by hand and rely on the software to fill in the rest.

Many storyboarding apps include the ability to automatically import your script from a screen-writing program, sophisticated Web-based storyboard sharing, and more. At the high end, previsualization apps help you create a full 3D virtual set that mimics your location and lets you program camera movements with the real limitations of the physical space in mind. They offer several different rendering styles and have advanced expandable libraries of objects, characters, backgrounds, and so on to help you create very specific environments. At the lower end, storyboarding apps let you quickly build a 2D environment by dragging and dropping a set of predrawn objects, characters, and backgrounds that are often customizable.

Here are some of the top apps that are currently available:

- **PowerProduction's StoryBoard Quick:** Available for Mac or Windows, StoryBoard Quick has been around longer than any other dedicated storyboarding app. Providing a simple interface, the program lets you drag and drop characters, props, and locations to create nice-looking colored storyboards. Although primarily a 2D environment, characters and certain objects can rotate in three dimensions. Because it offers robust import of screenplay formats and export of finished boards to print or the Web, StoryBoard Quick is an excellent solution with a very short learning curve (see Figure 5.4).

Figure 5.4

StoryBoard Quick provides an easy-to-use interface for creating your own storyboards.

- **PowerProduction's StoryBoard Artist:** Offering sophisticated 3D storyboard generation, StoryBoard Artist allows you to create more complex storyboards than you can build with StoryBoard Quick. In addition, the program lets you create animatics complete with multi-track audio. An excellent tool for any type of previsualization, StoryBoard Artist is especially good for complex action and special effects scenes (Figure 5.5).

Figure 5.5

StoryBoard Artist provides a true 3D environment for quickly building sets, blocking positions, and adding storyboarding symbols.

- **FrameForge 3D Studio:** Also a 3D storyboard app, FrameForge is built around the idea of creating a 3D environment that mimics your set and features sophisticated controls for the built-in cameras. You can easily build a 3D model of your actual location using blueprints or measurements, set up the lighting with models of real cinema light sources, and choose from a list of popular high-end cameras. You can even choose the f-stop, the focal length, and use accurate 3D models of camera accessories, such as jib arms and dollies. If you want to know that your RED camera on a Fisher jib arm will be able to track your lead actor down a hallway and out the door, FrameForge will help you find out. FrameForge also offers a special application for previsualizing stereoscopic productions (see Figure 5.6).

- **SketchUp Film & Stage:** SketchUp is an excellent 3D modeling program that was originally designed to provide a way for architects and designers to quickly create 3D visualizations of their designs. The Film & Stage plug-in provides a few extra features that add additional storyboard and previsualization functionality. Like StoryBoard Artist and FrameForge 3D Studio, SketchUp Film & Stage offers various render styles that look like beautifully hand-drawn or painted storyboards.

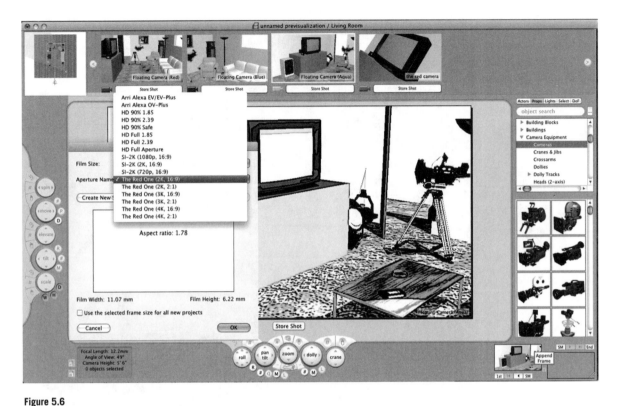

Figure 5.6

FrameForge 3D Studio offers a multi-cam 3D environment where you can use accurate 3D models to set up the lighting, camera, and other variables to match your set.

Less Is More

Remember, storyboards are a visualization tool, not an end product. The most important thing about them is that creating them forces you to really think about the camera angles you will need to tell your story and whether or not they are doable. If you show crew members detailed, photorealistic storyboards, they'll be inclined to think that those images are what your final scene will look like. It's better to give designers, costumers, set builders, and actors rough, sketchy storyboards. Let them use their expertise to design and create the details for which they're responsible.

Storyboarding is only one of your previsualization tasks, and you'll probably refine and change your storyboards throughout your preproduction and production phases.

Camera Diagrams and Shot Lists

For scenes that have a lot of complicated action like the James Bond scene mentioned earlier, you might find it useful to create a camera diagram. This is a simple visual reference that will help you understand what camera setups you need once you're on the set. In addition to helping you plan your shoot, camera diagrams can help ensure that you get all of the coverage that you need. Camera diagrams can also include information about light placement, to help your lighting crew stay organized.

Take a look at the scene below.

```
INT. THE UPTOWN BAR - DAY


A woman, DEBRA, sits drinking alone at the bar. She doesn't look up as
JOE, a greasy-looking character in his mid-thirties, enters.


MAX, the bartender, comes out from behind the bar.
Joe stops dead in his tracks.


JOE
I thought you quit. Left town. Something about cleaning up your act.


Debra looks uneasily from Joe to Max.


MAX
Doesn't look that way, does it?


JOE
She's with me. Aren't you, Deb?


Debra nods nervously.


MAX
I don't think so.


Max pulls out a gun and, without waiting for Joe's reaction, shoots.
Joe falls to the floor, dead.
```

According to the corresponding storyboards in Figure 5.7, this scene needs a master shot, three close-ups, and a two-shot.

Figure 5.7

A simple storyboard of the scene in the previous script.

These storyboards are based on master shot style coverage. Shot 1 is a master shot that covers the entire scene and serves as the foundation onto which you will add the close-ups (shots 2, 3, and 5) and other shots in the editing room (see Figure 5.8).

Camera diagrams can also include information about light placement and other crucial objects. Figure 5.2 is an example of a much more complicated camera diagram.

Legal Legwork

Here's a quick list of some legal issues to be aware of in advance of your shoot:

- If you are shooting on private property, you need to get a location release from the owner. This includes schools, universities, shopping malls, etc.

- You will need a license for any original artwork, photographs, book covers, music, etc., in your film. All of this work is copyrighted and you'll need permission, or license, from the owner of the copyright. Sometimes getting copyright licenses can take months.

- You will need an actor or model release from any person in your film, including voice actors, people in photos stuck on the fridge in the background of a shot, celebrities on the cover of magazines, and so on. Always get names, contact info, and releases for anyone who ends up in your footage as soon as possible. It is much harder to track those people down later. There's a great iPhone app called *iRelease* for getting releases on the fly.

- Most feature film production companies have a standard liability insurance policy with at least one million dollars worth of coverage. You'll need proof of this insurance to rent locations, stages, and more expensive camera and lighting gear. If you're in film school, your school might be able to provide this for you.

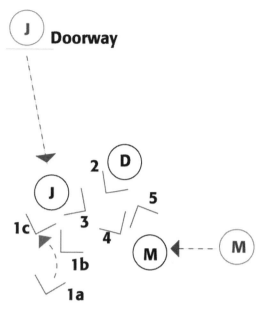

1. Master shot of scene:
Wide shot (1a) ,
dolly in, hold on 3-shot (1b),
dolly in to ECU of Joe (1c).
2. C.U. of Debra
3. C.U. of Joe
4. Two-shot of Debra and Joe
5. C.U. of Max

Cutaways: E.C.U. of gun, details of bar, etc.

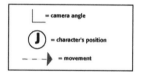

Figure 5.8

The corresponding camera diagram and shot list to the storyboard in Figure 5.7.

Legal Legwork (continued)

- You may need permission from companies to feature their product logos in your film. As a rule, it's best to avoid logos if you can.

- If you didn't write the script yourself, you will need proof that you own the rights to the script when you sell your movie to a distributor.

- If you are making a documentary, the right to use copyrighted images, footage, etc. might be available to you under the "Fair Use Doctrine," but only under certain conditions.

- When you sell your film to a distributor, you will need E&O (Errors and Omissions) insurance to protect you in case you made a mistake in your legal dealings along the way.

Location Scouting

The locations and sets on which you choose to shoot will convey some of the most vital visual information in your story. Sometimes, set and location will convey even more than your script or your actors.

There's no real rule for finding a location; you simply have to get out of the house and start looking around. There are, however, some things to remember and some questions to ask when looking for and selecting a location. Moreover, depending on the type of equipment you will be using, your location needs might vary. Consider the following when scouting locations:

- **Will the owners of the property let you shoot there?** You should, of course, always ask permission before shooting on private property. Though many people will let you shoot for free simply because they'll be excited by the idea of a movie shoot, in other situations you might have to work a deal—either for cash or donations of improvements to the property. If you are planning to sell your finished project to a distributor, you'll need to get a location release from the owners of the property.

- **Do you need a permit to shoot?** For shooting on civic or government-owned property, you'll often need to get special permits from your local city hall or municipal government. Most large cities have film commissions whose primary purpose is to help film production crews get permits. Permits do cost money, though, so you'll need to add this into the cost of shooting at a particular location. You can often get away with shooting clandestinely, without a permit, but there can be risks to this. Here in San Francisco, we've heard stories of permit-less production crews having all of their equipment confiscated by the local cops.

- **Do you need both the inside and outside?** You may not necessarily need access to both the inside and outside of a location. After all, you can always shoot your interiors on a set or in a building to which you have better, less expensive access. Storyboard carefully for these situations.

- **Can you find the same type of location in a cheaper town?** The inside of an office is the inside of an office. See if you can find office space nearby, but in a cheaper location.

- **Is the location a reasonable distance from the rest of your shoot?** Lugging equipment, cast, and crew to faraway locations can quickly become prohibitively expensive, particularly on a union shoot.

- **Does the location require redressing or modification?** Removal of signs, addition of new signs, changing the look or "period" of the environs. This can be done through practical set dressings or through digital "dressing" and postprocessing, but it will add expense to that particular location.

- **Does the location afford the coverage you need?** If the shots you plan require many different angles, you'll need to consider your location carefully. For example, although your location might look great, be sure you can shoot it from multiple angles and reverse angles without getting unwanted scenery (see Figure 5.9).

WHAT TO WATCH

For his movie **Do the Right Thing,** Spike Lee made major modifications to an entire city block in Brooklyn. With a clear idea of the storefronts he needed for his set—as well as their proximity to one another—his set designers proceeded to modify existing buildings to fit his needs. Because he had the use of an entire city block, he got all of the "in-between" locations (sidewalks, street corners, etc.), in addition to getting the individual storefronts he needed, and all within walking distance of each other. In the process of preparing the set, his location security guards cleared out and renovated a crack house, a set change that, obviously, made a lasting improvement in the neighborhood.

Figure 5.9

(Left) This Spanish-style mission might be just the location for some exteriors in your turn-of-the-century drama. (Middle) Unfortunately, it sits on a very busy, four-lane thoroughfare, which will make shooting clean audio very difficult. (Right) Also, across the street from the mission are very modern buildings and parking lots, which will make reverse angles difficult. (On the other hand, this location—San Francisco's Mission Dolores—was good enough for Hitchcock! He featured it prominently in *Vertigo*. Of course, it wasn't a period piece, and there was much less traffic in 1958.

- **Does your location have the physical space required for the size of your shoot?** See Figure 5.10. In addition to your equipment, don't forget the support needs of your crew (power generators, trucks, dressing rooms, catering, portable toilets, and so on).

- **Does the location have access to sufficient practical resources such as power?** Remote locations pose other logistical problems, such as access to restrooms and refrigeration. Is there enough parking for your cast and crew?

- **Is the location too noisy?** Refrigerators, outside traffic, and air-conditioning are just a few things that will add a hum to your sound recordings. Overhead airplanes and other intermittent noises will require constant halting of your production while you wait for the noise to pass.

- **What are the location requirements of your equipment?** If you are shooting at night, you might be able to get away with more or less lighting, depending on the type of camera you are using. In addition, video cameras can have difficulty dealing with certain repeating patterns and textures. Closely spaced horizontal or vertical lines can create annoying interference patterns on your screen. Does your location contain such textures? If so, can you shoot around them?

Figure 5.10

These cozy little houses could make a great location; however, the narrow street could make things difficult if you're expecting to use a large crew. In addition, clearing the street of cars could require expensive city permits, making what seemed like a cheap location into a big expense.

- **What about light and sound?** Can you adequately light and mic your location for the needs of your particular equipment? Different cameras and formats have different needs in regard to light and sound. Plan for these accordingly.

- **Can you improve the authenticity of your set with sound effects?** Adding some simple ambient sounds to a shot—adding the cries of a circus barker to a shot of a tent, for example—can improve the authenticity of your set.

- **Can you fake it?** Cutting from a good, convincing establishing shot of a sun-dappled vineyard with appropriate ambient sound effects to an interior set that's been properly decorated might be all you need to make your audience believe that you paid for a long shoot in the hills of Tuscany (see Figure 5.11).

Talk to your principal crew members when scouting locations. Does the production designer agree with your assessment of the feel of the set? Can he dress it accordingly? Does the cinematographer feel that she can shoot it in the way that you want? And can it be done affordably? Does your gaffer think the set can be outfitted? Careful location scouting will help you explore these issues and formulate questions to present to your crew.

Figure 5.11

A few well-planned establishing shots combined with the right audio can quickly establish a Mid-Eastern location. When, in fact, you've only gone as far as a busy American street corner.

WHAT TO WATCH

John Sayles's, *Matewan,* a 1987 tale of union troubles among West Virginia coal miners is an all-around example of excellent filmmaking. For the independent producer, it's especially informative as it shows that a convincing period piece (a type of movie that can be very expensive) can be produced with an indie budget. You can read more about the production design of this movie in John Sayles's excellent book *Thinking in Pictures: The Making of the Movie Matewan.*

Production Design

An important part of preproduction is the chance to work with your crew to create the "look" of your movie—from the elements on the set, to the way the movie will be shot and cut—a process also known as *production design*.

Whether you do it yourself or attach a professional production designer or art director to your project, defining the look is more than just creating a style; it's a chance to explore how all of the elements at your disposal can be used to strengthen your visual image and, consequently, your story.

The goal of production design is to enhance the story by adding to the available visual palette. For example, in *Trainspotting*, every wall is painted a striking color, often covered in a thick layer of grime: turquoise, red, green, and mustard yellow. This dark, rich palette conveys an atmosphere of opiate sensuality appropriate to the film. In the film *Red,* the color palette is biased toward occasional touches of bright reds against a background of charcoal grays and rich dark browns. In *American Beauty*, the sets are dressed in typical suburban furniture just verging on "kitsch." The comfortable excess of the main family's house lies in sharp contrast to the austere, traditional Americana furniture in the house of the family next door. In *Do the Right Thing*, bright reds in the sets and clothing are used to increase both the feeling of hot summer and the emotional intensity of the drama (see Color Plates 8–10).

Just as the director of photography is head of the camera department, the production designer is head of the art department. The production designer usually starts working early in the process, helping to generate storyboards and an overall "look" for the project. The title of this position might vary—you might use an art director or a set designer instead of a production designer, but their duties will be relatively the same. On a big movie, the production designer is responsible for the overall vision, while the art director implements that vision and manages the art department crew, which includes set designers, set dressers, prop masters, modelers, scenic painters, set construction workers, and production assistants.

Art Directing Basics

Good art direction is a combination of the symbolic and the practical. If your story is about a young girl growing up in Kansas in 1850, you'll be limited to certain types of buildings, furniture, and clothes. However, you still have the choice of giving her a sunlit, whitewashed bedroom with furnishings upholstered in bright calico fabrics, or an age-darkened room with indirect sunlight and dull, dark fabrics. These simple details tell two very different stories.

One of the easiest ways to add visual symbolism to a scene is via lighting. Colors also have strong connotations for people. Black often connotes death, while red conjures feelings of blood and violence, but also love and passion; blue is peaceful and calming, but can also create a feeling of sadness, and so on. Similarly, styles of furniture and clothing can say a lot about a character. An elderly woman living alone in a house decorated in sparse Eames furniture from the 1960s might indicate someone who won't let go of the past. Change the character to a young man, and the same furniture indicates a trendy sense of style. Clutter can be comfortable or claustrophobic; sparseness can be clean or indicative of emotional emptiness. In addition to externalizing the themes of the story, production design should also aid in focusing the viewer's eye, a challenge that goes hand in hand with lighting and framing the shot.

WHAT TO WATCH

Narc, this gritty tale of undercover narcotics agents is set in modern-day Detroit, but the lack of modern props and recognizable establishing shots give it a timeless, placeless feeling: this is a story that could happen anywhere in America.

Building a Set

If your location needs are very specific, it might be easier to build a set than to find the right location. Whether you build your set on a stage or at a location, you'll need to spend some extra effort to make it look real. Sets are usually built out of *flats,* large, hollow wooden walls that are held up from the rear with supports. If you rent a soundstage, you might find that several flats come with the stage rental. You can paint them the color of your choice.

Typically, a room built on a stage will have three solid walls and a fourth wall on wheels for use when needed. Many flats have doors or windows built into them. When shopping for a soundstage, look for one that has the type of flats you need. If your needs are very specialized, you may have to build your own flats and color or texture them appropriately. For example, you can easily create a stucco or adobe look by gluing foamcore to a flat and then spray painting it. (Spray paint dissolves foamcore.) Hiring a set carpenter can save lots of time and trouble.

Retail Therapy

Good set dressers and wardrobe people spend a lot of time browsing in the shops in their city. A thorough knowledge of where to buy odds and ends is one of the secrets of their profession.

Set Dressing and Props

Whether you have a found location or a built set, the next step is to dress it. Because they're completely empty, dressing a built set takes more work than handling a found location. On the other hand, your options might be limited when dressing a found location because you'll want to avoid disturbing the occupants or ruining their property. Either way, a good prop (short for *property*) can really sell a weak location. A giant gilded Victorian mirror, a barber's chair, a mirrored disco ball—the mere presence of these objects tells you where you are and makes the location believable. Props can be very expensive to rent, but if you can find that one key piece, it might be worth the money. In addition to prop rental houses, you can sometimes rent props from retailers. Usually, this will involve a hefty deposit and the requirement that it be returned in perfect condition.

If your film involves weapons and fight scenes, you'll need special props such as breakaway furniture and glass, fake knife sets, and realistic-looking guns. Fake knife sets usually include a real version of the knife, a rubber version, a collapsible version, and a broken-off version. Renting a realistic-looking gun usually involves some extra paperwork, and you are required to keep it concealed at all times. If you have a really specialized object that you need—like the *Get Smart* shoe-phone—you'll probably need to have a fabricator or modeler make it for you.

DIY Art Direction

Creative art direction can be one of the most effective ways to add production values to your film cheaply. A lot can be done with a couple gallons of paint, some elbow grease, and a trip to the local thrift store.

Here's a list of some basic ways to upgrade your set without spending a lot of money:

- **Get rid of the white walls.** Most offices, houses, and apartments have white walls. They might look fine in real life, but not on camera. First of all, if you are shooting in a small room, such as a bedroom, the white walls are going to act as giant bounce cards and blow out your set. It's very hard to control the lighting in a small room with white walls. Secondly, because they are so common, white walls are meaningless, visually. If you give a female character a bedroom with blood red walls, that says a lot about her personality. If you give her pastel pink walls, it says a lot, too. If you give her white walls, it says nothing. For less than $100 and a few hours of labor, you can have a set that speaks to your audience.

- **Paint over the dirt.** Keeping your color palette in mind, a fresh coat of paint can really transform ugly furniture and anything else that doesn't look so hot. Your goal isn't restoration so don't bother with sanding or primer or even the right type of paint. Just get the cheapest water-based household enamel in the right color and cover it up. It might not look that great close up, but it will look great in your film.

- **Thrifty props.** A few key props can change a room from ordinary to specific. Take a trip to the local thrift store and see what you can find that would work for your set. Don't make a shopping list; instead, make a list of problems to solve: "Something to put on Martina's desk to show that she is a control freak." "Something to cover the wall in Joel's bathroom and show that he's been living here for 40 years." What's also great about thrift store finds is that they usually look a bit worn, which is often ideal for dressing a set. If you don't have any thrift stores nearby, spend some time surfing eBay and Craigslist.

- **Negative space.** Sometimes you can achieve as much or more by removing things from the set. Stuff like junk mail on the table, trash cans, cables and wires, and other forms of visual clutter can make an otherwise fine location look cheap or ugly. Also keep an eye out for things that don't suit your story. You might love books, but if your character is an obsessive hacker, the towering bookshelves filled with classics won't help your film.

- **Foreground objects.** Objects that can fill part of the foreground of the frame, such as window frames, plants, and curtains, can add depth to shots in otherwise tight locations. As you dress the set, think about what you can add to the set that will serve to create an interesting foreground. At the very least, some gauzy sheer curtains in a couple of colors (white, taupe, dark gray) from Ikea are always good things to have on hand and cost under $20.

- **Be wary of mirrors.** Not because you might be a vampire but because mirrors and other reflective surfaces tend to reflect your entire crew into your shot.

WHAT TO WATCH

In his last film, **Eyes Wide Shut,** Stanley Kubrick used the religious images and iconography of the Middle Ages, particularly the works of Hieronymous Bosch, and their famous depictions of hell to create a frightening but fascinating secret world.

Art Directing Equipment Checklist

- Staple gun
- Hammer, screwdriver, and other tools
- Nails, tacks, and push-pins
- Various types of glue (Elmer's, superglue)
- House paint and spray paint, various colors including black
- Paint brushes and rollers
- Bucket
- Dark brown and amber water-based stains, Streaks and Tips, etc.
- Dulling spray (to take the shine off reflective objects)
- Contact paper
- Window cleaner (with ammonia)
- Cleaning products
- Rags, towels, cheesecloth
- Dust mask

Visual Planning for Documentaries

Sometimes people think that all you need to do to make a documentary is turn on the camera and start shooting. Nothing could be further from the truth. Like all great films, great documentaries start with a strong vision. Although you're not likely to build your sets from the ground up, documentaries still have lots of opportunities for designing shots, choosing interesting locations, and developing a "look."

Are you going to feature highly composed, wide-angle static shots or rough, dynamic handheld camerawork that gets in close to the subject? What is the color palette of the film? Are you going to position your subject inside the house in the shadows or out in front in the sunny garden? You may not want to interfere with your subjects' wardrobe choices, but it's highly likely they'll ask you whether you want "dressy" or "casual." At every moment while shooting a doc, visual choices are made and at those times, documentarians have a chance to create a stylish film.

In addition to planning the visual style of the film, there is also the issue of planning for coverage. Some people think you're just supposed to go out there and "wing it," and sometimes that is true, but documentaries can also benefit from shot lists and camera diagrams. Imagine that you are making a documentary about a woman who has a phobia and can't leave her house. What kind of shots would you need to show that she spends most of her time isolated and alone? Will you use lots of close-ups? Or fluid handheld shots that track her movements as she prepares dinner for one? A quick list can really help you visualize the shots in advance and will come in handy when you're actually shooting and things are a bit more hectic.

An important piece of the documentary puzzle is the interviews. Although not all documentaries rely on interviews, for many they form the narrative through-line of the film. If your film is going to rely on interviews, it's important to remember that they will have a big impact on the overall "look" of the film. Another issue that some documentarians face is the use of archival footage. Will you try to make the footage you are shooting now match the archival footage in some way? Or do you prefer a strong contrast? Even if you plan on only using the interviews as voice-overs, it's still worth shooting nice-looking video that matches your overall look. In post, this will give you the option of covering bad shots or cuts with interview footage, or completely changing the approach of your documentary if it turns out that your original idea isn't working out.

There are many decisions to make for documentary filmmakers and because the shooting of a documentary can often span years, it's even more important to have a vision of the film at the outset and stick to it.

WHAT TO WATCH

Dogtown and Z-boys is a documentary about Venice Beach skateboarding culture in the late 70s and it uses lots of archival footage and still photos from the era. However, director Stacy Peralta used lots of fast cuts, zooms, and spins that mimic the movements of the skateboarders themselves to make all the various types of footage work together.

Try These Planning Exercises

1. **Storyboarding:** In Chapter 2, "Writing and Scheduling," you were introduced to a scene from Shakespeare's *Richard III*. If you performed the script breakdown exercise at the end of that chapter, then you've already acquainted yourself with that scene. The script is located in the Chapter 2 folder on the companion Web site. Though it's a simple dialogue scene between two characters, there's a lot of dramatic tension and rhythmic interplay. Finding a way to shoot this scene to showcase the actors, enhance the drama, and reveal the tension is an excellent exercise. (After all, this is one of the rare instances as a director where you know you can trust your material.) Create a set of storyboards for this scene. In addition to planning your shots, go ahead and give some thought as to how and where you might like to stage it. Do you want to shoot it in a traditional period British setting? Or restage it for a different location. Because it's primarily talking heads, you don't need any exceptional rendering skill, even stick figures will do.

2. **Shot Lists:** Now that you've created a set of storyboards for the *Richard III* scene, create the associated camera diagrams and shot lists. In addition to helping you understand where you're going to want your camera, this process will also give you an idea of how many times you might have to run the scene to get the shots you want, and when you might need to shoot some things out of sequence. Remember, to get all the angles that you need, because your actors will have to be prepared to perform many takes.

3. **Production Design:** Don't worry, we're not going to send you shopping or set-building. Rather, we're simply going to ask you to write up a narrative description of how you might design the *Richard III* scene. You should have already chosen a setting during the storyboarding exercise. (If you really want to exercise your skills, go ahead and scout around for some locations, take some pictures of them, and determine if you think you could shoot your storyboarded scene there.)

   Now you can start thinking about how you might want to dress your location, what kind of wardrobe you might want the actors to wear, and what sorts of props you'll want to use. In addition, give some thought to overall color palette and tone of the scene. The obvious palette and tone choice is dark and muted, but perhaps there are other options—not so obvious—that are equally as powerful.

4. **Budget:** You've now done the bulk of the planning that you need to actually pull off a shoot of this scene. With your breakdown sheets, production design, and shot lists in hand, give some thought as to how much it would cost to shoot it. Write up a budget to generate a cost estimate to cover the shoot. Obviously, you'll need a camera, and possibly lights and audio gear, as well as two actors and a crew of at least one person and a camera operator. In addition, you might need to rent props or costumes, or pay for access to your location. If you're really going gung-ho on this, then you might even need to budget for set dressing or construction. (Bear in mind that it's also possible to do this scene for free with a skeleton crew. That's one reason we picked it. One great thing about Shakespeare: everything you need is in the text, so you can pull off this scene with minimal production. Nevertheless, it's fun to imagine a lavish production as well.)

Effects Planning

If your shoot requires any special effects, then you have a whole extra planning job ahead of you. Special effects must be carefully planned out for all the reasons that any shot needs to be planned (to save time on the set and to make sure you get the footage you need). But effects planning is also the time when you have to figure out how you're going to create the effect you want.

Your first question when creating a special effect shot should always be, "Do I really need it?" Effects are time-consuming, complicated, and expensive. You should never include anything in a story if it doesn't really belong there, but you *definitely* shouldn't include something as complex as a special effects shot if it doesn't really belong there.

If you decide that you do need the effect, your next question is to determine if the effect is going to be created digitally (in the computer), or practically (using "real" props and sets, and clever camerawork), or some combination of both. As amazing as digital effects can be, it's often easier and faster to create an effect using special props and backdrops on the set.

Obviously, to determine the best way to create an effect, you need to know something about creating effects, both digital and practical. We talk much more about effects creation in Chapter 17, "Titles and Effects." Hopefully, if you're not comfortable with effects work, you can find someone who is and get him or her to help you with your effects planning.

Once you've determined how to create the effect you need, you might want to shoot some simple test shots and see if the effect really works. Alternatively, maybe you'll want to create *animatics*, animated shots (usually 3D) that serve as a "moving storyboard." Animatics can provide good visual references for everyone, from designers to effects crews to actors. For example, you can use a 3D program to create animatics that can be shown to actors and crew and that can even be used as placeholder video while you're editing.

Perhaps the best way to understand the importance of effects planning is with an example. The shot in Figure 5.12 is from a short film about a guy with a remote control. In one scene, the script calls for a painting of the Mona Lisa to appear on the wall behind the man and for the wall to change color.

When shooting, we first thought about compositing the Mona Lisa in digitally, but then realized it would be easier to simply create a Mona Lisa prop (which we did by printing a digital file of the Mona Lisa on a large-format printer and then mounting it inside a rented frame).

The change in wall color, though, was achieved through a digital effect called *rotoscoping*. Simply put, we repainted the wall color in postproduction. Unfortunately, the first time we shot, we didn't realize that the actor's head needed to remain in front of the painting at all times, to ease the rotoscoping process.

With better planning and some good tests, we could have avoided this. As it was, we had to reshoot, or face an incredibly difficult rotoscoping job.

WHAT TO WATCH

Animated works, such as *The Incredible Adventures of Wallace and Gromit*, offer the most extreme production design examples, because *everything* that you see on-screen has to be designed. Even if you've already seen these excellent animated shorts, take a look at them again with an eye toward the production design. From the custom-designed wallpaper themes to the characteristic "industrial era" look of Wallace's inventions, these works are masterpieces of production design.

Figure 5.12

Due to bad effects planning, this shot was unusable. Since the actor's head did not remain in front of the Mona Lisa at all times, repainting the wall became prohibitively difficult.

Creating Rough Effects Shots

If your feature requires complex effects shots—battling spaceships, giant flying insects, waving computer-generated cornfields—you'll want to start preparing such shots early in production. There's no reason you can't have your effects department quickly rough-out low-res, low-detail animations that can serve as animated storyboards. With these rough animations, you can more easily plan and direct shots. Having low-res proxy footage also means that you can go ahead and start editing before your final effects are rendered.

Filmmakers have always had to engage in meticulous planning before rolling their cameras. As a digital filmmaker, you have a decided advantage. With digital tools for storyboarding, you can more easily try out different visualizations. Moreover, with digital editing, your storyboards, animatics, and early work files can actually be repurposed to save time in postproduction.

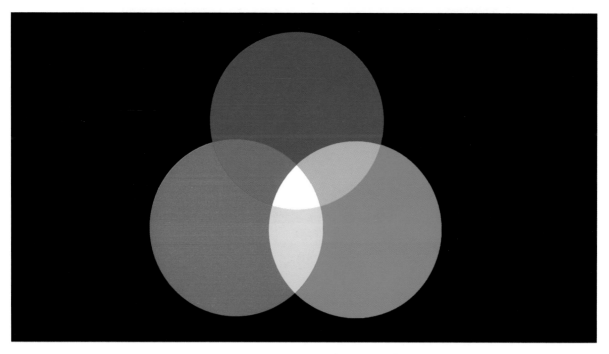

Color Plate 1

Red, green, and blue are the three primary colors of light, a system called *additive color*. You can create any other color of light by mixing those primaries together, and if you mix enough light together, you eventually get white.

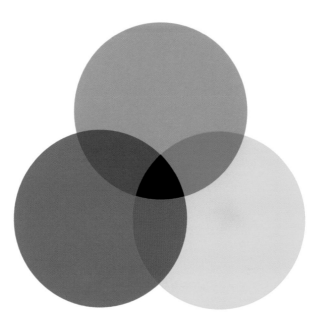

Color Plate 2

In a subtractive color system, mixing the colors together results in black.

Full Image

Luma Only

Chroma Only

Color Plate 3

A full-color HD image (top) consists of luma (middle) and chroma (bottom). In this example, you can see that most of the important image information is contained in the luminance channel.

Color Plate 4

The color in a video image (top) is comprised of a red channel (R), a green channel (G), and a blue channel (B). Note the differences in her lips and the shadows on her face across the RGB channels.

Color Plate 5

Same happy face, same PostIt—increasing the gain (lower image) yields better exposure but introduces noise.

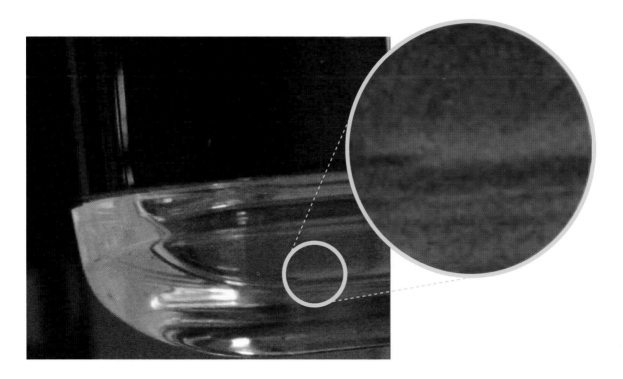

Color Plate 6

This object is almost monochrome, but due to heavy gain boosting, chrominance noise, consisting of brightly colored pixels, is introduced.

Color Plate 7

Chromatic aberration looks like a colorful halo or fringe between dark and light areas in an image. Instead of a clean edge, the leaves in this image are fringed with red and yellow tones.

Color Plate 8

This color palette was inspired by the images to the right and used to communicate ideas about the look of the film to the art director, costume designer, and others.

Color Plate 9

The Adobe Kuler Web site automatically creates a color palette using an uploaded still photograph.

Color Plate 10

This color palette was inspired by a location scout photograph of an old classroom.

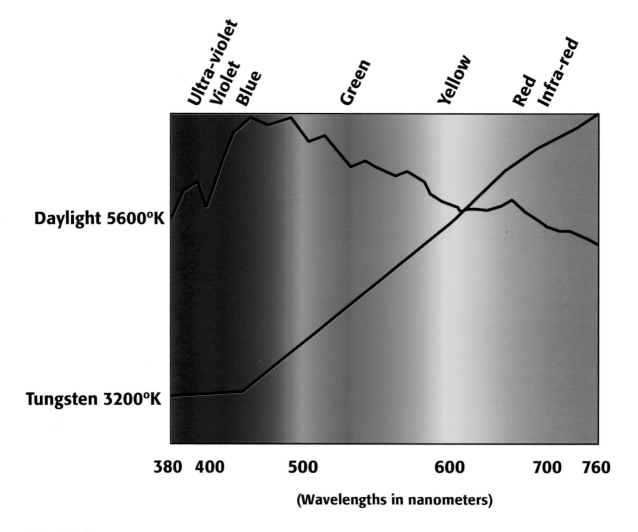

Color Plate 11

This chart shows the visible color spectrum and the spectral energy distributions of sunlight and tungsten light. Both cover the entire range of color, but sunlight has much more blue, whereas tungsten has more red.

Color Plate 12

There is a huge selection of colored lighting gels, reflectors, and diffusion materials available. Swatch books like these from Lee Filters are great to have on hand as you plan the lighting for your project.

Color Plate 13

Lighting crews use a lot of equipment to light the green background on this green screen set.

Color Plate 14

This green screen set was lit and art-directed to match a CGI environment.

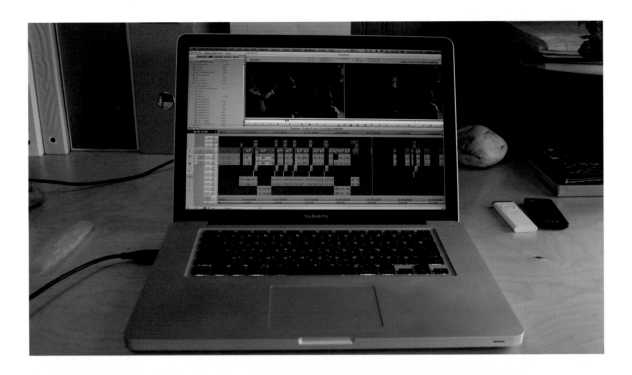

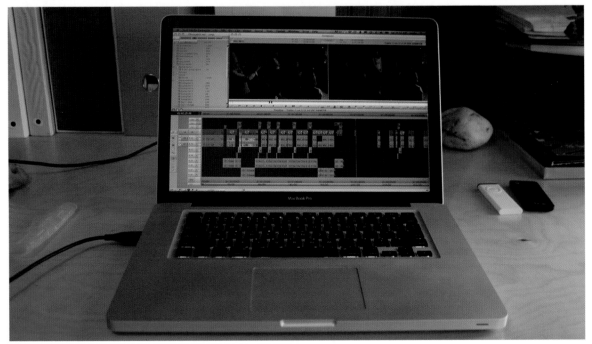

Color Plate 15

The image on the top has the white balance set for fluorescent interior light, but there is a window to the right, out of frame, so the best choice is to set the white balance for daylight (bottom).

Color Plate 16

This actor was recorded against a blue-screen backdrop (left) and the background image (middle) was keyed in to get the composite image (right). For this particular composite, the goal was to blend a modern day video image of an actor with colorized film footage from the 1920s.

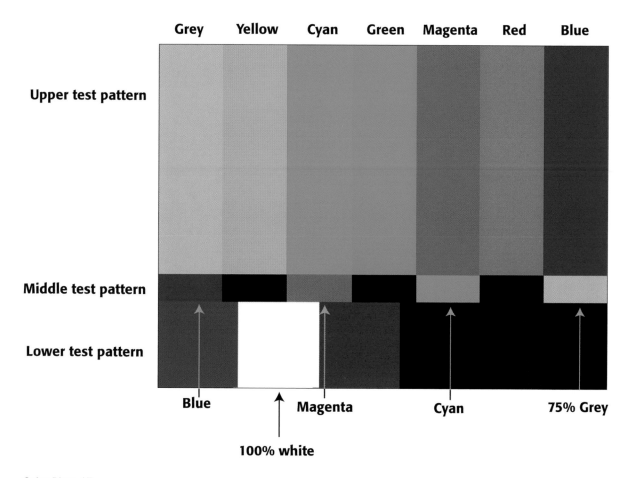

Color Plate 17

The SMPTE color bars image contains three test patterns that are designed to calibrate color on NTSC monitors.

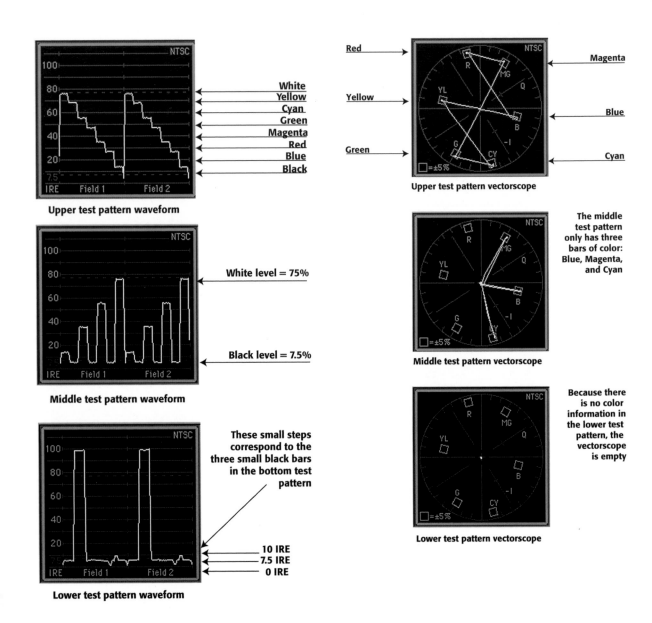

Upper test pattern waveform

White
Yellow
Cyan
Green
Magenta
Red
Blue
Black

Upper test pattern vectorscope

Red
Yellow
Green
Magenta
Blue
Cyan

Middle test pattern waveform

White level = 75%

Black level = 7.5%

Middle test pattern vectorscope

The middle test pattern only has three bars of color: Blue, Magenta, and Cyan

Lower test pattern waveform

These small steps correspond to the three small black bars in the bottom test pattern

10 IRE
7.5 IRE
0 IRE

Lower test pattern vectorscope

Because there is no color information in the lower test pattern, the vectorscope is empty

Color Plate 18

The waveforms (left) and vectorscopes (right) that correspond with the SMPTE color bars test patterns.

6

Lighting

Photo credit: Jason Hampton

Camera choice, of course, has a huge impact on the quality and look of your final project. But picking the right gear is only half the shooting battle. It doesn't matter how good your camera is; if you do a lousy lighting job, you'll get a lousy final product. A well-lit scene shot with an inferior camera can look much better than a poorly lit scene shot with a great camera. Fortunately, of all of the things that can affect the look of your production, lighting is something that you can actually control.

Lighting is not just a way of making your video look better. Lighting is an essential element in your visual vocabulary. Lighting conveys mood and atmosphere, and is the key to achieving a "film look." In this chapter, we will discuss tips for film-style lighting (whether you're shooting video or film), basic lighting setups, lighting for different exterior and interior situations, and lighting for special situations, such as video-to-film transfers and blue-screen photography.

Film-Style Lighting

If you've done any research on using video to shoot feature-length projects, you've probably encountered this piece of advice: "If you want your video to look like film, you need to light it like film." What's the difference between lighting for film and lighting for video? (If you're just starting out and don't know anything about "lighting for video," then you're in great shape, because you have nothing to unlearn, and no preconceived notions to jettison.)

Shooting on film is technically more challenging than shooting on video, because film stocks are much less forgiving of bad exposure, and proper film exposure requires lots of light. But film lighting specialists, known as cinematographers or directors of photography (DPs), do more than just pile lots of lights onto the set. They use special equipment to control the path of the light, the quality of the lights, the brightness of the lights, and the color of the lights. The amount of light coming from every light source is meticulously measured with a light meter in order to achieve the desired contrast ratio between the highlights and shadows. By controlling these elements, the cinematographer is able to direct the viewer's eye within the frame.

Lighting, along with focus and framing, which we'll cover in Chapters 7, "Using the Camera," and 10, "DSLRs and Other Advanced Shooting Situations," all add to the visual vocabulary used in filmic storytelling. Film-style lighting is not so much a distinct visual style as an artistic choice that helps tell the story, and it is useful for traditional film cinematographers and videographers alike.

WHAT TO WATCH

Barry Lyndon (Stanley Kubrick) was famously shot with only natural light. Jonathan Demme's film *Rachel Getting Married* also used natural lighting, combined with handheld camerawork to create a documentary-like feel.

In the past, it has been generally accepted that video looks lousy when compared to film. But thanks to HD, video has come a long way and is used for lots of great looking indie films. The key is to create the same sort of moody, subtle, expressive lighting that you see in a movie shot on film.

First, a film look is not appropriate for all projects. News footage and other documentary-style productions that use run-and-gun, shot-on-the-fly footage are designed simply to convey some specific factual (hopefully) content. Style is not a concern. Similarly, your production may not need a traditional film look either because the material doesn't need such a look, or simply because you can't afford the time and expense of shooting with complex lighting setups. These are decisions you'll need to make early in your preproduction process.

However, no matter what type of lighting you ultimately decide to use—even if it's none at all—a knowledge of film-style lighting can be very important. Though you may not be setting actual lights, you can still make decisions about where to position your camera, or choose to use some simple lighting implements such as reflectors, that can make a substantial difference in your image quality.

Throughout this chapter, we'll cover both film-style lighting and also the special needs that arise when lighting for video, especially when circumstances do not allow for traditional film-style lighting. But first, the basics . . .

WHAT TO WATCH

The Godfather employs a style of lighting that was developed in the Italian Renaissance known as "chiaroscuro," which literally means "light/dark" and is often described as pools of light. The paintings of Caravaggio are the most famous example of chiaroscuro lighting and *The Godfather* trilogy borrows heavily from paintings of this era for its lighting design, color palette, shot design, and symbolism.

The Art of Lighting

Lighting is one of the most powerful, yet subtle, filmmaking tools available. *Film noir* classics, such as *The Maltese Falcon,* are known for their creative use of light and shadow, while modern comedies often feature a bright, simple lighting style that is similar to television. No matter what your film is about, creative lighting can enhance the mood and emotion of your story.

Three-Point Lighting

Three-point lighting is the basic, jumping-off point for more complicated lighting setups. Three lights are used to light a single subject—usually an actor—from three directions (or points). The primary light source, called the *key light,* is used to illuminate the subject and is usually positioned at an angle (see Figure 6.1). The key light is a strong, dominant light source and is often designed to replicate a light source in the scene such as the sun or a lamp (see Figure 6.2 [top]).

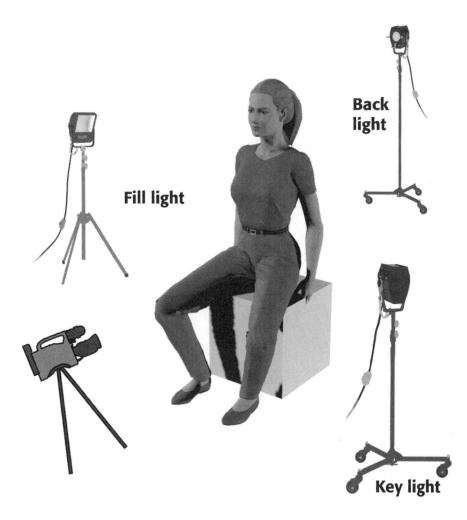

Back light

Fill light

Key light

Figure 6.1

A diagram of a typical three-point lighting setup, including camera placement and subject.

The second light, called the *back light* or sometimes the *kicker,* is positioned behind the subject and is used to separate the subject from the background (Figure 6.2 [middle]). This separation lends a sense of depth to the image and helps make your subject "stand out" better. You can see the effect of the back light in just about any type of video production, even the evening news. Note that well-lit newscasters usually have a ring of light around the top of their heads, or at least a good strong highlight on the top of their head. This rim lighting is created by the back light, and serves to give their head a more discernible shape. Sometimes the back light is a different color—bluish or orange. Making choices about the relationship between the key, fill, and back lights is part of the art of cinematography. After we present a few more key lighting concepts, you'll be ready to try your hand at the three-point lighting tutorial later in the chapter.

A third light, called the *fill light,* is used to "fill in" the strong shadows caused by the key light. Usually the fill light is quite a bit dimmer and more diffuse than the key light (Figure 6.2 [bottom]). The idea is not necessarily to get rid of the shadows, but to achieve a pleasing contrast ratio between the lights and shadows on the subject, so that neither bright lights nor dark shadows are dominant.

Key light only

Key light and back light

Figure 6.2

In this example of three-point lighting, the actor is first lit with a diffuse key light (top), then a hard back light is added (middle), and a soft, subtle fill light brings out the left side of his face without losing the high-contrast look (bottom).

Key light, back light and fill light

Types of Light

Knowing the types of lights that are available for shooting is like knowing what colors of paint you have available to paint a portrait. Professional lights fall into two basic categories: tungsten balanced (or indoor lights) and daylight balanced (or sunlight). These two categories represent two very different areas of the color spectrum. The light from a conventional indoor light-bulb tends to look orange or yellow, whereas the light outside at midday tends to appear more white or blue. Your camera probably has a setting that lets you choose a lightbulb icon (for tungsten) or a sun icon (for daylight). By informing your camera whether you are in daylight or tungsten light, you are letting it know the overall color cast of the scene. Setting this control is known as *white balancing*. We will discuss white balancing in detail in Chapter 7, but in order to understand it, you first need to understand how light and color are related.

Color Temperature

First, a quick science lesson: light is measured in terms of color temperature, which is calculated in *degrees Kelvin* (K). Indoor tungsten lights have a color temperature of 3200°K, whereas daylight has an approximate color temperature of 5500°K.

Color Plate 11 shows the color difference between tungsten light and typical daylight. As you can see, tungsten light at 3200°K is heavily shifted toward the orange part of the spectrum, which results in the warm, golden cast of household lights. On the other hand, daylight at 5600°K is heavily biased toward the blue part of the spectrum, which results in more of a bluish-white light. Be aware that as the sun rises and sets, its color temperature changes, and it decreases into the orange part of the spectrum.

While you might not be able to discern that household light looks orange and sunlight looks blue, the main thing to realize is that daylight is much stronger. (Think of the hotter, blue flames in a burning fire.) Daylight-balanced lights, such as HMIs and LED lights, are over 2000°K stronger than tungsten lights, and if you try to mix them together, the daylight will certainly overpower the tungsten light. If you can't avoid mixing tungsten and daylight—for example, if you're shooting a day interior scene that absolutely requires that a real window be in the shot—you need to account for the color temperature differences by *balancing* your light sources. Balancing your light sources means that you'll use special lighting gels to change the color temperature of some of the lights (or windows) so that they are all either tungsten-balanced or all daylight-balanced. We'll talk more about lighting gels and mixing daylight and interior light later in this chapter.

Types of Lights

Tungsten lights and daylight-balanced lights aren't the only types of lights. Fluorescent lights have a color temperature that ranges from 2700° to 6500°K, and sodium vapor lights, with a color temperature of about 2100°K, are yellow-orange. *Neon* lights vary wildly in temperature. All of these lights introduce special challenges.

- Tungsten lights range from standard household bulbs to large lights that require a generator for power.

- HMI lights are daylight balanced.

- LED lights offer lighting similar to HMIs and can be either daylight or tungsten-balanced. They are extremely low energy users, so it takes about 30 watts of power to put out 250–500 watts of light, which means they are great for use in household settings without generators for indie filmmakers. They are also very sturdy, so no worries about broken bulbs, and they do not put out much heat and can run on batteries. Be aware that LEDs with focused Fresnel beams use more power than flat light panel-style LEDS.

- Standard household fluorescents are notorious for flicker and for having a greenish tint, which can be exacerbated on film or video. But you can buy or rent special fluorescent tubes designed for cinema shooting that fit into normal fluorescent fixtures and get rid of the flicker and the green color. Cinema fluorescents can be either daylight-balanced or tungsten-balanced.

- Yellowish-orange sodium lights use a very limited section of the visible color spectrum. The result is an almost monochrome image. If you try to color correct later, you'll have very little color information with which to work.

- Neon lights can easily exceed the range of colors that your camera can capture (these lights produce colors that are outside of the NTSC color gamut), especially red and magenta neon. Even though they tend to be quite dim in terms of lux or footcandles, neon lights appear bright and overexposed due to their extremely saturated colors. (See Color Plate 23.)

Wattage

Lights are also measured in terms of the amount of electric power they require, or wattage. The higher the wattage, the brighter the light. Typical film lights range from 250 watts to 10K (10,000 watts). The powerful HMI lights used to mimic the sun and to light night exteriors require as much as 20,000 watts, whereas a typical household light needs a mere 60 watts. The professional lights best suited for use with video are those with a wattage of 2K or less.

Nowadays, you can get special low wattage HMIs, such as the Kobold series by Bron (see Figure 6.3). These lights use less power and give off less heat than traditional tungsten lights. LED lights, such as LitePanels (see Figure 6.4), come in a variety of sizes, can be battery-powered, and can switch between tungsten and daylight color balance. They use very little power so they are perfect if you are shooting with household power, and they give off little or no heat.

Camera Mount Lights

Camera mount lights have improved dramatically in recent years, thanks to LED lighting. Ring lights are fitted around the lens and camera-top lights (Figure 6.4) use the flash mount. Professional LED lights can switch between tungsten and daylight color balance.

Figure 6.3

A low-wattage HMI light by Bron (with diffusion) and a 1K tungsten light by Arri on a soundstage.

Figure 6.4

This battery-powered LitePanels Micro LED light can be mounted on top of a camera or taped somewhere on the set.

The Basic Light Kit for Video

A basic light kit for video provides the minimum lighting equipment necessary for three-point lighting (see Figure 6.5). The typical cinematographer won't be happy with it, but it's a considerable step above single source lighting. A basic video kit includes something like the following:

- Two 650-watt lights (with Fresnel lenses)
- Two single scrims
- Two single half-scrims
- Two double scrims
- Two double half-scrims
- Two sets of barn doors
- One 1K or 650W soft light
- One egg crate (used to make the soft light more directional)
- Three gel frames
- Three light stands

If you don't have access to a simple light kit at school or through a friend, you can rent one at most professional still photography suppliers, as long as you can provide a credit card for a deposit. They generally cost about $50 for a weekend. Be sure to avoid light kits with high-wattage lights if you're shooting video—it's likely they'll overpower your set.

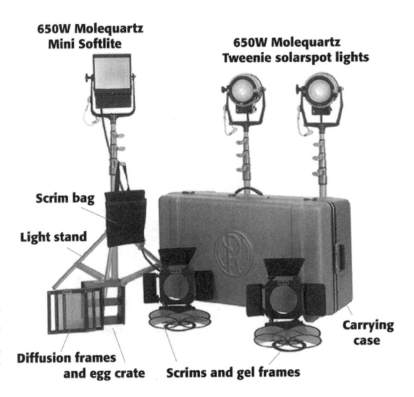

650W Molequartz Mini Softlite

650W Molequartz Tweenie solarspot lights

Scrim bag

Light stand

Diffusion frames and egg crate

Scrims and gel frames

Carrying case

Figure 6.5

This Teenie-weenie/Softlite combo kit from Mole-Richardson is a good example of a typical tungsten video lighting kit.

Measuring Light

It used to be that cinematographers always had a light meter in hand. But for digital video, handheld light meters are used with diminishing frequency. Instead, digital video cameras offer built-in tools that can help you determine the best lighting for a scene:

- Zebra stripes in the viewfinder help you identify which parts of an image are overexposed.

- In-camera light meters help you adjust the f-stop to get proper exposure. Some cinematographers choose an f-stop and then set all the lighting to expose correctly at that f-stop.

- Histogram displays show you the range of lights and darks in an image.

Be aware that not all cameras offer all of these tools. We discuss using these camera features in detail in Chapter 7.

Make a Lighting Plot

Obviously, lighting is a very hands-on stage of production. However, there's still plenty of planning that you can do to make sure you have the gear you need and to make the best use of your time on the set. Once you've chosen your locations, you should meet with your lighting crew or director of photography and try to plan exactly what type of lights you'll want and where. Try to rough out some floor plan sketches and determine where you'll need each piece of equipment. This is also a good time to assess how much power you'll need, and whether you'll need extra power generators. If your shoot involves any special effects, you'll want to take extra care in planning the lighting for those shots.

Controlling the Quality of Light

In addition to having different color temperatures, lights have different qualities. They can be direct or hard, they can be soft or diffuse, or they can be focused, like a spotlight. Figure 6.6 shows the same subject lit with a diffuse key light (top) and a hard key light (bottom).

There are many types of lighting accessories that can be used to control the quality of professional lights. A special Fresnel lens attachment lets you adjust the angle of the light beam from flood to spotlight (see Figure 6.7). Barn doors attach to the light itself to help you control where the light falls. Round scrims fit into a slot between the light and the barn doors and allow you to decrease the strength of a light without changing the quality. Single scrims (with a green edge) take the brightness down by one-half f-stop, and double scrims (with a red edge) take it down a whole f-stop. (See Chapter 7 for more about f-stops.)

- **Lighting gels** are translucent sheets of colored plastic that are placed in front of the light, not only to alter the color of the light, but also to decrease the brightness (see Color Plate 12). The most common use of lighting gels involves converting tungsten to daylight or vice versa. **Diffusion** gels are usually frosty white plastic sheets that make the light source appear softer. **Gel frames** allow you to place lighting gels behind the barn doors, but it's usually easier to use clothespins to attach gels directly to the barn doors.

- **Bounce cards** (often just pieces of white foam core) are also used to create soft, indirect lighting, while reflectors (shiny boards) are used to redirect lighting from a bright light source, such as the sun.

- **C-stands** (short for *Century stands*) hold flags, nets, and other objects in front of the lights to manipulate and shape the light that falls on the subject. We'll talk more about how to use these items as we cover traditional interior and exterior lighting.

Soft key light

Figure 6.6

The choice between a hard or diffuse key is an aesthetic one. This actor is lit with a diffuse key (top) and a hard key (bottom).

Hard key light

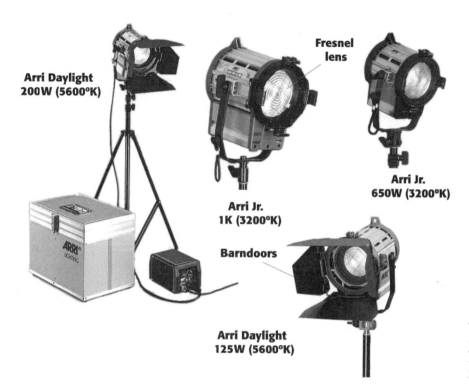

Arri Daylight
200W (5600°K)

Fresnel
lens

Arri Jr.
650W (3200°K)

Arri Jr.
1K (3200°K)

Barndoors

Arri Daylight
125W (5600°K)

Figure 6.7

These tungsten lights by Arriflex range from 200W to 1K and are each equipped with a Fresnel lens to allow for focused or flood lighting.

Lighting Gels

Gels are an indispensable tool if you're serious about lighting. Rosco and Lee make swatch books like the one in Color Plate 12 that contain samples of the different gels they produce. Gel swatch books are usually available at any professional camera store.

Colored gels can be used to add just about any color in the rainbow to your light sources. It's a good idea to have a choice of colors on hand. Remember that the brighter the light shining through the gel, the less intense the color will be. Adding colored gels will always decrease the brightness of the light.

Color temperature orange (CTO) and color temperature blue (CTB) gels can change the color temperature of a daylight-balanced light to tungsten, or tungsten to daylight.

Neutral density gels cut down the intensity of light without changing the color temperature. These gels are extremely useful when shooting video, where too much light is often a problem. They are especially handy when it's necessary to shoot in front of windows.

Diffusion

Because digital video can have a "hard" look, using softer, diffuse lighting is increasingly popular, and there are a range of tools and techniques to add diffusion. The simplest way is to cover the lights with diffusion fabric. Diffusion gels, as mentioned previously, can be clipped to the barn doors on the light itself. Special diffusion bags, like the one on the HMI light in Figure 6.3, are designed to fit over the light entirely. Large silks are special diffusion fabrics that fit into a frame that you place in-between your lights and the subject. In addition, you can also use fog machines to create a smoky, atmospheric haze in the air itself.

Lighting Your Actors

Lighting a person is always a bit more challenging than lighting an object. The human face has many angles, and it's easy for bright lights to cast strange and unflattering shadows. In addition, bright lights can magnify every little flaw on a person's face, while the wrong color lighting can result in an unnatural-looking skin tone. Whether your goal is to make your actors look beautiful or ugly, the right lighting will enhance your characters and story. The following three-point lighting tutorial provides a tried-and-true method for lighting an actor.

 Three-Point Lighting

This tutorial assumes that you have access to a typical video light kit (like the one described in the sidebar "The Basic Light Kit for Video"), a selection of gels (see the section "Lighting Gels"), and a suitable subject to light, preferably a person. If possible, you should also have your camera set up on a tripod in order to see how the different lighting possibilities look through the lens and to check for good exposure using the zebra stripes, built-in light meter, or histogram display. If you have a field monitor, you should use that, too. If you don't have a field monitor, consider recording video as you experiment with your lighting, so that you can later view the results on a full-size monitor. You'll also need a pair of work gloves for handling hot lights. Finally, you should start with a large, dark room. A soundstage is ideal, but any dark room will work. If you're doing this tutorial at home, see the following tip on how to avoid blowing a bulb.

STEP 1: PLACE THE KEY LIGHT

To begin, set up your key light. Take one of the 650-watt lights from your kit and set it up on one of the stands. Attach the barn doors to the light itself—they usually just slide into place. Direct the light toward your subject and turn it on. Don't worry about the background yet; we'll deal with that later. For now, focus on lighting your subject as best you can.

Now that you have light on your subject, find a pleasing angle at which to place the light. The human eye is used to seeing light that comes from a high angle, usually from over our shoulder, so low-placed, low-angle lights often yield results that look a little strange. Extend the stand to its full height and then aim the light down at your actor. Experiment with different heights to see what works best. Try placing the light at different distances from your subject. Does it look better close or farther away? You can set up the lights any way that looks good to your eye. Just make sure that the light is not so bright that it overexposes in your viewfinder. (If your viewfinder provides a Zebra display, turn it on to help identify hot spots.)

Because of the shadows cast by a person's nose, the key light is usually placed about 30 to 45 degrees off-center from the person's face. This position gives definition to the features of the face and allows the shadow from the nose to fall to the side without becoming huge or distorted. (Consult the diagram back in Figure 6.1 to re-visit a typical three-point lighting setup.) Once you're happy with the angle, play with the focus knob on the Fresnel lens. Does it look better tightly focused or flooded? (Figure 6.6 shows the difference between a hard key and a soft key.) Try adding some diffusion. Play around until you find a look you like, and then move on to the next step.

Don't Waste Expensive Lightbulbs

Avoid touching high-wattage lightbulbs, (or *globes*, as they are professionally known). The oil from your fingers can overheat and cause them to explode (the globes, not your fingers).

STEP 2: SET UP THE BACK LIGHT

Now it's time to add the back light. As with the key light, set it up on a stand and play around with different positions. Back lights are usually quite bright and often filtered with lightly colored gels. Usually, the best position for a back light is either high overhead pointing down at the back of the subject's head, or way down near the ground pointing up at the back of the subject's head. The reason for this is that you need to avoid having the light itself visible in the shot, as well as avoid having it pointed directly at the camera (which will cause a lens flare). Figure 6.8 shows the actor illuminated with the back light only, and Figure 6.2 (center photo) shows the actor illuminated with the back light and key light.

Fire Hazards

Avoid putting diffusion gels, lighting gels, and any flammable materials too close to professional light globes. You might end up with a stinky, smoldering mess stuck to your light, or worse, you might start a fire! In addition, use your gaffer's tape to tape down your light's power cords. It can be easy to trip over cords and pull over your lights as you work around them. Finally, use sandbags to weigh down light stands so that they aren't easily knocked over.

Figure 6.8

The actor lit with a back light only.

STEP 3: ADD SOME FILL LIGHT

Now you are ready to set up the fill light. Take the 1K soft light from the kit and set it up on the stand. Your goal with the fill light is to make the shadows cast by the key light less severe. Usually, this means placing the light on the opposite side of the subject from the key light, typically at a 30- to 45-degree angle directed at the unlit side of the actor's face (see the diagram in Figure 6.1).

The brightness of the fill light is very important, since this is how you control the contrast ratio of your scene. Remember that video doesn't handle high-contrast lighting as well as film does. Try placing the light at different distances from the subject to see how the contrast ratio changes. It's often nice to have a fill light that's a different color than the key light. Experiment with different colored gels until you're satisfied with the fill light. Figure 6.9 shows the actor illuminated with a soft 1K fill light only, and Figure 6.2 (bottom photo) shows a subject lit with key, back, and fill lights.

Figure 6.9

The same actor lit with a fill light only.

STEP 4: MAKE ADJUSTMENTS

Now that you have your three lights set up, it's time to look at the overall scene. Are colored areas washing out to white? Are there hot spots, bright reflections from cheekbones or foreheads? In other words, is it overlit? Try adding single or double scrims to the lights that seem too bright.

How does the background look? It's pretty hard to light the subject and the background with only three lights, but see if you can move the fill light so that it fills in the background as well as the shadows on the subject. Is there too much light falling on the background? Try using the barn doors on the key light to direct the light onto the subject only. If you have barn doors for the fill and back lights, adjust them as well. Remember to wear gloves when you're adjusting lights that have been on for a while—they get very hot. If your lights are still too bright, try moving them further from the subject, or add more scrims or diffusion to your setup.

Lighting for Darker Skin Tones

When an actor has darker-toned skin, it can be difficult to get enough light on their face without overlighting the background, because darker complexions simply require more light. If you can, keep the actor farther away from the background so that the light falls on the actor but not the background.

Interior Lighting

Lighting an interior scene can present all sorts of challenges, not the least of which is choosing a location that can facilitate your lights. Ideally, you would use a soundstage with an overhead lighting grid, lots of available power, and plenty of space for setting up lights as far from your subject as needed. Shooting in a normal house or office building will save you the trouble of having to build a realistic set, but you'll be hampered by less space, a limited power supply, and less control over how much exterior light enters the set.

Power Supply

If you're using professional lights at a location, you'll have to be careful not to overload the electrical circuits. A little preshoot prep work can save lots of headaches later. First, you need to map out the electrical circuits at the location. Arm yourself with some masking tape and a socket tester or an easily moveable household lamp. Plug the lamp into the first outlet and turn it on. Go to the breaker box and turn the circuits on and off until you find the one that controls the lamp. If the circuits aren't labeled, use the masking tape to label each with a number. Then use the masking tape to label the outlet to correspond with the circuit number. Work your way around until you find and label several outlets on different circuit breakers. To be safe when lighting, use one light for each 10-amp circuit. Most household circuits range from 10 to 40 amps, and the amperage of each circuit should be clearly engraved on the switches in the breaker box.

Mixing Daylight and Interior Light

Because of the different color temperatures of daylight and interior light, mixing them together can present a challenge. The simplest solution is to choose which light source you want to have dominant and balance the other light sources to match the color temperature of that source.

For example, if the dominant light source in your scene is the light streaming through a window, you should balance your light sources for daylight by using daylight balanced lights. You can also use CTB lighting gels on tungsten lights, but remember that CTB gels decrease the intensity of the lights and might render them useless. If your dominant light source is a 650W tungsten light, you should balance your light sources for tungsten light using CTO lighting gels on daylight-balanced lights and windows with daylight streaming through. You might also need to add neutral density (ND) gels to control the brightness of the daylight coming through the window. In general, shooting a daytime interior against a bright window is best avoided.

Using Household Lights

Because video requires less light than film does, you can get away with using normal household lights. Generally, household lamps are less than 3200° K and lean more toward the orange side of the spectrum.

Unfortunately, ordinary household lights are not directional, which makes it harder to control where the light falls in your scene. There are a couple of ways to make household lights directional. You can buy directional or "spot" lightbulbs, or you can surround the bulb with tin foil or some other lightproof material. Filter manufacturers such as Rosco and Lee sell black wrap, a heavy-duty tin foil with a black matte coating that can be used to create makeshift barn doors.

Even if you're not concerned with the light being directional, replacing low-wattage lightbulbs with brighter bulbs is a good way to create "practical" lights. "Practical" lights are those that are actually visible in the scene, such as a household lamp that the actor turns on. You can hide diffusion materials or gels in the lampshade for more lighting control. By using a low-wattage bulb and keeping it several feet away from the actor, the household lamp in the background of Figure 6.2 does not cast any light on the subject. You can also buy special bulbs that are very low wattage so that they cast almost no actual light on the scene but serve to make the prop lamps in the scene appear lit.

Do a Test Shoot

Big budget features test everything before they shoot—they even use "screen tests" to determine if the actors are photogenic, and whether they have "screen chemistry" with each other. Spending a weekend testing your lighting and other tricky elements of your production can be invaluable. For blue/green screen shoots, start out by familiarizing yourself with the blue (or green) screen compositing software that you'll be using. Follow any recommendations in the software manual, such as shooting a reference image. Use miniatures or stand-ins against a blue or green background and try different lighting setups. If you are planning on a video-to-film transfer, include the transfer facility in your test. Be sure to follow the tips listed in this chapter but play around with some of the variables to see what works best.

Exterior Lighting

The concept of exterior lighting might sound silly. Who needs lights outside when you have the sun? However, if you're bent on a film-style look for your project, you'll need to do more than just point and shoot. Daylight, defined as a combination of skylight and sunlight, is an intense source of light—often too intense for video. Think of the sky as a big giant bounce card reflecting the sun. It's a powerful light source in its own right, comparable to a 30,000-watt fixture on the ground and more than 50 times the illumination of a 650W tungsten light. Your light kit will be useless on an exterior shoot unless it includes HMIs or a 2K light. The art of exterior "lighting" has to do with blocking, diffusing, filtering, reflecting, and controlling the light of the sun and sky.

Enhancing Existing Daylight

If you're shooting outside on a sunny day at noon, you'll get a brightly lit image with very harsh shadows. If you're armed with the items listed in the "Lighting Equipment Checklist" sidebar, you will be able to exert some control over the harsh conditions of bright daylight. Here are a few tips for brightening up those dark shadows:

- Try positioning a piece of foam core below your subject and off to one side, so that the light of the sun bounces off the white foam core and up into the shadows on your subject's face. This is a variation of three-point lighting—think of the sun as your key light and the bounced light as your fill. Use a C-stand to secure the foam core.

- Use flags, black screens, and diffusion to cut down the intensity of the sun on the subject.

- Use a reflector or a bounce card to create a back light.

- If the contrast ratio is still too high, you need a stronger fill light. Try placing the sun behind your subject and use the bounce card as a soft key light from the front.

- Change locations. If you can't get the look you want in direct sunlight, try moving to a shadier location and using a bounce card to add highlights or positioning a large silk over your subject.

Golden Hour

The hour or so before sunset, also known as the "golden hour," is one of the best times of day to shoot exteriors. The warm cast of the light is very flattering to human skin tones, and the chance of your scene being overlit is reduced. In addition, the low angle of the sun creates sharp, dark shadows, throwing everything in your scene into sharp relief. Unfortunately, you'll have to work fast to take advantage of this quality of light, as it does not last long.

Lighting Equipment Checklist

You should have the following items on-hand and easily accessible during your shoot:

- Cloth tape—to tape down cables so that people won't trip over them.
- Power cables and heavy-duty extension cords (25 ft, 50 ft, 100 ft).
- Three-prong to two-prong adapters for older locations.
- Clothespins—used to attach lighting gels or diffusion to barn doors, and so forth.
- Heavy work gloves—for handling light globes and hot equipment.
- Lighting gels.
- Diffusion materials.
- Reflectors.
- Bounce cards—often nothing more than a big piece of white foam core, bounce cards can help you get more mileage out of your lights.
- Duvetine, black felt, or black garbage bags for blocking windows. Also, black wrap (a sort of black matte tin foil) or regular tin foil.

Lighting Equipment Checklist (continued)

- Kino-Flo bulbs—these color, temperature-corrected, flicker-free lightbulbs are used to replace standard fluorescent light tubes in location fixtures.

- Grip clips—clamps with rubber handles—similar in function to clothespins, but with more grip and a variety of sizes.

- Extra light globes—650W and 1K bulbs to go with your light kit, household bulbs in high wattages, and so forth. You should have at least one extra globe for every light in your kit.

- Clamp lights and China globes—easily found at hardware and household lighting stores, these lights are cheap and can be handy to have on hand in a pinch.

- C-stands.

- Flags and nets.

Video Lighting

Today's digital video cameras have an impressive ability to shoot in low-light situations. As a result, one of the challenges of shooting video is that there is often *too much* light. In Chapter 7, we discuss neutral density filters and other ways to control the amount of light that your video camera records, but it's also good to know some of the ways to limit the light on your set. Whether you're shooting a daytime or a nighttime interior scene, it can be hard to avoid overlighting the set, especially if you're in a small room. "Flat" lighting means there is not enough contrast between your key and fill lights, which will result in a lack of sculpting. Here are some ways to deal with an overlit scene:

- **Block out sunlight.** Because sunlight is so powerful, it might be the cause of your overlighting. *Duvetine* is a black, light-blocking fabric that can be used to cover windows. A cheaper alternative is to cover them with black plastic garbage bags. If windows are in the shot, you can use ND gels (see the section "Lighting Gels" earlier in the chapter) to tone down the light coming through the windows.

- **Turn off lights, especially overhead fixtures.** If your set is small, you simply might not be able to use all the lights you want without overlighting the scene.

- **Move lights away from the subject.** If space allows, move your lights back. The farther they are from your subject, the less illumination they'll cast on your subject.

- **Black nets and black flags.** Black nets and flags attach to C-stands and are versatile tools for controlling and blocking light.

- **Studio wallpaper.** Shooting in a room with white walls is like having four giant bounce cards surrounding your scene. If you can't repaint the locations, you can buy different colors of studio wallpaper to tone down the walls or to create blue/green backdrops for compositing. If you're shooting a night scene, use black studio wallpaper to make a room look bigger than it is, but be careful not to allow any light or hot spots to fall on the black paper.

- **Scrims.** If one or more of your lights is too bright, add scrims to take it down. Most lights will take at least two scrims at once.

- **Barn doors.** Narrow the opening between the barn doors to make a light more directional.

Low-Light Shooting

Modern digital video cameras can do a good job of producing an image when there is very little light. Unfortunately, they accomplish this by electronically boosting the gain of the camera, which adds noise. If you turn off the gain boost, you'll have noise-free video, but unless you have a fast lens, you'll have little or no image. The only solution in this case is to use lights. You'll have to weigh the benefit of noise-free video against the difficulty of lighting. If your eventual goal is a video-to-film transfer, noise should be avoided at all costs. (More on gain in Chapter 9, "Shooting and Directing.")

DSLRs are a popular choice for low-light shooting. Large image sensors, combined with fast lenses add up to very high-quality low-light images with little or no gain.

Battery-Operated Lights and Generators

Renting a generator might be out of your league, but for those situations where electrical power is unavailable, try using battery-operated lights.

Special Lighting Situations

Lighting does more than illuminate actors and locations. It also plays a key role in creating a believable setting, pulling off some types of special effects, and producing successful blue- or green-screen photography.

With a little imagination, lights can be used to suggest a location. Here are a few typical ways to create a scene with lights:

- **Car interiors:** A nighttime driving scene can be shot on a soundstage using a few focused lights placed outside a car, along with a fill light. The focused lights should be gelled to match the lights of passing cars, street lights, and brake lights. Each light (except the fill) needs to be manned by a grip who will move the light past the car at irregular intervals to replicate passing lights. For actual driving scenes, small battery-operated LED lights can be taped to the dashboard of the car for natural-looking car lighting.

- **Day-for-night:** Use slightly blue-colored gels to create light that looks like nighttime and ND filters on your camera to make the image darker. Later, use digital compositing tools to matte out the sky and tweak the contrast ratio. There are several vendors that make day-for-night software plug-ins that can be used to treat your daylight footage so that it will look like it was shot at night. Check out *www.thedigitalfilmmakinghandbook. com/chapter6* for more info.

- **Firelight:** Dark orange gels can make your light source the same color as firelight. Wave flags in front of the light source to create a fire-like flicker. A fan with paper streamers in front of the light can add hands-free flicker.

- **Other illusional spaces:** Carefully flagged lights in the background can create the illusion of space, such as a doorway.

Lighting for 360° Shooting

Documentaries and other run-and-gun shooting situations require lighting that allows for shooting in all directions without any advance warning. Bigger reality shows typically hang lights from the ceiling to avoid visible lighting hardware. Another solution is to put HMIs outside the windows to create a fake source of "sunlight."

Lighting for Video-to-Film Transfers

Lighting for video-to-film transfers can be a little tricky if you've never done it before. This is because the way your lit set looks to the naked eye will bear very little resemblance to how it will look after it's been transferred to film. There are many theories on how to achieve the best results, but here are a few guidelines to help make your shoot a success:

- **Avoid high-contrast lighting.** Transferring your video footage to film will increase the contrast ratio between light and dark areas so it's important to avoid too much contrast in the original video footage. Low-contrast lighting won't look very "film-like" when you view your original video footage, but it will acquire a higher-contrast, film-like look after you transfer it to film.

- **Make sure your images are sharp.** Sharpness, or focus, is related to your camera and the lens, but it's also dependent on good lighting. Any softness in your video image will be exacerbated once it's transferred to film and projected on a big screen. Often, you won't be able to see that your image is out of focus until it's blown up and projected onto a big screen.

- **Avoid hot spots**. Overexposed areas in the video will look even worse when transferred to film.

- **Light to avoid video noise.** Low-light situations require that you boost the gain on your video camera, which in turn increases video artifacts or "noise." Noise is similar to film grain, but larger and more distracting, especially when transferred to film and projected. So make sure that your on-set lighting is sufficient enough to avoid video noise.

Shooting Video for Film

If you are going to finish your video project by transferring it to 35mm film, you should research and find a film recordist now. Each film recording company uses a different process, and they'll have specific tips for how to light and shoot in order to achieve the best look for your project. (More on transferring video to film in Chapter 18, "Finishing.")

Lighting for Blue and Green Screen

If you will be shooting blue- or green-screen shots for later compositing with other elements, it's critical that you light your screen smoothly and evenly. For best results, consider the following:

- **Choose your compositing software before you shoot.** Different apps have different needs. Becoming familiar with your compositing software and its specific needs will save you time and headaches later. See Chapter 17, "Titles and Effects," for more on compositing apps.

- **Place your subject as far from the blue/green background as possible.** If your subject is too close to the background, you'll end up with blue spill (or green spill)—reflections of blue light that bounce off the blue screen and onto the back of your actor, resulting in a bluish backlight. This can make it extremely difficult to pull a clean matte later. If you can't avoid blue spill, try to make up for it by adding a hotter orange back light to cancel it out.

- **Light your subject and the background separately.** This also helps avoid blue spill and makes it easier to create the matte. The set in Color Plate 13 shows how much trouble a professional crew has to go to in order to light the set and the green screen separately.

- **Light to minimize video noise.** Video noise can make pulling a matte difficult. Be sure the scene is well lit so that there's no need for gain-boosting on your camera. If you can, disable the automatic gain boost feature.

- **Try to make sure the blue/green screen is evenly lit.** Because you want an even shade of blue across your entire blue-screen background, having consistent lighting across the surface of your screen is essential. A spot meter reads reflective light instead of incident or direct light, and can be a real asset when trying to even out the light levels on your blue screen. Most camera shops rent them on a daily or weekly basis.

- **Art direct to avoid blue or green in your subject/foreground.** This might seem obvious, but blue can be a hard color to avoid, which is why the option of green screen exists and vice versa. In Color Plate 14, the warm oranges and browns of the set lie in sharp contrast to the green screen in the background.

- **Dress the floor.** If you're going to see the actor's feet in the shot, it will be much easier to dress the floor with something that matches your final composite shot—carpeting, wood, stones, and so on—rather than attempting to composite it later.

- **Screen correction shots.** Several compositing applications can use a screen correction shot to make creating a matte easier. Either before or after every take, get a few seconds of footage of the empty blue/green screen with the same framing as the action. Refer to your compositing software documentation for other specific tips regarding screen correction shots.

- **Have a visual effects supervisor on set.** They might see problems you won't notice.

- **Pay attention to shadows.** Shadows can tend toward blue, which can make creating a matte difficult.

- **Light to match your CGI material.** If you're going to be compositing live action and CGI environments, be sure the live-action lighting matches the CGI environment lighting. If your digital background has an orange hue, it will look strange if your subject is lit with a blue backlight. The green screen set in Color Plate 14 is lit to match a CGI background.

- **Use a 3D program to practice lighting.** Believe it or not, 3D applications like Maya and Studio Max are great tools for mapping out lighting, because their lights do a great job of simulating real-world lights. You can use preprogrammed figure models in place of your actors and try out different kinds of lighting on them. You can even use a 3D application to do the three-point lighting tutorial earlier in this chapter. You can also use a 3D previsualization application like FrameForge 3D Studio. These types of 3D packages are complex, but learning enough to perform simple lighting studies is fairly simple, and worth the investment in time.

Lighting provides the backdrop in which your story will take place. Once you've tackled it, you're ready to move over to the other side of the set—the camera.

7

Using the Camera

Photo credit: Jason Hampton

The sweeping panoramas of *Lawrence of Arabia*, the evocative shadows and compositions of *The Third Man*, the famous dolly/crane shot that opens *A Touch of Evil*—when we remember great films, striking images usually come to mind. Digital video cameras are the hot topic among filmmakers these days, and shooting your film is the single most important step in a live-action production. Shooting good video requires more than just recording pretty images. As a director, the ability to unite the actors' performances with the compositions of the cinematographer, while managing all of the other minutiae that one must deal with on a set, will be key to the success of your project. Central to all of the above is the ability to use the camera.

The camera is the primary piece of equipment in any type of production, so in this chapter, you're going to get familiar with your camera. Professional cinematographers know their cameras inside and out. Many of them will only work with certain types of cameras, and some will only work with equipment from specific rental houses. The advantage of most digital video cameras is that you can point and shoot and still get a good image. However, if you want to get the most from your camera, you should follow the example of the pros and take the time to learn the details of your gear.

In Chapter 4, "Choosing a Camera," we explained how digital video cameras work, in Chapter 5, "Planning Your Shoot," we discussed different types of shots. In this chapter, we'll show you how to use the various features of a typical film or video camera and we'll discuss how to put it all together using exposure, strong compositions, and camera movement to tell your story.

Shooting good footage involves much more than simply knowing what button to push and when. There are many creative decisions involved in setting up your shots, and in this chapter, we're going to cover all of the controls at your disposal and learn how they affect your final image.

Shooting with DSLRs

Shooting HD video with still cameras differs significantly from shooting with "normal" video cameras. We discuss shooting with DSLRs in detail in Chapter 10 "DSLRs and Other Advanced Shooting Situations."

Setting Focus

Focus is possibly the most basic part of using a camera. All modern cameras come with autofocus mechanisms, but in order to truly master the camera, you need to learn how to set and control the focus yourself.

Before you can focus your camera, make sure the viewfinder is adjusted to match your vision. Most cameras, like the ones in Figures 7.1 and 7.2, have an adjustment ring, or diopter, on the viewfinder. (Refer to your camera documentation for specifics.) Set the camera lens out of focus, then look through the viewfinder and move the viewfinder focus adjustment until you can see the grains of glass or the display information in the viewfinder itself.

Figure 7.1

A typical entry-level professional camcorder from Sony.

Figure 7.2

Typical features of a professional-level shoulder-mount camcorder.

If your camera allows, turn off the auto-focus mechanism. Auto focus will always focus on the middle of the frame. Since you might want to be more creative than this, stick with manual focus.

To focus a zoom lens manually, zoom all the way in to your subject and focus the image. Now you can zoom back to compose the shot at the focal length you desire. As long as your subject doesn't move forward or backward, your image will be in focus at any focal length available.

Many video cameras have a special focus assist view that displays a zoomed in portion of the frame so that you can double-check the focus. This is especially helpful if you do not have a field monitor (see Figure 7.3)

You can also focus by composing your shot first and then adjusting the focus ring on the lens, the same way you would with a prime lens. The only problem with this method is that the wider your shot, the harder it will be to tell if your subject is truly in focus and if the subject or camera moves, you will have to make an adjustment to keep the shot in focus.

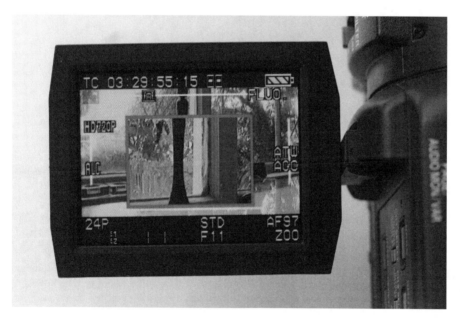

Figure 7.3

The focus assist button makes it easier to check focus on the fly.

Luckily, most images have a depth of field that exceeds the depth of focus. In Figure 7.4, the depth of focus is eight feet from the camera, but the depth of field—the part of the image that *appears* in focus—starts a couple of feet in front of the subject and extends to infinity. Anything behind the subject will appear in focus, even though it is not on the plane of focus.

If you're having trouble focusing, use your manual iris control to iris down (go to a higher f-stop number). This will increase your depth of field and improve your chances of shooting focused. Under most normal, bright lighting conditions, especially daylight, the field of focus will extend from your subject (the plane of focus) to infinity (see Figure 7.4).

Figure 7.4

In this illustration, the plane of focus is eight feet from the lens, but the depth of field is much bigger. Everything behind the plane of focus appears in focus as well.

Generally, focus won't present much of a problem. In fact, one of the biggest complaints about the look of digital video is that the focus is too sharp throughout the image. Film typically has a much more shallow depth of field than video, so often only the subject is in focus (see Figure 7.13). One way to get more of a film-like image is to control the lighting and exposure so that the depth of field is shallow. With a video camera, this is very difficult to do under bright, uncontrolled lighting conditions such as daylight. (More about how to get shallow depth of field in Chapter 10.)

The only time you're likely to encounter a focus problem is when you're shooting in low-light conditions. When there isn't a lot of light, the field of focus becomes very small, and it's hard to judge focus in the viewfinder or LCD display when there isn't much light on the subject.

If focus is critical and the lighting conditions are challenging, the only way to be absolutely sure that your shot is in focus is to measure the focus with a tape measure and then change, or "pull" the focus on the lens as the camera or subject moves. We explain how to measure and pull focus in Chapter 10.

Use a Field Monitor

Feature film directors connect "video assist" monitors to their 35mm film cameras so that they can see what the camera operator sees through the viewfinder. A field monitor lets you do the same thing with a video camera. Even if you'll be operating the camera yourself, a field monitor can be an asset, making it much easier to focus and frame your shots, and it lets others see what the camera operator is seeing. To see a true HD image, you'll need to use the HD output on the camera and the HD input on the monitor. (For more on monitoring video on the set, see Chapter 10.)

Using the Zoom Lens

Once you've set the focus, the next basic skill is learning how to use a zoom lens.

Camera lenses fall into two categories: prime lenses and zoom lenses. Prime lenses have a fixed focal length, measured in millimeters, that determines their angle of view. Prime lenses are known for producing a sharper image than zoom lenses, and DPs who work in feature films are used to having a selection of high-quality prime lenses for their 35mm film or digital cinema cameras.

If your camera can use interchangeable lenses, you will have the choice of using primes or zooms, or a combination of both for different shooting situations. However, most video cameras are equipped with built-in zoom lenses (Figure 7.5) that offer a range of focal lengths from telephoto (or close-up) to wide angles.

And that's why learning to use the camera starts with learning to use a zoom lens. (Using prime lenses is discussed in Chapter 10.)

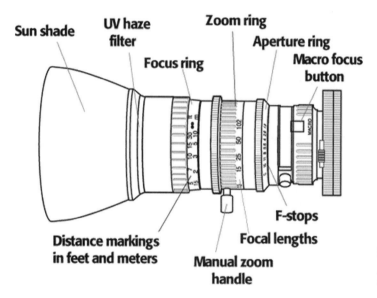

Figure 7.5

A professional zoom lens will be equipped something like this.

Focal Length Equivalency

Many people are familiar with the focal lengths of lenses used in 35mm. But whenever you use a camera with an image sensor that is smaller than 35mm film, the focal lengths are designed at a different scale. You can use a focal length multiplier to figure out the focal length equivalency of different lenses. For example, a 7mm DV lens has a focal length multiplier of 7 and is the equivalent of a 50mm lens on a 35mm still camera. Refer to the manufacturer's documentation to get the focal length multiplier for your camera/lens.

The great thing about a zoom lens is that it provides great flexibility when you frame a shot. Without changing your position, you can quickly zoom in to a subject to get a tighter view and a different framing. However, it's essential that you pay attention to the elements of your image that change when you zoom in and out.

It's easy to think of your zoom lens as a big magnifying glass and, to a degree, that is what it is. As you zoom in, your subject appears larger. This is why digital video camera manufacturers label their lenses with a magnification factor—2x, 3x, and so forth. However, a few other things happen to your image when you zoom.

Focal Length Defined

Focal length is the distance from the lens to the camera's image sensor(s), usually measured in millimeters.

As you go to a longer focal length (zoom in), your field of view gets narrower. The human eye has a field of view of about 50 to 55°. This is considered a "normal" field of view (see Figure 7.6).

More important, though, is to pay attention to the way that a lens magnifies different parts of your image, and how it compresses depth overall as you zoom in and out.

At wider focal lengths (that is, when you are zoomed out), objects that are closer to the lens get magnified *more* than objects that are farther away. Telephoto lenses, on the other hand, magnify all objects in a scene equally, no matter how far away they are.

Here is an example. At some time, you've probably looked at a photograph or video of yourself and thought "that doesn't really look like me." One reason for the poor result might be that the photographer was using a wide-angle lens. Shooting a portrait with a wide-angle lens is problematic because some parts of your subject's face are closer to the lens than others are. Consequently, those parts, particularly the nose, will be magnified more than the parts that are farther away.

Check out the pictures in Figure 7.7. The image on the left was shot with a slightly telephoto lens and really does look like the actual person. The image on the right is not a very good likeness (though it might be truer to this person's character). The nose is too big and the ears have been rendered too small. In addition, the distance between the nose and ears—the depth of the picture—is too long. In other words, the sense of depth in the second image has been expanded, and the results look a bit weird.

Now consider the images in Figure 7.8. For these images, we zoomed the lens in, *but we also changed the camera's position to keep the framing the same.* In other words, we adjusted the camera's position (by moving it farther away) to maintain the same field of view as we zoomed the camera in. Therefore, the man appears to be the same size in each image, but notice what happens to the tree. It gets bigger! This is because, as we zoom in, we're compressing the sense of depth in the image, just as we compressed the face of the man in Figure 7.7.

The lesson here is that there's a price to pay for being lazy. Many people think "Great, I can stand here, zoom in, and get the shot I need, rather than having to take my camera all the way over there." However, as you can see, the camera's position and distance from the subject has a huge effect on the final image. A tight shot created by a zoom can feel voyeuristic, while a tight shot created by moving the camera up close can feel more intimate. In other words, your choice of camera position and corresponding focal length can greatly change the sense of space and atmosphere in your scene.

22mm

50mm

480mm

Figure 7.6

The middle 50mm image displays roughly the same field of view as the naked eye. As the focal length shortens to 22mm, the field of view gets very wide. Conversely, as the focal length extends to 480mm, the field of view gets very narrow.

Figure 7.7

These two pictures show what a difference focal length can make. The image on the left was shot with a slightly telephoto focal length, while the image on the right was shot with a very wide-angle focal length.

Next time you watch a comedy, pay attention to the focal length of most shots. If it's a particularly wacky comedy, you'll probably notice that most close-ups and many scenes are shot with a really wide-angle lens. The fact is that wide-angle lenses make people funny-looking. You'll be able to spot a wide-angle shot because actor's faces will appear distorted as they are in the top two photos in Figure 7.8. You'll also probably notice that objects behind the actors appear very far away, and you'll have an extremely wide angle of view that encompasses a lot of the set or location.

To sum up: As focal length increases, the sense of depth in the image decreases, so it's very important to carefully choose your focal length and camera position.

You'll learn more about the importance of focal length when we discuss composition and framing later in this chapter.

Care of the Lens

Always keep your lens cap on when your camera is not in use. Keep a UV haze filter on your lens as a protective layer. Avoid touching the lens with your bare hands, since the oil from your fingers can etch a permanent mark on the glass. Never clean a lens with dry fabric or tissue. Instead, use a lens tissue dampened with lens cleaning fluid to wipe it off.

Controlling the Zoom

In addition to letting you choose an appropriate focal length when you frame a shot, zoom lenses allow you to change focal length *during* a shot, using either a mechanical control button or by manually turning the zoom ring on the lens itself. Unless you're trying for that "caught-on-tape" look, a good zoom needs to start out slowly, ramp up to the desired speed, and then gradually slow to a halt. You can also conceal a zoom by combining it with a pan or tilt.

The mechanical zooms found on most low-end consumer video cameras can be difficult to control—they tend to start awkwardly, go too fast, and respond jerkily to any fluctuations in pressure on the button. And unfortunately, many low-end video cameras have lenses that do not have a manual zoom ring. In either case, practice makes perfect—give your camera operator (or yourself) time with the camera before the shoot to get a feel for how the camera's zoom works.

A word to the wise—if your camera doesn't let you make a smooth zoom, then zoom as quickly as possible. A snap zoom has two advantages: it hides shakiness, and it takes up a minimal amount of time, making it easier to cut around later when editing. Higher-end cameras have zoom lenses that have a handle that lets you change the focal length really fast for better snap zooms (refer to Figure 7.2).

Many consumer-grade video cameras also have digital zooms, which are accessed through a menu display. Digital zooms are best avoided, since they work by blowing up the image rather than moving the optics of the lens, resulting in a low-resolution, pixelated image.

Very wide angle

Wide angle

Normal angle

Telephoto

Figure 7.8

These four images were shot using four different focal length lenses: very wide, wide, normal, and telephoto. The camera's position was adjusted to keep the framing similar. Notice what happens to the tree in the background.

Exposure

Back when indie films were shot on 35mm film, the hardest part of shooting was getting proper exposure. It was entirely possible that your film stock would come back from the lab with no image at all on it. With video, the only way that will happen is if you leave the lens cap on. But getting good exposure is still important.

So what, exactly, is exposure? At the most basic level, exposure is the amount of light that is allowed onto the image sensor(s). When too much light falls on the image, it is overexposed and when there's not enough light, the image is considered underexposed.

Underexposure usually results in a dark or muddy-looking image, whereas overexposure causes bright areas to turn white, or get "blown out." Properly exposed film or video footage usually contains some areas of overexposure—usually reflective highlights and bright whites. With film, overexposed images are easier to fix than underexposed images because the brightness can be pulled down in the film lab. However, with digital video, overexposure can cause many problems because blown-out white areas contain no visual information. So, for digital video, underexposure is preferable to overexposure. Of course, proper exposure is always best of all.

Film shooters use light meters to judge exposure, but with digital video it's possible to judge exposure by eye. Instead of a traditional light meter, better-quality digital video cameras have the zebra stripes feature to let you know what parts of the frame are overexposed. Some video cameras, and most DSLRs, also have a histogram view that shows the range of lights and darks in any given frame (see Figure 7.9).

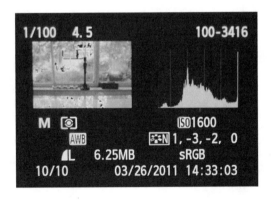

Figure 7.9

A frame of HD video with the zebra stripes feature enabled (right) and a histogram of that same frame ((left). In this image, the sky is overexposed.

Most higher-quality digital video cameras have video outputs that allow you to send the video signal out to a field monitor to immediately see if the image is properly exposed. Field monitors are bigger and make it much easier to check the quality of the image than the LCD displays on the camera itself. We recommend *always* using a field monitor when shooting video—think of it as your first and only line of defense against poor image quality. With a field monitor, you can make an immediate decision as to whether or not an overexposed image is acceptable for your project.

Most video cameras offer an auto-exposure setting, but auto exposure can be adversely affected by a change in the content of your scene. If an actor walks into a frame and blocks some light, for example, you might see your camera automatically open the iris up, resulting in a disturbing, overall contrast change. For this reason alone, you're usually better off controlling exposure manually. You might decide, for example, to purposely overexpose the sky, in favor of keeping a good exposure on an actor's face. Be aware that the auto-exposure mechanism in your camera will make exactly the opposite decision, and will properly expose the sky, causing the actor's face to fall into shadow.

Controlling the exposure manually involves setting the aperture (or f-stop), the shutter speed, and the gain (or ISO). These three controls have a reciprocal relationship—if you change one, you'll need to make a corresponding change with one of the others to maintain the same overall illumination.

What that means, practically speaking, is that you have three ways to adjust the camera to get proper exposure.

Aperture

Aperture refers to the opening at the rear of the lens. The camera's lens focuses light through the aperture and onto the image sensor mounted on the focal plane. The size of the aperture is controlled by the iris, a series of interlocking metal leaves that can expand and contract like the iris in your eye. The size of the opening of a camera's iris is measured in f-stops. Higher-numbered f-stop values stop more light. That is, a higher-numbered value represents a smaller aperture, which provides *more* light stoppage, resulting in less light passing through the lens (see Figure 7.10).

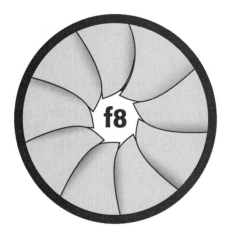 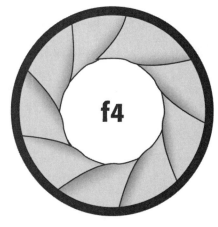

Figure 7.10

The iris on the left is stopping more light than the iris on the right is. Therefore, it has a higher f-stop value, and makes a smaller aperture.

Most high-end video cameras show f-stop markings on their lenses, which make it easy to set a particular aperture. Mid-range cameras do not have f-stop markings on their lenses, but provide control of the lens aperture with special dials, and with f-stop settings that appear in the digital menu display. Lower-end cameras do not display f-stops, but allow for manual iris adjustment and iris locking. Bottom-line cameras do not allow for any manual control of the lens aperture and rely solely on automated iris settings.

All video cameras include an auto-iris function, which constantly adjusts the size of the camera's iris according to the current lighting conditions. While the auto-iris function might work fine in "normal" lighting situations, it's usually the wrong choice in more complicated scenes. For example, if you have a subject who is in the shade, but a background that is sunny, the auto iris will probably expose for the bright background, since it fills the majority of the frame (see the top image in Figure 7.11). Because the camera is exposing for the brighter part of the image, the shadowy person in the foreground ends up underexposed and difficult to see. In order to expose for the darkened foreground figure (see the lower image in Figure 7.11), you'll need to use the manual iris control to overexpose. This will blow out the background, while keeping the subject exposed correctly.

As your camera moves, or the subjects in your scene move, your camera might re-evaluate what it thinks is a proper exposure. For example, as people walk in front of light sources in your scene, the iris will fluctuate, causing your scene to get lighter and darker. Though what the camera is doing is technically "correct," it will look awful. If your camera allows it, you should usually work with the auto-iris function turned off and control the iris manually while shooting.

Sometimes, it's not that easy to decide what the best aperture setting is for a tricky shot like the guy in front of the window. When that's the case, professionals use a technique called *bracketing*. They shoot the shot three times—once with the exposure they think is best, then one stop down from that and one stop up from that. The result is a higher likelihood of getting good exposure in one of the shots. This technique can be a bit time-consuming so it's not recommended for every shot in your film, just the ones that are really important and challenging.

Shutter Speed

The shutter determines how long the iris is open when you are shooting. With motion video and film, the lowest shutter speed is determined by the frame rate you are shooting at. For 30fps video or film, the slowest shutter speed possible is 1/30th of a second. But usually, the slowest speed available on most consumer cameras is 1/60th of a second, which corresponds with the fastest shutter speed available on most film cameras.

There are advantages to both slow and fast shutter speeds. Faster shutter speeds are better at capturing fast motion without blurring. Sports shooters typically shoot at very high shutter speeds. Fast shutter speeds also limit the amount of light allowed into the image sensor and are one way of reducing the exposure or stopping down.

Slow shutter speeds are considered more film-like. Additionally, they provide a way to increase the exposure in low-light situations.

In Chapter 4, we showed you an example of the difference between a fast shutter speed and a slower shutter speed. The resulting motion blur of the slow shutter speed will help make your video look more like film. (Refer to your camera manual for instructions on manually adjusting the shutter speed.) Sometimes adjusting the shutter speed can reduce on-set issues such as flickering monitors or lightbulbs.

Figure 7.11

In the upper image, the camera's automatic exposure exposed for the sunlit background, leaving our subject in shadow. In the lower image, we used the manual exposure control to expose for our subject. Although the background is blown out, at least now we can see our subject's face.

A Shutter by Any Other Name

Most digital video cameras don't have a mechanical shutter that opens and closes. Instead, they use an "electronic" shutter; that is, the image sensor inside the camera simply turns itself on and off for the appropriate duration.

Gain

All newer video cameras come with a gain boost feature for low-light situations. Gain boost makes everything in your image brighter, including the black areas of your image. A good video image should aim for dark, solid blacks and bright, clear whites. If the gain is boosted, the blacks tend toward gray. DSLR cameras allow for a choice of ISO settings, which is effectively the same as gain boosting.

With many digital video cameras, the color cast of the image tends to go red when you shoot with the gain boosted. In addition, video noise is introduced. Noise is the video equivalent of film grain, except it is much more noticeable and distracting (see Color Plates 5 and 6). If you are planning to go to film later or project your video, you should avoid any gain boosting. It only looks worse when it's bigger. Instead, use proper lighting to get a good exposure on your videotape and turn off the gain boost feature.

Gain boosting capabilities have improved greatly in newer cameras, but too much gain boosting will always look bad. However, sometimes using the gain is the choice between getting exposure and not (see Figure 7.12).

Figure 7.12

Thanks to a little gain boost, it was possible to shoot usable footage in this completely dark theater. However, gain boost is no substitute for good lighting. Dark is dark, and boosting the gain can only recover so much image. In addition, as can be seen here, boosting the gain dramatically increases the amount of noise.

Which One to Adjust?

As we mentioned earlier, you can adjust the aperture, the shutter speed, and the gain/ISO to change the exposure. So how do you choose which one to adjust? Because boosting the gain can introduce noise, this is typically used as a last resort. Ideally, you've lit your scene so that you don't need to increase the gain. Because different shutter speeds create different "looks," typically that is a choice you make in advance. So it's best to disable the gain, set the predetermined shutter speed, and then use the aperture settings to adjust for good exposure. However, if you find yourself shooting in a low-light situation, you have three ways to improve the exposure of your image.

Exposure and Depth of Field

Having control of the exposure gives you the freedom to control the depth of field in the image, which allows you to separate the subject from the background. Depth of field refers to how "deep" the range of focus is in an image. Modern HD cameras are very sensitive to light and very good at shooting in low-light situations. That means it is easy for the entire image to be in perfect focus. That might sound great at first, but when you look at a large, busy image like a crowd of people on a 50-inch plasma display, if the whole image is in perfect focus, it will be hard to decide what to look at. As a result, many filmmakers prefer a shallow depth of field so that they can put the main subject of the shot in focus and keep the rest of the image soft.

In Figure 7.13 (left), the depth of field is shallow, and only the subject is in focus. It is easy to focus your attention on the actor because he is completely separated from the background. In Figure 7.13 (right), the depth of field is longer, and more detail shows in the background.

Both of these images were shot under the same lighting conditions with the same lens. In Figure 7.13 (left), the depth of field is shallow because the lens aperture is wide open. In Figure 7.13 (right), the lens aperture is closed down all the way, resulting in a less shallow depth of field. Moreover, depth of field is shallower at longer focal lengths. Therefore, if you want a really shallow depth of field, you need to position your camera farther from your subject, zoom in, and open the iris as far as possible.

Shallow depth of field   **Less shallow depth of field**

Figure 7.13

By controlling the depth of field in your image, you can selectively blur out parts of your image.

However, as you open your aperture, you'll be letting in more light, which means you'll need to go to a faster shutter speed. A faster shutter speed might result in more stuttery motion, so you'll need to carefully balance your depth-of-field and shutter-speed concerns. As you'll see later, you can also use special neutral density filters to reduce the amount of light entering the camera, allowing you more shutter speed flexibility.

Camera Equipment Checklist

You should keep these items in your camera bag for easy access at all times:

- Your camera's original owner's manual
- Lens tissue
- Lens cleaning fluid
- Blower brush
- Measuring tape
- Rain cover, umbrella, or plastic garbage bags
- Sun shade
- Extra lenses (if applicable)
- Lens filters
- Extra batteries (charged)
- A/C adapter
- Flashlight
- Standard tool kit
- Slate (see Chapter 9, "Shooting and Directing")
- White pencil (for temporarily marking settings on the lens)
- Colored tape (for marking blocking, camera, and light placement)
- Gaffer's tape (for who-knows-what, but when you need it, you need it)
- Small bungee cords
- Small alligator clamps
- Large black cloth (to hide camera from reflective surfaces)

White Balancing

As you saw in Chapter 6, "Lighting," different types of lights shine at different temperatures, or colors. One of the amazing characteristics of your eyeballs is that they can adjust automatically to all of these different temperatures, and can even understand mixed lighting temperatures—sunlight shining through a window into a fluorescent-lit room, for example.

Film and video cameras are not as sophisticated. Film has to be specially formulated for different types of light to represent color accurately. This is why there is film for daylight and film for tungsten light.

Digital image sensors have the same trouble. Fortunately, though, a digital camera's understanding of color is entirely dependent on how the data coming off the sensor is processed by the camera's internal computer. Therefore, by telling the camera what kind of light you're shooting in, you can make sure that the camera interprets color data correctly.

White balancing is the process of getting a camera to represent white accurately. Because white light contains all other colors, if a camera can accurately reproduce white, then it can accurately render every other color. Color Plate 15 shows an example of an image that was incorrectly white balanced.

Your camera probably has an automatic white-balance setting that tries to white balance correctly on the fly. Automatic white-balance mechanisms can work very well, but for best results, you should take control of the white-balance process yourself.

Be aware that because the auto-white-balance mechanism is constantly white balancing, a sudden change in the luminance or color content of your scene can cause the camera to re-white balance, resulting in a weird color shift. For example, a giant pink elephant entering the frame might be enough to throw off the white balance for the entire scene. If you think your scene might be susceptible to such problems—or if you notice them when shooting—then you'll want to use a manual white balance as described next.

Most cameras offer white-balance presets for different types of light. Therefore, you'll have an option to select preset white-balance settings for daylight, or tungsten, or fluorescent lights. These can often prove better than auto-white-balance settings, especially if you're shooting in a mixed light situation.

White Balance in °K

3000°K	—	White Tungsten
3700°K	—	Yellow Tungsten
4000°K	—	Fluorescent
4500°K	—	Fluorescent
5600°K	—	Sunlight
6500°K	—	Cloudy
7500°K	—	Shade

For the absolute best results, though, you should use your camera's manual white-balance control. Getting yourself in the habit of always manually white balancing will help you shoot better footage and is essential for mixed-light situations.

To manually white balance, first set your lights. Then place something white in-frame, like a piece of foamcore or the back of a white script page. Make sure the white object is illuminated by the dominant light source(s) in your scene. Frame the camera so that only white shows in the viewfinder and activate the camera's manual white-balance control.

Remember that you'll need to re-white balance every time you significantly change the lighting, especially if you switch from daylight to tungsten light, or vice versa. Also, note that some cameras lose their manual white-balance reading if they are switched off or even placed in standby mode. If your camera functions like this, then you must remember to manually white balance when you restart the camera.

Alternative White Balancing

You can use the white-balancing feature on your camera to achieve different color effects. White balancing against a bluish surface will result in a warmer-looking image, while balancing against an orange-ish surface results in a cool-looking image. Since white balancing affects the scene's overall color temperature, it is sometimes easier to adjust the white balance than it is to place colored lighting gels on all your light sources. However, you'll be hard-pressed to get your footage back to a normal color if you decide later that that's what you need. As such, it's almost always better to shoot good, normal-looking footage and then add any color effects later in postproduction.

Lens Filters

If your camera has threads on the end of its lens (Figure 7.14), you can attach special filters that will help you control color and composition better, as well as create special effects. Filters are simply specially prepared pieces of glass housed in a screw-on attachment. Most filters are threaded so that you can screw filters onto other filters to stack up effects. Filters come in different sizes, so the selection of filters available for your lens size might vary. Many filters come in different "strengths" whose values are usually measured with a simple number scheme—the higher the number, the stronger the effect you'll get from the filter.

Figure 7.14

A selection of diffusion filters from Schneider.

UV Filters

As mentioned earlier, you should get at least one UV filter to protect your lens. In addition, UV filters will stop ultraviolet light from coming into the lens and will help reduce haze. There are a number of variations of UV filters, including stronger haze filters and warm UV filters, which will add warmth to your image.

Polarizing Filters

Polarizers are used to deepen saturation and improve contrast. Shooting with a polarizer will greatly improve images of cloudy skies, and they are valuable for all landscape shooting.

Polarizers can also be used to eliminate reflections when shooting through glass or windows (see Figure 7.15) and to eliminate hot spots on a reflective surface created by a light source.

Lens Filters (continued)

Figure 7.15

The window reflections in the left image can be easily eliminated with a polarizing filter in the right image.

Neutral Density Filters

Neutral density (ND) filters reduce the amount of light entering the lens in single f-stop increments, without changing the quality or color of the light. Therefore, if you're shooting in bright sunlight (which normally requires a small aperture), but you want to shoot with a very shallow depth of field (which requires a large aperture), you can use ND filters to cut out enough light to facilitate a smaller f-stop value. ND filters can also be used to slow shutter speeds from fast, stuttery speeds to something a little more natural looking.

Your camera might have a built-in electronic ND filter. Check your manual to see how many f-stops this feature provides (see Figure 7.16).

You can also get gradated ND filters that are designed to darken bright skies, which can easily overexpose.

Figure 7.16

Many cameras offer built-in ND filters.

Lens Filters (continued)

Diffusion Filters

Digital video images can be very crisp and sometimes that sharp look is not pleasing to the eye. Diffusion filters are designed to change the sharpness of digital video. High-contrast filters can be used to improve the contrast ratio (and therefore, apparent sharpness) in an image, while filters such as Tiffen's ProMist and Black ProMist can be used to reduce contrast resulting in a softer image, as shown in Figure 7.17.

Figure 7.17

Tiffen's ProMist and Black ProMist can be used to reduce the contrast in an image and make light flares bloom, creating a softer-looking image.

Aspect Ratios

Your camera might offer the choice between a 4:3 image and a 16:9 (or widescreen) image. Just because a camera can switch between 16:9 and 4:3 doesn't mean that the camera records a true native 16:9 image. The change in aspect ratio might simply mean that the image is being reshaped to fit that ratio by letterboxing or squeezing the image.

Know Thy Camera

By now, you should be comfortable with the idea of experimenting to discover what your camera is capable of and how it reacts in different lighting situations, such as low light, night exteriors, and backlight situations. Try to learn where the camera's controls are by feel. While shooting, you might want to switch a feature on or off without taking your eye from the viewfinder. It's better to learn about your camera during test shoots, rather than during your production.

Composition

Composition is simply the way that elements on-screen are arranged. Composition determines which visual elements are included in the image and how they're arranged. While shooting, you'll frame each shot using your camera's viewfinder to create compositions. Composition is essential to creating moving images that are attractive and that serve to tell the story.

Begin your shot setup by roughly positioning your camera. This is your first stab at getting the composition you want. Make sure you can frame and position all of the elements the way you want them. Is the subject and action best shown in a static shot or in a moving shot? Make a choice and take a rough camera stance. You might need to reposition the actors and props to get the framing you want. What's more, you might need to reposition them in a way that is completely unrealistic; that is, in positions that wouldn't occur in real life.

Good composition skills let you do far more than simply create pretty images. By carefully crafting each shot, you can convey important information to your audience. For example, look at the images in Figure 7.18.

Figure 7.18

The different compositions of these two shots present two very different impressions of this man.

In the upper image, the man looks confident and powerful, while in the lower image, the same man looks lonely and possibly afraid. In both of these images, the man is striking a similar pose and a somewhat neutral expression. Your sense of how powerful or weak he is comes mostly from the composition and framing of the shot.

In the upper image, he has been shot from below and framed so that he fills the frame. In this image, he is a very strong-looking, imposing figure. By contrast, the lower image shows a man who seems small. He is literally lower than we are, and therefore appears to be overwhelmed and weak. When used well, compositional differences can add a lot of depth to your story.

Mastering composition requires not only study, but also practice. Great camera operators are able to compose beautiful shots on the fly, a skill that's crucial for documentary-style shooting. Nevertheless, there are some basic compositional rules that you can learn quickly.

Headroom

One of the most common mistakes that beginning photographers and cinematographers make is that they don't pay attention. Your brain has an incredible ability to focus your attention on something. If you pay attention to what your brain is "seeing" instead of what your eyes are seeing, you might end up with a shot like the one shown in Figure 7.19.

If you were intending to show a wide shot of the entire scene, then this shot might be okay—boring, but okay. If you were intending to show the person in the scene, though, you'd be better off with something like the image shown in the bottom part of Figure 7.19.

When composing a shot, it's very important to get in the habit of looking *at* the image in the viewfinder, rather than looking *through* the viewfinder at your scene.

The top picture in Figure 7.19 has too much extra space around it—its subject is not clearly presented and framed. If you get in the habit of checking the edges of your frame when you're composing, then you'll force yourself to notice any extraneous space that needs to be cropped out.

Lead Your Subject

Composition and framing can also be used to help your audience understand the physical relationships of the people and objects in your scene—to help them better understand the space in which your scene takes place. When you have a single shot of someone speaking, you should usually "lead" them by putting some empty screen space in front of them. For example, Figure 7.20 shows a person talking to another person who is off-frame. If we put the blank space in front of them, we get a much more comfortable sense than if we put the space behind them.

Figure 7.19

Framing with too much headroom is one of the most common compositional mistakes of beginning cinematographers (as shown in the top figure). Less headroom brings more focus to your subject (bottom figure).

Figure 7.20

By "leading" your subject with empty space, you give your audience a better understanding of the physical relationships of the actors in your scene.

Following Versus Anticipating

Both documentary and scripted projects will include very mundane events and actions that present a challenge for the camera operator: sitting down, standing up, opening a door, following a subject as they walk. Often, these sorts of movements happen spontaneously and unpredictably. In general, the rule is that the camera should slightly follow any action of the subject. If your actor decides to stand suddenly in a scene that you blocked as seated, it will look okay if the camera is a little behind the movement of the actor, following their movement. But if the camera operator senses that the actor is about to stand and tilts up before the actor actually stands, then the camera will be perceived as anticipating the actor's movement, which will result in footage that looks awkward and sloppy. If you do accidentally anticipate a movement, resist the urge to correct the movement by moving back to your original position unless you are fairly certain the movement you anticipated isn't going to happen in the next few moments.

Don't Be Afraid to Get Too Close

Although it's important to have the proper headroom and leading in a shot, there are times when a shot calls for something more dramatic. Don't be afraid to get in close to the actors and to crop their heads and bodies out of the frame, as shown in Figure 7.21.

Figure 7.21

You can increase the drama and suspense of a scene by getting in really close to your subject. Although this "tight" framing cuts off some of our actor's head, it's still a well-composed, effective image.

This is a very "dramatic" type of framing. In Figure 7.21, tight framing is used to heighten suspense. In a more dramatic moment, it could be used to give the audience the perspective to see an actor's mood change or develop.

Listen

It might sound funny, but listening is one of the most important skills of any camera operator. Whether you're shooting a documentary or a scripted drama, listening and paying attention to what is going on beyond the visual elements of the scene is often the key to achieving the most brilliantly captured moments or performances. Many camera operators think that anything that isn't visual is not of their concern. This is a big mistake, and the result is that the camera operator fails to capture the moments of the high drama, emotion, or spontaneity.

Eyelines

If you're shooting a conversation between two or more actors, you need to make sure the eyelines in each close-up match, so that when the shots are edited together, the performers appear to be looking at each other (Figure 7.22). It's also a good idea to shoot separate close-ups within a dialogue scene using the same focal length and from the same distance, so that the shots match in terms of scale, composition, and lens distortions as well.

Figure 7.22

The upper images have eyelines that don't match, while the lower images have eyelines that match—in other words, they appear to be looking at each other.

Clearing Frame

When framing a static shot that might be used to start or end a scene, have the actors enter the frame from off-screen, perform, and then exit the frame entirely. You might not need to show them both entering and exiting frame in the final edited project, but you'll at least have the option.

Beware of the Stage Line

Crossing the 180° axis, also known as the *stage line,* or *axis of action,* is jarring. If you think of your set as a theatrical stage, the 180° axis falls along the proscenium (the front of the stage). Once you've set up your camera on one side of the axis, avoid moving it to the other side, or you might end up with camera angles that don't cut together (see Figure 7.23), as well as mismatched eyelines. Be aware that this primarily concerns action and dialogue shots. Cutaways and establishing shots can often get away with crossing the stage line, as can handheld moving shots in documentaries.

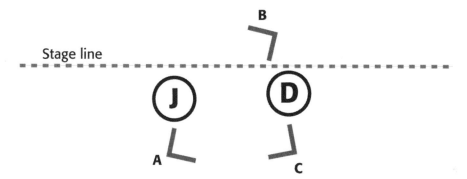

Figure 7.23

This camera diagram corresponds to the images in Figure 7.22. Camera angle B is on the wrong side of the stage line, which results in the mismatched eyelines in Figure 7.22.

TV Framing

The portion of the video image that is visible varies from one TV set to another. To ensure that all viewers can see the action and read the titles, there are standard guidelines for the action-safe and title-safe areas of the image. If any elements of your image fall outside of these lines, there's no guarantee that they'll be visible on all TV sets.

Professional lenses have visual guides visible in the viewfinder that show where the title-safe and action-safe boundaries lie. Unfortunately, not all video camera manufacturers include these guides in their viewfinders. When shooting, it's imperative to remember that your LCD viewfinder is showing the *entire* image, much of which will not be visible on many TVs. If your viewfinder doesn't have action-safe and title-safe guides, you'll simply have to try to approximate where the safe areas are and remember to try to keep important action within them.

Also, remember to frame your subject appropriately if you think you might need to put any text over the image. If you are shooting a documentary that is destined for television broadcast, be sure to frame your interviews with enough room for lower thirds. Lower thirds are titles in the bottom third of the frame that state the person's name, job title and other information (Figure 7.24).

Figure 7.24

A "lower third" is a title that identifies an interview subject used in television shows and documentaries. Remember the text must fall within the "title safe" guidelines. The figure on the left looks fine, but when a lower third is added, it becomes apparent that the subject is framed too tightly.

Breaking the Rules

In Western culture, our ideas about good framing are heavily dependent on the tradition of fine art painting. The shape of the film and video frame is similar to that of a traditional landscape painting, and the concept of how a medium close-up should be framed is similar to a traditional portrait. Breaking from these traditions can be interesting and exciting when it looks intentional, but beware: it can be disastrous when it looks like you didn't know any better.

Camera Movement

As if composition weren't complex enough, we're now going to complicate things and consider camera movement. Pans, tilts, zooms, dollies, and other types of camera movement are important parts of the language of film. (See Chapter 5, "Planning Your Shoot," for definitions of types of shots.) As with composition and editing, good camera movement is something that you don't always notice when you're watching a movie. When planning your shots, your goal is simply to create movements that will allow you to cover the action in your scene in an elegant, attractive manner.

Panning and Tilting

Pans and tilts are movements around the camera's axes. When you swivel the camera from side to side around its center, you are panning the camera. When you swivel it up and down around its center, you are tilting the camera. These are the most common camera movements you'll make, especially if your camera is locked down on a tripod. Like most camera moves, good pans and tilts are smooth and slow, never jarring or sudden. They always start with a static image and eventually come to rest on a static image, even if these static parts of the shot are edited out later on.

Zooms and Dolly Shots

These types of shots use movement that goes forward and backward along the Z-axis. We've already discussed zooms and techniques for zooming earlier in this chapter. It's important to know that, aesthetically, zooms are considered the low-rent cousin of dolly shots. Dollying the camera means to move it closer or farther from the subject. The feeling is similar to walking through space, rather than simply magnifying it. When you zoom the camera, you change the sense of depth in your scene, which results in the objects in your scene appearing to have a different spatial relationship to one another. Consequently, dolly shots usually appear more natural. Dolly shots require a camera dolly or some type of wheeled conveyance. Therefore, if you really need to pull off a good dolly shot, you'll want to rent some extra gear.

Tracking Shots

Tracking shots are akin to dolly shots, in that you physically move the camera, but tracking shots are used to follow action, or to create a camera movement parallel to the action within the scene, such as following a car by shooting from another car. As with dolly shots, you'll need some type of wheeled camera dolly to create a tracking shot.

Practice Camera Movements

Even if your script isn't ready, you can still practice the use of a moving camera. Choose some mundane actions—a person opens a letter and reacts to the contents while sitting down in a chair—and practice shooting with different types of camera movements. Try some versions of this shot with multiple angles, and then try editing them together so that you can get a feel for how moving shots can be pieced together.

Handholding

Traditionally, handheld shots were used in documentaries because it's easier to capture unscripted events when the cameraperson isn't bogged down by a tripod. In features, this verité style of shooting is often used intentionally to give a raw, documentary feeling that implies that the camera operator was involved in the scene. Think of dramatic footage you've seen on the news where the cameraperson starts running without turning off the camera, in an obvious attempt to escape personal danger. Even big budget movies occasionally have their camera operators handhold shots to capture moments of extreme action or violence. In the hands of a skilled operator, a handheld shot can be indistinguishable from a shot on a tripod, but a wobbly handheld camera draws attention to itself and makes the audience question whether the event was real or fictional (think *Blair Witch Project*). Nowadays, handheld cameras have additional meaning within the lexicon of visual literacy. Thanks to "reality" TV shows, home-video TV shows, and amateur news footage, we've learned to see handheld shots as amateur, caught-on-tape verité footage. As more and more people shoot more and more video, the lines between real and fictional, professional and amateur continue to blur.

Handheld shots often imply a point-of-view change. If you use a tripod to shoot a scene of a scared person walking fearfully through a dark, deserted house, the audience will feel like they're simply watching that action. If you shoot the same scene handheld, though, the audience will feel like they're watching the action from the point of view of someone else—probably someone rather unsavory. This can greatly heighten the tension in your scene. Switching from locked down to handheld is often a way of switching the viewer's perspective from outside the action to inside, from objective to subjective.

Handholding a lightweight video camera can be a challenge. Some prefer to hold the camera at waist level, balanced against their torso; others prefer holding it at eye level. You can also use the shoulder strap to try to steady the camera, while standing with your legs shoulder-width apart to help steady your stance. As with most camera-operating skills, practice makes perfect. Handholding a medium-sized 16mm film camera or a professional video camera is actually a little easier because the weight of the camera helps the operator hold it steady. Many gear-laden 35mm and HD cameras are not designed for handholding at all, and projects that use these cameras often use a secondary camera for any handheld shots.

In many ways, the camera operator who handholds is free from the restrictions that others face when using tripods, dollies, jibs, and steadicams. But there are many challenges as well. Perhaps one of the most difficult things to shoot handheld is a subject who "walks and talks." Generally, the camera operator must get in front of the subject and walk backward, shooting the subject as they walk toward them. Believe it or not, skilled handheld operators can shoot footage in this manner that looks fluid and smooth. One trick of the trade is for the camera operator to match his stride to that of the subject. Not only does this ensure that the camera operator walks at the same pace, but it also ensures that the bobbing motion of a camera matches the bobbing motions of the subject. The result is that the subject's head stays in approximately the same place within the frame, which makes the footage appear "smoother" and less jarring than it would if the camera were moving up and down out of sync with the subject.

Practice Handholding

Video cameras are pretty easy to come by these days. If you don't own one yourself, you can probably borrow one from a friend or your school or your office. Start out by learning how to hold the camera steady by picking a static object and shooting it. The longer the shot, the harder it is to hold the camera without shaking. Next, try panning, zooming, and following moving objects—cars, your cat, birds, or airplanes in the sky. Try to make each pan part of a composed shot that starts and ends. Remember to keep the center of gravity in your body low, even if your arms are holding a camera pointed up overhead. Sometimes, slightly bending your knees helps. If your camera has electronic image stabilization, try shooting both with and without it.

WHAT TO WATCH

The Blair Witch Project is famous for its use of handheld camera shots. This gives a limited point of view, which made for a much scarier film.

Shooting for the Web

It used to be that shooting video for the Web required a lot of care to avoid compression artifacts. Today, thanks to high-quality codecs, such as H.264, that's no longer the case. If you've ever watched a movie trailer on the Internet, you know how good video on the Web can look. If small file size is an absolute must, though, try to limit the amount of motion in your image (both subject and camera motion), and stay away from sets and locations with lots of different colors and lots of fine detail. These will all contribute to the size of your final file.

Deciding When to Move

Choosing when to use a camera movement can be tricky. Not only do moving shots require special gear (dollies, cranes, jibs, steadicams, and so on) and a skilled cameraman, they can also be challenging to work with in the editing room. Editing moving shots into static shots, or moving shots that travel in different directions or at different speeds, can be difficult and may result in scenes that lack the emotional tone you were looking for.

A camera movement is usually used for two reasons:

1. **It's the only way to get the shot.** Sometimes, the decision to use a moving shot is obvious, as it's the only way to cover the action in your scene. If you're having trouble blocking your scene because you can't keep it all framed from one camera position, then try some very simple camera movements. Often, even a short tracking movement is all you need to get the camera into a new position that frames the rest of your action.

2. **A moving camera changes the level of tension in a scene.** Think of the extremely tense moments in a soap opera. A character has just learned some horrible news, and we're getting ready to break for a commercial. The music builds, the actor looks traumatized, and what happens? The camera slowly zooms into their face. (Never *ever* zoom for this type of effect. Dolly the camera in instead.) Camera movements are not just used to create tension, they can also be used to *release* tension. A swirling camera movement that circles two excited lovers as they finally embrace and kiss on a crowded street corner at rush hour can be a tremendous release of tension (since they were probably on the outs just a few scenes earlier).

It *is* possible to move the camera too much. A scene of an intimate private discussion between two people may not be served by lots of camera movements. In fact, the moving camera may simply distract the audience and upstage the action happening on-screen.

A well-conceived camera movement will be invisible to the viewer, which makes it hard to learn from skilled directors, because you simply won't notice their best work. Nevertheless, studying and practicing camera movements are the best ways to learn how to use them.

Corporate and industrial works usually benefit tremendously from moving cameras. Because these types of productions often include lots of footage of mundane actions, spicing up your shots with some nice camerawork not only allows you to show the same mundane actions in different ways, but it can also inject a lot of visual energy into what might be dry material. Next time you have to shoot an office worker talking on the phone or filing, consider renting a small jib or dolly and try shooting them a little more dynamically.

WHAT TO WATCH

Watching camera movements in movies can be a great way to understand how they can be used, how they are edited together, and what emotional impact they can have on a scene. As we mentioned earlier, a well-orchestrated camera movement won't necessarily be visible, so you may have to pay close attention to notice them. This means focusing less on the story, which is often easier with a movie with which you're very familiar. Being a little less compelled by the story will make it easier to concentrate on technical specifics. For complex movements, you'll probably need to watch a scene repeatedly.

For an interesting comparison, rent *Dr. Strangelove* and *The Shining*, both of which were directed by Stanley Kubrick. In *Dr. Strangelove,* pay particular attention to the scenes between Mandrake (Peter Sellers) and Ripper (Sterling Hayden). Note Kubrick's use of extremely wide-angle shots that contain no movement at all. Also, note how he's willing to only show Hayden's back. Now consider *The Shining*, a movie that is stunning for its dynamic camera movements and well known for being the first prominent use of a steadicam. These films represent two very different approaches to camera movement, from the same director.

Plan a Test Shoot

If you're really worried about how your footage is going to turn out, you should plan on a simple test shoot prior to going into production. This will give you a chance to look at the quality of your footage and determine if you need to make any changes in your shooting plan. If you're transferring to film, you might also want a film recordist to do a film print of your test shoot. Obviously, to be a useful test, your test shoot should replicate the lighting and shooting conditions of your real shoot.

Shooting Checklist

Do a camera test: depth of field, focal length, lens filters, white balance, and camera movement are all cinematic tools that you have at your disposal when composing a shot. Good composition involves balancing these choices along with the placement of your subject and background within your scene.

Here, then, is a simple list that you should get in the habit of following when setting up your shots:

1. **Consider depth of field.** Think about how deep or shallow you want the depth of field in your image. If you want a very shallow depth of field, then you're probably going to need to use a longer focal length, so you might need to move your camera away from your subject to get the framing you established in step 1. Remember also to manually control your camera's aperture, as described earlier.

2. **Pay attention to the effect of your focal length.** Whether or not you're trying to control the depth of field in your scene, you should take a minute to consider how your choice of focal length is affecting the sense of depth in your image. Are you trying to create a large sense of space? If you are, then you probably want a shorter focal length to reduce depth compression. However, if you go too short, you might distort your actors' faces. There's no right or wrong to focal length choice, but it is important to pay attention to how focal length is affecting your image.

3. **Double-check exposure and shutter speed.** Most of the time, your camera will be calculating at least one of these parameters, often both. If you're manually adjusting aperture to control depth of field, then make sure the camera hasn't switched to a shutter speed that's too high. Or perhaps you want to make your images darker, or to expose them in a particular way. Or perhaps you're worried about your actor's movements interfering with your camera's automatic exposure mechanism. If so, you'll want to manually pick an exposure that works well for the scene and set the camera to that aperture.

4. **White balance.** Assuming your set is already lit—and assuming you've decided to shoot using manual white balance—it's now time to white balance. Have someone hold something white in an appropriate spot and take your white balance. You might not have to do this every time, but remember that if your camera has shut off or been placed in stand-by mode, or if your lighting setup has changed, you need to take a new white balance.

If you follow the preceding steps when setting up your camera, you'll stand a better chance of using all of the creative tools at your disposal.

Like any other tool, when you're very familiar with how to use your camera, your hands will simply do what they need to do without you having to think about it. With all of the other things you'll have to think about when on set, worrying about a particular camera setting is a luxury you won't be able to afford. As such, a thorough working knowledge of your camera is essential.

8

Production Sound

Photo credit: Jason Hampton

With all this talk about storyboarding, cameras, and image quality, it's pretty easy to become something of a "visual chauvinist" and end up scrimping on your project's sound. Therefore, at this point, it's important to be reminded that *sound is one of the most powerful tools in your creative palette.* With the right music and sound effects, you can do everything from evoking locations to defining moods and building tension. In fact, in many ways, good sound is *more* important than good video.

As an example, there are plenty of movies that adopt a grungy, low-quality image as a stylistic choice. For *Rachel Getting Married,* Jonathan Demme went to great lengths to create a very rough-looking, image style. However, did he choose an equivalent low-fidelity for the audio? No way! (You'll regularly see similar visual styles in music videos—grungy, beat up video with high-fidelity sound.) Audiences are very forgiving of low-quality video—they even find it visually appealing—but if they can't understand the audio, especially the dialogue, they won't be engaged in the story.

Editing, mixing, adding music, and creating sound effects are each a crucial part of your postproduction process, but to be successful in those tasks, you have to have clean, high-quality audio recordings. In this chapter, we'll cover the basics of good production sound recording, including how to choose and use microphones, as well as what the best recording options are for different types of projects. Finally, at the end of this chapter, we'll detail simple recording setups for common shooting situations.

What You Want to Record

Most of your audio recording tasks will involve dialogue. (Obviously, if you're shooting a nature documentary or action sequence, dialogue is probably not as prevalent.) Therefore, your entire strategy when planning your audio recording will be built around the specific problems of recording dialogue.

Although it is possible to improve the quality of your audio in postproduction, don't expect to be able to make the type of content changes that you can make when editing video or still images. If you have extra sound, such as background noise, or low recording levels, correcting your audio will be extremely difficult. Your goal when recording audio is to get high-quality recordings of just the sounds you want. Although dialogue will make up the bulk of your audio recording, there are times when you'll want to record other things, such as actions that are critical to your story; for example, a hand turning the clicking dial of a safe, or the philandering husband trying, unsuccessfully, to quietly creep into his house late at night.

It's difficult or impossible to correct a sound, or remove an unwanted sound from a recording, but it's easy to mix sounds *in.* Therefore, if you've recorded high-quality sound of your primary foreground elements, you can always add background sound later.

For example, say you're recording two people talking in a crowded restaurant. You can spend a long time shooting multiple takes, trying to get a version where you can hear every word over the din of other diners. Alternatively, you can ask everyone else in the restaurant to be silent—but continue to pantomime talking—while you record your actors. Afterward, let your restaurant patrons go back to speaking, and record a few minutes of their sound (in the business, crowd noise is referred to as "walla"). In postproduction, you can mix together the sounds of your characters with your separately recorded background walla, and have full control over the loudness of the background, letting you mix the background to more easily hear your foreground characters.

Similarly, any other sounds—doorknobs, car doors opening, windows breaking—can be added later, during a process called *foley* (named for Jack Foley, the man who pioneered the technique). Foley is simply the process of recording all of the other incidental sounds that your scene needs and mixing them in during your final sound mix.

Recording good audio requires a lot of preparation, and it begins with selecting the right microphone.

Microphones

Although your video camera has a built-in microphone, you shouldn't use it for most feature and documentary work. On-camera mics are typically low quality and produce tinny sound recorded from all directions. In addition, because of their location on the camera, they frequently pick up camera noise such as motors and hand movements (see Figure 8.2). Consequently, to record good audio, you'll want to buy or rent one or more high-quality microphones, which you will connect to your camera or to a separate audio recorder such as the Fostex FR-2, as shown in Figure 8.1.

Different types of microphones are designed for different recording situations, so your choice of microphone will be based on matching microphone characteristics to your shooting needs.

Figure 8.1

The Fostex FR-2 audio recorder.

What a Mic Hears

Just as different lenses have different angles of view—some wider, some narrower—that define what they will see, microphones have different "directional" characteristics that define what they will hear (see Figures 8.2 and 8.3). The directional "coverage" of the mic that you choose will have a lot to do with both the content and quality of your recorded sound.

Figure 8.2

Higher-quality camcorders like this Panasonic HVX200 typically have a built-in directional microphone.

Figure 8.3

Even if your camera has a decent built-in microphone, you still may want to add a higher-quality, shotgun mic like this one from Rode to the mic mount on your camera.

Omnidirectional Mics

As their name implies, omnidirectional mics pick up sounds from all directions. While this might seem like a good idea for recording the sound of an entire room, omnidirectional mics are often not practical. With their wide coverage, omni mics can pick up far more sound than you might want, including camera noise (and camera operator noise!), as well as ambient sounds such as passing cars or people. Because they listen in all directions, omni mics tend to record echoes within the room, which makes for a much more "boomy" sound.

Omnidirectional mics work well if they are held close to the subject of the sound—within 12 inches or so—because the subject tends to overpower any background sound. However, keeping a mic in this position can be very difficult, particularly if you want it hidden, and especially if your subject is moving.

On the positive side, omnidirectional mics have a low sensitivity to wind and breath sounds, and many provide a "shaped" response that boosts higher-frequency sounds while dampening lower, rumbling sounds. Shaped-response mics are good for preserving the sound of a voice that is being recorded against loud sounds such as traffic or construction.

Unidirectional Mics

Unidirectional (or just "directional") mics, as you might expect, pick up sound from one direction. Because you can point a unidirectional mic at a particular subject, they are well suited to feature and documentary production, as they allow you to selectively record a particular person or event. Moreover, because a directional mic can be farther from the recording subject than an omnidirectional mic can, they are better suited to some feature production sets, where keeping a mic close to the subject is difficult. Some directional mics are more directional than others, and which type to choose depends on your shooting task.

Most directional mics are sensitive to sound in a cardioid pattern (so named because it looks vaguely heart shaped—see Figure 8.4). A cardioid microphone is more sensitive to sound coming from the front of the mic, and typically attenuates, or drops off, sounds around the sides of the mic. Typically, a cardioid pattern is wide enough that a cardioid mic placed more than seven or eight feet from its subject will pick up unwanted sounds.

A supercardioid mic has a tighter pickup pattern than a cardioid and is similar to the pickup pattern of the human ear. Supercardioid mics provide good results when used at a distance of 6 to 15 feet from the subject.

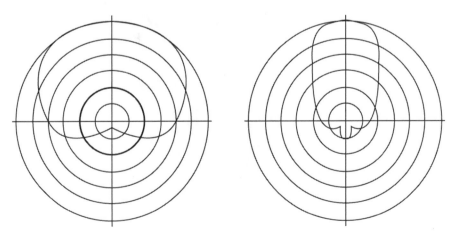

Figure 8.4

The cardioid patterns for an omnidirectional and a supercardioid mic.

Finally, hypercardioid mics have an even narrower pickup pattern that rejects most sounds that are "off-axis" from the direction the mic is pointed. Hypercardioids are, in fact, so directional that they can be somewhat difficult to use. If they stray even a little from their subject, they will not pick up the desired sound. You'll need a diligent mic operator to use a hypercardioid mic.

Contrary to common sense, it's the holes on a microphone that make it more or less directional. Take a look at a typical handheld or clip-on omnidirectional mic. You'll see that most of the holes in the microphone's case are in the very top of the mic, with just a few holes around the sides. Now look at a typical hypercardioid mic and you'll see a very long tube riddled with holes along its entire length. What's the deal?

The holes in a directional mic cause the sounds coming in from the sides of the mic to cancel each other out, leaving only the sounds from the front (and sometimes, back). In fact, you can turn a hypercardioid mic into an omnidirectional mic simply by covering up the holes along the sides (see Figure 8.5).

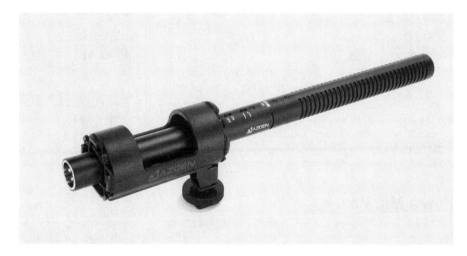

Figure 8.5

Extremely directional mics such as this one from Azden are ideal for mounting on a boom or fishpole or, in a pinch, mounting on the top of your camera. It is the holes in the side of the mic that give its directional qualities.

If you can't afford multiple mics or arrange for a boom operator on your shoot (more on this later), and you need to shoot dialogue scenes, then an omnidirectional mic will be the best choice. Ideally, though, you'll want a mic with a supercardioid pattern, and the personnel and equipment to use it right. Later in this chapter, we'll discuss how to mic your scene.

Most microphones come with a coverage chart that indicates the directional pattern of the microphone and how different parts of the field of coverage respond to different frequencies (see Figure 8.6). Although interesting, don't lose any sleep over trying to understand these charts. Most mics are clearly rated as cardioid, supercardioid, or hypercardioid.

Hands Off That Mic!

Because a mic's directional characteristics can be affected by the way you handle the mic, be very careful when attaching a mic to a stand or pole with a clamp or tape (or when holding a mic in your hand). Be certain you don't cover up any of the holes in the mic's case. Similarly, don't think that you can make a mic more directional by cupping your hands around the front of the mic.

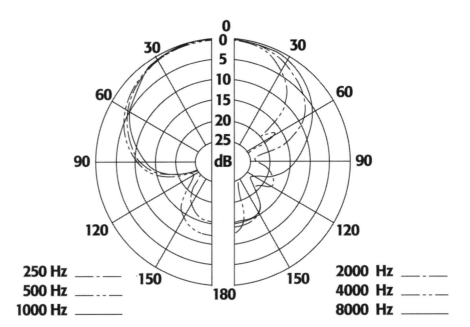

Figure 8.6

Most microphones include a polar chart that diagrams their directionality and sensitivity. The polar chart shows a cross-section of the mic's pickup pattern, with the mic laying in the middle of the chart, pointed toward the top. This chart diagrams a supercardioid mic.

Finally, parabolic mics are extremely directional mics that use a large parabolic dish to gather and focus sound onto the head of a unidirectional microphone. Parabolic mics are sensitive to sounds over 200 feet away and are not practical for most feature shoots. However, for difficult shooting situations where a subject is extremely far away (climbing the side of a mountain, for example), a parabolic mic might be the most reasonable way to record sound.

How a Mic Hears

All microphones work by converting sound waves into electrical impulses. There are different mechanisms for performing this conversion, and each has its own advantages and limitations. Typically, different mechanisms are used for different types of microphones.

A dynamic microphone is the most basic mechanism, consisting of a simple diaphragm attached to a coil of wire that is surrounded by a magnet. (It is, literally, the exact opposite of a speaker.) When the pressure of a sound wave hits the diaphragm, it moves the coil of wire within the magnetic field of the magnet. This generates a small electrical current that is fed out of the microphone.

Because of their simple design, dynamic microphones are incredibly rugged and require no external power or batteries. The dynamic mechanism has a very short range, and so is typically only used in handheld mics. Their short range makes dynamic mics well suited to narration and voice-over recording (they tend to pick up only the voice of the speaker), but frequently impractical for on-set recording.

In a condenser mic, a metal plate and a metal diaphragm are separated by a thin gap of air. Both plates are electrically polarized by an external power supply. Because of a property called capacitance, an electric charge is created between the plates. As incoming sound waves move the metal diaphragm, the amount of charge between the plates changes. The electrical charges produced by this mechanism are tiny and must be amplified using power from either a battery or a phantom power supply housed externally. Because the diaphragm in a condenser mic is so small, it requires very little acoustic pressure to make it move. Consequently, condenser mics are much more sensitive than dynamic mics.

An electret condenser is a somewhat cheaper, lower-quality version of the condenser mechanism. Electret condenser mics use a small battery to create a polarizing voltage, and so don't require an external power supply.

Because their pickup mechanisms are so tiny, condenser mics can be made very small—most clip-on mics use electret condenser mechanisms. Most condenser mics also include a small preamplifier, either built into the mic itself, or located outboard in a small box.

Ideally, you'll want to choose a condenser mic simply because it delivers the best quality. However, for recording voice-overs or narration, or for doing interviews in more harsh conditions (bad weather, extreme humidity, etc.), a handheld, dynamic mic might be a better choice.

Types of Mics

No matter what type of pickup element is used, mics typically fall into three categories: handheld, lavalier (clip-on), and shotgun. Which to choose depends on your set, and you might find yourself using multiple mics of different types. Obviously, for a dramatic production, keeping the mic hidden is your primary concern (after getting good audio!). However, even documentary producers might want unobtrusive mics, both for aesthetics and to record their subjects more clandestinely. (Note that we're not advocating illegal wiretapping! Rather, we're simply trying to remind you that a microphone can be a very intimidating object to someone who hasn't spent a lot of time "on-camera." To keep an interview or documentary subject calm and more spontaneous, a less-intrusive type of mic might be preferable.)

We've all seen the handheld mics used by talk show hosts, rock stars, and karaoke singers. Usually omnidirectional dynamic mics, these are the least useful mics for on-set use. Because they typically operate at short range, they have to be held close to the speaker's mouth, making it nearly impossible to keep them hidden (see Figure 8.7).

Figure 8.7

A handheld mic on a microphone stand.

Lavaliers

Lavalier, or clip-on mics, are the small condenser mics that you see clipped to the front of newscasters. Lavaliers are usually omnidirectional mics, but because they are kept so close to the speaker's mouth, they rarely pick up extraneous sound, making them well suited to record individual performers. Moreover, because of their small size, they can easily be hidden under clothing (see Figure 8.8).

Figure 8.8

A clip-on, or lavalier, mic.

Although laveliers are omnidirectional, they might still have some directional characteristics. A somewhat directional lavalier will produce a very clear recording, but might lack some ambient sound that makes for a full, realistic sound. (These lavs are typically used for newscasting where the sound of an authoritarian voice is all you're interested in recording.) A more omnidirectional lav can record a more natural sound, but you'll have to worry about controlling extra ambient noises on your set.

For scenes involving many actors, you'll probably need a separate lav for each performer, which means that you'll have to deal with the requisite logistical troubles, such as wiring multiple performers and managing lots of mic cables. (You'll also need a mixer, which we'll discuss later in this chapter.) Because keeping cables hidden (and keeping actors from tripping over them) can be a problem, wireless lavaliers are a good solution for complex shoots involving lots of mics. A wireless lav system consists of a normal lav microphone attached to a small transmitter worn by the actor. A receiver picks up the audio and routes it on to your recording device.

Although a great solution to the "obtrusive cable" problem, wireless lavaliers have complications of their own. First, you'll want to be sure you get a system that uses an FM transmitter, for higher quality. In addition, you'll have to worry about radio interference from other devices, cell phones, overhead power lines, and so on. These problems can be easy to solve, but they can take time.

Shotgun Mics

Those long, skinny microphones that you often see sticking off video cameras are referred to as shotgun mics. Although varied in pickup mechanism and directional characteristics, shotgun mics provide the greatest flexibility for miking. Most shotgun mics record stereo audio, usually by having two pickups inside, one each for left and right channels (see Figure 8.9).

Figure 8.9

A typical shotgun mic.

If your camera already has a shotgun mic attached, odds are it's not very high quality. Whatever its quality, the front of your camera is not the best location for a mic. Ideally, you'll want a supercardioid or hypercardioid shotgun mic attached to a boom pole. We'll discuss using a boom later in this chapter.

A Little of Each

The ideal audio setup involves several microphones, frequently of different types. If you can only afford one mic, then you'll want to get a directional shotgun mic and attach it to a boom. However, for better sound and greater postproduction audio editing flexibility, fitting actors with lavaliers while simultaneously miking them with a boom mic provides your sound editor with more options for mixing and correcting difficult-to-understand audio.

No matter what types of mics you choose, you'll ideally want to listen to them before you buy. Just like loudspeakers, different mics provide different sounds. Some will boost low frequencies to help create authoritative, booming voices. Others will have more of a "flat," realistic response. Although you can look at frequency response charts for a mic, such stats don't reveal everything about how a mic will sound. Your ear is the best judge of whether or not a mic is right for you.

Mixing

As you might have noticed, most cameras and tape decks only have one place to plug in a microphone. Therefore, if you're using multiple microphones, you'll have to plug them into a mixer to mix their signals down to two or four signals that can be plugged in to the inputs on your camera or deck.

When choosing a mixer, you'll need to pick a unit with enough inputs for the number of mics you'll be using (see Figure 8.10). You might also want to select a unit that has a built-in graphic equalizer. As we'll discuss later, an equalizer will let you slightly modify the sound coming through a mic to add more bass or treble. Equalizers are a great way of improving the sound of a weak voice or removing certain problems such as "shushing" S sounds or hisses.

Figure 8.10

The Azden FMX-42 is a portable
four-channel field mixer.

Headphones

Headphones are the audio equivalent of a field monitor—you need them to hear (or "monitor") the audio as it's being recorded. Headphones serve a dual purpose: they block out ambient noise from the set and allow the sound recordist to monitor the audio directly. Because the sound recordist is listening to what is being recorded, as opposed to what the human ear would hear on the set, he will often notice extra noises such as crackling mics and distracting background sounds. Even though you can use small "walkman" type headphones, it's best to use big, professional padded ones that block out as much ambient noise as possible.

Connecting It All Up

Unfortunately, connecting your mics to your camera, mixer, or deck involves a little more than just matching connectors. Although you might have the right-shaped plug on your microphone, it might not be wired properly for the jack on your deck or mixer.

There are two different types of inputs on a recording device: line-level inputs and mic-level inputs. Mic-level inputs are designed to receive weak, quieter audio signals. A preamplifier inside the mic input boosts the incoming signal to increase its level. Line-level inputs are designed for more powerful signals. Most newer video cameras and mixers or recorders provide both mic and line. Note that you can't tell the level of an input by its connector—RCA, TRS, or 1/4" phono connectors can all be either mic or line level (see Figure 8.11). However, most jacks are clearly labeled mic or line, and some can be changed from one to the other by flipping a switch, usually located near the jack.

There are two types of microphone connectors: balanced and unbalanced. You can generally tell whether a mic is balanced by looking at the type of plug it uses. RCA, 1/4" phono, and TRS plugs are all unbalanced connectors, while three-prong XLR plugs are usually balanced. One is not better than the other as far as audio quality goes, but if you want to use cables longer than about 25 feet, you'll need balanced connectors (see Figure 8.12).

If you're using a consumer grade camcorder, most likely, it has an unbalanced connector, usually a TRS jack. If you're using a mic with a balanced connector (usually a mic with an XLR plug), then you'll need to get a special adapter that not only provides an XLR jack, but also alters the mic's signal. A mixer, like the one in Figure 8.10 will also do the trick.

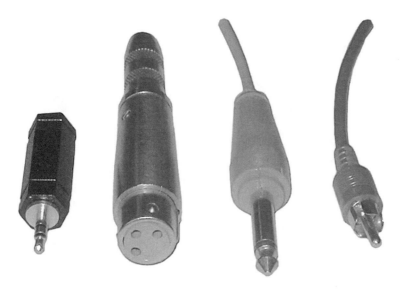

Figure 8.11

TRS, XLR, 1/4" phono, and RCA plugs.

Figure 8.12

Camcorders aimed at digital filmmakers, like the Sony F3, offer built-in balanced XLR audio inputs.

Wireless Mics

Wireless mics are usually lavalier (lav) mics attached to a transmitter (see Figure 8.13) that send the audio signal wirelessly to a recording device, thanks to a special receiver attachment.

Figure 8.13

A wireless mic is a lavalier
attached to a wireless transmitter.

Wireless mics are great for shooting in a way that's unobtrusive, but sometimes the quality can suffer. Like all wireless technologies, wireless mics are susceptible to interference. They are great for run-and-gun shooting, guerilla shooting, and documentaries where you want your subject to forget they are being recorded. Typically, the lavalier is attached to the collar, and the transmitter is placed at the small of the back and taped to the wearer's torso.

Double-System Sound

Recording audio to a device other than the camera, aka double-system sound, is an important technique that involves careful coordination of both the audio crew and the camera crew. We cover it in depth in Chapter 10, "DSLRs and Other Advanced Shooting Situations."

Setting Up

Getting good sound requires much more than just clipping a mic on an actor and pressing the Record button. Good sound recording also involves choosing appropriate mic setups for the type of image you're shooting and careful management of your set or location.

Placing Your Mics

As we've seen, different types of mics have very different characteristics, both in terms of sound quality and in what they can "hear." To get the most from your mic, you need to place it correctly.

Handheld Mics

Because they're usually omnidirectional, handheld mics need to be placed close to your subject to ensure that they record more of your subject than anything else. Handheld mics can be placed on a microphone stand, either a tall, floor-standing device or a small desktop stand. Your talent should not speak directly into the top of the mic; rather, tilt the mic at about a 30° angle.

Windscreens

No matter what type of mic you're using, you might need a windscreen—a foam covering that slips over your mic—to cut out the sound of wind, or particularly breathy voices. Some camcorders include an electronic windscreen, which automatically cuts out certain frequencies to reduce wind sounds. Although these features can work well, they can also cut out more frequencies than you might want. You'll need to test in your particular situation to ensure that it's not degrading the quality of your audio.

Lavalier Mics

For feature film production, you'll usually do more than simply clip a lavalier onto someone's collar or tie. To keep the microphone invisible, you'll most likely want to hide it under the talent's clothing, or somewhere on the set—in a plant, on the dashboard of a car, or on a prop. In these cases, try to choose a location that's roughly at mouth level to the actor and in the direction in which the actor will be speaking. For close-ups, the easiest way to hide a mic is simply to place it out-of-frame. Wherever you attach a lavalier, consider the following:

- Try to position the mic so that it sits about 8 to 12 inches from the performer's mouth.

- As the speaker turns her head back and forth, she might tend to speak more or less into the microphone, making her voice get louder or softer. When attaching her mic, try to predict which direction she will favor and place the mic on that side. For example, if the actor will be "cheating out" a bit to stay open to the camera when talking to someone on her right, then her head will probably be turned a little to the right side. Place the mic more to that side of her body. The clip on most lavaliers is reversible, making it easier to clip the mic in one direction or another.

- If you're trying to hide the mic inside of clothing, you'll need to make sure that it doesn't rub against skin or clothing when the actors move, as this will create extremely loud noise. With some cleverly placed gaffer's tape, you can usually secure the mic and any surrounding clothing. If the talent is moving a lot, or wearing tight clothes, a lav mic might not be the best choice.

- After clipping the mic to a shirt, arrange the cable, as shown in Figure 8.14 (obviously, we're not concerned about hiding the mic in this shot, but you'll want the same cable arrangement, even if it's inside someone's shirt). With the cable looped as shown in the figure, the sound of cable bumps or movements will not be conducted up the cable to the microphone.

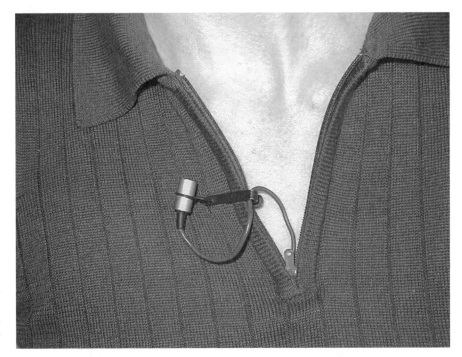

Figure 8.14

When placing a lavalier mic, make sure that the mic cable is secured to prevent cable noise and bumps.

- Run the rest of the cable down the inside front of the talent's shirt and around the waist to the back.

- For most work, you'll need to attach the connection end of the mic cable to a cable extension. These couplers are usually large and just a little bit heavy. Place the connector in the subject's back pocket or attach it to his waistband using gaffer's tape, clothespins, or binder clips. If clipping the cable, be careful that the clip is not so strong that it damages the cable.

- Once you've wired the talent, let them move around to test their freedom of movement. Make certain that your rigging holds. When you test the level of the mic (more on this later), make sure that you've positioned the mic well to get the best recording of their voices. You might need to move it.

- If you're using a wireless lavalier, then you'll need to test the reception of your system. Make sure that you're getting a clean signal on your receiver. Noise or other interference might be caused by cell phones, other pieces of equipment, or any large transmitters that might be in the area. In addition to the difficulty in keeping the transmitter hidden, wireless lavs are also prone to picking up static when the actor's clothes move across the antenna.

Wireless lavaliers can also be confused by transmitter reflections, wherein the transmitter's signal, and reflections of that signal, are both picked up by the receiver. Moving the receiver can often alleviate these troubles.

Shotgun Mics

Because they're usually very directional, it's crucial that you pay attention to what a shotgun mic is pointed at. This means taking note of not just your foreground elements, but your background as well.

For example, if there is a shotgun mic attached to your camera, it will be pointed at your subject when you've framed him or her with the camera. Unfortunately, it will also be pointed at everything *behind* your subject. Whether it's other sounds, or an echo-producing wall, there will be little differentiation between the sounds of your foreground and the sounds of your background. Because you can always add background sound in postproduction, your primary concern when recording is to get good audio from your foreground elements. Consequently, a shotgun mic mounted on your camera is not the ideal shotgun setup. Although fine for stand-up interviews where the subject is directly in front of your camera, a camera-mounted shotgun is a bad choice for recording dialogue.

A better choice is to mic your scene from above with the microphone pointed down toward the ground. The easiest way to do this is to attach the mic to a fishpole or boom and have it held in position by a boom operator. A fishpole is a long, telescoping pole with a super- or hypercardioid mic attached to one end. The boom operator holds the mic above the performer and tries to keep the mic as close to the performers as possible, without letting it dip into the shot. Because the mic is above the performers and pointed down toward the ground, there is little or no background noise for it to pick up. Consequently, you'll get a very clean recording of just your actors. In addition, this type of miking affords your cast much more freedom to move around without worrying about hitting a microphone or tripping over a cable. Because it's overhead, the mic will also pick up a good mix of footsteps, prop sounds, and other environmental noises that will make for a richer soundtrack. For almost all situations, a fishpole or boom mic will be the best miking option.

(Although people will use the terms *boom* and *fishpole* interchangeably, technically a boom is a beefed-up version of a fishpole and is usually only used in a studio situation. Booms are typically much larger than a fishpole, with a capacity to extend a mic over 100 feet. Frequently hydraulically controlled, they're not the sort of apparatus the independent filmmaker will take on location.)

Operating a mic fishpole can be difficult work. In addition to the physical strain of holding a long pole overhead for hours at a time, the boom operator must be very focused and diligent to ensure that the best sound is recorded. Remember, because the microphone that is used is typically very directional, even a little mic movement can change the quality of the sound. Moreover, if your subjects are moving, boom operation gets even more difficult.

Listen Up!

The boom operator must wear a set of headphones to monitor the audio that is being recorded!

In addition, consider the following:

- **Properly rig the pole.** Although you can try to get away with a makeshift pole, a commercial boom has a number of advantages. First, a shock-resistant mount attaches the mic to the pole and reduces noise from the boom itself. In addition, in a professional boom pole, the inside of the pole will often be insulated to reduce sound conduction along the length of the pole. To keep the cable from slapping against the pole, you'll want to hold it taut against the pole when in use, and you'll need to secure any cable slack at the end of the pole to ensure that the cable doesn't slide or move. Professional boom poles come with clips to hold the mic cable against the pole (Figure 8.15).

Figure 8.15

A typical boom kit with collapsible boom pole, microphone holder, and windscreen.

- **Mounting the mic.** Although the mic will be pointed at the actors, don't forget that directional mics pick up sounds from the side and back as well as the front. Therefore, be aware of where other parts of the microphone are pointing. In some situations, you might need to angle the mic to ensure that it's not picking up sounds from other directions.

- **Directional mics** are more susceptible to wind noise than other types of mics are. You might need a special "blimp" or "zeppelin" style windscreen (see Figure 8.16).

- **Choose the right amount of extension for the shot.** How long your pole will need to be depends on how wide the shot will be. For most feature work, a pole between 8 and 15 feet will be adequate. Experiment with the mic and pole before shooting to learn where its center of gravity is and what is most comfortable. To be able to grip the pole more toward its center, you might want to extend the pole farther than you actually need for the shot. This will provide a more balanced grip. Many poles have locking mechanisms at each extension. Extending to a point just short of these locks will usually make for a stronger pole.

- **Choose your position.** Make sure that you choose a position that affords you access to the entire shot, allows you to get the mic as close to the subject as possible, and isn't so uncomfortable that you'll be unable to do your job.

Figure 8.16

A supercardioid mic and windscreen.

- **Watch your grip.** Remember, noise from your hands—scraping, drumming, and so forth—can be transmitted up the pole to the mic, so you want to get a good grip on the mic before you start shooting and then hold it for the duration of the shot. Gloves are often a good idea in extreme temperatures, both for comfort and to eliminate the sound of your skin sticking to the metal pole.

- **Holding the pole.** The pole should be held parallel to the ground with your arms straight up, close to your head, and your elbows locked. Microphone poles aren't too heavy, and you should be able to hold this position for a while. Your lead arm will act as a fulcrum for the mic, while your trailing arm can be used to steer. From this position, you can quickly get the mic into the right position. In addition to tilting the pole around, you might need to spin the pole to point the microphone in the right direction. Make sure that your grip and stance allow for all the motions you'll need.

- **Positioning the mic.** Remember: if you're a boom operator, your job is to get the best audio possible, and this means getting the microphone *close to your subject!* Don't be shy, get the mic in as low and close as you can. Depending on the framing of the shot, your mic can be a few inches to a few feet above the talent's head. Although you might screw up some takes by dipping the mic into the shot, this is better than discovering later that the audio is lousy because the mic was too far away. To make the mic easier to see in the frame, use a brightly colored windscreen or place a bright-colored label on the front of the windscreen.

- **Booms don't have to be held above your subject.** Remember that you can also hold your mic boom below your subject and point it upward. This is often easier on your boom operator, and sometimes less intimidating to your talent (particularly in a documentary shoot). However, if you're outdoors or in a high-ceilinged room, overhead positioning will probably sound a little better. Have your sound person do some tests before committing to a particular boom positioning.

- **Adjusting for echo.** If the surface that you're standing on is hard tile or stone, there is a chance that it will reflect sound back up toward the microphone. In your mic tests, if your sound is a little too "echoey," consider putting cardboard, carpet, or some other sound-absorbing surface on the floor, below the frame.

- **Talk to your director and cinematographer!** You'll need to maintain good communication with both of these people to ensure that you're not letting the mic enter the frame, and to remind them that you're only trying to get the best audio you can. With all the troubles present on a shoot, it's easy for nerves to get a little frayed. Stay in communication with the rest of your crew to ensure that everyone stays calm.

Hanging Mics

Mics can be hung to record large groups of people or presentations. Typically, an omnidirectional or cardioid mic is best, and you might need more than one if you're covering a large area. You usually need a lot of cable when hanging a mic, so you'll need balanced mics and connectors. Alternatively, a high-quality, omnidirectional wireless lavalier can be used—obviating the need for lots of cable—if you're not miking an area that's too large.

Multiple Mics

If your subjects are too far apart to reach with one boom, consider using multiple mics. Some sound people like to use multiple mics as backups. For example, you can feed a lavalier mic into the left channel and a boom mic covering the same actor into the right channel. When mixing and editing, you can select between channels to get the best sound.

Think Batteries

Accept it right now: at some point in your moviemaking career, a mic battery will die in the middle of the best take you've ever shot. Your sound will be useless. Although frustrating, the situation will be more frustrating if you don't have any extra batteries! Always pack several extra batteries for each type of mic you plan on using, and be sure to test your mics throughout the day to make sure their batteries haven't died. For shots where you only get one take—pyrotechnic or other special effects shots—consider using more than one mic so that if a battery dies in one mic, you'll still get sound from the other.

Using Your Mixer

If you're feeding multiple mics through a mixer, then you might want to consider "arranging" the different mics onto the separate left and right channels that you're feeding to your camera. This will allow you to keep different actors (or groups of actors) on separate channels. If there are two people who have a lot of overlapping dialogue, then consider using your mixer's *pan* control to place one person at the extreme left and the other person at the extreme right. This will help you maintain separation during overlapping dialogue, which will ease your audio editing chores.

Getting the Right Sound for the Picture

No matter which type of microphone you use, it's important to consider what the audio "feel" of the shot should be. An extreme wide shot, for example, should sound far away, while a close-up should have a more intimate sound. Consider this when selecting the type of mic to use for a shot.

When using an overhead mic, you'll tend to automatically compensate for these types of shot changes. Since the mic will have to be farther away from its subject during wider shots, but can afford to be brought in closer during close-ups, your audio recording will have a natural shift of audio "space."

The bass response of any microphone drops off over distance. Consequently, handheld mics and lavalier mics often have a richer, bassier tone—sometimes too rich and bassy—than an overhead mic. This difference in bass tone is called the *proximity effect,* and some microphones have special filters to reduce the amount of bass response in the mic. It's important to be aware of the proximity effect while miking so that you don't create mixing hassles in postproduction.

If a bass-heavy lavalier is used in a close-up, but a less-bassy overhead mic is used in a cutaway, the actor's voice will sound distractingly different from shot to shot. A good pair of headphones and careful attention to EQ while shooting will help you prevent such problems.

Testing Sound

After connecting your mics, you'll want to do a mic check to ensure that the microphones are working and that their input levels are set properly. Your camera might not have manual control of input levels, in which case, there's little you can do in the way of testing and preparing to record. Simply connect the mic to your camera, attach headphones to your camera, ask the subject to speak, and make sure you can hear her in your headphones. If her voice is too quiet, consider moving the microphone closer to her mouth, and then test again.

Hopefully, you're running your audio through a mixer. A mixer will not only allow you to use multiple microphones, but will also provide you with level controls—for adjusting the volume of each microphone. Level adjustment is crucial to getting good audio. If the record levels for a mic are too low, then the resulting sound will be too quiet. If they're too high, however, then distortion and noise can be introduced, and the resulting sound will be ugly and unintelligible.

Sound is measured in decibels, although there are two types of decibel scales. dBSPL (or decibel sound pressure loudness) is a measure of the actual acoustic power of a sound. This is the sound that we hear with our ears. A faint whisper from a few feet away might register at about 30 decibels, while a jackhammer usually meters at about 85 decibels. You should know that 135dB is considered painful, and is the point at which permanent hearing damage can occur.

A dBm (or decibel milliwatt) measures sound as units of electrical power and is measured using a VU meter that is displayed on your camera, record deck, or mixer. Through careful use of a meter, you can ensure that your audio level is set properly (see Figure 8.17).

Figure 8.17

An Edirol 4-channel portable mixer with a display featuring digital level meters.

Analog audio meters—the type you'll usually find on a video camera or deck—can seem a little strange at first, because they place "0" in the middle of the scale. The zero point does not mean *no sound*, but rather, *ideal sound*. Your goal when setting a level is to keep the VU meter readout as close to the ideal as possible. Using your mixer controls, you'll set the level when you test the mic, and then ride the level during your production (but not too much!), adjusting the level control to compensate for changes in the loudness of your subject.

With digital audio, the ideal level is somewhere between −12 and −20dB. This is the point where you'll want your audio level to peak on your VU meter. Try to set the level so that any spikes in the audio level don't go beyond this point. When digital audio peaks, the parts of the signal that go into the red are clipped out of the signal altogether. (If you're recording on an analog recording device, such as an analog video camera or tape deck, then you'll want the audio to peak a bit higher, at 0dB.)

It is during the mic test that you'll also perform any sweetening of the subject using a graphic equalizer (if your mixer has one). We'll discuss this type of EQ in detail in Chapter 15, "Sound Editing."

Reference Tone

Not all pieces of hardware and software use the exact same scales and meters for measuring the loudness of audio. Consequently, "ideal" sound on your camera might be too quiet on your editing system. Fortunately, there's a simple way to work around this. Just as you record color bars on your videotape to help calibrate color when editing, you should record some 60Hz audio reference tone on your videotape before you start shooting. You can then use this tone in postproduction to set your audio levels (more on this in Chapter 13, "Preparing to Edit").

Any camera that can generate color bars should be able to generate reference tone as well. If you're shooting double-system sound, you'll also need to record tone with your DAT or miniDisc recorder. If your camera can't generate bars and tone, then you can use your editing software to prerecord the tapes with bars and tone before you shoot.

Managing Your Set

Although it is possible to edit your sound in postproduction, you simply can't do many things. For example, you're not going to be able to remove the sound of a passing semitruck or of that obnoxious couple that was having an argument across the street from your shoot. Consequently, you're going to have to pay close attention to what your set sounds like.

This involves more than just yelling "Quiet on the set!" and then waiting for everyone to stop talking. Your ears have an incredible ability to adjust to—and eventually tune out—sounds that might ruin an otherwise good shoot. You'll need to stop and listen to—as well as look at—the set to pick out any potential audio troubles. Once you start paying attention, you might be surprised at all the "white noise" you didn't hear before: air conditioners, refrigerators, fans from computers and equipment. Any one of these things can render a soundtrack muddy and useless.

Recording Your Sound

With all your preparations complete (not just of sound, but of lighting, blocking, camera movement, cast preparation, costuming, set dressing, and so on), you're finally ready to start shooting. First, you'll need to get everything quiet on your set or location. When recording, "quiet" doesn't mean "no sound," but rather means to reduce the sound of your set to the natural ambience that belongs there. For example, if you're on a busy street, "quiet" will mean the sounds of car and foot traffic.

If you are recording your dialogue separate from the background—for example, a conversation being held in a crowded room full of people—the "quiet" might mean completely quiet. As explained earlier, after recording your dialogue takes with the crowd pantomiming silent conversation, you'll do a final take to record the sound of the crowd talking. These two elements will be mixed together later.

Once you've achieved quiet, you're ready to begin.

- **Tell your tape operator to start rolling.** If you're recording sound onto your camera, then the camera is all that will roll, but if you're recording non-sync sound on a separate recording deck, then that deck will have to be started also. For non-sync sound, you'll next need to use a slate.

- **Tell your performers and crew to get ready.** At this point, if you have a boom person, she will need to position the mic and double-check with the director of photography to ensure that the mic isn't in the frame.

- **After the call to *action*, your boom operator will begin following the sound.** At the same time, your sound person will monitor your audio levels (if you have such hardware) and adjust them to ensure proper recording.

- **Finally, with your take completed, *all* your decks will need to be stopped.** Next, you do it all again, and again, and again.

If there is a pause between takes, your sound person should take the opportunity to ensure that the sound was properly recorded. He should play back a little bit of both the beginning and end, and listen to the sound on headphones. This will help to ensure that good sound was recorded throughout the take. If sound was not recorded, it is the sound person's job to fix the problem and break the bad news that another take will be required.

Documentary filmmakers frequently don't have the downtime between multiple takes that narrative filmmakers have. Consequently, whenever he can get a break, the sound engineer should listen to ensure that the recorded audio sounds good. If there's no break during the day, then he should double-check different sections of the entire tape to make sure it's all usable. If not, then another day at the location might be required.

Room Tone

At some point during your shoot, your sound recordist will need to record 30 seconds to a minute of room tone. Room tone is nothing more than the sound of the room when no one is talking or making sound. This "empty" sound will be used by the sound editor to patch gaps in the soundtrack and to cover rough sound edits.

Because you are trying to record the natural ambient sound of your location, be sure to record your room tone after your set has been fully dressed. Recording it before might produce a different quality tone, as there will be fewer sound-absorbing set pieces and props. The end of your shooting day is usually the best time to record room tone. Simply ask everyone on the set to be quiet and start your recorder.

Run-and-Gun Audio

If you're shooting corporate videos, documentaries, "reality" productions, or any type of project where you need to shoot quickly on-the-fly, then you won't have the time or opportunity for complex audio setups, and you'll need to have your gear organized and ready to move at all times (see Figure 8.18). At best, you might be able to get people outfitted with wireless lavs or be able to give them a handheld microphone. Ideally, you'll want to have a boom mic and operator, but if you're a single-person crew, or don't have the budget for a boom, then you should at least invest in a quality, very directional shotgun mic and mount it on your camera.

As we said earlier, one problem with shotgun mics is that they can also pick up sounds coming from behind your subject. A directional mic will minimize these problems, and you can further improve your chances of getting good audio by moving in close to your subject. (Obviously, you don't want to get so close that you must use a wide-angle focal length that will make their face look weird.)

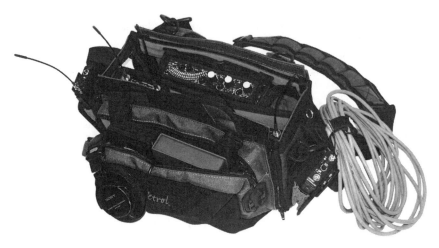

Figure 8.18

A typical carrying case for run-and-gun sound recording.

A Crew of One

If you're really working on a shoestring, you might not have a crew of any kind, leaving yourself in the position of having to do *everything* while shooting. If you're shooting a scene with actors, you can often get your performers to assume some of your crew duties, but if you're shooting a low-budget documentary on your own, you'll usually have access to only your own two hands. Unfortunately, lack of personnel doesn't mean you can scrimp on the issues and details presented here. However, you might want to adjust your gear if you're shooting on your own.

Obviously, managing multiple recording devices is going to be more complicated than recording audio to your camera, so unless there's some special reason for outboard audio recording, stick to recording directly into your camera.

Since you don't have a boom operator, you'll be forced to rely on lavaliers or a high-quality, on-camera shotgun mic. Lavaliers are the best option in this instance because they can deliver excellent quality with little work on your part. (Wireless lavs are even better for single-person shoots, as they save you the trouble of managing cables.) If you must use an on-camera mic, opt for a very directional microphone, so as to minimize the recording of extra background sounds, echoes, and room noises.

Because audio is so critical, when budgeting your project, you should prioritize the purchase or rental of a good mic and boom over just about anything else. Finally, hire, beg, cajole, bribe, blackmail—use whatever techniques you have to get someone to operate your boom for you so that you don't have to face a single-person shoot.

As with any kind of audio recording, your most important task will be to monitor the audio recording through headphones while shooting. Because this can make things more difficult if you're conducting an interview, you might opt to only periodically monitor your audio, but you should check in on it fairly regularly. Dead batteries, the unnoticed activation of an air conditioner, power problems—all of these things can cause your audio to turn bad. Monitoring is the only way to ensure you're recording the sounds you need.

Gear Checklist

Your audio equipment usually requires a big assortment of little items. Cables, adapters, batteries, stands, the microphones themselves—if you forget any of these things, you'll be severely audio challenged when you get to your set. Before you walk out the door, set up all of your audio equipment and make sure it works. Then make a list of every item—even the smallest adapters and cables. If you want to be extra secure, get some tape and mark each item with a number, and code each item appropriately on your list. Then, when you're in a hurry, you can simply make sure that you have the right number of items. If a number is missing, a quick glance at your list should tell you what you need to find.

We recommend taking the same approach to audio that you should take to video: record the cleanest, least-modified sound you can. Then, in postproduction, add whatever modifications, effects, grunge, and extra sound you want. In addition to more flexibility (if you decide you don't want a particular sound, you'll be able to move it), this approach will probably yield higher-quality results. We'll cover sound editing in Chapter 15.

9

Shooting and Directing

Photo credit: William MacCollum

This is it. You have a script or outline. You've determined a production schedule based on your budget. You've selected a film or video format, and chosen a camera to purchase or rent. You've planned the shoot, using storyboards, shot lists, and camera diagrams. You've secured a location or created a set. You have a cast. You've researched and tested tricky lighting setups and any special effects shots that you might need. You've learned how to use the camera and carefully selected the audio equipment necessary for your production. You may have even devoted a day or two to a test shoot.

Now, all the hard work you've done is about to pay off. You're ready to start using your camera to shoot some footage. In many ways, shooting is the best part of the entire movie-making process. You get to go out to fun locations, you get to boss people around, and you get to use cool gear. It's also the first time that you can start to see the ideas in your head turn into something real. Unfortunately, shooting can also be really difficult. Many things can go wrong, there's lots to keep track of, and you're usually working against the clock. During the shoot, you're going to have to muster all of your artistic, logistical, and managerial sensibilities to create each shot.

Up to this point, almost everything in the book has been about preparing to shoot, and there still are some things to do in the week, days, or even hours before the shoot begins. Arriving on set fully prepared will save you time and money, and you won't have to worry about appeasing a bored, frustrated cast and crew.

The Shooting Script

By now, it's been a while since the final draft of your script was completed. You've probably gotten comments on the script from higher-ups: producers, your boss, your professor, and so on. The script has been read by the cast and crew, and you've heard their opinions as well. Now is the time to decide if you want to incorporate or ignore their ideas and suggestions. It's also the time to a take a good look at the dialogue in your script and revise it if needed. Perhaps the age of a character has changed due to a casting choice. Or you have to shoot a love scene in an apartment instead of a castle because of budgetary constraints. By this point, you should have staged a table reading and read through a rehearsal of (at the very least) the key elements of your script. If you noticed actors tripping over too many words, awkward phrasing, and unnecessary repetition, now is the time to fix it. Finally, you may need to resolve technical issues, logistical problems, or reorganize the order of the scenes.

Once you've made these types of content changes, it's time to "number" the script, and each scene gets a number. (In case you're confused, if it has a slugline, it's considered a separate scene.) Later on, if you decide to omit a scene, you can cross it out on the script and write "omit" on the scene, but you do not have to renumber the script. These scene numbers will be recorded on the slate and used later on to organize the media.

When you are done, clearly date the draft and label it the "shooting script." Distribute copies of the shooting script to anyone who needs it: actors, producers, the director of photography, and other crew members. Everyone on the set should have read this version of the script by the time you are ready to roll.

Updating the Shooting Script

It's very common to make script changes once you start shooting. Locations fall out, you realize a scene is redundant, and so on. After you number and distribute the script, you should "lock" the page numbers in your screenplay writing software. This means that the page numbers will stay the same, even if rewrites occur. So you can simply email any new or changed material, and the cast and crew can insert it into their scripts without having to reprint the entire script again. That way, the page numbers will stay the same, and you can all be on the same page—literally and figuratively. Traditional Hollywood productions use different colors of paper for each revision so that you can quickly tell if a script is up-to-date.

Script Changes

Script changes during the shoot can be the biggest cause of confusion on the set, so take care to make sure that everyone is kept up-to-date and give your actors time to learn any new lines.

Directing

The job of directing a movie is huge and in a way, this entire book encompasses the subject, because, after all the director is responsible for everything. On the set, everyone listens to what the director says, even if the director is making a bad choice. A typical film set is run like a military hierarchy, and no one is supposed to question the director. From time to time, someone may subtly suggest that there is an alternate way of doing something, but it is rare to be directly confronted by anyone except the highest ranking crew members unless you have a very inexperienced crew. In other words, as director, the successes are yours, but so are the failures.

To be a good director, you need to know everyone else's job. It may not be feasible to know the gory details of each position on the crew, but you need to know what they do and why they do it and also what can go wrong. On low budget sets, everyone wears lots of hats because the crew is usually small. On big budget sets, each job has a very specific description and is often regulated by union rules. You cannot ask the grip to hand you a prop, for example.

With so much going on technically and with crew members, it's easy to lose sight of the director's primary focus: storytelling. Many directors set aside a few minutes or an hour at the beginning or end of the day to review the scenes for the next day's shoot. If you are the director, this is the time to remind yourself what is important, what the key beats of the story are, and what you need to shoot to make sure the scene is successful. In other words, it is the time to really focus on what your vision for the scene/film is and make sure that you can articulate it to yourself and others.

For example, if you have a comedic scene where the lead character bursts into tears after losing a call on a cell phone, you'll need to keep in mind that the comedy comes from the extreme over-reaction on the part of the main character to a mundane event. When your actor suggests that it would be funnier to get angry and throw the phone instead of crying, you'll need to decide if this is a good suggestion or not. If you've clarified your vision of the scene in your head, it will be easier to know the best response. In addition, if you've successfully communicated your vision to the cast (and crew), it will be more likely that the suggestions you get from them are good ones.

Sometimes cast or crew members make brilliant suggestions, and those can often be the hardest to recognize as wrong. The more compelling the idea, the harder it is to not say yes. This is where your vision of the big picture of the project is key. Often, actors make suggestions with their own character in mind, directors of photography and production designers make suggestions with the visuals in mind, and so on. That doesn't mean they are self-serving; it simply means they are doing their job and focusing on the part of the filmmaking process that they are responsible for. The director, however, is responsible for everything. Knowing your vision for the film and therefore the details of the film is invaluable. If there is a simple definition for directing, it is having a vision for the story and keeping everything in line with that vision. The stronger your vision is, the easier it is to direct.

Rehearsals

Film and video productions are notorious for scheduling little or no rehearsal time for actors. However, rehearsals can be a valuable experience for both actors and directors.

Many big budget Hollywood movies set aside two weeks to rehearse an entire feature film. Other directors, like John Cassavetes, are famous for rehearsing for months. How you decide to work with actors is up to you, but at the very least, plan on spending some time choreographing the movement of the actors—also known as *blocking*—for the camera. The more action you have in your scene, the more time you should spend blocking. Blocking a fight scene in a way that looks realistic, but also fits with the visual style of your film, can be a big challenge. If your film has an important fight scene, consider using a fight choreographer. If you have time, consider shooting the rehearsals to get a feel for the flow of the scene and for planning a shot list. If you can, avoid waiting until the day of the shoot to start blocking. Working out the blocking of a scene can reveal many unforeseen problems in advance of the shoot itself.

If your rehearsal will go beyond basic blocking, you should consider coming up with a plan for the rehearsal. Take some time to re-read the scenes you will be rehearsing and think about what is most important to you as a director in these scenes. Having this sort of clarity about what the scene is about can be invaluable in rehearsals and on the set as well. We highly recommend the book, *Directing Actors* by Judith Weston, for detailed information on rehearsal techniques and directing actors in general.

Sometimes, actors aren't the only ones who need to rehearse. If you have complicated lighting effects or camera movements or challenging special effects scenes, schedule some time with the camera, lighting, and special effects crew members for a tech rehearsal.

Rehearsals aren't necessary for documentary-style productions. However, commentators, on-camera hosts, and voice-over talent can benefit from a quick warm-up or read-through of the material. Seasoned producers often take a few minutes to speak with interview subjects before they shoot to break the ice and make sure everyone is on the same page before the interview begins.

Stage a Table Reading

Before you shoot your project, gather a group of actors or friends to do a table reading of your script, which is the reading of a script from start to end using either actors or non-actors. It is called a "table reading" because usually the group reads while seated at a table, rather than standing or going through the motions of acting. Try to avoid having anyone play more than one character in the same scene, and cast a separate person as the narrator who will read the stage directions in the script—often the majority of the reading. Invite friends and colleagues to participate, and either hand out a questionnaire or initiate an informal discussion of the project afterward. Use this information to revise the shooting script.

Managing the Set

There are many things to keep track of during a shoot, no matter how big or small your production is. If you're directing a small crew, you might find yourself performing many of the tasks that would normally be delegated to others on a bigger crew. If you have a large crew, then you'll have crew members who can take care of some of your management concerns, but you may feel like you're losing control of your own project. Whatever the size of the crew, good on-set management skills are always an asset. Part of good management includes setting a tone for the day. Is it going to be casual and relaxed or tightly scheduled and serious? It's worth considering the tone of the material you are shooting on that day and taking cues from there to establish an appropriate mood for the actors. As the director or producer, the cast and crew will look at your attitude and act accordingly. If you spend 20 minutes chatting socially with a friend who is helping out on the set, you'll give the impression that there's plenty of time to get what you need, whether or not this is actually true.

When you first get to your set or location, you (or the person with the appropriate job—usually a producer or production manager) need to ensure that all crew and cast members have arrived with their gear. In addition, you need to check that you have all power, cables, lights, and other necessary pieces of hardware. Make certain that nothing unexpected has developed at your location—bad weather, noisy construction workers, and so forth. Finally, talk to the actors and key crew members to find out if they have any questions about what they'll be doing in the scenes that you'll be shooting.

Camera Crew Who's Who

Lighting and shooting a feature film is a big job that requires many people. Here's a list of the camera and lighting crew members you'll find on a typical big-budget film set:

- **Director of photography (DP), a.k.a. cinematographer:** This is the person in charge of all camera operations and lighting. With a skeleton crew, the DP might operate the camera. With a bigger crew, the DP will hire a camera operator.

- **Camera operator:** This is the person behind the camera, who works in tandem with the DP.

- **First assistant camera (AC):** The first AC is responsible for loading the camera, setting up the lenses and filters for each shot, and making sure the shot is in focus.

Camera Crew Who's Who (continued)

- **Second AC:** The second assistant camera (AC) is responsible for keeping camera reports, slating each shot, and sometimes loading film or videotape into the camera.

- **Gaffer:** The gaffer is the head electrician on the set and is responsible for directing the setup of the lights and other electrical equipment.

- **Best boy and electricians:** The best boy is the first assistant under the gaffer and is responsible for managing the other set electricians in the setting of lights and other electrical work.

- **Key grip:** The key grip assists the gaffer with lighting and is responsible for coordinating the placement of grip equipment (flags, nets, and so on), special riggings, and the hardware used to move the camera.

- **Dolly grip:** Big movies have special grips who are employed to operate cranes, dollies, and other heavy equipment.

- **Camera department production assistant (PA):** The camera department often needs a PA (or two) to run errands to the equipment rental house, purchase film stock or videotape, and so on.

Putting Plans into Action

In Chapter 5, "Planning Your Shoot," we discussed storyboards, camera diagrams, and shot lists. Now they'll come in handy. It's possible that weeks or months have gone by since you first planned your shoot, so it's likely that you'll need to revise these elements so that they match the shooting script.

Whatever the nature of your project, you should always arrive on the set with a shot list. Documentary filmmakers will find it useful to second-guess what will happen during the shoot and plan their coverage in advance. Is a close-up of a sign or other object needed? An establishing shot? A shot list serves as a simple checklist detailing the day's plan, and it can go a long way toward helping you achieve your goals and communicating your vision to the crew so that you get the coverage you need for each scene.

Get Releases on the Set

For documentary producers and anyone else shooting in a "real" location, it is important that you get releases from anyone in the shot and from the owner of the location. It is much easier to obtain releases as you shoot than it is to go back later and track people down. If you succeed in selling your project to a TV network or other distributor, their legal department will require these releases. For locations filled with lots of people, it is standard to post a sign at the entrance of the location informing those who enter that they will be taped. For legal purposes, have your camera person get a quick shot of this sign.

Double-Check Your Camera Settings

Right before you shoot, go over all of the controls and settings on your camera to make sure they are all set appropriately. Be certain that any features you don't want, such as auto iris, are turned off. Ensure that your sharpening and white-balance settings are configured appropriately. Make sure you have the correct frame rate, image resolution and aspect ratio set. Bear in mind that some settings might change back to their defaults when you power down the camera or even put it in standby mode. So you'll need to double-check your settings anytime you change tape or do anything else that takes the camera out of recording mode.

If you are shooting from a tripod or some other image-stabilizing device, turn off any electronic or optical image-stabilization features on your camera. Electronic image-stabilization (EIS) algorithms typically shoot at higher shutter speeds. In addition to producing a harsher image, you'll see a reduction in gain. Some EIS mechanisms will also soften your image, even when the camera is sitting still.

Optical image-stabilization mechanisms won't change your image quality, but they will drain your battery life. Since you won't need stabilization if you're using a tripod, turn off optical stabilization when your camera is tripod-mounted.

And don't forget to make sure your audio equipment is working properly as well.

The Protocol of Shooting

Because a movie shoot requires the coordination of many people, each with unique job concerns, it's important to stay organized and follow a regular procedure on your set.

Believe it or not, there is a very specific protocol to follow when calling "Action" on a traditional film shoot. Shooting a shot begins when the assistant director yells "Roll sound." The sound recordist starts the sound recorder and replies "Speed" when his equipment is ready. Next, the assistant director calls "Roll camera," and the camera person answers "Speed" once the camera is ready. The assistant director calls "Marker," and the slate is clapped for synchronization (see Figure 9.1). Finally, the director calls "Action!" Even if you're not using a sound recordist, assistant director, or a camera operator, it's still good practice to warn everyone on the set vocally that you're about to start shooting, and give your camera and audio equipment a few seconds to get going before you call "Action." Additionally, actors and crew members are expected to keep going until the director calls "Cut." If the disk, tape, or film stock runs out in the middle of a take, the camera or sound operator calls "Roll out" to end the take.

Respect for Acting

In the sea of technical details, you might forget the most important thing on your set: the cast. Here are a few quick tips on how to help them give a great performance:

- **Try to maintain some type of story continuity as you shoot.** It's often necessary to shoot out of sequence, but at least try to stay continuous within each scene.

- **Have a closed set if you're doing a scene that involves highly emotional performances or nudity.** In addition, try to keep your crew as small as possible for these shots.

Figure 9.1

A typical camera slate marked with the scene number and take number.

- **Respect actors' opinions about the characters they're playing.** Even if you wrote the script yourself, you might find that they have new ideas that make your script even better. Remember, they've probably spent the last week or two thinking a lot about that character, and they might have come to a deeper understanding than you have.

- **Try to remain sensitive to the mood and material of the scene.** If the actor must play a sad scene when everyone is joking around on the set, the actor might have a hard time concentrating or getting in the right mood.

Make a Shot List

Take your shooting script or outline and use it to make a shot list. Think about how you want the final edited project to look and make sure the shots you've listed will get the results you desire. Take into account the assets and limitations of the crew, locations, cast, and other key elements. Take the most complicated scene in your script and make a camera and lighting diagram as well. If you already have storyboards, shot lists, and camera diagrams, go over them and make sure they are appropriate for the actual conditions of your pending shoot.

Organization on the Set

All productions benefit from having someone keep a record of what happens on the set. The traditional Hollywood method uses a script supervisor to record all the shots as they occur, along with important details. Using a script supervisor is not necessary for non-scripted projects, such as documentaries and corporate videos. Instead, a field producer keeps careful notes about the shoot. Either way, on-set records are used later during postproduction to help the editor and others who were not present on the set understand what was shot, how it was shot, and why it was shot. When problems occur during the shoot, the script supervisor's or field producer's notes offer an explanation and often point to a solution.

Script Supervising for Scripted Projects

The script supervisor's job is to keep track of the number of pages that are shot each day and to make sure that the camera angles and eyelines are framed correctly to cut together later on, that continuity is maintained, and that the camera slates are marked with the correct take numbers and other information. As if this weren't enough to keep track of, they are also responsible for creating a lined script during the shoot (see Figure 9.2).

Continuity

During a shoot, continuity is the process of keeping track of dialogue changes, matching camera angles, actors' positions, and wardrobe and props so that the footage from shot-to-shot, and day-to-day, will cut together. You can use a digital still camera to take photos to keep track of continuity.

When a script is prepared for production, each scene is given a scene number. In turn, each shot in that scene is given its own shot number. Generally, the master shot is named according to the scene number; for example, scene 23, and each take is numbered consecutively: 23-1, 23-2, 23-3, and so on. The next shot in the scene, say a close-up of the lead actor, would be called 23a, and so on. This information is recorded on the slate and also on the notes kept on the shooting script by the script supervisor, usually handwritten on the facing page of the shooting script itself (see Figure 9.2). Usually, the best takes are marked with a circle around the shot number. These circled takes are the shots that the director thought were the best takes during the shoot.

For complicated scenes, a script supervisor's notes might include diagrams of the set, still images for continuity, and more. In addition, the script supervisor lines the script, drawing lines with arrows to show the portion of the script that each shot covers. Be aware that these lines indicate the dialogue that was *actually* covered during the shot, as opposed to the director's idea of what should be covered.

Clearly, script supervising isn't necessary for every shoot, but the longer your project and the more complicated the shoot, the more valuable this information can be later on.

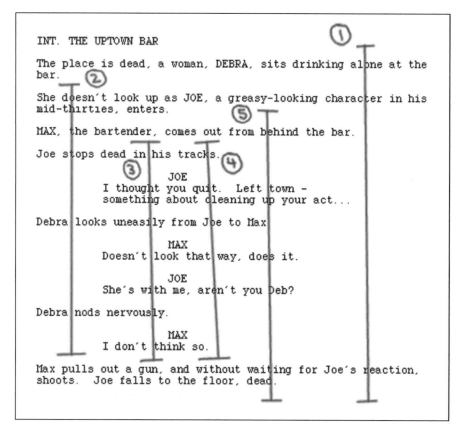

Figure 9.2

A lined script and script supervisor's marks.

Documentary Field Notes

For documentaries, there is no such thing as a script supervisor; however, there is usually someone on the set to take field notes. Field notes are not as formalized as script supervisor notes, but they contain the same sorts of information: content, technical notes, and so on. If the shoot involves multiple takes—such as the taping of an on-camera host—the takes are numbered, and the director selects circled takes, just as they do on a scripted project. With documentaries, separate "takes" don't always exist—rather the camera operators simply cover the scene as best they can without stopping the camera unnecessarily. The field notes serve to describe what happened and to give the timecodes of key moments so that later on, people working in postproduction can quickly find important material.

Once your project is shot, and you've got it "in the can," it's time to move on to postproduction. The rest of this book covers building a workstation for postproduction, editing picture and sound, color correction, titling, rotoscoping for special effects, and outputting your final project.

10

DSLRs and Other Advanced Shooting Situations

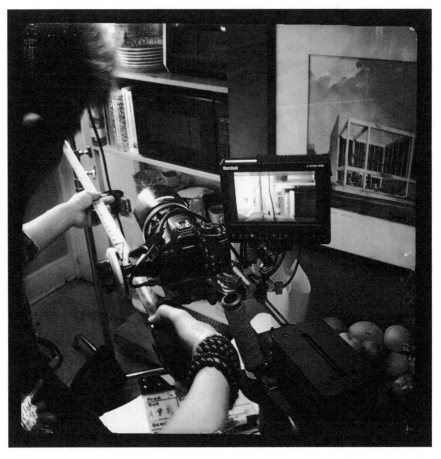

Photo credit: William MacCollum

One of the biggest recent trends in digital filmmaking is the use of DSLR cameras to shoot HD video. With their extremely good image quality, low price, great low-light performance, and huge selection of lenses, a DSLR can be a great option for the filmmaker on a budget. But since DSLR cameras weren't designed for shooting moving images, there are many challenges associated with their use, and shooting video with them is complicated. In this chapter, we'll go over all of the special issues and gear that can make your DSLR video shoot a success.

Many of the advanced shooting techniques in this chapter apply to shooting with DSLR cameras, but they are not limited to DSLRs. In fact, many of these techniques are used when shooting traditional 35mm film and also high-end digital cinema. Interchangeable lenses, double-system sound, advanced camera rigging and supports, viewing live video on the set, and using tapeless media are all covered in this chapter. In addition, we provide a discussion of shooting with multiple cameras, recording double-system sound and the special requirements that are necessary for shooting blue- or green-screen special effects footage.

Thanks to the DSLR trend, advanced filmmaking technology is now affordable for indie filmmakers. Using this technology requires more equipment, and more expertise on the set, but in return you'll get extremely high production values.

What's Different with a DSLR?

DSLR cameras that shoot HD video can be found on all types of shoots, from indie features to network TV shows. Why? Because they're cheap, and the footage looks fantastic.

So what's different when shooting with a DSLR?

Still camera bodies differ greatly from video camera bodies. Still cameras are designed with a handgrip on the right side, which leaves your left hand free to make adjustments to the lens. This works great for still photographs, but it can be a challenge when shooting handheld video. A professional camera has a body style that lets you balance the camera on your right shoulder. This allows you to use your body to stabilize the camera, takes the weight of the camera off your arms, and serves to make the camera an extension of your body: when you turn, the camera turns as well.

To make a DSLR more ergonomic, and to provide a shooting experience that is more like a "real" video camera, you'll want to buy a special rig that eases handholding (Figure 10.1). Think of a rig as a hard exoskeleton that your still camera failed to develop on its own, or a video camera–shaped cage for your DSLR. Even if you are not going to be doing much handholding, a rig includes a rod that can be used to provide support for a large lens, especially if the lens is bigger than your camera.

Follow focus

Weights

Figure 10.1

A still camera enhanced with the Cinema Field Bundle from Red Rock Micro. This rig is designed to provide better handholding ergonomics and includes rods, counter weights, grips, and a follow focus mechanism.

Grips

Rods

Shoulder rest

One of the big advantages of a DSLR is that you can change the lens, which opens up a huge arena of custom shooting options. A standard video camera has a built-in zoom lens that is designed to cover a variety of shooting situations from wide field of view to very telephoto. But if you want an extreme wide angle or an extreme telephoto shot, you are out of luck. With a DSLR, you can have a selection of lenses on hand for any special shooting needs.

Or you might select a lens that can handle low-light situations. Lenses with an f-stop rating of 1.2 or 1.4 can do very well shooting on a city street at night without the need for additional lighting or heavy gain boosting. This can be a huge advantage to filmmakers who want to shoot night exteriors with a limited budget.

Those wider apertures (and the larger sensors used in DSLRs) also give you the option for a more shallow depth of field, something that is very difficult to achieve with a normal video camera. While the ability to shoot shallow depth of field gives you more creative options, it also means you have to be extra careful about focus, and focusing with a DSLR can be a challenge, especially if the camera or subject is moving. Most DLSRs do not allow for auto focusing while recording video, and if they do, auto focus is often slow and jerky. To get the most out of your camera, you'll need to use manual focus.

Another difference is that there is no motorized zoom when using a DSLR. Some filmmakers do not like zooms, preferring to use a dolly or other device to move the camera closer to the subject, to preserve a uniform sense of depth in the scene. But for documentaries and other unscripted projects, zooming can be an invaluable tool. Any lens that is equipped with a manual zoom knob will work great, and you might find you prefer it to a motorized zoom. If zooming is important to you, be sure to use a lens that has a zoom knob (or a place to install one).

We mentioned in Chapter 4, "Choosing a Camera," that DSLRs are not great at recording audio. They only have two channels of audio, they don't have high-quality XLR audio inputs, and every time you touch the camera body or lens, that noise will get recorded. The most common work-around for this is to record your audio to a separate device, a process known as double-system sound. We'll explain how to record double-system sound later in this chapter.

While shooting HD video, the optical viewfinder in most DSLRs is disabled, leaving only the LCD viewfinder. It can be tough to judge focus or even see an LCD display at times, so there are several types of enhanced viewfinders on the market to compensate for this, such as the one shown in Figure 10.2.

Figure 10.2

A still camera outfitted with a Zacuto base plate and Z-finder enhanced viewfinder.

And finally, DSLRs can overheat. While overheating doesn't mean that you end up with a melted handful of plastic and metal slag, it does mean that the camera might shut itself down after about 20 minutes to cool down. So, if your project requires very long takes, a DSLR might not be practical.

All told, these various accessories can add up to a lot of gear attached to your camera (Figure 10.3). That's another reason that DSLR rigs are popular. We've got a selection of photos throughout this chapter showing different types of DSLR rigging.

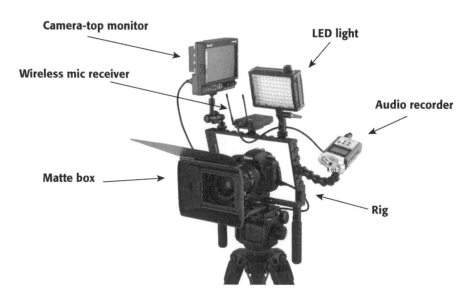

Figure 10.3

A fully-accessorized Canon DSLR camera outfitted with a matte box, camera-top monitor, double-system audio recording device, LED light and wireless microphone receiver—all held in place with a Norbert Filmmaker rig by K-Tek.

Guerrilla Shooting

DSLR cameras are very low profile (if they're not outfitted with all the gear discussed in this chapter) and that means they're better for shooting guerilla-style (for example, without a permit or permission).

DSLR Camera Settings for HD Video

Still cameras that shoot HD video are still cameras first, and video cameras second. So the first step in shooting HD video with a DSLR is to change the camera settings to accommodate video capture. Also, if you have a lot of video camera experience and are new to using a still camera, there are some camera settings that you might not be familiar with.

- **Start by setting the camera to video mode.** The available menu options and other settings on the camera will change accordingly.

- **Select a frame rate and size.** We chose 1920x1080 at 30fps (see Figure 10.4)

- **Select manual exposure.** This lets you choose the ISO, shutter speed, and f-stop yourself.

- **Set the ISO.** ISO is a rating system originally used in still photography to describe the light sensitivity of various film stocks. Digital still cameras don't use film stock, but the light sensitivity of the image sensor is measured using the same ISO scale used to rate film. Increasing the ISO is the same as boosting the gain on a standard video camera. How high you can push the ISO before you see visible noise in your footage depends on which camera you have, so you'll want to do some tests before you commit to a specific high ISO.

- **Set the shutter speed.** High-end video cameras let you adjust the shutter speed and so do DSLRs. A "normal" shutter speed is usually about 1/50th of a second for 24fps shooting and 1/60th of a second for 30fps shooting. If you want to reduce motion blur and other movement artifacts, choose a higher shutter speed although be aware that some people find video shot with a high shutter speed aesthetically unappealing. If you want to increase motion blur, choose a slower shutter speed.

- **Set the f-stop.** Again, depth-of-field control is one of the great advantages of a DSLR over a video camera, and you'll manipulate depth of field by carefully choosing an aperture. Wider apertures (lower f-numbers) will give you shallower depth of field, letting you blur out backgrounds to bring more attention to your subject.

- **Set the focus.** Although some DSLRs can auto focus while recording, the usefulness of this feature is extremely limited because the auto focus on still cameras seeks focus by zooming in and out until focus is achieved—not something that makes for great video. Manual focusing can be a complex process, and we will discuss it in greater detail later in this chapter.

- **Set the white balance.** Most digital still cameras offer a selection of white-balance presets: tungsten, daylight, overcast, fluorescent, and so on. But for complex lighting situations, it's best to custom white balance. On most DSLRs, you'll set custom white balance by shooting a still photo of a white object (such as a piece of paper) in your lighting setup. This picture will be used as the source for the custom white-balance setting.

- **Decide if you need image stabilization**. If your lens has image stabilization (IS), it can help you get smoother footage when handholding. If you're shooting from a tripod, it's usually best to turn image stabilization off, as many IS systems can be confused by the smooth pans that a tripod allows.

Figure 10.4

Carefully go through your camera's menu to select the settings for recording HD video.

In addition to the above settings, there are several features offered on your DSLR that you will want to avoid:

- **Disable any image enhancement settings.** Canon cameras offer a selection of "Picture styles." Other manufacturers use their own terminology, but whatever it's called, you don't need it when you're shooting HD video. Image enhancement settings are primarily designed for still photographs. Instead, choose "Neutral" and if you want to enhance the image, you can do so later in postproduction.

- **Avoid cropping or any other image manipulation.** Again, you can do this stuff in post.

- **Turn off auto exposure and auto white-balance.** It's not so much that the camera can't choose a good exposure or white balance for you, it's that you don't want it to do so in the middle of your shot.

Hacking Your DSLR

Magic Lantern is a product that enhances the firmware in Canon cameras to add features such as on-screen audio meters and zebra stripes. But be aware that installing it may void your warranty.

Working with Interchangeable Lenses

Until very recently, standard low- to mid-level video cameras came with a lens that was built-in and could not be changed. However, thanks to the DSLR trend, that is changing fast, and there are several lower-priced cameras on the market that offer the best of both worlds: the image sensor size and lens interchangeability of DSLRs housed in a camera body that is designed for motion (see Figure 10.5).

Figure 10.5

The latest generation of video cameras in the $5,000 range, such as the Panasonic AG AF-100, offer large image sensors and interchangeable lenses.

So why is changing the lens so great?

Primarily because it results in a truly customizable camera. You can opt for an ultra-wide fisheye lens or an extreme telephoto lens—both of which are far out of the range of a standard built-in lens. You can also have a selection of lenses on hand to suit your shooting needs (Figure 10.6).

Because you can change lenses, you might opt for an extremely high-quality lens. Lenses by Zeiss, Schneider, Nikon, and the Canon L series are known for their high-quality optics that will result in better looking footage.

Also important is that some modern prime lenses are extremely good at shooting in low-light situations. Look for lenses with an f-stop rating of 1.2 or 1.4 like the one in Figure 10.7.

What Lenses Do I Need?

At the most basic level, you will need a wide-angle lens, a normal lens (one with a field of view roughly equivalent to the human eye), and a telephoto lens. Another option is to choose three zoom lenses: one in the wide-angle range, one in the middle, and one that covers a range of telephoto angles.

Figure 10.6

Prime lenses for cinema shooting usually come in matched sets, like this set of Zeiss CP2 Compact Primes. Note the distance markings on the lenses for setting focus.

Some lenses such as the 50mm Canon f1.4 lens shown in Figure 10.7 are more suited to portrait-like shots, and you'll use them a lot for singles of your actors or for interview setups. Their wide maximum aperture makes it easy to achieve a shallow depth of field. Wider lenses are more suited to big panoramas and can help when shooting in cramped spaces. Comedies are typically shot with wide images, because they make people look a little distorted, and typically make them appear much smaller in their environment. If your schedule is tight, using zoom lenses means you won't have to change lenses as frequently. Certain camera functions are lens-specific: zoom control, focusing, and image stabilization.

The lenses you choose will ultimately be tied to the story you are shooting so there is no quick answer to what the right lens selection is for your project. But the good news is that most major cities have rental houses that rent lenses at a reasonable price, and you can always send someone to go pick one up if you find you need a specific lens mid-shoot. If you don't have access to a rental house, consider an online rental source such as *borrowlenses.com* or *rentglass.com*.

Figure 10.7

This 50mm Canon lens has an f-stop rating of 1.4 and has distance markings for measuring focus. Note the use of paper tape to set focus marks for pulling focus.

How to Get a Shallow Depth of Field

Shallow depth of field is a look that many filmmakers covet, but achieving it is technically challenging and involves many different variables. The lighting, the lens, the placement of the subject, and the camera all play a role. Here are some basics for getting shallow depth of field.

- **Shoot in low light.** This will let you use a lower f-stop, which results in a more shallow depth of field.

- **Use ND filters** (see Figures 10.8 and 10.9). If you need to shoot in brighter light, you can still change the amount of light coming into the camera by adding ND filters so that you can use a lower f-stop.

- **Use a longer lens.** Longer lenses need more light so you can use a lower f-stop. They also compress distance within the image, which separates your subject from the background even more.

- **Increase the shutter speed.** A faster shutter speed lets in less light.

- **Decrease the gain/ISO.**

Figure 10.8

Matte boxes like this one by Chrosziel fit onto the lens and let you change filters quickly and easily.

Figure 10.9

Filters, like these by Schneider Optics, are designed to simply drop into the frame of the matte box.

A shallow depth of field can look very pleasing but it means that setting the focus is crucial. If you don't know much about setting focus manually, read on.

Measuring and Pulling Focus

If you plan to project your video in a theater, proper focus is critical. Things that look focused on a small LCD screen might, in fact, be slightly out of focus. When these images are blown up to the big screen, the focus problems will become visible. Nowadays, even a large TV monitor can expose focus problems.

Video assist monitors like the ones shown later in this chapter can help, but even they are very small when compared to a large flat panel TV or a screen in a theater.

The easiest way to keep your footage in focus is to shoot in bright daylight with a high f-stop. Shooting with a wide-angle lens also helps hide any focus or depth-of -field issues, because things in the background will likely appear smaller, due to the wide angle. So as long as you don't have anything coming too close to the camera, you can rest assured that everything will be in focus.

Unfortunately, the look of a wide lens and bright daylight isn't always the ideal choice, aesthetically. If you're shooting mostly at night, or you want a shallow depth of field, chances are high that you'll need more advanced techniques for setting focus.

In Chapter 7, "Using the Camera," we discussed the basic technique of zooming in or using focus assist to set the focus by eye. This method will work, and it is sufficient for a project that will be viewed on a small scale, such as a Web video. But for projects destined for bigger screens, the only safe way to set the focus is to measure it. Measuring focus takes the guesswork out of the equation and means that you can feel confident in your footage, even if you can't judge the focus by eye.

Measuring Focus

If your camera lens has a focus ring with distance measurements marked, it can measure the distance between your subject and the camera to ensure perfect focus. Most cameras have a mark somewhere on the camera body to indicate where you should measure focus from—check your camera manual if you can't find it. In the case of digital cameras, the focal plane is where the image sensor is positioned. In some instances, focus is measured from a mark on the lens instead of the camera body. Note that you can't be sure of the focus markings on your lens or camera unless you've tested them and found the marks to be accurate. To measure focus, a standard measuring tape is used to check the distance between the mark on the camera/lens and the subject in the shot. Often, the biggest challenge in measuring focus has to do with figuring out where the actors will end up during the course of a shot and also the fact that you may need to plan on several points of focus during a shot.

Pulling Focus

Everyone's heard of actors "missing their mark." The mark is actually the focus mark. The assistant camera operator will put marks with colored tape on the floor (out of view) and the actors will know to hit that mark for a certain line. There will usually be at least two marks for each actor in every shot, if not more. Once the marks are established, focus is measured for each mark and then focus marks are recorded on the lens, either using a Sharpie marker on a piece of paper tape or using a china marker on the follow focus mechanism (Figure 10.10).

During the take, the camera assistant will adjust the focus, following the movements of the actors—a process called *pulling focus*. Pulling focus requires choreographing the movement of the actors and the camera during blocking. There is an art to pulling focus, especially when shooting with a shallow depth of field. A *rack focus* is an intentionally visible shift in focus when there are two subjects in the frame and the focus is pulled from one subject to the other.

Figure 10.10

A camera equipped with a follow focus mechanism by Red Rock Micro and an assortment of gears to fit various lens sizes.

Advanced Camera Rigging and Supports

When people talk about camera supports, the first thing that comes to mind is the tripod. Tripods are very important and a good tripod for recording moving images is a little more complicated than tripods that are designed for still photography. Top-of-the-line video tripods have a fluid head and are often designed with the size and weight of the camera in mind. But tripods are just the beginning, there are many other types of camera supports that can help you get the shot you want.

- **Base plate** is a metal piece that attaches to the bottom of your camera using a screw through the tripod mount. A base plate gives you a quick way of attaching your camera to various camera accessories. Baseplates usually feature a quick release mechanism so that you can take your camera on and off the tripod or other device without having to unthread the screw (refer to Figure 10.2).

- **Rods** are used to support large lenses and lens accessories such as follow focus mechanisms. They are especially useful when putting a big lens on a small camera.

- **Follow focus mechanisms** are a set of gears that let you pull focus smoothly while shooting. They are much larger than the focus rings found on the lens itself and make it easier for a second person to do the focus pulling (Figure 10.10).

- **Matte boxes** are used to hold filters on the lens. They can speed up the process of adding or removing filters because the filters are dropped in rather than screwed on. They also provide bigger adjustable sunshades, also known as *eyebrows* that can help you avoid lens flares (see Figure 10.8).

- **DSLR camera riggings,** such as the Zacuto Striker (Figure 10.11) and the Red Rock Micro Cinema Field Bundle (Figure 10.1), serve to make DSLR cameras function more like video cameras. The Cam Caddie (Figure 10.12) features a different design that is very useful when holding the camera low and when moving. Other DSLR riggings are designed to help hold various accessories while the camera is mounted on a tripod (Figure 10.3).

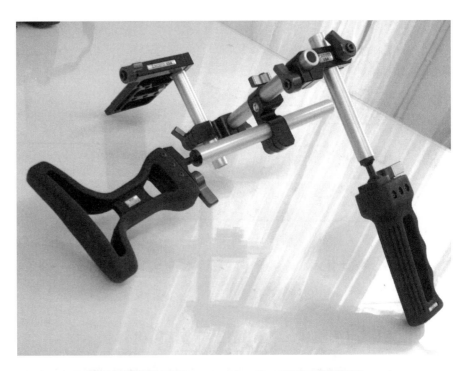

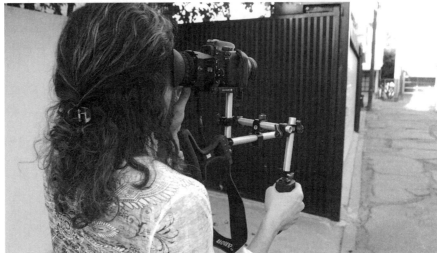

Figure 10.11

Zacuto Striker rig adds video functionality to DSLR cameras. Shown here is the rig on its own (top) and in use with a DSLR camera (bottom).

Figure 10.12

The Cam Caddie offers a
different kind of handholding
rig for DSLRs that is especially
well-suited to tracking
movement from a low angle.

- **Glidecams and steadicams** are devices used to smooth out the movement in a handheld
  shot. A clever arrangement of gimbals and counterweights, these stabilizers work by
  mounting the camera on an apparatus that has a lot of rotational inertia, but little reason
  to rotate. Though the physics are complicated, the result is simple: a camera that mostly
  floats in place, but that can be adjusted and moved in simple, tiny movements. Both
  Steadicam and Glidecam produce a number of different types of units for cameras of
  different weights. These devices are not cheap, and if you really need one, you'll probably do better to rent it. Note that if you have a very large camera that requires a large
  Steadicam, you'll also need to spring for a trained Steadicam operator.

- **Dollies** are special camera-holding carts that travel along special tracks and are used for
  creating tracking shots. Dollies and tracks require some extra effort to set up and use,
  but they're often the only way to achieve certain shots. Most good production houses
  rent dolly gear at very reasonable rates.

- **Sliders** are used to move the camera closer to or farther away from the subject during a
  shot. Sliders fit onto a tripod and let you move the camera a couple of feet in either direction. They can mimic the look of a short dolly shot without all the extra gear.

- **Jibs and cranes** provide high- to low-angle movement for swooping shots, and they are
  especially popular for establishing shots.

- **Aerials, car mounts, and shotmakers** are a few of the many devices used in tandem
  with transportation vehicles to create a different type of moving shot.

Viewing Video on the Set

Viewing video on the set falls into two basic categories: viewing aids for the camera crew and viewing aids for the director.

Camera operators and assistants need to see a calibrated, high-quality image in order to set focus and other variables during the shoot. The camera crew also needs to view video as close to the camera as possible. Most traditional video cameras offer an optical viewfinder and an LCD display that can suffice for the viewing needs of the camera crew, but often viewing with a separate video assist monitor is preferred. With DSLR cameras, the optical viewfinder is disabled during video recording, and LCD viewfinders are difficult to work with, especially in bright sunlight. Camera crews shooting with DSLR cameras typically use camera top monitors (Figure 10.13) or enhanced viewfinders (Figure 10.14) to view video as the camera is rolling. Very high-end digital cinema or effects footage often requires having a larger video assist monitor set up on or near the camera so that the director of photography can make very precise image adjustments.

Directors also need to be able to see a live video image of what is being shot in order to judge whether or not they are getting the material needed for their project. Unfortunately, it is often inconvenient or physically impossible for the director to be physically close to the cameras. Typically, a monitor (or several monitors if the shoot is multi-cam) is set up in what is called a video village where the director and others, such as the script supervisor, can watch exactly what is being recorded. Higher-end video cameras can be outfitted with wireless transmitters to send a video signal wirelessly to the video village. Mid-range and lower-end cameras use cables and splitters to send the signal the old-fashioned way.

Figure 10.13

Marshall camera-top monitor.

Figure 10.14

The Hoodman enhanced viewfinder is a lower-priced solution that straps onto the camera.

Although the process of setting up a video village is not really any more complicated than connecting your home television to your game console, the physical realities of being on the set can make it challenging. Unless you are shooting on a soundstage, your camera crew will need to move the video village around every time you change setups. In addition, just like your home theater, building a video village will involve lots of small parts: cables, adaptors, splitters, power supplies, and so on. And unfortunately, there is no "plug-and-play" option here. You'll have to figure out how to connect from the camera to the director's monitor(s) on a case-by-case basis, depending on the gear you're using, who you rented it from, quirks of your particular camera or monitor, and so on.

No matter how high-budget your project, there are always challenges attached to viewing video on the set. Wireless signals can be subject to interference, cables fail or come loose, and space limitations can make it difficult to find space for all the extra gear. But having the ability to view your footage is well worth the hassle.

Here are the parts of the video viewing food chain:

- **Enhanced viewfinders** like the Hoodman (Figure 10.14) and the Zacuto Z-finder (Figure 10.2) fit over the LCD of a camera to block out light and make it easier to see the image. There are also many types of hoods, shades, and bags to fit over LCD displays to block out ambient light.

- **Camera-top monitors** like those made by Marshall are very popular solutions and a little pricey, but you definitely get what you pay for (see Figure 10.13). At the top of the line, the Marshall offers a full-res HD image, SDI outputs, and "pass-through," which means you can send a video signal out to your video village without the need for extra splitters. These high-end monitors also offer image calibration features, such as the Marshall false color and peaking filters, which provide an enhanced way to check exposure similar to histograms and zebra stripes.

- **Field monitors** are basically any monitor that you use on the set. However, monitors designed exclusively for field use are usually compact and portable. The best ones are carefully calibrated so that you know you are watching an accurate image of what the camera is recording. But if you are on a restricted budget, you can make do with a small-ish flat panel television, a computer display, or even a laptop (Figure 10.15). There are also wireless field monitors that work in tandem with cameras that have wireless microwave transmitters, but these devices are subject to interference, and therefore not always of the best quality.

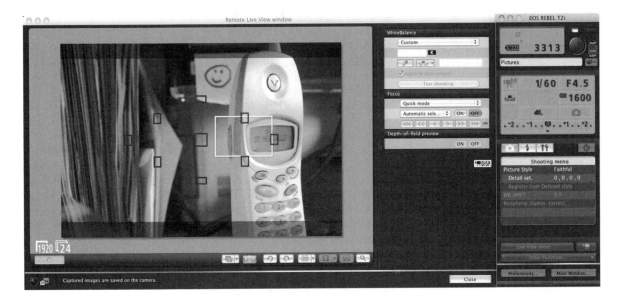

Figure 10.15

Poor man's video assist: the Canon camera utility offers a live view from your camera when connected by a cable and even lets you adjust camera settings if you wish.

- **Splitters** are little boxes that split a single video signal into two (or more) signals (Figure 10.16). The video signal coming out of the camera will need to be split if you are sending it to two different monitors, typically the camera-top monitor and the field monitor in the video village.

- **HDMI cables** are found on most lower-end HD cameras and also DSLR cameras (Figure 10.17). They provide a full quality HD signal, but are not really designed for fieldwork. They do not handle the stresses of the shooting environment well and tend to break or fall out of the camera due to all the movement on set.

- **SDI cables** are available on higher-end cameras (see Figure 10.17). They are sturdy and lock into place using a BNC connector and are therefore much better for use when shooting.

- **Power supplies** can be a limited resource when shooting. Most camera-top monitors and field monitors can be powered by rechargeable batteries. Standard video monitors and TV flat panels will require an AC power source. Most splitters also require a separate power source.

Figure 10.16

An HDMI splitter can send your HD video signal to two monitors.

Figure 10.17

Not all HD cables are created equal: SDI (left) has a mechanism for locking into position and HDMI (right) does not.

Double-System Audio Recording

Although your HD camera can potentially do a great job of recording audio, there will be times when you'll want to record audio onto a separate recording device like the digital audio recorder shown in Figure 10.18.

Here are a few common reasons to record audio to a separate device:

- If you have a very small video camera and are planning on doing a lot of handheld camera movements, it might not be practical to have an external microphone or mixer plugged into the camera.

- Most cameras only record two channels of audio, but the ideal sound recording scenario is that each actor wears a wireless lav. In addition, the sound recordist holds a boom mic to make an additional recording. So even if you only have two actors in a scene, that's three channels of audio. You'll need a 4-channel recorder to record all three tracks.

Figure 10.18

The Olympus LS-11 handheld
PCM audio recorder.

- Any scene in which actors are inside a car having a conversation, but you're shooting the exterior of the car from a chase vehicle. In this case, you'll need to have an audio recorder inside the car with the actors.

- Any scene in which the logistics of your set or camera movements make it impractical to keep your camera cabled to your microphones.

- A scene in which the action is a long way from the camera—for example, action scenes, wide landscape shots, or any time you want to shoot something from far away.

- Multi-camera shoots— where all cameras will share the same audio later in post.

Recording audio separately from your video makes the shoot more involved and postproduction more complicated. But that doesn't mean you should avoid it. Recent developments in postproduction software, such as Plural Eyes and Dual Eyes, have made synchronizing easier, and the result is well worth the trouble. Plus, by recording with both boom and lavs, you'll have an instant backup of your audio. If one mic goes bad, there is a good chance the dialogue will be covered in the boom audio track. And you'll also have the audio from the camera mic as a backup or guide track.

Be Sure to Record Camera Mic Audio, Too

Automated synchronizing apps like Plural Eyes use the audio recorded with your onboard camera mic and compare it to the audio recorded on a separate audio recording device in order to synchronize sound and video later in post. So be sure to record audio with your camera even though it won't be of high quality. Some producers actually add a decent camera-top shot gun mic to insure that the camera records audible audio.

How to Record Double-System Audio

Shooting double-system sound is, obviously, more involved than shooting standard, synched audio, and it requires the careful cooperation of a number of people. First, you'll want to have an operator for your audio recording device. This person, the production recording mixer, will monitor the recording levels and take care of starting and stopping the recording device. You'll also want a camera assistant to handle the slate.

We've all seen the classic shot of the black-and-white chalkboard with the clapper bar that is held before a camera. "Scene 1, take 1" says a voice, and then the top of the board is clapped down to make a loud cracking sound. Slating is used both to label the shot and to provide an audio/visual cue that can be used to synchronize the video and audio. Once in the editing room, the editor looks for the frame where the clapper bar is down and lines this up with the sharp crack of the audio. If all has gone well, the rest of the scene will be in sync. You can use this same method when shooting HD.

Today, most productions that shoot with double-system sound use a timecode slate (Figure 10.19). These are electronic devices that, in addition to displaying scene, shot, and take numbers, also display an electronic timecode readout. The electronic slate is connected to a timecode-capable audio deck or camera through a special cable. When editing, rather than having to sync your audio manually, by looking at the clap of the slate, you can simply line up the timecode on your audio and video.

Timecode audio recorders are more expensive to buy or rent, and a timecode slate adds even more money. It's easy enough to sync audio the old-fashioned way or use a postproduction tool like Singulary Software's Dual Eyes, so don't avoid double-system sound just because the timecode devices are too expensive.

Figure 10.19

PureBlend MovieSlate is an iPhone and iPad digital slating app useful for shooting double-system sound or multi-cam footage. It can generate timecode, accept timecode from a camera with the right cabling and synchronize timecode across iOS devices via Bluetooth and WiFi.

If you're not going to invest in timecoded audio recording, then buy or build yourself a clapping slate board, and be sure to enlist a responsible person to handle the job of filling out and clapping the slate. When slating, make sure the slate fills the frame clearly so that you can read what it says, and make sure the clap is quick and somewhat loud, so that it will appear as a sharp spike in your audio track. (But try not to deafen your sound recordist in the process.) In addition, don't forget that if you missed slating the head of the shot, you can always do a tail slate at the end of the shot, as long as camera and sound are still rolling.

Finally, be sure that you've chosen the right audio sampling rate (usually 48kHz) and that the frame rate on your audio recording device matches the frame rate on your video or film camera.

The Sound of Two Hands Clapping

As long as you can see it clearly through your viewfinder and hear it from your recording device, clapping your hands together can be a sufficient slate for synchronizing video and audio later on. You can also rely on software like Plural Eyes to help you out in post (more on that in Chapter 13, "Preparing to Edit"). Remember that even with automated synchronizing software, it can help to have slate claps and a guide track recorded with your camera's onboard mic.

Multi-Cam Shooting

Shooting with two or more cameras at the same time was developed in the early days of live television. With at least two cameras rolling, the person controlling the broadcast feed could switch back and forth between the two on the fly. That would give the other camera a chance to find a better shot or the director the opportunity to focus on a particular performance.

The standard for televised studio shoots is four cameras, typically a wide or master and three roving close-up cameras. A technical director sits in the control room and directs the cameras via headset, using a switcher to edit on the fly. Even today, most game shows, talk shows, and sitcoms are shot this way. Sporting events and concerts are done in a similar manner as well.

There have been many technological developments that have improved the way that multi-cam shoots are done, but the reason for its popularity has remained the same since the 1950s: it's better at capturing spontaneous action and requires less postproduction editing.

Multi-cam is a natural fit for sports and other unpredictable subject matter, such as reality TV shows. It's also a natural choice for comedy. The editor's bane of overlapping dialogue is less of a problem when there's a second camera covering that same turn of phrase. It's especially well suited to improvisation: both "The Office" and "Curb Your Enthusiasm" take advantage of multi-cam shooting to allow for creative freedom for the cast. Even feature filmmakers like Judd Apatow use multi-cam setups at times, for all of these same reasons.

Shooting with multiple cameras is not really that hard, and as with most filmmaking technologies, there's the big budget way and the low budget way, which we'll discuss here.

Multi-Cam Basics

The first rule of shooting multi-cam is that the cameras need to be synchronized. This synchronization can happen while filming or later, in postproduction.

Synchronizing cameras on the set with wired hardware connections, also known as jam synching, requires some extra gear: a timecode slate or other device that generates timecode and cameras that can accept a hard-wired signal from that slate through their timecode input (Figures 10.19 and 10.20). Consumer-grade camcorders and DSLRs typically do not have a timecode input. Jam synching on the set makes things faster and easier in post, but will cost more since you'll need higher-level cameras and technical expertise to make it work.

Figure 10.20

The Canon XL1H1 camera features a timecode input for jam synching to other devices, such as a timecode slate in a multi-cam shoot.

If jam synching is not possible for your production, you can still shoot multi-cam. Synchronizing cameras in post doesn't require any special gear and uses the same process as double-system sound recording: you will need a slate clap, and you need to make sure all cameras are running at the same frame rate. In other words, if you are already planning to record double-system sound, you'll already be synchronizing the audio and the footage from one camera in post. Adding a second or third camera isn't really going to be that much trouble.

The second rule of multi-cam shooting is match your cameras. Here's a quick list of what should match:

- Camera model/type
- Lens or focal length
- F-stop setting/aperture
- White balance
- Shutter speed
- Frame rate (*** this one is crucial)
- Frame size (for example, 1080, 720, and so on)
- Codec (if your camera offers more than one codec)
- Any other special image enhancement features in your camera's settings
- Filters such as NDs, ProMist, and so on

Rules are meant to be broken, and you can decide to purposely have your cameras have different looks, but the one thing you will not want to ever have mismatched is the frame rate. Having two different frame rates creates a potential nightmare in post and serves no purpose on the set. If you want a special effect on one camera, such as the look of Super 8 film, save any messing with the frame rate for post.

Challenges of Multi-Cam Shoots

Synchronizing two or more cameras is actually the easy part. What's a little more challenging is lighting and framing shots with multiple cameras on the set. Typically, lighting for multi-cam shoots is designed for 360-degree shooting. That usually means there is a grid on the ceiling with lights hanging from it to keep the lights out of your shots. Shooting outside is a little easier since you can use natural daylight and not worry about lights getting in your shots.

Framing for multi-cam is tricky as well. Typically, you want all your cameras to cut together. That means they all need to be on the same side of the stage line and that each camera needs to be shooting at an angle that is sufficiently different from the others so that cutting between them doesn't result in a jump cut (Figure 10.21). A traditional television studio is designed similarly to a stage in a theater. The stage line is literally the line at the edge of the stage between the audience and the actors. The cameras never cross this line and as a result, there is no risk of, in this case literally, crossing the stage line. Documentaries, reality TV shows, and sporting events are less rigorous about the rules regarding the stage line, in part because the nature of what they are shooting does not fit into clean, defined areas of "stage" and "audience." You will need to decide what rules apply to your project and frame your shots accordingly.

Also challenging for multi-cam shooting is finding a position for the boom operator so they don't appear in any of the shots. For this reason, wireless mics are a must on multi-cam shoots.

Figure 10.21

Three angles from a three-camera shoot, and a camera diagram.

WHAT TO WATCH

Single camera editing has a style and so does multi-cam editing. But you don't need to edit multi-cam style just because you shot multi-cam. *Survivor* is a TV show that shoots mostly multi-cam, but the editors use single cam editing techniques to avoid a multi-cam style. More on editing styles and multi-cam footage in Chapter 14, "Editing."

Going Tapeless

More and more cameras use media cards rather than videotape. Tapeless is much less of a hassle, but still has its own challenges, the biggest being the fact that it is very easy to accidentally delete or write over media that is recorded to cards.

Here's a quick guide to going tapeless.

First, you have a big decision to make: Will you use each media card only once or will you recycle them as you shoot? The first option is *much* safer, but it's not always possible. For example, some proprietary card formats like Panasonic's P2 will set you back several hundred dollars a card. However, with standard SD cards, single use is a viable option. You will likely need 30–50 cards, so it won't be cheap, but it will be secure.

The second option, recycling your cards as you go, is the choice of most indie filmmakers at present. The best way to do this is to have one day's worth of cards on hand—typically, about 8–10 16GB cards. With a day's worth of cards, you won't be forced to delete any media while you are actually shooting. By recycling as you go, you'll save several hundred dollars, but you'll have the added stress of deleting media from your cards after a long day of shooting, when perhaps you are tired and a bit prone to error.

Whichever option you chose, you should plan on having an on-set media workstation and a DIT (digital imaging technician) to collect the media from the camera crew, copy it onto your hard drives, organize it, and possibly rename the files. You'll also want a backup scheme and will only want to erase the cards after you're certain that everything is in order. Then you can put the cards back into play.

This is a job that might seem simple, and yet you want to make sure that it's done by someone you have complete confidence in, because your film will literally be in their hands.

On-set Media Workstations

A typical on-set media workstation consists of a laptop and two backup drives. Typically, these drives will end up as part of your editing workstation, so you might as well get drives that are up to the job. You'll need 7200RPM (or greater) drives that use a fast connection: eSATA, FireWire 400, or FireWire 800. (USB drives are cheap and prevalent, but they are just too slow for HD.) A typical feature film shoots about 30–60GB per day, and by the end of your shoot, you are likely to have about 1TB of media, so two 1TB drives should suffice for most projects.

The media workstation will need to be somewhat mobile/portable, and it will need a guaranteed power supply. Often, a small rolling cart and folding chair will do the job, but if you're shooting exteriors without a generator, be aware that getting power to the drives can be tricky.

Media Cards and Workflow

Once the workstation is set up, the next order of business is working out the details of getting drives to and from the cameras. You should have two containers for media cards— one for cards that are empty and ready to be used by the camera crew and one for cards that are full and waiting to be ingested into the media workstation. Ziplock bags work well for this. You should clearly label these containers because there is no margin for error here. If you hand a full card to the assistant camera operator and she reformats it in the camera, thinking the media has already been transferred to the hard drives, you just lost your footage.

Traditionally, every roll of film or piece of videotape that goes into the camera is given a number by the assistant camera crew, and this number is recorded on the slate. Similarly, each media card should be given a camera roll number (Figure 10.22). This extra step of numbering will help make it clearer which cards have been used in the camera and which haven't, in case there is any confusion on the set. Even if your project isn't scripted, having camera roll numbers can be a helpful way of organizing media for post. It's also a good policy not to have any folders on your drive share the same name so that you don't accidentally copy over anything. Instead of having several folders called "A-cam," you can name each folder by camera letter and roll number.

Figure 10.22

These SD cards were used during the shoot and given roll numbers by the assistant camera operator. Note that the tape on these drives is positioned so as not to interfere with drive operations.

Organizing Media on the Set

Once a card is filled with media, it should be immediately loaded into the computer and the contents copied onto one of the hard drives. At this point, it's considered a good idea to rename the raw camera files (Figure 10.23). Unless your camera lets you name files, each shot will be on the card with a name like *0001.mov*, which isn't too helpful for post. The file should be renamed to match the info on the slate so that *0001.mov* becomes *54A-1.mov*. Sometimes if it's a multi-cam shoot, it's wise to add the camera letter to the filename as well, such as *54A-1a.mov*.

You should make a folder for each date that you shoot, a subfolder for each camera (if multi-cam), and then another subfolder for each camera roll. DSLR cameras tend to create extra thumbnail files that you can delete at this point.

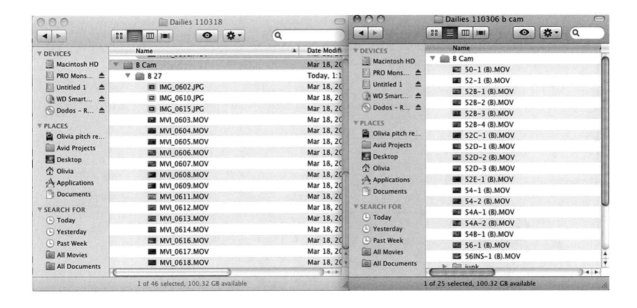

Figure 10.23

The folder on the left has the raw media files from the camera; the folder on the right has files that have been renamed according to information on the slate.

File Naming Conventions

Always name your files in a way that is compatible with the operating system and editing software used by your editing workstation. And always make sure to use the same naming conventions for all the media in your production.

After the files are renamed, they should be backed up to the second hard drive as well. This is purely a security measure, but drives are known to fail, and it's better to be safe than sorry. Once the media is renamed and stored on two hard drives, you can delete the media from the card. Once again, we recommend being extra careful before you delete anything. Check that the files on the hard drive are working properly. If time permits, you should watch them all the way through. This isn't always feasible, but it is the best way to know that the media is secure before you delete your camera originals.

If you follow these steps shown in Figure 10.24, your media will be organized and ready to import into your editing software when the shoot is finished.

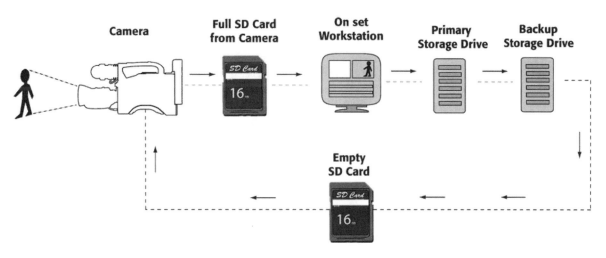

Figure 10.24

A diagram of tapeless workflow on the set.

Audio Media Workflow

For double-system sound, most sound recordists name the media files by scene and take numbers on the fly. Because audio files are relatively small, you can usually record all the day's media onto one card and hand it over to copy at the end of the day.

Shooting Blue-Screen Effects

One of the most important processes used in creating special effects is compositing, which means building a single shot out of two or more shots, or layers. And a key tool for compositing is shooting with a blue or green screen. Blue/green-screen sets are designed with a blue or green area, usually the backdrop, that can later be removed and filled with another shot or image.

If you have a special effect that is dependent on blue-screen shooting, then there are a few things to remember when shooting. Most of the work of getting a good blue-screen plate comes in the lighting (see Color Plate 16 and also Chapter 6, "Lighting"). However, there are still some things to remember when shooting blue-screen shots:

- Use a field monitor and pay close attention to the quality of the blue screen in your shot. Are the actors casting shadows on the screen? Is the blue screen reflecting on their clothing?

- If you have access to a laptop computer, consider taking it to the set with you. There, you can shoot some quick test footage and do a simple composite on your computer. This is the best way to determine if your blue-screen effect is working.

- Shoot at a high shutter speed. Motion blur makes keying very difficult, if not impossible and it can always be added later in post.

- Finally, be very careful of your camera's built-in sharpening mechanism. One of the byproducts of sharpening is that high-contrast areas—like the border between an actor and a blue screen—can develop "halos" of color. These halos can interfere with your post-production compositing process.

As an example, consider Figure 10.25. This shot shows a custom-made prop—a "universal remote control" that was painted blue to facilitate compositing of a computer-generated control panel. Check the edge of the blue area, though. Because the camera oversharpened, there's a discernible halo that is visible even after compositing.

By simply dialing down the camera's sharpening feature, you can usually eliminate these artifacts.

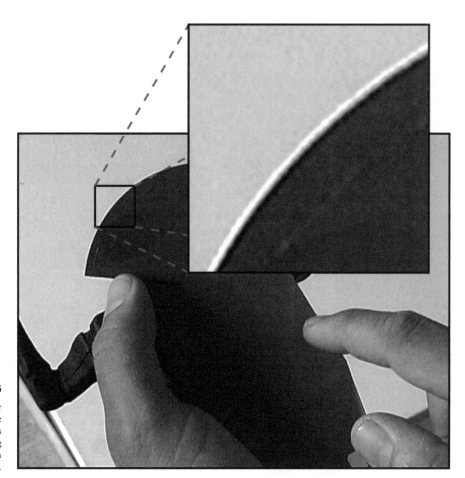

Figure 10.25

When shooting elements for blue-screen compositing, make sure that your camera's sharpening setting is not causing halos that will prevent you from getting a good composite.

11

Editing Gear

Photo credit: Sonja Schenk

B ack in the first chapter of this book, we said that digital filmmaking is better, cheaper, and easier than it was several years ago. Editing gear is where the most dramatic simplification has occurred. In fact, it's gotten so much simpler that we streamlined two chapters into one rather short chapter.

Full-resolution HD video involves huge file sizes and very intense computer processing capabilities and throughput. But somewhere along the way, computers caught up. The average high-end personal computer is more than capable of editing full-res HD video right out of the box. Things like media capture cards and breakout boxes are pretty much a thing of the past. Sure they still exist, and in some cases, you might find them useful, but for the most part, you can just plug and play.

The same is true for all the editing peripherals that were staples of the editing room. Thanks to HD integration and tapeless workflow, NTSC monitors, calibration tools, video decks, and all the assorted gear that once surrounded your computer are no longer required.

So what exactly do you need to set up your editing workstation?

Setting Up a Workstation

These days, the first step of setting up an editing workstation is to buy a new computer (see Figure 11.1). Any new Mac that you buy, be it a laptop or desktop machine, will come with built-in FireWire and HDMI ports and a hard drive that's fast enough to handle any HD editing tasks. Similarly, just about any Windows machine that you buy that includes built-in FireWire or eSATA ports will also include speedy disk storage that will be suitable for video editing. What's more, you can easily expand your storage options with external hard drives.

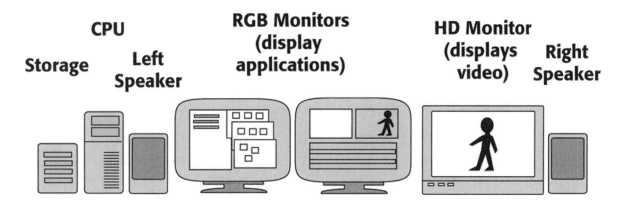

Figure 11.1

Components of a typical tapeless HD editing workstation.

CPU

Working with video requires a lot of processing power, but most new computers with 2GHz or greater processors are up to the job. But don't forget that you'll be doing more than just editing video. Be sure to get enough computing muscle to run the various image editors, compositing, and special effects programs that you'll want to use.

When we wrote the first edition of this book, it was still possible to buy a new computer that didn't have enough processing power to handle an HD stream. Nowadays, you'd have to look really hard to find a new machine that was similarly hobbled. For the most part, any CPU you buy today should be plenty speedy for video editing and that includes most laptops.

If you acquired your footage using a proprietary card or optical disk format, such as P2, you will need a special card or disk reader.

RAM

HD video editing can use a fair amount of RAM, so a safe bet is 1–2GB of RAM for most editing applications.

However, if you're going beyond simple editing with basic dissolves and effects, you should spring for extra memory. To prepare titles and special effects, you might be depending on an image editor such as Photoshop. In addition, specialized applications that load video segments into RAM—After Effects, for example—need *lots* of memory.

We guarantee that no one who edits video has ever said, "Gosh, I wish I hadn't bought all that extra RAM."

Storage

Buying enough storage used to be the bane of digital video editing. However, with recent changes in technology and pricing, storage has become surprisingly affordable. How much storage you'll need depends largely on the nature of your project. We mentioned in Chapter 10, "DSLRs and Other Advanced Shooting Situations," that the raw footage for a feature film will probably add up to 1TB. You'll want to store a copy of that footage on a separate drive as an off-site backup. Then you'll want a separate set of drives for your editing workstation.

Once you are ready to edit, you'll probably transcode the footage to an intermediary codec, such as Apple ProRes or Avid DNxHD. Depending on which resolution you choose, transcoding can actually increase your file sizes. We'll talk more about importing and transcoding media in Chapter 13, "Preparing to Edit," but be aware that odds are high that transcoding will increase your raw media by a ratio of about 2.5:1. That means you'll need at least 2.5TB for your media, and then you'll probably need extra space for music, renders, and other stuff. 4TB is a safe place to start. Luckily, that will only set you back about $500.

When buying drives, you have the choice of purchasing a RAID or daisy-chaining several non-RAID drives together. RAID stands for *Redundant Array of Independent Disks*—usually referred to simply as an *array*—and consists of two or more identical hard drives that have been logically striped with indexing information so that they can be treated as a single drive. For video, the advantage of an array is speed. Because the computer can interleave information between both drives, one drive can be reading or writing while the other drive is preparing to read or write.

RAIDs are very fast, but we don't recommend putting all your media on one single RAID. If it fails, you could lose it all. Instead, daisy chain a couple of smaller RAIDS (1–2TB each) together. In a bad situation when one drive fails, you'll still have half your media to work with. (And, of course, you'll have your off-site backup in case of a bigger media disaster.)

RAIDs are nice, but not required. What you do need, however, are drives that use a fast interface—eSATA or FireWire—and have a spin rate of 7200rpms or higher. USB drives are plentiful and cheap, but the USB interface is simply not up to the task of moving around giant HD video files in real-time. They make great backup drives, however.

Monitors

Video applications tend to consume a lot of screen real estate. Consequently, even the most basic editing workstations have two computer monitors (see Figure 11.2). Any HD flat panel monitors will do, and the prices can be very reasonable. However, keep in mind that you get what you pay for with monitors, and at the lower-priced end of the spectrum, monitors can be uneven across the screen in terms of brightness, contrast, and color.

In addition to the two computer monitors, most editing workstations have a third monitor for viewing full-screen playback. This can be a third HD computer monitor or a flat panel television. To view true HD footage, you will need to make sure that you have an HDMI or SDI signal coming out of your computer and going into your video monitor.

Figure 11.2

Even the most basic editing workstations have two computer monitors.

If you are planning to do lots of color grading on your system, you should consider adding a hard-ware waveform monitor and vectorscope. These are tools used to view the video signal in differ-ent ways to help you set the white levels, the black levels, and the colors. We discuss how to use waveform monitors and vectorscopes in Chapter 16, "Color Correction" and also in the Chapter 13 materials provided on the companion Web site at *www.thedigitalfilmmakinghandbook.com.*

Videotape Interface

If you acquired your footage on videotape, you will need a video interface to get the video off the videotapes and into your computer. Also, if you want to make outputs of your project on videotape, you will need a video interface, regardless of your acquisition format.

If your videotape format is FireWire-based, such as DVCPro-HD or HDV, then you can sim-ply use FireWire cables to move media off your tapes and into your computer (see Figure 11.3). As long as your computer has a FireWire port, you can simply use FireWire cables to attach your computer to a videotape deck (VTR) or camcorder. If you plan to capture lots of media, we recommend investing in a VTR and saving the wear and tear on your camcorder.

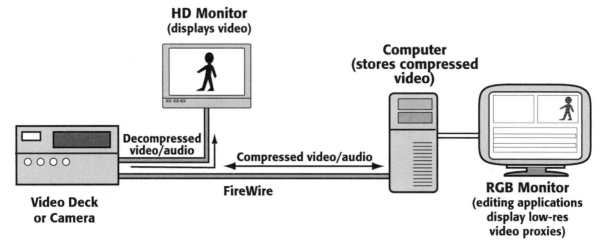

Figure 11.3

Components of a typical FireWire-based editing workstation.

If your videotape format is not FireWire-based, you will need a video card or a breakout box with HD-SDI input and output in order to move your media into your workstation (see Figures 11.4 and 11.5). You'll also need a VTR that can play back your videotape format (see Figure 11.6). High-end VTRs are a big investment.

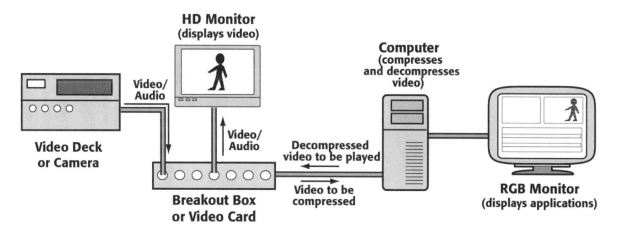

Figure 11.4

Components of a typical SDI-based editing workstation.

Figure 11.5

This AJA Kona HD video card offers HD-SDI input and output that allows for input and output to a variety of HD videotape formats. It can be used in tandem with a breakout box (shown later in this chapter) and also adds increased performance to your system.

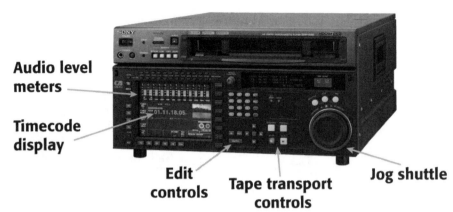

Audio level meters

Timecode display

Edit controls

Tape transport controls

Jog shuttle

Figure 11.6
A high-end HDCAM VTR.

Working with Analog or DV Video

If your project involves analog video, check out the Analog Video Primer and the DV Primer on the Web site at *www.thedigitalfilmmakinghandbook.com/chapter3*. It's a compilation of all the information on working with analog video from past editions of the book.

Custom Keyboards and Controllers

Although you can drive an editing program with your mouse, having keyboard control allows you to make edits without stopping to move the mouse around. In addition to being much faster, driving your editor from the keyboard allows you to work more fluidly and to develop a rhythm. Editing is a very tactile process, so good keyboard control is essential.

However, complex editing programs can have dozens of keyboard commands and shortcuts. Although a good program will have keyboard controls that are logically arranged, learning these layouts can take some time. A custom keyboard like the one shown in Figure 11.7 can make learning your system much easier. These keyboards feature color-coded keys with custom icons that allow you to easily see exactly what each key does.

In addition to custom keyboards, you might also find a higher-quality mouse is a worthwhile investment. There are also a number of specialized edit controllers on the market.

Backing Up

Everyone who has used a computer for any amount of time knows the importance of backing up. And though losing that critical text document can be a drag, losing hours and hours of transcoded video in addition to your editing project file and weeks' worth of complex 3D renderings can completely destroy a project. As you might surmise, good backup is essential. Consequently, you should consider your backup strategy when constructing your system.

The best backup system to implement and use is to simply buy additional external hard drives and copy your files over at regular intervals. Using hard drives as backup is also the speediest backup strategy. Hard drives are also fairly cheap to buy these days, making them a cost-effective backup solution.

Figure 11.7

A keyboard with custom-colored keycaps designed for your editing program of choice can make learning a new editing app much easier.

In addition to backing up your media, you should also back up your project files. Project files created by editing systems are usually very small and can easily be backed up to a USB key, DVD, external hard drive, or uploaded to Web-based storage, or an email server. If you have carefully organized all of your files, then your project file contains a database that tells exactly where each clip is on your original storage drives. If your system crashes, you can simply restore it from your backed-up project file and your off-site backup media drive, and then tell your editing system where to find all the duplicate footage.

Networked Systems

Now that you've hassled out the details of picking a single computer, you might consider picking up a few more of them. Large projects often require more than one editor, and having multiple editing systems on a network allows for instant access to shared resources, and consequently less downtime while waiting for files to transfer. High-end systems, like Avid's Media Composer, offer special network solutions, like the Avid Unity network, which includes hardware and special software. But just because you're not using Avid Unity doesn't mean you need to stay out of the loop if networking will benefit your project. However, be aware that the limitations of your editing software will be a factor in terms of just exactly how and what parts of your editing workflow can be shared over a network.

Storage Area Networks (SANs) and Network-Attached Storage (NAS)

Storage area networks (SANs) and network-attached storage (NAS) let you share drives (and media) between multiple workstations. As with local storage drives, the key to choosing the right system is bandwidth. You want to be sure that you can move media quickly enough through your pipeline to maintain real-time video and audio. A high-bandwidth format, such as uncompressed HD, will require a network that uses Fibre channel. Creating your own SAN will require special software, such as Apple XSAN, Charismac Fibre Share, or Studio Network Solutions SANmp, to help manage your drives and your media across multiple workstations.

Cloud Storage

Storing your media on the "cloud"—in other words, on a remote server via the Internet—is an exciting idea, but not likely to help editors of full-resolution HD video at the present. Data rates and bandwidth are just too slow for real-time functionality. But if you are working with very low bandwidth media—video that is intended for Web or cell phone delivery—then this might be a great option for you in the near future.

Render Farms

If you plan to do lots of effects work, or if speedy workflow is an absolute essential for your production needs, a "farm" of networked computers will let you distribute your rendering tasks across multiple machines. With this type of system, separate ranges of frames are distributed to each machine for rendering. As each computer finishes its batch, the rendered frames are returned to the host system, which assembles them into a completed piece.

Most 3D applications offer network rendering, as do most high-end compositing programs. There are few editing programs that are able to distribute their rendering tasks, but these rendering chores are not usually as time-consuming as 3D and compositing rendering, so distributed rendering is not as critical.

If you want to build a render farm, you'll need networking gear in addition to a bunch of computers. Because they are so computing-intensive, 3D programs see a bigger performance boost from distributed rendering than do compositing programs. Fortunately, because 3D project data is so small, you don't need an especially speedy network to create a rendering farm.

Using a render farm for compositing tasks usually requires the movement of a fair amount of data, which means you'll need to use computers on your local area network. These can be connected using a standard Ethernet network or wireless network.

No matter what type of distributed rendering you want to do, you'll need to install special client software on all of the computers that you want to include in your render farm. Most programs that provide a distributed rendering option include a license for installing render clients on an additional number of machines, or *nodes*. How many nodes you can install varies from package to package; check your particular software for details. Purchasing additional rendering nodes is far less expensive than having to buy a full copy of the software.

Battery Backup

Many editing systems include a battery backup in case of a power failure. These batteries act as a central power switch for the system, and in the case of a power failure, keep the system running long enough for you to save your work and shut down properly.

Grounding Your Electronic Equipment

Heavy-duty electronic equipment, such as video editing system hardware, should always be grounded. This means using three-prong AC cables plugged into a grounded (three-prong) outlet.

Audio Equipment

If you're in a hurry to get started editing, you can make do with a pair of earbuds or your computer speakers, but if you're serious about audio, you'll need to plan on upgrading your audio environment.

Unlike computer video monitors, built-in computer speakers are generally terrible. At the very least, you'll want to add a pair of good quality external computer speakers. But bear in mind that at the low end, most add-on speakers are designed for music with lots of bass boosting that isn't ideal for editing dialogue. You can also use the type of speakers that come with a home stereo system, by sending the audio from your computer or mixer through the Video/Auxiliary input on your stereo.

There are several manufacturers of professional grade, self-powered speakers made specially for editing systems. These can be a bit pricey, but are definitely more suited to the task of editing than home stereo or computer speakers.

If you have more serious sound editing in mind—for example, if you plan to edit and mix 5.1 surround sound—you'll need some additional hardware. A surround sound audio interface, 6-channel (or greater) mixing board (Figure 11.8), and at least six speakers are needed to play back each stream of audio separately. Bear in mind that most people opt to hire a special audio mixer (a person, not the hardware) to do the surround sound mix for them.

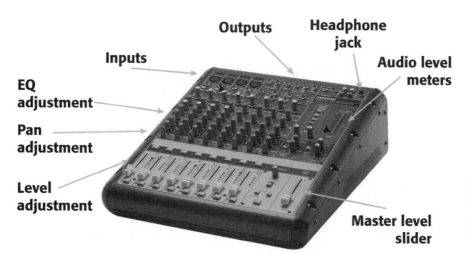

Figure 11.8

An audio mixing board, like this 12-channel FireWire-based mixer from Mackie, can connect audio from various sources (computer, VTRs, and so on) and send it out to various devices (speakers, computer, VTRs) in different configurations. In addition, mixing boards allow for on-the-fly adjustment of levels, balance and EQ.

Digital Video Cables and Connectors

Building an editing system is much easier than it used to be, but it helps to know the different ins and outs of your gear (see Figure 11.9)

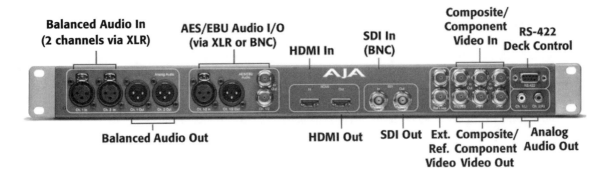

Figure 11.9

A breakout box, like this one from AJA Kona, offers many different ins and outs to make it easy to hook up your gear.

FireWire

FireWire was developed by Apple in 1986 as a replacement for several older interfaces: serial, parallel, SCSI, and, to a lesser degree, Ethernet. Nowadays, many computers only have two interfaces for connecting peripherals: USB for slow devices such as keyboards, mice, and printers, and FireWire 400 or 800 for high-speed connectivity to mass storage, cameras, scanners, and even networks since FireWire allows you to daisy-chain up to 64 devices.

HDMI

High-definition multimedia interface (HDMI) is designed to transmit uncompressed digital media to computers, television sets, and other media devices. HDMI is great, but the cables do not lock into place, which can make them unstable when used with hardware such as cameras.

SDI and HD-SDI

Developed by Sony as an interface between high-end digital video formats and non-linear editing systems, SDI (for Serial Digital Interface) is designed to handle uncompressed digital video and provides a data rate ranging from 140Mbps to 570Mbps. SDI supports much longer cables than FireWire does, which is useful for postproduction facilities that keep their equipment in a special climate-controlled machine room and need to send high-quality video signals to other rooms in the building. HD-SDI has a data rate of 1.485Gbps (Gigabits per second), which is necessary for moving uncompressed HD data. SDI uses BNC connectors that lock into place for maximum stability.

Fibre Channel

Fibre Channel is a high-speed data transfer protocol that is currently the most popular solution for networked editing workstations. Fibre Channel is similar to Ethernet but with greater bandwidth, supporting up to 4Gbps data transfer rates, which means that SANs using Fibre Channel connectivity can support real-time transfer of HD video and maintain synchronization of audio and video streams.

Thunderbolt

Thunderbolt is a new high-speed I/O protocol developed by Intel and Apple that can handle 10Gbps in data transfer. That's more than five times faster than HD-SDI. It was specifically designed for professional audio and video applications, where high data transfer rates with accurate synchronization is crucial for real-time playback and processing. The Thunderbolt interface can support multiple daisy-chained devices, so in theory at least, you'll be able to use a single port on your computer to connect HD displays, drives, cameras, audio mixers, and any other part of an editing system together. At the time of this writing, Thunderbolt is brand new technology so look for new products and developments to take advantage of it in the very near future.

RS-422

If you are using a high-end VTR, you'll need support for an RS-422 cable to remotely control the deck via your computer. RS-422 is a serial device protocol that is found on almost all high-end VTRs.

Audio Interfaces

The cables and connections listed in the preceding section carry both audio and video signals, but there are also several audio-only interfaces out there.

TRS is the standard audio interface used with earbuds, iPods, cell phones, and other small devices. It is an analog, consumer-grade audio interface. Some higher-end audio devices and cameras, though, use BNC or XLR connectors. If you find yourself trying to connect a TRS-equipped device into something that only has BNC or XLR connectors, then you'll need to get appropriate adapters. RCA is another type of consumer-grade audio connector used a lot in older television sets, video decks, and home stereos.

If you're working with a high-end digital audio device, it might have a digital interface such as SP/DIF or AES/EBU, in addition to an RCA or XLR interface. (Note that some SP/DIF or AES/EBU connections use the same cables—RCA, BNC, or XLR—to carry a digital audio signal.)

If you need to take audio from a mixer or microphone, you'll probably need XLR connectors.

Know What You Need

Before you head to the computer store (or before you start surfing online for a good deal), there are a few technical specs that you need to be sure of.

- How fast a processor do you need?

- How much storage will you need for your intended project?

- How much RAM will your editing and effects packages require?

- How important is portability? Will you use this system on the set for organizing file-based media? If so you may want to consider a laptop.

- Do you want a second or third computer monitor?

- How many backup drives will you need?

- Will you need to input or output videotape? If so, you'll need a video card and a video deck.

- Do you have lots of audio sources? If so, you may want to incorporate a mixing board into your system.

- Do you have multiple workstations that you want to share media over a network? If so, do you want to invest in a networked storage server?

- Does your editing, compositing, or 3D software support network rendering? If so, do you want to build a render farm?

There are many products and options out there for the digital filmmaker. If you're making a traditional film with limited special effects, you don't need to worry about most of them because your needs are fairly simple, so don't go overboard in building your system. If you are working on a project with lots of graphics and effects, you'll need a more robust system with all the bells and whistles and a way for multiple editors to share media. Stick with what will work best for your production and aim for a system that can support the software that you prefer to use. You can always upgrade along the way.

Photo credit: William MacCollum

12

Editing Software

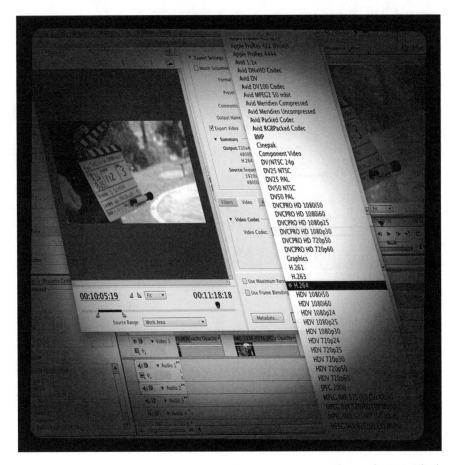

Photo credit: Sonja Schenk

N ow that you've assembled your workstation, it's time to choose the editing software that you'll run on your new workstation.

A typical non-linear editing program is a very complicated piece of software. However, by identifying the features you need for your project, you can zero in on the package more easily that's right for you.

In this chapter, we'll cover all of the issues, concepts, and terminology you'll need to understand when choosing an editing application. Your editing software will be the heart of your postproduction system, so choose carefully. The following are factors to consider when choosing an editing program.

The Interface

Most editing applications share a similar interface (see Figure 12.1). A project window contains bins or folders, which hold video clips and other media. Double-clicking on a clip will open it in the source viewer, a window on the left side of the screen. The source viewer lets you view the shot and select the part of it that you want to use in your edited sequence.

You assemble shots into a sequence using a timeline window that displays representations of your clips in their edited order. The timeline window is divided into tracks that contain video or audio. When editing, you can target particular tracks, letting you choose to add both the audio and video from a clip into your project, or just the audio or video. For example, by targeting the video track only, you can perform a cutaway from one piece of video to another, without altering the underlying audio. Most editing applications can support unlimited tracks of audio and video, but you may find it easier to work with just a few.

On the right side of the screen is the record viewer, a window that displays the video from the timeline—that is, your edited sequence, as shown in Figure 12.1. Some simpler editing programs like Apple iMovie use a less-complicated interface with only one viewer, but we don't recommend them for larger scale projects like feature films.

For maximum flexibility, look for a package with robust editing controls (many of which are described next). For faster learning, look for a program with a more streamlined interface, but beware: with a simpler program, you might not get all the tools you need to create a high-quality final product.

Project Window　　　　**Source Viewer**　　　　**Record Viewer**

Bins

Clips

Timeline

Figure 12.1

The Avid Media Composer interface includes a project window, bins containing clips, source and record viewers, and a timeline.

Editing Tools

One of the best things about a good editing application is that there are many different ways to make an edit. The following is a list of editing tools found in most editing applications. If you are new to editing, selecting a package with lots of these features will ensure the most editing flexibility. If you have some experience editing, you'll want to be sure to find a package that provides the editing controls that you prefer.

Drag-and-Drop Editing

With drag-and-drop editing, you use the mouse to drag shots into the timeline window from a bin. Once there, you can rearrange shots by dragging them into the order you prefer. Drag-and-drop editing is often the best way to build your first rough string-up of a scene. You can arrange and select multiple shots in a bin and then drag them into the timeline all at once.

Three-Point Editing

Three-point editing lets you define the part of a source clip that will be used in your edited sequence, by selecting a beginning, or in-point, and an ending, or out-point, within the clip (these are the first two points), and then selecting where the clip will begin or end in your edited sequence (the third point). This allows you to build an edited sequence more precisely than you can with drag-and-drop editing. After setting the in- and out-points, press the Edit button and the selected part of your source clip will be placed on the timeline at the selected destination.

JKL Editing

If your program provides JKL editing controls, the J on your keyboard will play your video in reverse, the K will pause, and the L will play forward. This simple mechanism allows you to shuttle quickly around a video clip to find an in- or out-point. Since you can usually select an in-point with the I on your keyboard and an out-point with the O, JKL turns your standard keyboard into an efficient, one-handed edit controller (see Figure 12.2).

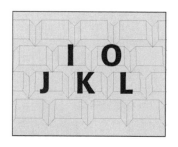

Figure 12.2

Keyboard, or JKL, editing provides a simple, one-handed editing interface.

Insert and Overwrite Editing

Whether you're using drag-and-drop, three-point editing, or switching between the two, your editing package should provide for insert and overwrite editing modes. These two options allow you to choose *how* your footage is added into an already-cut sequence.

When inserting, all of the footage after the in-point is pushed down the timeline to accommodate the footage that is being added. In other words, the new footage—whether audio, video, or both—is inserted into the timeline.

Conversely, overwrite leaves all clips in place, but writes the new clip over any existing video or audio (depending on which tracks are targeted), as shown in Figure 12.3.

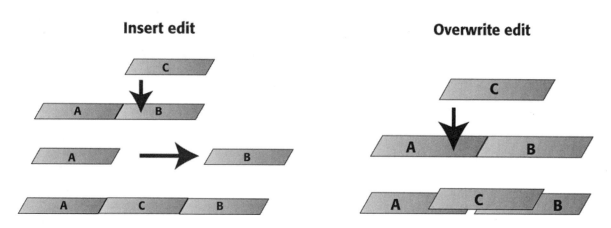

Figure 12.3

Insert edits allow you to add a shot between two existing shots (left), while overwrite edits allow you to easily add a shot to cover an edit, like a cutaway (right).

Trimming

Once you have a decent rough cut of a scene, it's time to fine-tune it. For example, you might want to add beats of silence between certain lines of dialogue to show a character's hesitation, or you might want to extend a shot of a character to show his reaction as another character speaks. One way to do this is by trimming the edit. A trimming interface has a familiar two-viewer window, but instead of source and record viewers, you see the last frame of the outgoing shot in the left viewer and the first frame of the incoming shot of the edit that you are going to trim in the right (see Figure 12.4). In trim mode, you can extend or shorten the end of the outgoing shot (the "A-side" of the edit), or you can extend or shorten the incoming shot (the "B-side" of the edit), or both.

Figure 12.4

The trimming interface in Apple Final Cut Pro.

Ripple and Roll, Slip and Slide

There are a number of different types of edits that you can make once you've built a sequence. The following are four advanced ways to fine-tune an edited sequence. Depending on your software, they can be executed in the timeline, in trim mode, or both.

Ripple and roll are two ways to change an existing edit between two shots. Ripple allows you to extend or shorten either the outgoing shot (the A-side) or the incoming shot (the B-side). All of the shots in your sequence will move farther down in the timeline to accommodate these added frames. Roll lets you extend the outgoing shot and tighten the incoming shot simultaneously (or vice versa). The overall length of the sequence will remain unchanged, which makes rolling edits well suited to creating overlapping edits.

Three shot sequence

Center shot slides to the right

Center shot slides to the left

Figure 12.5

By using a slide edit, you can move the center shot in the top sequence to the right (middle) or to the left (bottom) without changing the length of the overall sequence.

Slip-and-slide edits involve three shots, as in Figure 12.5 (top). If you use a slide edit to drag the middle shot forward in time, the first shot automatically will be extended to fill the gap, while the last shot will be shortened automatically to keep the overall length of the three shots the same (see Figures 12.5 [center] and 12.5 [bottom]). Slip allows you to change the footage contained in the middle shot, starting it at a different place without affecting the shots surrounding it or the duration of the sequence.

Multi-Camera Editing

If your software allows for multi-camera editing, you can group shots from different cameras together in your timeline and then select which video you want to see at any given time. You can group the audio and video for each shot using either matching timecode or a slate sync mark. Figure 12.6 shows multi-camera editing in Avid Media Composer.

Grouped Source Clips   Record Viewer

Figure 12.6

Multi-camera editing in Avid Media Composer.

Advanced Features

In addition to editing methods, there are a number of interface and utility features that you should look for when choosing an editing package.

Good keyboard controls are a must, as it's much easier to develop an editing rhythm by punching keys than by moving a mouse. Also look for multiple Undos (at least 15 levels) and automatic Save and Backup features, all of which will help you recover from mistakes.

In addition, look for the following features when assessing editing apps:

- **Match Frame:** Instead of having to search through all your bins and shots to find a source file that you've already added to your timeline, if your editor provides a Match Frame feature, you simply park your cursor on a frame in your timeline and then press the Match Frame button. The source clip appears in your source viewer. Related to Match Frame is the Find Clip or Find Bin command that opens the bin in which a shot is located.

- **Audio scrubbing:** Most editing systems let you scrub through the audio, which means that as you slowly scroll through a clip, the audio plays back in slow motion along with the video. This is a must for finding a particular sound, such as a pause in a line of dialogue or the beat in a piece of music.

- **Lockable tracks:** Locking a track can prevent you from making accidental edits. If you follow the traditional motion picture workflow and lock picture before you begin fine-cutting your sound, then locking the picture track in your software will help ensure that the edited picture doesn't get changed.

- **Network editing:** For projects that need multiple editors and workstations, software support for networked editing can save lots of headaches. The biggest danger with networked editing lies in accidentally writing over a project that someone else has worked on and losing all their work. Software support for networked editing helps prevent these sorts of mistakes.

Organizational Tools

A good non-linear editing system should provide you with tools that will help you keep track of all of the media in your project.

In applications with good organizational tools, bins will display columns showing information about each piece of media—for example, start and end timecode, source tape number, frame rate, number and types of tracks, audio sampling rate, and more. For long projects, you'll want editing software that lets you customize and add columns for your own comments, keywords, and so on. You should be able to Sort and Sift bins according to your needs, and use Search or Find commands to locate clips (see Figure 12.7).

	Name	Comments	Duration	Tracks	Source File	Format	Audio SR	Creation Date	Drive	Video File Format	Can
	13-2 (A).MOV	Best take	1:46:15	V1 A1-2	13-2 (A).MOV	HD 1080p/23.976	48000	3/12/11 11:52:18 PM	PRO Monsoon 1TB	MXF	
	13A-3 (A).MOV	ng	1:13:21	V1 A1-2	13A-3 (A).MOV	HD 1080p/23.976	48000	3/13/11 12:03:07 AM	PRO Monsoon 1TB	MXF	
	13A-4 (A).MOV	flub	1:10:22	V1 A1-2	13A-4 (A).MOV	HD 1080p/23.976	48000	3/13/11 12:06:38 AM	PRO Monsoon 1TB	MXF	
	13B-4 (A).MOV	Great!	52:08	V1 A1-2	13B-4 (A).MOV	HD 1080p/23.976	48000	3/13/11 12:17:41 AM	PRO Monsoon 1TB	MXF	
	25-3 (A).MOV		3:53:21	V1 A1-2	25-3 (A).MOV	HD 1080p/23.976	48000	3/13/11 12:25:52 AM	PRO Monsoon 1TB	MXF	
	25D-1 (A).MOV		4:19:22	V1 A1-2	25D-1 (A).MOV	HD 1080p/23.976	48000	3/13/11 1:19:35 AM	PRO Monsoon 1TB	MXF	
	30-3 (A).MOV		1:08:12	V1 A1-2	30-3 (A).MOV	HD 1080p/23.976	48000	3/13/11 1:36:09 AM	PRO Monsoon 1TB	MXF	
	30A-4 (A).MOV		2:07:08	V1 A1-2	30A-4 (A).MOV	HD 1080p/23.976	48000	3/13/11 1:52:06 AM	PRO Monsoon 1TB	MXF	
	52-2 (A).MOV		1:37:00	V1 A1-2	52-2 (A).MOV	HD 1080p/23.976	48000	3/13/11 2:00:44 AM	PRO Monsoon 1TB	MXF	
	52A-1 (A).MOV		1:34:10	V1 A1-2	52A-1 (A).MOV	HD 1080p/23.976	48000	3/13/11 2:05:04 AM	PRO Monsoon 1TB	MXF	
	52B-3 (A).MOV		1:15:12	V1 A1-2	52B-3 (A).MOV	HD 1080p/23.976	48000	3/13/11 2:13:57 AM	PRO Monsoon 1TB	MXF	
	52C-1 (A).MOV		2:03:13	V1 A1-2	52C-1 (A).MOV	HD 1080p/23.976	48000	3/13/11 2:19:36 AM	PRO Monsoon 1TB	MXF	
	52G-2 (A).MOV		1:34:20	V1 A1-2	52G-2 (A).MOV	HD 1080p/23.976	48000	3/13/11 2:27:17 AM	PRO Monsoon 1TB	MXF	
	52H-2 (A).MOV		1:23:12	V1 A1-2	52H-2 (A).MOV	HD 1080p/23.976	48000	3/13/11 2:35:19 AM	PRO Monsoon 1TB	MXF	
	52J-3 (A).MOV		1:02:17	V1 A1-2	52J-3 (A).MOV	HD 1080p/23.976	48000	3/13/11 2:42:45 AM	PRO Monsoon 1TB	MXF	
	54-2 (A).MOV		1:19:20	V1 A1-2	54-2 (A).MOV	HD 1080p/23.976	48000	3/13/11 2:52:24 AM	PRO Monsoon 1TB	MXF	
	56-1 (A).MOV		1:17:10	V1 A1-2	56-1 (A).MOV	HD 1080p/23.976	48000	3/13/11 4:07:46 AM	PRO Monsoon 1TB	MXF	
	30B-1		2:32:16	V1 A1-2	MVI_2792.MOV	HD 1080p/23.976	48000	3/13/11 4:12:38 AM	PRO Monsoon 1TB	MXF	

Figure 12.7

Most editing applications let you add customized columns and headings when you view your clips in text view; shown here is a bin created in Adobe Premiere Pro.

Importing Media

If your footage is file-based, you'll simply copy your files onto a storage drive and then import them into your editing application.

Most editing packages work best when you transcode your camera-raw media to an intermediary codec (see Figure 12.8). This process can take a while, but you'll be rewarded with improved playback performance that is crucial to editing. Be aware that different editing apps support different codecs, so make sure that the app you choose can work with the codec you need.

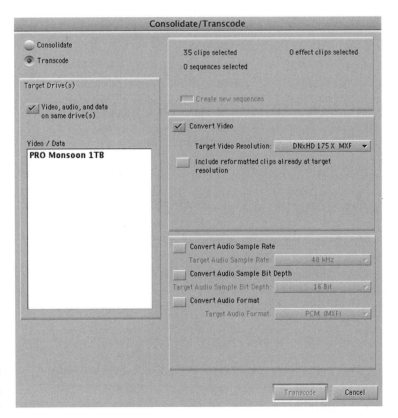

Figure 12.8

The transcoding interface in Avid Media Composer.

If your footage is tape-based, you'll have to capture the media first. Capturing digital media is much easier than capturing analog media because you don't have to use custom settings. You will, however, want a capture interface that offers deck control so that you can let the application batch capture your footage after you've logged it (see Figure 12.9).

Preview Window   **Capture Settings**

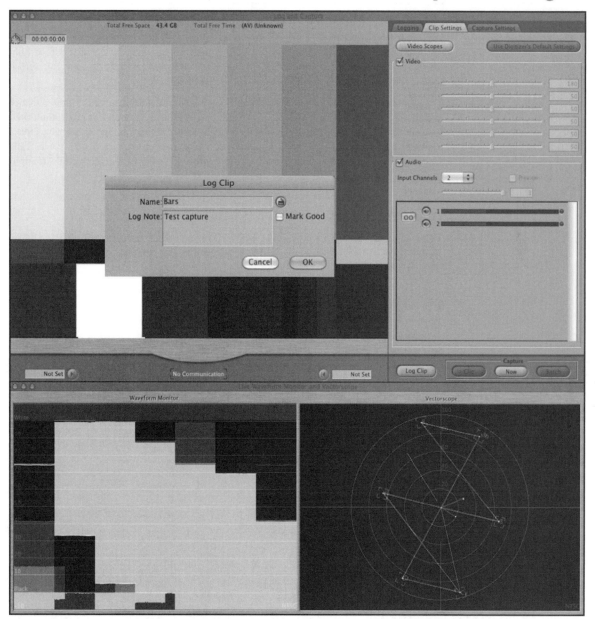

Waveform   **Vectorscope**

Figure 12.9

The tape-based capture utility in Final Cut Pro.

Effects and Titles

Most editing applications come packed with all types of fancy transitions and wipes. However, for a dramatic feature, you probably won't want to use anything more complex than a cross-dissolve. (Just think of those tacky wipes and iris transitions in *Star Wars,* and you'll see what we mean.) However, if you're working on a project that's more stylized, or on a commercial or corporate presentation, fancy transitions might be necessary.

Because transitions are notorious for quickly falling in and out of fashion, don't let the presence of the "wipe du jour" play too much of a role in your purchase decision—it might look tired by the time you're up and running. Instead, look for software that has a good practical effects package: color correction, internal titling, motion effects, and compositing. And if you're really serious about special effects, look for software that integrates easily with dedicated effects applications, such as Adobe After Effects.

Types of Effects

Nowadays, even the cheapest editing package includes a mind-boggling number of effects. In fact, sometimes the cheaper the software, the more effects you get! Nevertheless, all effects fall into one of the categories discussed next.

Transitions

Transition effects create a bridge from one shot to another. The most often-used transition is the cross-dissolve. Others include various wipes, pushes, page turns, and white flashes, to name only a few. If you're planning on using lots of these, look for software with plug-in support and keyframing (see Figure 12.10).

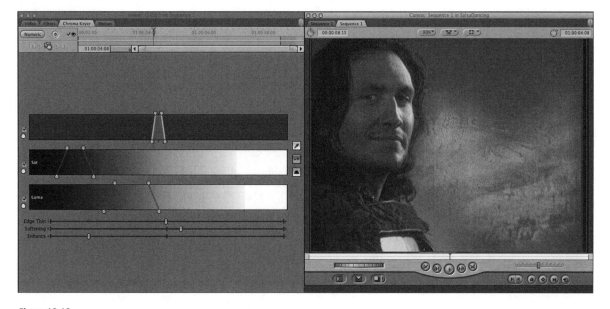

Figure 12.10

The effects editor showing luma keying and keyframes in Final Cut Pro.

Image Enhancement Effects

There's a limit to how much you can improve poorly shot video, but your editing software should offer some control over the brightness, contrast, saturation, and hue of your footage (see Figure 12.11). A lot of editing packages now offer elaborate color correction tools. These are especially useful if you are planning to finish your project using your editing software.

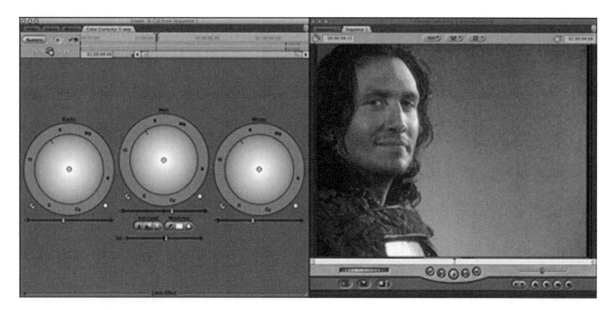

Figure 12.11

Color correction in Final Cut Pro.

Motion Effects

One of the most basic video effects is the ability to freeze, slow down, or speed up a shot. If you're going to do lots of motion effects, look for software that lets you specify a variable frame rate from 0% (freeze frame) to 3000% (the maximum that most programs will allow) so that you can do speed ramps.

Compositing

Compositing tools are used for everything from complex titling and video collage to sophisticated special effects, including virtual sets and locations. The compositing tools offered by most editing applications (alpha channel compositing, luma keying, chroma keying, and matte keying) are good enough for creating simple composites, but they lack the precision and control needed for serious special effects.

3D Effects

Another hot property these days is the ability to move a video layer in true 3D space. Used primarily for fancy transitions and simple effects, the feature filmmaker will find little use for these effects. If you want to create true 3D objects and environments, you'll be better off using a specialized 3D animation application.

Titles

Most film projects need three types of titles: the opening title sequence, the credit roll at the end, and possibly subtitles. Most editing applications can create simple titles, subtitles, and credit rolls (Figure 12.12). An opening credit sequence is another story. Complicated title sequences such as the one in *The Matrix* are really more like short animated films and will probably require using a dedicated 2D animation application such as Adobe After Effects.

Figure 12.12

Creating titles in Adobe Premiere Pro.

Audio Tools

Audio editing can often make or break a film. Good audio can enhance atmosphere, create drama, and provide a reason for what would otherwise seem like a bad edit. Editing software can tend to skimp on audio features, so if you're serious about sound editing, we recommend using a dedicated sound editing application, such as Avid ProTools. We'll talk about sound editing applications in Chapter 15, "Sound Editing." That said, you'll still need some decent sound editing tools before the film is handed off to the sound editor.

The following are some things to look for that will help you create better sound tracks in your non-linear editing application.

Equalization

Good equalization features (or EQ) let you do everything from removing the hiss from a bad tape recording to adding presence to someone with a weak voice.

Audio Effects and Filters

Just like video effects, audio effects and filters let you change the nature of the sound in a clip. And, just like video effects, many programs support audio plug-ins for adding everything from echo, reverb, delay, and pitch-shifting, to specialized effects that make a voice sound like it's coming through a telephone. When selecting editing software, you should assess the audio filters that are included and determine if the package supports audio plug-ins. See Chapter 15 for more on audio editing.

Audio Plug-In Formats

Although there are a number of audio plug-in formats, including TDM, SoundDesigner, AudioSuite, Apple's Audio Units, and Premiere, it's best to look for an editing package that is compatible with the plug-ins that you or your sound editor will use to edit the audio.

Mixing

No editing system is complete without the ability to set the audio levels on each individual piece of sound in your sequence, a process called *mixing*. Look for software that has a mixing interface with gain sliders and dB (decibel) markings. Some editing packages offer real-time mixing, which allows you to adjust audio levels while your sequence plays. This can be a time-saving way to get a rough mix that you can fine-tune later (see Figure 12.13).

Figure 12.13

Audio EQ and mixing interface in Avid Media Composer.

OMF Export

If you plan on using a dedicated sound editing application to complete the sound design of your film, software that can export OMF files will make your life a lot easier. OMF files contain the audio portion of your timeline and can be imported directly into an audio editing system such as ProTools. OMF support saves lots of time if you need to reconstruct your audio in another application.

Finishing Tools

Finally, the editing software you choose needs to be capable of creating an output of your final product. Outputting can be very complicated, and we've dedicated an entire chapter to it at the end of this book. Most professional-level editing applications offer support for low-res Web-oriented outputs and full-res HD outputs, as well as everything in-between.

Our Software Recommendations

There are many editing applications on the market, so we decided to stick with some of the most popular, and, in our opinion, most successful products out there. All of these programs are capable of being the centerpiece of a high-end, professional editing workstation. All of them share a similar, customizable interface with strong mouse support and lots of keyboard shortcuts. All of them offer drag-and-drop editing, three-point editing, and trimming. They have multiple levels of Undo, auto save and auto backup functions, as well as support for multiple video and audio tracks. They all offer decent audio editing tools and basic special effects capabilities, including title generators. Finally, they all support the importing and exporting of QuickTime movies and are capable of high-quality videotape outputs. In short, any one of these applications is up to the task of editing a movie. Finally, be aware that this list is not comprehensive. We chose not to talk about the myriad low-end editing apps—such as Apple iMovie—simply because there are so many of them, and they do not offer the advanced features necessary for longer format or more complex projects.

- **Adobe Premiere Pro:** The original QuickTime editing program, Premiere, is the least robust editing application listed here, but as a result, it is also the easiest to learn to use. It offers impressive integration with the Adobe Creative Suite, especially Photoshop, After Effects, Encore (for DVD/Blu-ray authoring), Media Encoder, and Soundbooth, not to mention Flash and Dreamweaver for Web-oriented projects.

- **Apple Final Cut Pro:** Apple's popular editing application is a complete, Mac platform–only editing system that is often the application of choice for indie filmmakers. The Final Cut Studio package includes several other great apps: Compressor, Soundtrack Pro, Motion, DVD Studio Pro, and Color.

- **Avid Media Composer:** It has a line of products that offer all of the features discussed in this chapter and then some. Designed for multiple users who need to manage large projects and finally available as a software-only app, Avid Media Composer is a great choice for the high-end market and indie filmmaker alike. The stand-alone software application comes bundled with Sorenson Squeeze, Boris FX Continuum, Avid DVD, and the SmartSound Sonicfire Pro music scoring application.

- **Sony Vegas:** It is a mid-range Windows-only application with support for native HD editing.

Know What You Need

By this point, you've thought long and hard about your project. Look at the following list of editing software features and decide which ones are important for your project.

- Will your project require multi-camera editing?

- Will you need to network two or more editing workstations together?

- Does the application have native support for the codec you shot your footage on? Or is the application's intermediary codec right for your project?

- Is color correction important for your project?

- Can the application import and export the file formats you need: Flash, Photoshop, and so on?

- What kind of special effects will your project require?

- Will you be doing your final mix in your editing app or in a dedicated audio editing app?

- Do you need to be able to export audio OMF files or 2K film res frames?

Most software-only editing applications offer downloadable demo versions of their products, so try out the ones that sound promising.

13

Preparing to Edit

Photo credit: Sonja Schenk

etting ready to edit is a three-part process: organizing your media, getting the media into your editing system, and preparing it for editing, especially if it's double-system sound or multi-cam footage that needs to be synchronized.

The biggest change when it comes to setting up a project for editing is that most projects are now file-based, instead of tape-based (see Figure 13.1). Even projects that were shot on video-tape typically capture full-resolution video and maintain a file-based workflow from that point on. 35mm film projects also maintain a file-based workflow once the film footage is transferred to a digital intermediate.

File-based Media

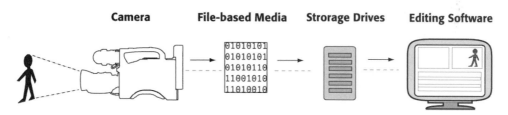

35mm Film

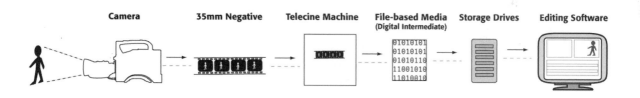

Tape-based Media

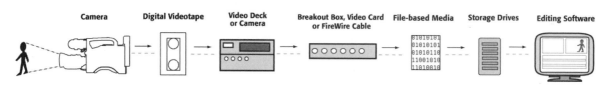

Figure 13.1

No matter how you acquired your media, your postproduction workflow will ultimately be file-based, as shown in this diagram.

File-based media is great, but without a set of videotapes or film negative as a backup, there is a serious risk of losing (or maybe just losing track of) your media.

In this chapter, we'll explain how to set up your project for the highest quality and the lowest margin for error.

Organizing Your Media

Making a movie requires a lot of media. Scripted feature films have a shooting ratio of 5:1 for lower budget films and upward of 10:1 for bigger movies. That means 8–15 hours of footage, not including additional sound media, effects, graphics, and any other elements that will factor into your postproduction process. Unscripted projects have even more media—a ratio of 100:1 is not unheard of for documentaries and reality TV shows. Whatever the scale of your project, organizing your media carefully *before* you start to edit will save you lots of headaches later on.

Setting up your project will involve the following steps, and they should be done in this order:

1. If tapeless, back up your camera original media and store it off-site.

2. Create a naming system and rename your files.

3. Transcode (file-based) or capture (tape-based) your media to an intermediate codec for editing.

4. Sort and organize your media within your editing application.

5. Synchronize sound and picture if you shot double-system.

6. Group multi-cam clips (if applicable).

7. Start editing.

Because a typical editing project can contain hundreds of separate pieces of media—video clips, audio clips, still images, and computer-generated media—spread across several hard drives, it's crucial to have a numbering and cataloging system that lets you find any piece of media quickly and easily.

Imagine this scenario: you've just finished whittling 30 hours of dailies into a 90-minute feature film. You're about to screen the final cut for an executive producer who may invest finishing funds into your film, and then your computer crashes. After you restart, you realize that about 30 percent of your media is corrupted or missing. What do you do?

If your project is well organized, you will probably be able to reconstruct your edited sequence in a few hours, possibly even using batch operations. If not, you'll have to reconstruct from memory. Depending on the degree of disorganization, you might have to search through several drives to find the correct shots, re-import your footage, and so on. Worse, you may have lost or accidentally deleted media without knowing it. The resulting cleanup job could take days or even weeks.

The longer and more complex your project, the more likely it is that you'll encounter problems such as corrupted or lost media, the need to re-import or work on a different editing system, and the need to bring in many different types of media from various sources.

Even without these troubles, staying organized will speed your editing process and make changes easier later on.

Create a Naming System

If your project is a scripted feature film with slates and a lined script, the numbering process has already begun. Each shot will be named according to scene/shot and take number, such as *35A-1.mov*. In addition, if the film was shot with double-system sound, there is probably a corresponding audio file called *35A-1.wav*.

If the project you are editing did not have a media person on the set, the raw media files from the camera may not follow these naming conventions. If that is the case, we recommend renaming the raw files according to the information on the slate. The best way to do this is at the OS level of your computer *before* you import or transcode any media into your editing application.

If you are doing an unscripted project or don't have slates, you will need to figure out your own file naming system. *Every file in your system should have a unique name.* Usually, a combination of the shoot date followed by numbers in the shoot order will do, such as *082511-001.mov*. However you decide to name your files, keep them short. We recommend no more than 10 characters (not including the extension). If your project is tape-based, hopefully the tapes will have been named in the field. If not, a numbering system based on the shoot date should suffice. As with files, each tape should have a unique name.

Back Up Your Camera Originals

Before you do anything to change your raw media files, be sure to keep a backup copy on a special hard drive that you store somewhere safe (not integrated into your workstation).

When you import digital files, the editing application will use the existing filename and keep track of where it is on your drives. If you end up moving the file to another folder, the application will ask you where the file went. As a result, it's important to know the name of the file and also the location. Many applications will let you change the name of the file once you've imported it into a project, but the name of the original file on your drives will remain unchanged. This can lead to much confusion, so it's best to name your digital files intelligently from the beginning at the OS level and avoid changing them after that.

There are several utility programs available, such as the BatchFileRename droplet for the Mac OS, which make it easier to rename large numbers of files in batches. If for some reason at a later date you need to re-transcode or re-import your media, the file names of your source media files are extremely important because your editing system will use these file names, along with the location of each file (for example, the hard drive, folder, etc., where it is stored) to find the source files. That means that the directory structure is also crucial. However you organize your media at this point, it is very important not to change it. If this link is lost or broken, you will have to tell the editing application where to find each source file on a case-by-case basis. That means that any organizing of the source media files on the OS level needs to happen before the files are imported or transcoded into your editing system. After that point, you should use your OS to lock or protect theses files so that no one can accidentally move them. Your editing system will not need them on a day-to-day basis to work with once the media is transcoded—they will exist as a secondary backup.

If your project is tape-based, your editing software will use the tape name and timecode to keep track of the original location of each shot. If you need to re-capture your media from the source tapes, your editing application will ask you for each tape based on the tape names you entered when you captured the media the first time. Because your project is likely to be file-based from this point forward, you should now make a backup of your captured media files and store it on a separate drive. You can, however, always recapture your clips from videotape.

Don't Overorganize Your Media in the OS

Too many levels of folders will make it complicated to find and import media. Stick with one folder for each day of shooting.

For large unscripted projects, you should also consider developing some keywords that will be assigned to your media before you start editing. Keywords allow you to sift and filter your media bins easily to find categories of clips. Keywords can be an invaluable tool for organizing, logging, and finding shots later in the editing process. Consider using the names of characters, topics in a documentary, and the locations.

Setting Up Your Project

At the simplest level, an editing application acts as a link between you and the hard drive(s) where your media is stored. Exactly how does the computer handle the massive amount of data that is being processed when you edit?

Each project that you create is stored in a folder, usually on the main hard drive. Some applications create a special folder for all the projects they create; others let you decide where to store the project folder. Inside the project folder are all the files that make up your project. Some applications store a master project file that includes just about everything. Others, like Avid Media Composer, store a master project file, a file for each edited sequence, a file for each bin, and a settings file for each project and each user.

What you won't find in the project folder is the actual media for your project—the video and audio files that make up your source clips. These will be stored on your storage drives (see Figure 13.2). Some applications will ask you to define the storage drives, or scratch disks. Others will simply store media on the drive with the most available space. Whatever the case, you will want to make sure that your media is getting stored in the right place. In the last chapter we talked about how some storage drives aren't fast enough to handle real-time playback of large digital video files. If you have a slow USB backup drive attached to your system, you want to make sure your editing application doesn't store any media on that drive. Refer to your software documentation for details.

When you create your project, your editing application will ask you to choose video and audio settings. You should set the project up for whatever type of media you'll be editing with the most. This will reduce the need for rendering later on.

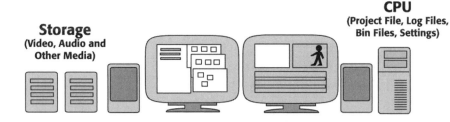

Editing Workstation

Storage
(Video, Audio and
Other Media)

CPU
(Project File, Log Files,
Bin Files, Settings)

Figure 13.2

Project files and other data files
are usually stored on your main
hard drive; media is usually
stored on fast external drives.

Other Helpful Tools

Editing applications are designed to be all-in-one packages for capturing, organizing, editing, mixing audio, creating special effects, and outputting a final master. Sometimes, though, they can stand to have a little help from the outside:

- **Media cataloguing software** like Final Cut Server or Adobe Bridge, and so on (see Figure 13.3 for organizing video, stills, and audio clips). Especially useful if you have multiple projects or multiple editors.

- **Still image editing applications** like Adobe Photoshop for preparing still images (if you have any) and for certain types of graphics and titling operations.

- **Database software** such as DevonThink Pro and FileMaker for keeping track of text-based documents; for example, field logs, camera reports, script versions, and so on.

- **Synchronizing software** such as Singular Software's Plural Eyes and Dual Eyes. Especially useful for projects that require synchronizing and were shot without slates.

- **Project Management applications** such as Movie Magic Scheduling and OmniFocus.

- **Cloud-based filesharing** such as Google Docs and Dropbox.

- **Large-sized file transfer tools** such as You Send It or a private FTP site, for digitally distributing work-in-progress cuts of your project to people who can't be there to screen in person.

- **Blu-ray and DVD authoring software** such as Roxio Toast and Apple iDVD. These simpler applications are great for creating work-in-progress DVDs. Later when you are creating a more complex DVD/Blu-ray Disc for distribution, you will want a more robust application like Apple DVD Studio Pro.

- **Web-based design tools** such as Adobe Dreamweaver and Flash.

- **Third-party compressors** such as Handbrake or MPEG Streamclip for encoding or transcoding media in the background so that you can continue to use your editing application to edit. (More about these later in this chapter.)

Figure 13.3

Adobe Bridge cataloging software is a great tool for cataloging and organizing all of the media that you'll use for a project, including video, stills, and audio.

Importing and Transcoding

Now that your source files are named and organized, you can start importing media into your editing application. In Chapter 3, "Digital Video Primer," we mentioned that most people choose to transcode their camera's original footage into an intermediate codec for editing. The codec you choose will most likely be based on the software you are using. Final Cut Pro users will choose the Apple ProRes codec (see Figure 13.4), and Media Composer users will choose the Avid DNxHD codec (see Figure 13.5). Although some will argue that one is better than the other, both are excellent and offer a wide range of quality levels, from very low-resolution, or proxy quality, to 4K digital cinema quality.

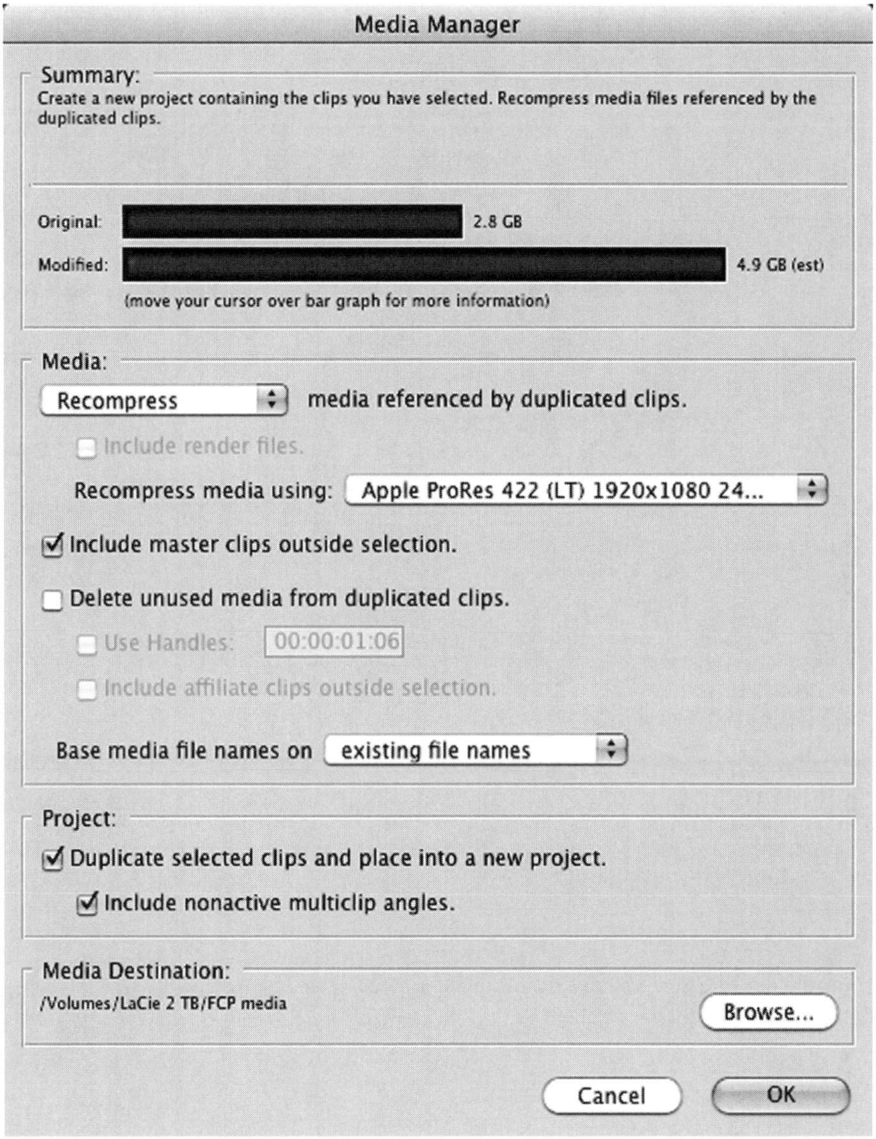

Media Manager

Summary:
Create a new project containing the clips you have selected. Recompress media files referenced by the duplicated clips.

Original:	2.8 GB
Modified:	4.9 GB (est)

(move your cursor over bar graph for more information)

Media:

[Recompress ⬍] media referenced by duplicated clips.

☐ Include render files.

Recompress media using: [Apple ProRes 422 (LT) 1920x1080 24... ⬍]

☑ Include master clips outside selection.

☐ Delete unused media from duplicated clips.

☐ Use Handles: [00:00:01:06]

☐ Include affiliate clips outside selection.

Base media file names on [existing file names ⬍]

Project:

☑ Duplicate selected clips and place into a new project.

☑ Include nonactive multiclip angles.

Media Destination:
/Volumes/LaCie 2 TB/FCP media   (Browse...)

(Cancel)   (OK)

Figure 13.4

The Media Manager in Final Cut Pro makes it easy to take your camera original files, transcode them to the Apple ProRes codec, and create a new project using the new files. Note that this h.264 footage almost doubles in size when transcoded to ProRes 422.

Typically, you will want to choose a codec that has the same resolution as your camera's raw media or better. In other words, since you are going to use these files to create your final master at the very end of your editing process, you don't want to downgrade the image quality of your camera's original footage when you transcode it. Choosing a codec that's higher quality than your original files won't make any improvements but choosing a codec that's of lesser quality will result in a loss of image quality. When in doubt, choose a higher quality codec. After all, storage drives are relatively cheap.

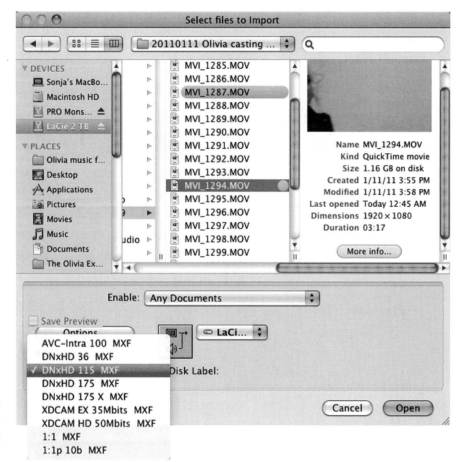

Figure 13.5

Avid Media Composer lets you select a codec and transcode as you import files into the project for the first time.

If you are not sure how to judge the quality of a codec, remember to compare the following components of a digital video file:

- Resolution or image size

- Frame rate

- Interlaced versus progressive scanning

- Color sampling ratio

- Bit depth

- Data rate

To maintain image quality, each of the above items should be the same as your camera's original media or better. If you don't know much about your camera's original media, open a clip in your editing software and select Clip Info (Media Composer) or Edit > Item Properties > Format in Final Cut Pro (see Figure 13.6).

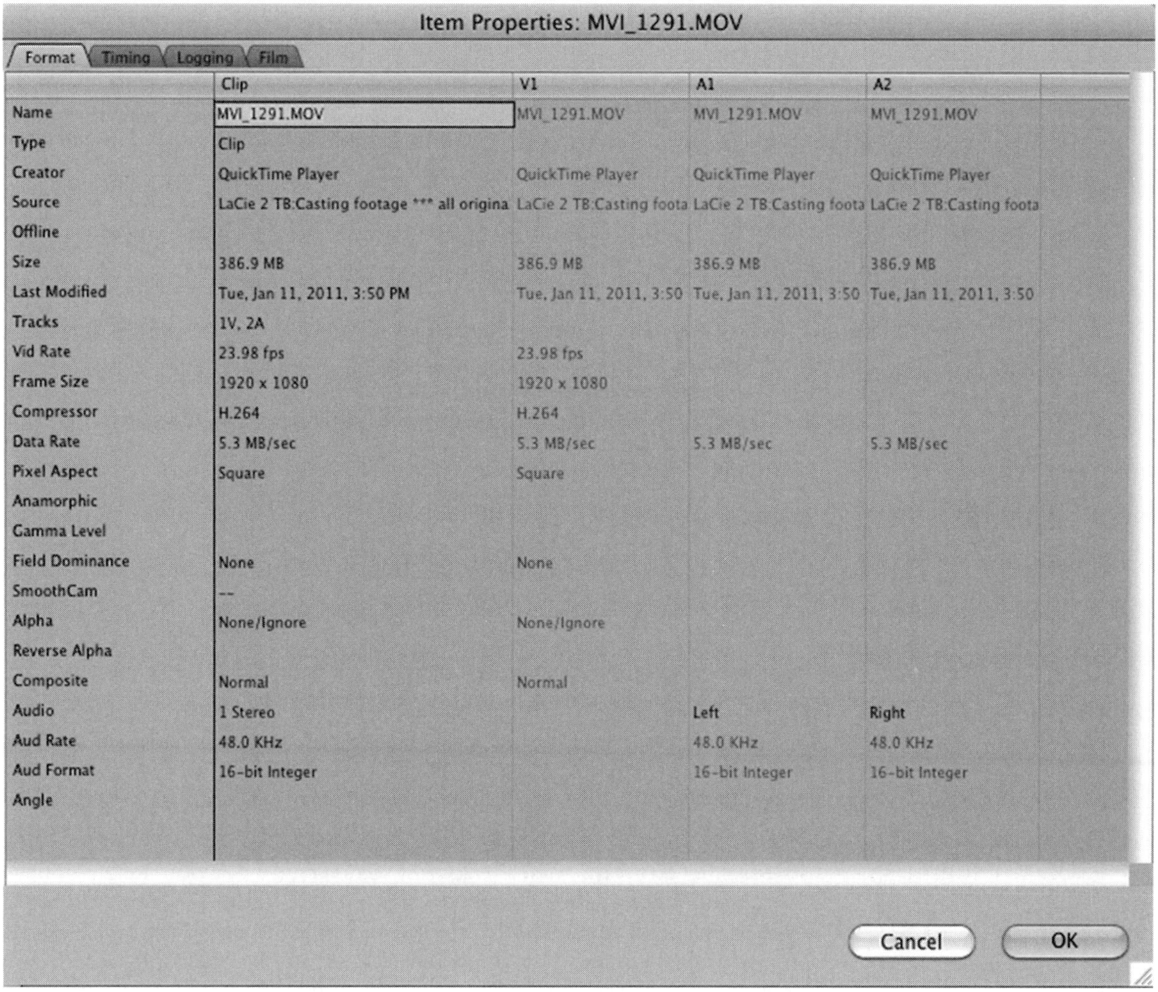

Figure 13.6

Most editing applications provide detailed information about each video clip. Shown here is the Item Properties window in Apple Final Cut Pro.

Just to make things a little more complicated, you can choose from several different applications to transcode your media. You can use your editing application or you can use a stand-alone encoder such as Apple Compressor, MPEG Streamclip, or Handbrake. Stand-alone compressors can run in the background or on another computer, and sometimes they are faster at compressing media than editing applications. But be aware, not all compressors are equal, and media compressed by different applications can look very different, *even though you are transcoding to the same codec.* Do some tests before you start, in order to find the compressor that gets the look you like the best and then stick with it.

Transcoding DSLR Media

If you shot your project with a DSLR, your camera original footage was most likely acquired with the h.264 codec, which uses 4:2:0 color sampling and 8-bit color. Choose an intermediate codec that offers 4:2:2 color sampling and 8-bit color that matches the frame rate and image size of your camera's original footage.

Capturing Tape-based Media

Most editing packages offer a capture utility to get video into your computer (see Figure 13.7). The simplest packages will work like a tape recorder: tell them to start recording, and they'll record any video that's fed into them. More sophisticated applications will let you specify, or log, which sections of a tape to capture, and can be configured for unattended capturing of whole batches of clips.

Logging

Because digital videotape isn't broken down into files the way tapeless media is, you'll have to help your editing software by telling it where each shot starts and ends before you have it ingest the media.

Following these technical tips can save time and frustration in the editing room, both now and later:

- **Log first, and then capture.** Logging your tapes lets you skip unusable takes that would waste disk space if captured. Usually, it's best to log all the takes, whether good or bad, during a first pass. Then you can capture only the good takes during a second pass. This way, you have a complete log of your tapes and can later easily grab additional takes.

- **Avoid logging across timecode breaks.** Any section on the tape that displays no timecode in your deck's counter is a break, and they tend to occur whenever the camera was turned on and off. If that is the case, it's likely that what follows the timecode break is a new shot, so log it separately. Some timecode breaks are very short and hard to spot so most editing apps let you choose to "capture across timecode breaks" in the project capture settings.

- **Log with "handles."** It's best to log each shot with a few seconds of padding at the head and tail. These handles give you flexibility to extend a shot or add dissolves. Some programs enable you to set up a predetermined handle length for your shots.

- **Avoid logging extremely long takes.** As you log your tapes, you might find yourself faced with a seemingly endless series of uninterrupted multiple takes. Rather than logging these as one giant shot, it's better to pick the best usable sections and log them separately. After you decide which take to use, you can delete, or take "off-line," the media that you're not using. You don't want to log a shot that's ten minutes long if you only use five seconds of it. Remember, the goal of logging is to make some initial decisions about the content of your project. While it's nice to have lots of choices in the editing room, too many choices can bog down the editing process.

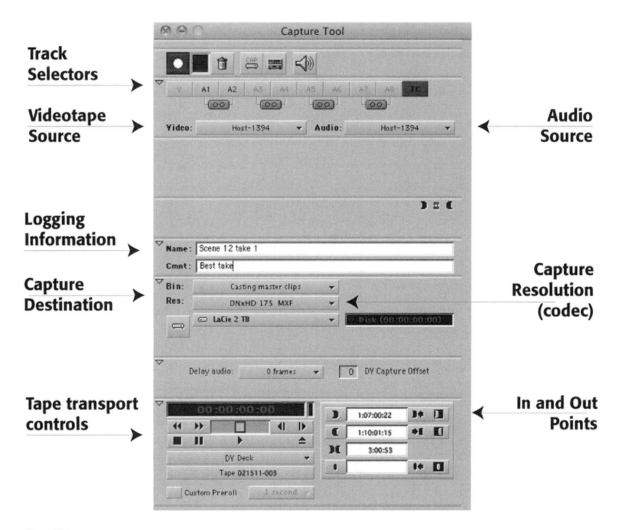

Track Selectors

Videotape Source

Audio Source

Logging Information

Capture Destination

Capture Resolution (codec)

Tape transport controls

In and Out Points

Figure 13.7

Tape-based capturing in Avid Media Composer.

- **Log the blue-screen correction shot.** If you're logging blue-screen footage, log the empty blue-screen shots that either proceed or follow each shot. These are important for compositing.

Capturing

Ingesting media from digital videotape can be a very simple process. The goal is simply to make sure that you do nothing to degrade the original image (and audio) quality as you capture it. Just as with file-based media, you'll want to select a codec that has the same image quality as your camera original media or better.

Typically, digital video files are captured straight across, meaning without any custom adjustment of the video signal during capture. Analog video (composite, component, and S-video) is calibrated using SMPTE color bars (if recorded on your source tape) and hardware or software-based waveforms and vectorscopes (see Figure 13.8 and Color Plates 17 and 18). We provide a detailed discussion of capturing analog video, including two tutorials, on the companion Web site, at *www.thedigitalfilmmakinghandbook.com/chapter13*.

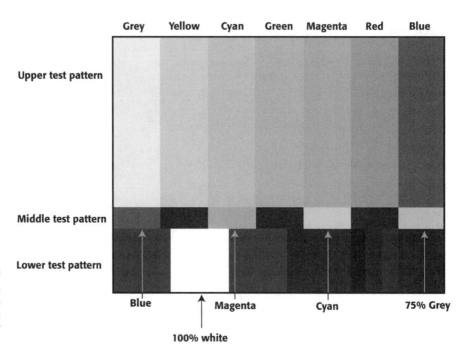

Figure 13.8

The SMPTE color bars test pattern provides a way to calibrate analog video when capturing (see also Color Plates 17 and 18).

Importing Audio

Audio files are much smaller, so there's simply no good reason to import low-res audio. For optimal quality, the audio files you import into your editing system should have been saved with the same sampling rate as they were recorded with, usually 48kHz (see Figure 13.9).

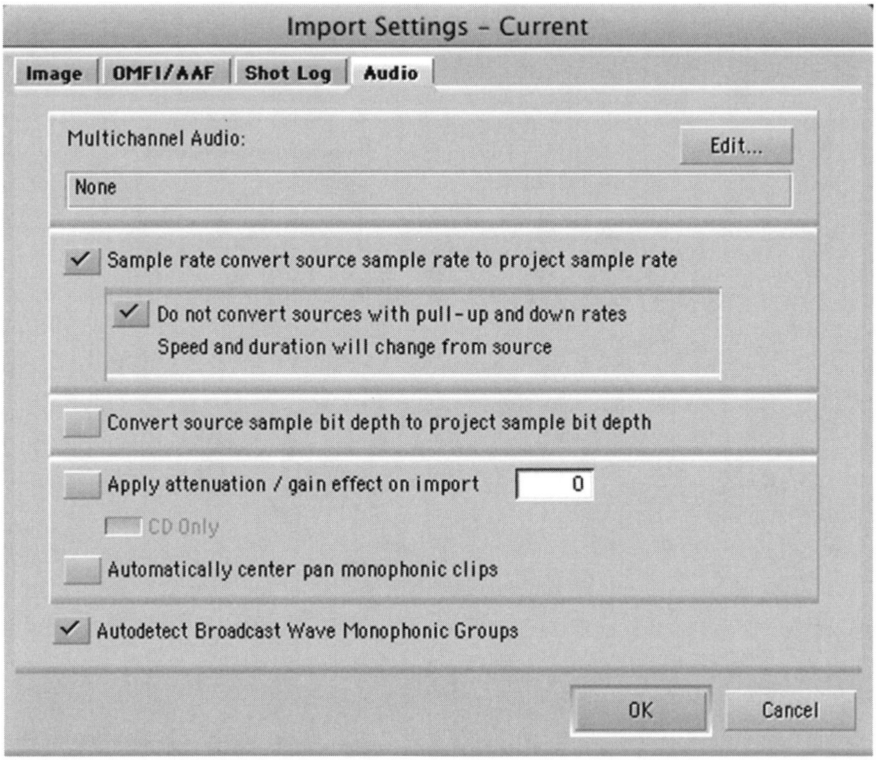

Figure 13.9

Most editing applications import audio files according to your project settings unless you specify otherwise. Shown here, Media Composer's audio import dialogue window.

Importing Still Images

Digital stills (TIFF, PICT, JPEG, PSD, BMP, and so on) can be a little tricky to import. Some editing applications will let you import images of any size, while others require that they fit the resolution and aspect ratio that you've set for the project (see Figure 13.10). The standard resolution for video is 72dpi, and the aspect ratio is the same as the resolution of the video you're working with. You may find that you need to use a still image editing application like Adobe Photoshop to resize your images to match your video resolution. Always be certain that the pixel shape of the still image matches that of the video. Otherwise, the still image might get distorted on import. And remember that it is better to work with an uncompressed still image file format like TIFF, than a compressed file format like JPEG. Some applications import Photoshop files with the layers intact—they appear as elements on separate video tracks—others will flatten them on import.

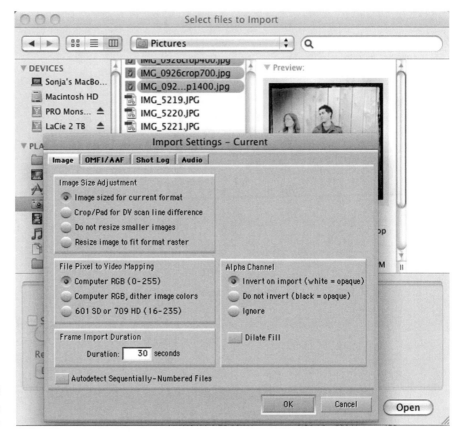

Figure 13.10

Still image import settings in
Avid Media Composer.

Moving Media

Digital video projects can have huge amounts of media associated with them, and the editing process can take a long time. That mean odds are high that you'll end up needing to move your media to another system or another set of drives at some point. Perhaps you decide to add a second editor, or maybe you want to send some media to your visual effects person. Or maybe you have a drive that is acting a little funny, and you think it's best to replace it.

Moving media can be tricky and can cause a world of pain if you aren't careful. Earlier, we mentioned how crucial file names and directory structure are, in order for your editing software to keep track of your file-based media. The safest way to move media around is by using your editing application to do it, rather than doing it manually at the operating system level. Avid users can use the Media Tool (see Figure 13.11) to manage their files and Final Cut Pro Users can use the Media Manager (shown earlier in this chapter). By using these internal media management tools, you can rest assured that your editing application won't lose track of your files.

Figure 13.11

The Media Tool in Avid Media Composer.

Moving Media from Mac to Windows

If you have to move media from one platform to another, take extra care to make sure that your filenames are compatible with the naming conventions for both the Mac and Windows operating systems.

Sorting Media After Ingest

Once you've got all your footage ingested into your editing application, you can organize it within the application. You can move files into different bins or folders so that it's organized in a way that's more intuitive to the way you want to work. The files on your hard drive won't be affected so you can rearrange and reorganize however you desire. You can also duplicate media so that you have, for example, an establishing shot of the Taj Mahal in a bin with all the other establishing shots in your movie and also in another bin with the rest of the scenes shot in the Taj Mahal.

It's a good idea to create a separate bin (or folder) for each set of dailies in your project. That way, if you want a reminder of what was shot on a particular day, you can simply open that day's source bin and see a list of all the shots on the tape. Figure 12.7 shows aan Adobe Premiere Pro bin that displays all of the information that was logged with each shot. As you can see, there's a lot of information there; much of this information was added automatically by Final Cut Pro.

Once you have each set of dailies in a bin, the next step is to create a bin for each scene. Between these two sets of bins, you should have everything you need to edit your project. If your project was recorded with double-system sound, you'll probably have another set of bins that contain all the synchronized clips, and you'll use the synchronized clips to build your scene bins.

How to Sort by Content

When sorting your footage, you should think about what you'll need to edit each scene properly. If you're logging tapes that were shot film-style—in other words, with slates, scene numbers, and script supervisor notes—your job will be relatively simple: just look at each slate and name each shot accordingly. However, if you're logging something that couldn't be meticulously organized on the set, like a typical documentary shoot, you might benefit from the following tips:

- **Listen to the dialogue first.** Dialogue is the framework of any scene, whether scripted or documentary. Use the dialogue to separate different topics into bins.

- **Find the cutaways that go with the dialogue.** These are usually reaction shots of the other characters in the scene. Sometimes, cutaways will be on the tape before or after the scene itself.

- **Make sure all the movements and geography are covered.** Put all of the action necessary to complete a scene into the bin for that scene. For example, if a scene involves two people going out to dinner, make sure you get all the "action" or movement in the scene (entering the restaurant, sitting, ordering, and so on). Make sure that you have all of the moments that set up the scene and that define how the characters are arranged physically.

- **If you're sorting interviews, separate each Q&A as a single subclip.** In other words, keep the question and the answer together, rather than only getting the answer, and don't include more than one question and one answer in a single clip.

- **Find the establishing and wide shots that set up the scene.** Separate out all the "b-roll" or scenery shots of the location.

- **Make a bin for any particularly nice or interesting-looking shots.** The camera operator might have shot something that's not in the script but that will prove useful later, or maybe that beauty shot of the beach in Hawaii will serve as an establishing shot later on.

- **Find the "room tone."** Room tone is the background sound at a location, whether it's party chatter or what sounds like "silence." You might need it for audio editing. Hopefully, the person who recorded the room tone voice slated it so that you know what it is—room tone, naturally, often sounds like nothing.

Synchronizing Double-System Sound and Picture

Synchronizing sound and picture is a process that has been around since the 1930s, and although some find it a little intimidating, it's actually pretty simple.

- If your project has matching timecode or slates, you can synchronize your media quickly in your editing application.

- If your project doesn't have slates, we recommend using one of the various synchronizing applications by Singular Software, Plural Eyes or Dual Eyes.

To synchronize in Media Composer, drag your sound and video files into the same bin or folder. If your clips have matching timecode, you can simply select the timecode, and they will be synched automatically. If not, load the video clip in the source monitor and find the frame where the slate is clapped. Set an in-point on that frame. Now find the slate clap in the audio file and put an in-point on that frame as well. Go into the Bin menu and select Auto Sync. A subclip will be created with the video clip and the audio file synched together. Once clips are synched together, Media Composer will treat them as a unit.

The synchronizing application Plural Eyes comes in a variety of flavors (stand-alone Dual Eyes, Final Cut Pro plug in, Adobe Premiere plug-in, and more) and works by comparing the waveforms on the audio tracks of the two files and synchronizing them accordingly (see Figure 13.12).

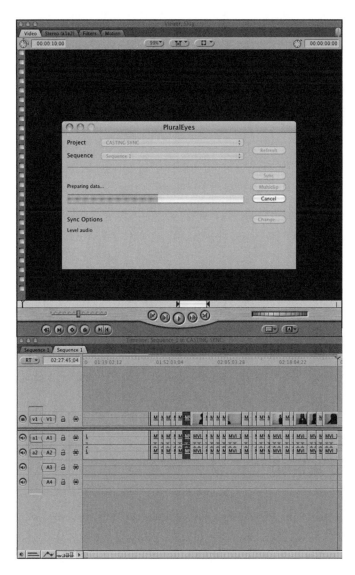

Figure 13.12

Singular Software Plural Eyes works within Final Cut Pro and other editing applications to synchronize audio and video automatically. It is especially useful if your media doesn't have timecode or slates.

Probably the best thing about the Plural Eyes app is that it can synchronize across breaks in the timecode or clips (for example, if your camera operator paused the camera during a scene but your sound recordist kept rolling). You might have five video clips but only one audio clip. This is especially common with unscripted shoots. Synchronizing media like this is a potential nightmare, but Plural Eyes makes it automatic. However, if for some reason you didn't record audio with your camera, it won't be able to synchronize your files because it needs the audio track to determine sync.

Preparing Multi-Camera Media

All of the editing applications we recommended in Chapter 12, "Editing Software," support multi-cam editing. As with double-system sound, each clip of video is imported as a separate piece of media, and the process for grouping multiple clips is similar to synchronizing. If your footage was shot with jammed sync, you can use the source timecode of each media file to synchronize the clips. If not, you can use the slate mark (see Figure 13.13).

Grouping multi-cam shots is pretty easy unless the cameras are stopping and starting at very different times during the shooting; in that case, it can be a time-consuming process.

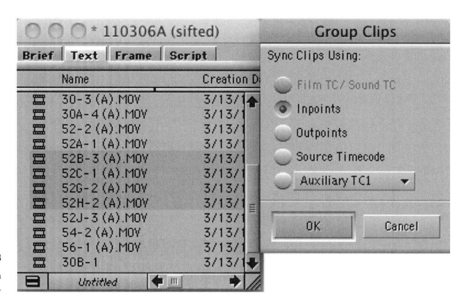

Figure 13.13

Grouping multi-cam footage in Avid Media Composer.

Troubleshooting

Sometimes you run into mystifying problems when you're editing, especially if you are working on a new system. Here's a checklist of what to look for when you're having problems:

- **Check your software settings.** Be certain that all preferences are set properly. Video editing apps have *lots* of settings. Re-launch. Refer to your software documentation.

- **Check your computer.** Do you have enough RAM for your editing software? Are other applications running? Are your drives full or fragmented? Mac OS users should try rebuilding the desktop, zapping the PRAM, and restarting the computer. Remember, when you shut down your computer, count to 10 before restarting.

- **Check your cables.** With your computer shut down, check all your cables, connections, and routers (if you have any), and make sure everything is secure. Check to make sure that cable lengths are within the approved limits.

- **Check your hardware.** Check all the settings on your hardware accessories. Refer to your equipment documentation. Make certain all your components are receiving power.

- **Dropped frames or stuttery playback.** Frame-dropping often stems from performance bottlenecks: fragmented disk drives, an overtaxed processor, or lack of RAM. In addition, check for system conflicts, especially codecs that aren't compatible with your editing application. External hard drives that are too slow (USB, drives with less than 7200rpms) are another culprit.

- **Audio is distorted.** Check the levels in your software. Are they overmodulating? If so, the problem is either due to the level settings in your software or a problem with the media file itself. If the levels in your editing app are good, use a pair of headphones. It may be a hardware problem with your mixer, cables, or speakers.

- **Your software refuses to batch import a previously imported shot.** This is almost always because the original source file was moved or changed, and the software can't find it. Check to make sure all your drives are online and working properly. Also make sure that there is space on your drives for the new media that you are trying to create. If a file or folder was accidentally moved, try to restore it to its original location.

- **Audio and video are out of sync.** This is usually a playback problem. Some software apps are known to be unable to maintain sync in longer edits. Moreover, some low-resolution codecs aren't capable of maintaining true sync. See also the suggestions for dropped frames and stuttery playback above. If none of those are the problem, it might be that the tracks in your timeline have accidentally gotten out of sync.

- **Audio plays too fast.** Make sure the audio settings in your software match the audio settings at which you recorded your sound.

- **Corrupted video.** Check the camera-original media. Is the problem on there as well? If the corrupted video is only in your imported clip and not the original file itself, simply re-import the clip. If it is in your original camera file, you're probably stuck with it. You'll have to try to fix it using your effects tools in your editing software—more about this in Chapter 17, "Titles and Effects."

- **Video looks bad on the computer screen.** Remember, if you're using a low-res codec, your video *will* look lossy on your computer, especially for wide or very complicated shots. If image quality is a concern, remember to always use an intermediate codec that has the same image quality as your camera originals or better.

14

Editing

Photo credit: Sonja Schenk

By the time you get to this stage, you've probably been working on your project for a long time: writing, researching, planning, and shooting. Now it's time to play with it. The history of filmmaking is rife with examples of films that have been rebuilt, restructured, and sometimes resurrected in the editing room.

If the script is weak, it is the editor's job to try to find a way to make it work. If the director was tired one day and forgot to get the cutaways, it's the editor's job to cut the scene regardless. The notorious "cutting room floor" has saved many actors from the embarrassment of a weak performance, and many cinematographers from the embarrassment of poorly shot footage. There's a saying that editing is a no-win situation—if the editor saves the film, the director gets the credit, but if the editor fails to save the film, the editor takes the blame. While it's true that for many people, editing is an invisible art, it's also well appreciated by those who know better, and it can be lots of fun.

Editing Basics

Motion picture film was invented in the late nineteenth century, but editing as we know it today developed slowly over the next 40 years as new technologies were introduced and more sophisticated ways to tell stories became the norm. The earliest films, like the Lumière brothers' *Workers Leaving the Lumière Factory* (1895), consisted of nothing more than *shots*, the most basic building blocks for an edited sequence. Turn-of-the-century French filmmaker Georges Meliès introduced the use of in-camera special effects such as slow-motion, dissolves, fade-outs, and super-impositions. These "magic tricks" developed into the rudiments of a filmic language: fade-ins to signify the beginning, dissolves to transition between one shot and another, and fade-outs to signify the ending.

Around the same time, Edwin S. Porter made *The Great Train Robbery* (1903), a film considered to be the beginning of modern editing. Porter developed the technique of jumping to different points of view and different locations, something we now take for granted. In the controversial *Birth of a Nation* (1915), D.W. Griffith took the concept of editing a step further, introducing the use of the close-up, the long shot (long as in length of time, not as in camera angle), and panning to develop story and intensify emotion. He also innovated the intercutting of scenes and parallel plot lines.

Russian filmmaker Sergei Eisenstein took Griffith's techniques even further and invented the concept of montage, as exemplified by the famous Odessa steps scene in *The Battleship Potemkin* (1925). In 1929, another Russian, Dziga Vertov, made the early cinema verité film, *Man with a Movie Camera*, documenting daily life in Russia with fast-cutting to create intensity and energy.

The invention of sync sound added an entirely new level of sophistication in filmmaking, and this turning point is exemplified by Orson Welles's *Citizen Kane* (1941), which used off-screen dialogue, voice-over, overlapping dialogue, and music to enhance the mood and power of the story. Editing styles and techniques have continued to grow and change since *Citizen Kane*, but the early history of film and editing is repeated on a small scale in every editing room as films are cut together using dissolves, close-ups, cutaways, intercutting, montage, and sound to build the final cut (see Figure 14.1).

Figure 14.1

If we first show a shot of the *San Joaquin Valley Swiss Club* and then show a clip of our actor, he looks confused or disappointed (top). However, if we show a clip of a knife-wielding maniac, and then show the same clip of our actor, the actor will appear terrified (bottom). The same images "edited" two different ways yield a very different emotional impact.

Whether you prefer the quick-cutting MTV style, a more traditional feature film-cutting style, or something you come up with all by yourself, the goal of editing is to successfully tell a story. In this regard, editing can be considered a continuation of the writing process: now that the film has been shot, the editor needs to do a "rewrite" of the script using the footage that exists. Because the footage has already been shot, this rewrite, or cut, will be limited to what was recorded by the camera. The editor might find that he can't always remain true to the original story—the dialogue that looked great on paper seems long and tedious, the "montage scene" that was supposed to play for several minutes ended up consisting of a mere three shots, and so on. The editor's job is to use the screenplay as a blueprint for the final story that will emerge from the footage that was shot.

Applied Three-Act Structure

If you've studied screenwriting (or read Chapter 2, "Writing and Scheduling"), you've probably heard the phrase three-act structure tossed about. Three-act structure originated with the plays of ancient Greece and is the basis for most Western visual storytelling forms. Three-act structure, put simply, means that every story has a beginning, a middle, and an end. In a typical feature film, the first act, or beginning, ends about 30 minutes into the story; the second act, or middle, ends 45 to 60 minutes later; and the third act, or ending, comprises the last 30 minutes.

When editing, three-act structure can be applied to each scene and each sequence of scenes, as well as the film as a whole. The beginning, middle, and end of a scene are referred to as *beats* rather than acts. Another way to think of these three beats is the setup, the action, and the payoff. A typical chase sequence might start with a burglar breaking into a convenience store and setting off the alarm (the setup); he flees and is chased by the police (the action); but he escapes by gunning his car across a rising drawbridge (the payoff). Sometimes, there is an additional half beat at the end for comic effect—a shot of the frustrated cops sitting in their car on the wrong side of the bridge. If a scene is missing one of these elements, it might seem odd, nonsensical, or boring. Keeping the idea of three story beats in mind can help if a scene or sequence you're cutting seems awkward or unwieldy.

Building a Rough Cut

Doing the first cut of a film requires juggling many different elements: visuals, performance, sound, story, and music. And that's just the start. There's also pacing, tone, and structure. The first cut of a film or scene is called the *rough cut* because it's pretty much impossible to get all those things right the first time. Rather than attempting perfection, its better to just take a stab at the material and worry about making it perfect later.

There are several ways to build the first cut of a scene using editing software. The simplest method is known as *drag-and-drop editing*. If your shots are named by scene number, shot number, and take number, sort them in that order. Select the good takes of each shot, and drag and drop them into the timeline in your editing app. The result will be a rough string-up of all the good takes of your scene in the order you selected them. If your software allows, switch to a thumbnail view in your bin and arrange the shots visually in an order that you think will work, and then select and drag and drop them into the timeline. If your scene is a complicated montage or action sequence, you might want to use three-point editing to create a more refined first cut of your scene.

Watch Everything

Back in the heyday of Hollywood filmmaking, during the shooting process, the film stock would get processed overnight and the next day the director, cast, and crew would watch the "dailies." These days, directors can watch their footage on the set, so dailies are rarely screened the way they used to do it. However, it's common for the director and editor to screen footage in the editing room after the shoot.

Some people like to spend the first half of the day cutting new material and the latter half of the day watching footage for the next day. If it's a documentary, the watching footage process can go on for weeks. However you decide to work, you'll need to watch all the footage in order to do the best possible cut of the film.

Take Notes

You'll never get a second chance to have a first impression of the raw material of your project, so take notes the first time you watch it. You don't need to write down much—just ideas, things that stand out as great or problematic, and so on.

Radio Cuts

If the scene you're cutting is based on dialogue, interviews, or a voice-over, a good way to build the first cut is to create a radio cut. The idea of a radio cut is to create an edit that sounds good first, without worrying about how it looks. You don't have to avoid editing the visuals during a radio cut—it's just not your first priority.

This method works equally well for scripted and unscripted projects. Using three-point editing, you can watch your footage, select the in- and out-points for each line of dialogue, and then press the Edit button to add each line, in order, to your sequence in the timeline. Once you've created a rough string-up of all the dialogue, go through the scene and make sure all the dialogue edits sound good and that you're happy with the overall flow of the dialogue. Now is the time to trim out extra lines, or add a pause where you think the content of the scene calls for it— such as after a particularly emotional, funny, or shocking line.

Master Shot—Style Coverage

If your scene was shot master shot–style (that is, a wide establishing shot and series of cut-aways), you'll want to set up a series of multiple tracks. Start by editing the entire master shot into your sequence as a guide track. Your scene probably has a selection of camera angles that can then be worked into your master shot. By adding extra video and audio tracks, you can edit other shots into the sequence by laying them in higher tracks, rather than by cutting up the master shot.

Editing Tutorials

In this chapter, we'll use two tutorials to walk you through the basic concepts of editing. These tutorials use footage from a short film shot in HD with a DSLR camera. You can use any editing application, but we opted for Avid Media Composer, which is available for download as a free demo on the Avid Web site. However, the tutorial will work just as well with Apple Final Cut Pro, Adobe Premiere Pro, or any other professional-grade editing package.

The media for the tutorial is available at our companion Web site. Go to *www.thedigitalfilmmaking handbook.com/chapter14* and follow the links.

If you've never done any editing at all before, you should take some time to get to know your editing application before you dive in. Basic editing software functions are covered in Chapter 12, "Editing Software," and also in the tutorials and manuals that come with your editing application. Give yourself a chance to get familiar with the editing software interface before you continue.

Last, but not least, in previous editions of this book, we featured a scene from Shakespeare's *Richard III* for these tutorials. It's a much longer scene and you can find the media and the tutorials for that scene on the companion Web site at *www.thedigitalfilmmakinghandbook.com/chapter14* as well.

Creating a First Cut

In this tutorial, you'll create a project and import media and create the first rough cut of a scene. See the sidebar above to get started downloading the media.

STEP 1: SET UP THE PROJECT

Setting up an editing project isn't hard, but you need to have some technical information on hand at the outset. It's always best to know the acquisition format of the media you're working with, including the native codec, the frame rate, and the audio sampling rate. You'll also need to decide if you want to transcode your media as you import it and what the resolution is that you want to work with.

If you don't know these things, don't worry—we're here to walk you through the technical stuff.

Launch the editing application. Create a new project and call it "Salsa Dancing." When the New Project dialog box appears (see Figure 14.2), set up the project according to the following specifications:

- Format: 1080/23.975
- Color space: YCbCr 709
- Render dimensions: 1920 × 1080

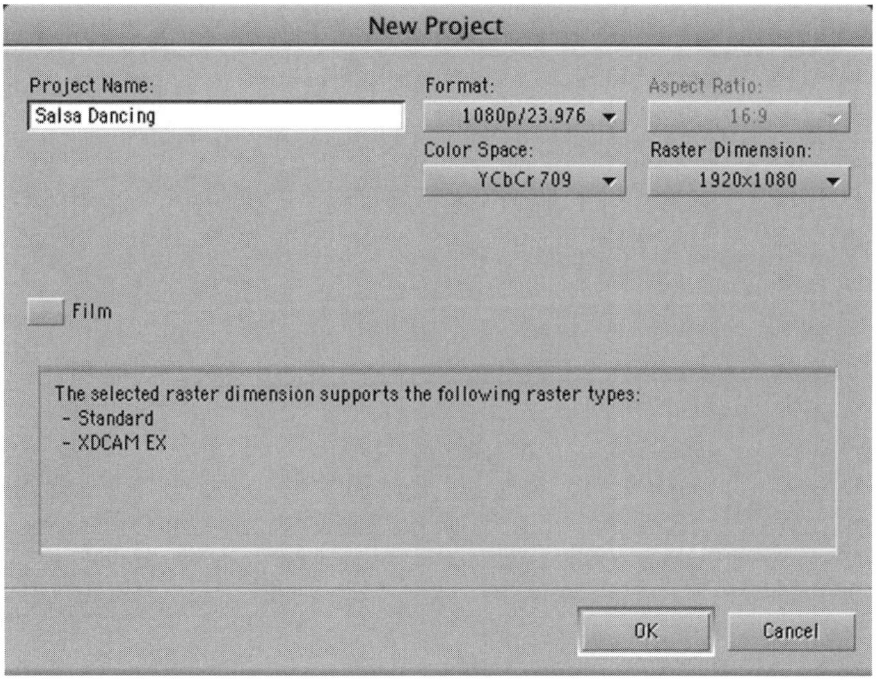

Figure 14.2

Your settings should match this figure when you create a new project in Media Composer.

STEP 2: BRING IN THE MEDIA

Your new project will open and a bin called "Salsa Dancing Bin" will automatically be created. Bins work like folders: they contain clips and edited sequences. Double-click on the "Salsa Dancing Bin" to open it and then go to File > Import and navigate to the media that you downloaded from the companion Web site. Select the files and tell Media Composer to transcode the media to DNxHD 36 (see Figure 14.3).

STEP 3: WATCH THE FOOTAGE

The first step in editing is always to watch the footage.

But first, a little back story: this is a scene where James is trying to practice some salsa dancing steps in the mirror. He is embarrassed when Sherrie, his roommate's mother who is visiting from out of town, walks in on him. Sherrie offers to help James with his dancing and uses it as an opportunity to grill him about her daughter.

Now that you know what the scene is about, go ahead and watch all the shots that comprise the scene.

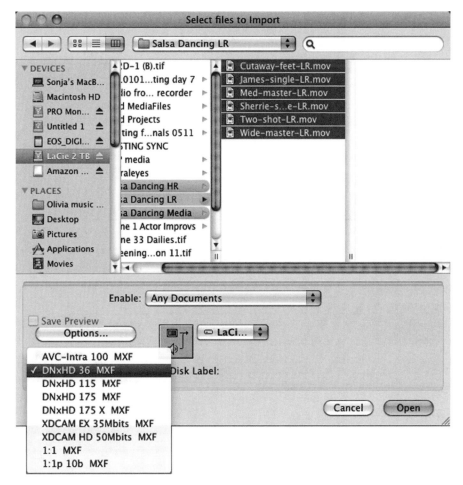

Figure 14.3

Import the media and transcode it using the Avid DNxHD 36 codec.

Select the Script tab at the top of the bin. This will show you a thumbnail image of each shot and also let you take notes in the text area (see Figure 14.4). To watch a shot, double-click to open it in the source viewer on the left side of your screen and then press the spacebar, or click on the Play button.

As you watch, you can also add locators (Avid) or marks (Final Cut Pro). Locators are a way to make a note that stays associated with a specific frame in a shot. So if you want to make a note of the moment that a character enters frame, for example, adding a locator is the way to go. The locator button is on the far right under the source display and when you click on it, a dialog box will open that lets you add a comment that will stay on that frame until you delete it (see Figure 14.5).

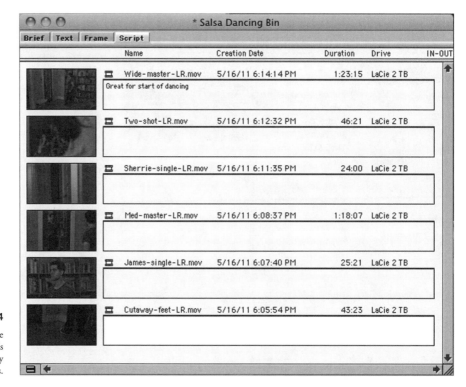

Figure 14.4

Select the Script view tab at the top of the bin to see thumbnails for each shot and a text entry area where you can take notes.

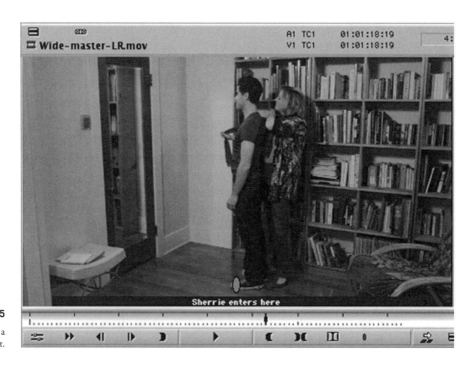

Figure 14.5

Locators let you make notes on a specific frame in your shot.

STEP 4: BUILD THE FOUNDATION OF YOUR CUT

Now you've watched all the shots, and you have probably developed some opinions along the way. Hopefully, you've taken notes or marked the takes you liked as good using locators. As you watched the raw, you probably noticed that there was a bit of a plan in place, in terms of the coverage. The scene is intended to begin with James dancing in the mirror and then cuts to Sherrie as she enters. They dance and end up at the mirror, where Sherrie grills him about her daughter.

Here is a list of the coverage for the scene:

- **Wide-master-LR.mov** is the wide master shot, which covers all of the action in the whole scene.

- **Med-master-LR.mov** is the medium master shot. This shot favors "James" and covers the entire scene with a medium-wide 2-shot.

- **Sherrie-single-LR.mov** is a single on Sherrie as she enters, and it only covers the beginning of the scene.

- **James-single-LR.mov** is a single on James up to Sherrie's entrance, and it also only covers the beginning of the scene.

- **Cutaway-feet-LR.mov** is a cutaway of that actor's feet during the salsa dancing portion of the scene.

- **Two-shot-LR.mov** is a two-shot of James and Sherrie's dialogue in mirror.

As you can see, there are two master shots of the scene—the wide master and the medium master. Even if you have an idea in your head of how the scene should be cut together, the wide master shot provides an easy way to create a very simple cut of the scene. You'll have all the action and dialogue in one shot.

Double-click on the wide master shot to load it into the source display. Press Play and find the start of the scene. Set an in-point by pressing the "I" key and then set an out-point at the end of the scene by pressing the "O" key. Click on the "Overwrite" button in the center of your screen and the master shot will be added to a new sequence in the Timeline (see Figure 14.6). Note that the new sequence will appear in your bin as "Untitled Sequence." Give it a name and save your project.

STEP 5: ADD SOME OTHER SHOTS

Now that you have the spine of your cut in place, you'll build up the scene by adding coverage. The first order of business is to add the shot of Sherrie entering the scene. Double-click on Sherrie-Single-LR.mov and set in (I) and out (O) points for the part of the shot you want to insert into your master shot.

There are many different ways to build a scene, but one of the easiest is to roughly position new shots on different tracks in the Timeline. So this time, we are going to target video track 2 and some unused audio tracks by clicking on the V2, A3, and A4 track selectors on the left side of the timeline (see Figure 14.7). Press the Overwrite button and the new shot will be positioned around your master shot.

Source Display

Overwrite edit button

In and Out Points Set

Timeline

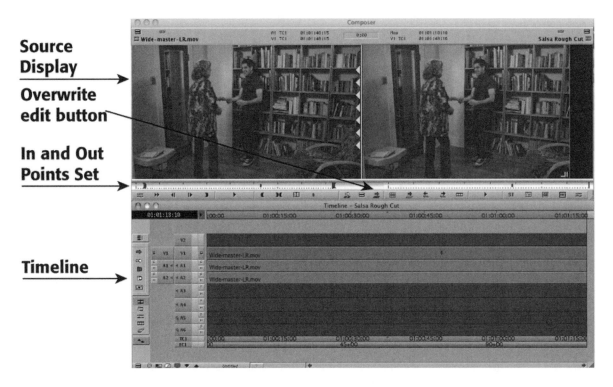

Figure 14.6

Load the wide master shot into the source display, set an in-point and an out-point, position the cursor in the timeline, and press the Overwrite button to create the foundation of your scene in the Timeline.

V2 targeted

A3 & A4 targeted

Figure 14.7

Use the Track Selector buttons to choose V2, A3, and A4.

Don't worry about the cut to the new shot being perfect. We'll adjust that later in the next tutorial. For now, we'll focus on covering the scene with the shots we like best. The medium master shot is the best choice for the dancing section, so double-click on it and use the same technique described earlier to select in and out points and edit it onto V2, A3, and A4. Next, move on to the shot that best covers the dialogue portion of the scene, Two-shot-LR.mov, and edit it onto V2, A3, and A4 as well. Your sequence should look something like Figure 14.8.

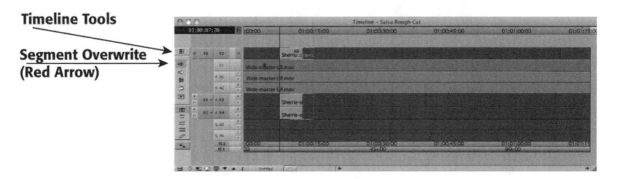

Figure 14.8
Use the red arrow to select the first shot on V2 and drag it to a good position in the Timeline.

Don't Be Afraid to Try Different Versions

As long as you save copies of your sequences, you can always go back to an older version if you don't like the changes you made.

STEP 6: ADJUST THE SHOTS

Watch your sequence. Remember that your editing software will play your sequence from the top down, so the shots on Video track 2 will cover up any video on the tracks below it, and so on.

Most likely, your cut is very rough, and the double dialogue is distracting. That's okay. We're not trying to make a perfect cut just yet. Instead, we're trying to create a rough sketch of the basic structure of the scene.

Now we'll use the Red arrow tool in the timeline to adjust the shots we added. Select the Red arrow from the Timeline toolbar and hold the Shift key as you select the video and audio for the single of Sherrie. The clips will turn a light blue color to indicate that they are selected. You can now drag and drop *within* the timeline to adjust the timing of each shot.

Notice that the displays above the Timeline have changed to Trim Mode. Drag the shot around until you think it's in the right place and then do the same for the other shots you added.

STEP 7: COLLAPSE THE VIDEO TRACKS

Now that you have the basic shots of your cut in position, collapse the tracks by using the red arrow tool to drag the video on V2 down onto V1. Hold the Cmd key (Mac) or Ctrl key (Win) to drag the shot down to V1 without shifting its position in time. Your sequence should look like Figure 14.9.

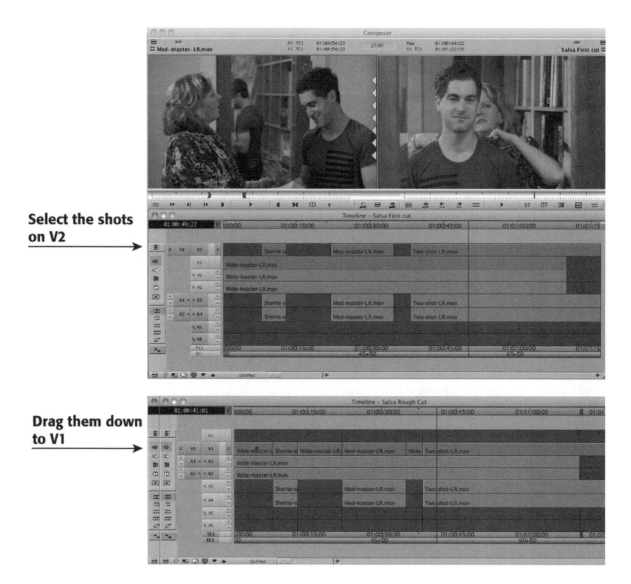

Select the shots on V2

Drag them down to V1

Figure 14.9

Use the red arrow tool to collapse all the video onto V1 in the Timeline.

STEP 8: CLEAN UP THE AUDIO

Now it's time to get rid of the double dialogue. But we want to keep the audio from each shot available in our sequence in case we need it later, so we aren't going to delete or overwrite any audio. Instead, we are going to use the Audio Mixer to turn down the volume of the audio we don't need.

Make sure the A1 and A2 tracks are selected on the left side of the Timeline; then go to the pop-up menu on the Record display (see Figure 14.10) and find the Add Edit button (also known as the *Razor button*). Drag through your sequence while holding the Cmd or Ctrl key. The cursor will stop at each edit in your V1 track. At each edit, click on the Add Edit button to make a splice. Your sequence should look like Figure 14.10 now.

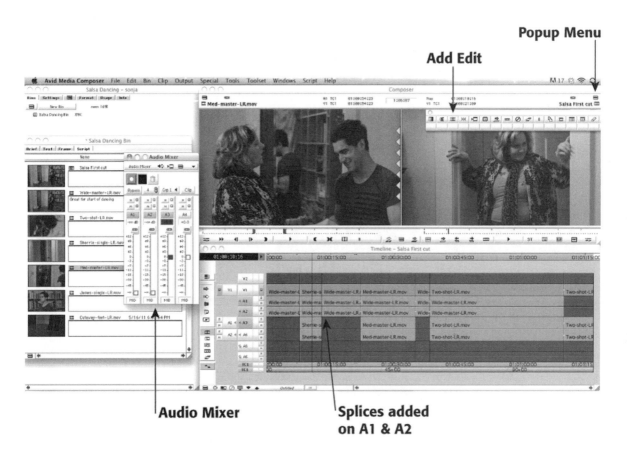

Figure 14.10

Use the Add Edit button to make splices in the audio tracks on A1 and A2.

From the Tools menu, select Audio Mixer. Position your cursor in the first place where you have double dialogue in the Timeline. This is the shot where Sherrie enters from the doorway. You want to keep the audio from Sherrie's single, but turn down the volume on the wide master, which is on A1 and A2. Go to the Audio Mixer and drag the levels sliders all the way down (see Figure 14.11). Now do the same for the other place where there is double dialogue.

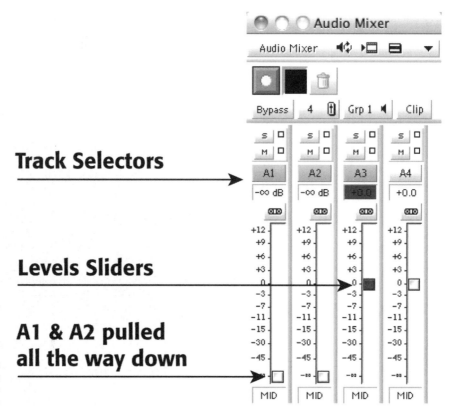

Track Selectors

Levels Sliders

A1 & A2 pulled all the way down

Figure 14.11

By adding splices, you can adjust the volume on the master shot but leave it intact in case you need it later on.

That's it. You have a first cut of the scene. It's not perfect, and there's a fair amount of work left to do, which we'll cover in the next tutorial but all of the beats are there and you've roughed in the basic visuals and the audio. Remember that a rough cut is meant to be rough. You should feel free to play around with it and not feel worried that you are destroying something amazing.

Save your cut and read on.

Auto Save and Auto Backup

Remember to save many copies of your sequences as you work. Use auto save and auto backup features offered by your editing application.

Editing Techniques

Once you have a first rough cut, it's time for the real editing to begin.

There's a saying that if you notice the editing, the film was poorly edited. Traditional Hollywood feature film editors strive for seamless edits—edits that don't call attention to themselves and that flow naturally with the action, dialogue, and tone of the scene. The key to creating seamless edits is to make sure each edit is motivated. A motivated edit is cued by a line of dialogue, a look or gesture from one of the actors, a sound effect, a music cue, or some other element in the film.

The opposite of a seamless edit is the jump cut. Jump cuts not only lack motivation, but also break up the basic continuity and linear progression of time. It used to be that jump cuts were to be avoided at all costs. Nowadays, even studio films feature carefully placed jump cuts to jar the viewer, add energy, or create a special effect. In *American Beauty*, jump cuts were used to accentuate the dream sequences, while the rest of the movie was edited seamlessly.

The following are different editing techniques you can use to smooth over a rough edit. All of them will work better if they are motivated in some way.

Cutaways and Reaction Shots

The easiest way to smooth a rough edit is to cover it up with another shot. It's almost like putting a Band-Aid over the cut. Cutaways are shots of other things in the scene, outside of the main area of action and dialogue: a fly on the wall, a hand moving to the handle of a gun, a foot tapping on the floor.

Reactions are shots of people reacting to the dialogue and action of the scene: a passerby looking on as the main characters yell at each other, a crowd cheering at a baseball game, a woman ducking as a gunshot rings out. Used properly, they not only cover rough edits, but also enhance the story.

Conversely, there's nothing worse than a random cutaway. In a scene showing a holdup in a bar, a cutaway to one of the bar patrons reacting when the robber pulls out the gun works well, while a cutaway to a static shot of a picture on the wall or a glass on the bar is unintentionally humorous. However, a cutaway to the glass right before the gunman puts a bullet through it can work well. In other words, using a cutaway or reaction shot in the proper context can be powerful and effective; using one that appears random will disrupt the dramatic intensity of a scene.

Avoid Overcutting

Too many unmotivated cutaways can result in the scene looking "cutty." Fast-cutting, as in *El Mariachi*, is not the same as overcutting.

Matching Action

If your scene involves movement, you might need to match action across an edit. Cutting from a wide shot of a man reaching for his gun to a close-up of the gun, from a hand turning a doorknob to the door opening, and from a shot of a man leading a woman dancing the tango to the reverse shot of her as she is dipped, are all examples of edits that need matching action.

Often, if you edit two action shots together as they play out in real-time the cut won't work, especially if you are cutting from a wide shot to a close-up, or vice versa. Because the movement across the screen is small in a wide shot and big in a close-up (see Figure 14.12), you might need to show more of the action in the wide shot than in the close-up. Matching action becomes second nature after a while, but it might require some playing around to get the hang of it.

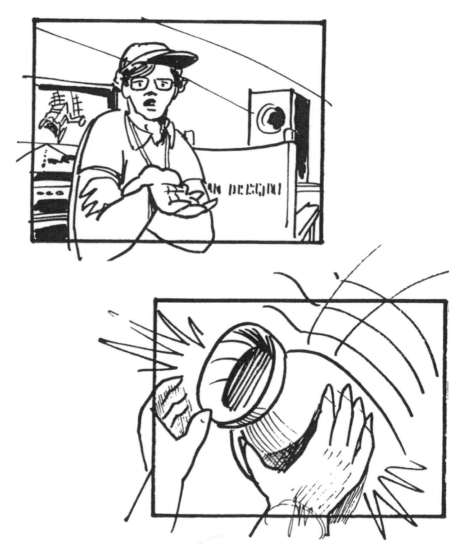

Figure 14.12

The movement across the screen is small in a wide shot (top) and big in a close-up (bottom).

Matching Screen Position

In a well-composed shot, it's pretty easy to figure out where the viewer's eye will be directed. In a close-up, the eye will be directed at the face of the actor; in an action shot, it will follow the line of movement; and if there are no people in the shot, it will be directed at the biggest, most colorful or dynamic thing in the frame. Once you determine where the screen position of the viewer's eye is on your outgoing shot, you can pick a similar screen position on your incoming shot (see Figure 14.13). This is especially helpful when you're trying to match action. You can also intentionally jar and disorient the viewer by mismatching the screen position (see Figure 14.14).

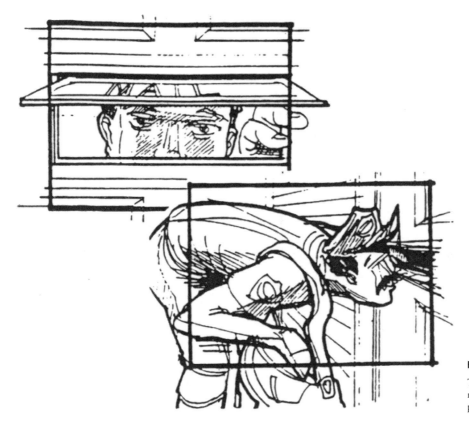

Figure 14.13

These two images of the mailman have matching screen positions.

Overlapping Edits

A common way to refine a dialogue scene is to use overlapping edits, also called *split edits* or *L-cuts*. If you cut from one actor to the other at the start of each line of dialogue, the scene can start to feel like a Ping-Pong match. Overlapping edits help break up this rhythm by extending or shortening the picture while leaving the dialogue the same, allowing you to see the reaction of one character as another talks. Trim mode and rolling edits are useful editing tools for creating overlapping edits.

Figure 14.14

These two images do not have
matching screen positions.

Matching Emotion and Tone

It's pretty obvious that you need to match emotion and tone in terms of the actors' performances when you cut from one shot to another. What's a little less obvious is that emotion and tone are carried in other things besides performance—the amount of camera movement in a shot, the amount of movement of the actors in the shot, the composition of the shot (wide, tight, etc.), the lighting and overall look of the shot, and the energy of the background elements. If your scene consists of an argument between two characters, it may work well to start out using wide shots and then get tighter and tighter as the scene heats up. However, cutting to a wide shot during the most intense part of the scene will most likely deflate the energy.

Pauses and Pull-Ups

Adding a few seconds of silence can intensify a moment. If one scene shows a man saying "I love you" to a woman, a well-placed pause can completely change the tone of the scene. Putting the pause before he speaks will imply hesitation; put the pause before she answers, and you'll have suspense.

Just as pauses in a scene can intensify the moment, shortening, or pulling-up the pauses in a scene can help pick up the pace. Whether you're cutting out the "ums" or trimming entire lines of dialogue, you can usually find a lot of "fat" in a scene once you start looking for it. Be careful, though—not every scene needs to be "tight" to be good.

Hard Sound Effects and Music

A hard sound effect is something short, precise, and fairly loud—a knock on a door, a burst of applause, a screech of tires. These sorts of sound effects startle the viewer a little bit and make it easy to hide a rough edit or smooth a jump cut. If your scene has music, it's a good idea to add it early on as you refine the edit. Music can change the pacing, add emotion, intensify action, and tell the viewer how they should be feeling. Many editors have a supply of film scores that they bring to a project as temporary soundtrack elements.

 ## Refining Your Cut

In the previous tutorial, you created a rough cut of the Salsa Dancing scene. In this tutorial, you'll use some of the techniques we described earlier to refine the cut. Open your project from the last tutorial and make a duplicate of your edited sequence. Call the duplicate "Salsa Rough Cut" and save your project.

STEP 1: OVERLAP SOME AUDIO

Load your sequence into the Timeline by double-clicking on it. The wide shot of James practicing his dance steps is fine, but the cut to Sherrie in the doorway might seem a little abrupt. By rolling the audio of Sherrie's shot back, we'll be able to hear the sound of her feet approaching, and the cut to her won't feel so unnatural.

Select A3 and A4 (the audio for Sherrie's single) and position your cursor near the edit. Then select the Trim Mode tool from the Timeline tool bar (see Figure 14.15). Now you can simply drag the end of the shot backward or forward in time to create an overlapping audio edit.

Go through the sequence and look for other places that overlapping audio can help the cuts.

STEP 2: ADD SOME CUTAWAYS

The shot called Cutaway-feet-LR.mov is a nice shot to enhance the scene. Drop it onto the V2 track at first to see where it works best and use the techniques described in the first tutorial to drag it around until you find the right spot for it. To get this shot to work, you'll need to match the action between the cutaway and the master shot. Play around with it until it looks good; then drag it down to V1.

Similarly, although the wide master is highly functional, you might find a more interesting shot to start the scene. One option is the medium master, which starts with a shot of James' feet and pans up to reveal his face.

STEP 3: CLEAN UP THE TRANSITION TO DIALOGUE

The next area to work on is the transition from the dancing to the dialogue that occurs in the mirror. Notice that the tone of the performances is quite different between the wide master and the two shot in front of the mirror. This is due to a choice the director made on the set. They are very different in pacing and energy, but it's still possible to make the cut between the two shots work.

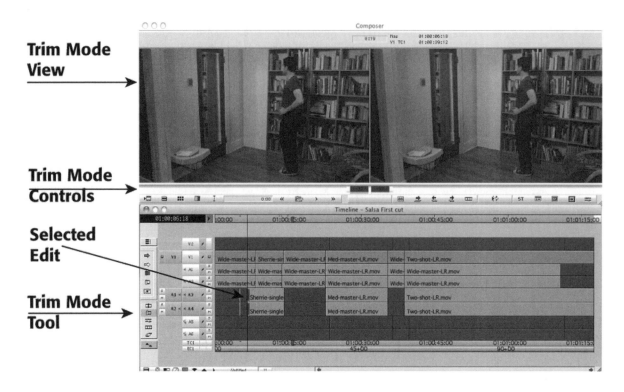

Trim Mode View

Trim Mode Controls

Selected Edit

Trim Mode Tool

Figure 14.15

Use the Trim Mode tool to roll the audio on A3 and A4 back so that you can hear the sound of Sherrie's footsteps approaching.

Luckily, in the wide master, Sherrie turns her back to the camera so you can get away with cheating dialogue here because we can't see her lips. Adjust the edit and roll the dialogue back to smooth the cut.

STEP 4: ADD SOME MUSIC

It's hard to watch a scene of two people dancing without any music. Go to the File menu and select Import and then navigate to a clip in your personal music library and import it. Edit it onto A5 and A6 and use it to cover both the beginning and the end as well. Try adding the wide master for the end of the scene since it allows us to clearly see the action (dancing) that ends the scene. 🔳

Watch Our Cuts

On the Chapter 14 page on the companion Web site, there are two files: Salsa Rough Cut and Salsa Final Cut. Click on the links to watch our cuts and compare them to yours.

Transitions Between Scenes

Once you have solid cuts of several scenes, it's time to string them together and start building the film as a whole. In addition to the edits within the scene, you'll need to work on how the scenes play against each other.

There are a number of things that happen "between scenes" in a feature film—a change in location, for example, or a jump forward or back in time, or a jump to an imagined sequence or dream scene. In the early days of filmmaking, each scene began with a fade-in and ended with a fade-out. Later, title cards were added to establish the scene. Both served the function of establishing a new location and a new point in time. Although filmmakers like Jim Jarmusch still use this technique (in films such as *Dead Man*), the typical modern filmmaker relies more on the techniques discussed next.

Hard Cuts

The phrase *hard cut* refers to an edit between two very different shots, without a dissolve or another effect to soften the transition. Hard cuts *within* a scene work best if they are smoothed out with matching action, screen position, and other cues. However, hard cuts can often be used to good comic effect, or to force the audience's imagination in a particular direction. Consider the scene in *Raiders of the Lost Ark* when Indiana Jones and Marion are finally onboard the freighter ship. While he suffers with his bruises, she looks at herself in a mirror. As she flips the mirror over to the clean side, we see the other end swinging up toward Jones's jaw, and then a hard cut to an extreme long shot of the entire ship, and an extremely loud, distant scream.

Hard cuts between scenes work best when they are surprising and jarring: a scene of two lovers kissing ends with a hard cut to an extreme close-up of the woman's hand on a gun as she plots to kill her lover. Or a close-up of a goalie missing the ball hard cuts to a wide shot of the goalie hanging up his uniform, and so on.

Dissolves, Fades, and Wipes

Using a dissolve to transition between scenes can add a feeling of smoothness and serve to slow the pacing of your story. Dissolves can imply a sense of "reflection" or "introspection" and give the audience a moment to chew on what has just transpired. Dissolves can also indicate the start of a dream sequence, flashback, or other jump in time.

Fades and wipes are looking out of date these days, but you never know when a fresh eye can make something old look new. The *Austin Powers* films employed a liberal use of wipes for comic effect, and the hard cuts to black between scenes in *Stranger Than Paradise* added a modern feel to a century-old technique.

Establishing Shots

Carefully placed establishing shots announce that a new scene is about to start, help to orient the audience, and serve to set the location. Without establishing shots, the audience can feel "lost." Often, the establishing shot is built into the first shot of the scene—a crane shot that starts high overhead and ends in a close-up on the main character, a slow reveal that pans across a series of objects on a desk and ends on the main character talking on the telephone, and so on. If the director didn't shoot a good establishing shot, then you'll have to find something to "cheat," such as the last few seconds of a wide shot after the cast has cleared frame. You don't need an establishing shot for every single scene in the film, just whenever a significant change in location takes place.

Spending more or less time on your establishing shots is an easy way to change the pacing of your project. A long establishing shot with supporting cutaways will slow things down and give your audience time to "settle in."

To speed things up, you can use a short establishing shot, or economize by combining an establishing shot with a split-audio voice-over. For example, cut to a wide crane-shot of a riverboat while playing audio of your main character saying something like, "The way your mother was driving, I never thought we'd get here." This simple split edit serves to establish the location of your new scene, identify which characters are participating, and provide a little exposition about what they have just done.

Clearing Frame and Natural "Wipes"

An easy way to create a smooth transition between two scenes is to cut out of a shot as the actor clears the frame, and cut into the next shot as she enters the frame in another location. This method can become repetitive very quickly if it is overused. When a large object passes through the frame, such as a passing car, a person in the foreground, and so on, it can be used as a natural "wipe" to easily transition to the next scene. In *Rope*, Alfred Hitchcock concealed his few edits in the film by hiding them under natural wipes.

Solving Technical Problems

Every film has a set of unique technical challenges that often fail to become evident until the editing process actually begins. The following are some of the most common technical issues that get resolved in the editing room.

Missing Elements

The problem you will face most frequently when editing is not having enough material, whether it's because an actor's mic didn't work, the pickups don't match the original performance, or there just aren't enough cutaways to allow you to edit the scene the way you want. Most of these types of problems require the on-your-feet, creative thinking that good editors are known for—restructuring the scene so that the bad mic or the pickups aren't necessary, or finding an inventive way to recut the scene using jump cuts to make up for the lack of cutaways.

Temporary Elements

When you start editing, it's rare to have all of the elements you need. Whether it's music, pickups, or special effects shots, if you don't have all your materials, you'll need some temporary elements in order to create a solid rough cut. Creating a temporary score is a necessity to help "sell" your rough cut, but be sure it's a score that is representative of what you'll be able to use in the final edit.

If you are missing shots because they haven't been shot yet, you can use a placeholder, such as a title, that describes the missing shot. If you have lots of effects shots and composites, you can use low-resolution proxies imported from your effects software (more about effects in Chapters 16, "Color Correction," and Chapter 17, "Titles and Effects,"), or you can create a temporary effects shot or composite in your editing project to use until you get the real thing. Managing lots of temp footage, proxies, and other elements can be an organizational nightmare if you let it get out of control. Be sure to develop some type of naming convention to indicate what's temporary and what's final.

High-Res HD Is Unforgiving

If you're editing with a low-res codec, be aware that when you up-res your project, you'll be able to see a lot more than what you saw in low-res. You may find focus problems, sync issues, and objects in the frame that you weren't aware of, such as microphones and cables. And if you "cheated" any dialogue or cutaways, you may find they are glaringly apparent on a bigger screen.

Multi-Cam Editing

Projects that are unscripted, involve lots of action, or cover a "live" event are often shot with multiple cameras. Sports events, talk shows, reality TV, and concert performances are typically shot multi-cam. As long as the cameras are properly synchronized with matching timecode, editing multi-cam footage is a breeze if you have editing software that can handle multi-cam footage.

The first step is to digitize the footage from each camera, breaking it up as needed and maintaining consistency in the clips across the different cameras. For example, if you're editing a boxing match, you could create a clip for each round that overlaps by 30 seconds or so. As you log and capture, you would do the same for all the cameras so that if you, say, have four cameras, you would then have four clips for round one, four clips for round two, and so on.

The next step is to link the clips from each camera together. The way this is done varies according to your editing software, so refer to your user documentation. Each group of camera clips is synched together using matching timecode from the shoot or a sync mark. If the film isn't recorded with timecode or properly slated, you'll have to find and set the sync marks yourself. You'll have to find a discrete frame—the moment a football flies out of the quarterback's hand, for example—and use that frame to sync all your cameras together.

Now that the clips are locked together, you can start editing. With Avid Media Composer, you load your grouped shot into the source monitor, switch to a multi-cam view (Media Composer allows you to view four or nine sources in a window), select the camera you want, set in-and-out points, and edit the shot into your sequence. The reference to the grouped shot remains intact so that at any time you can match back to the other shots in the grouped clip or use Multi-cam Mode to switch between cameras or, if you have your keyboard set up for it, use keystrokes to switch cameras on the fly. Apple Final Cut Pro now offers multi-cam editing, too.

The biggest issue with multi-cam editing is keeping the right audio in your cut. Traditionally, the best audio is linked to the "A camera." (The "A camera" is the primary camera, the next camera is the "B camera," and so on.) If your audio is organized this way, you can often simply use the A camera shot for audio, and it will sound great. However, some producers do not follow this convention. You may have to spend a lot of time listening to the various tracks on all the different cameras until you find the audio you need.

Fine Cutting

Now that you have a decent rough cut, it's time to take a harsher look at it. Is it working? Does the story work? Does the dialogue make sense? Does it flow naturally? Does it convey the desired mood? Fine cutting is when you will try to make the story and presentation work.

Usually, at this point, there's an important editing cliché to remember: the cutting room floor. If your film isn't working, you might need to cut it down. Maybe it's that montage sequence that you love, but comes out of nowhere and destroys the natural build of a love story between the main characters. Or maybe it's part of a secondary storyline that just doesn't fit anymore. Whether it's a scene, a shot, or just a line or two of dialogue, cutting out the things that don't work can do wonders for your film.

Woody Allen routinely makes drastic changes between his rough cuts and his fine cuts, often rewriting and reshooting *half* of the movie! This is true for films including *Interiors, The Purple Rose of Cairo, Hannah and Her Sisters, September,* and *Crimes and Misdemeanors.* Such massive reworking is often necessitated because Allen relies on very long master shots. If one line of a five-minute scene is wrong, no amount of editing can save it. In the case of *September,* several actors were no longer available, and were replaced (Sam Shepherd with Sam Waterston and Maureen O'Sullivan with Elaine Stritch).

After Allen saw the rough cut of *Crimes and Misdemeanors,* he threw out a third of the original story, rewrote it from scratch, and started reshooting. In the process, Mia Farrow's character changed from a geriatric social worker to a television producer; the documentary that Woody Allen's character was shooting changed from a film about retired vaudeville performers to a film about Allen's TV-producing brother-in-law; and a character played by Sean Young was cut completely.

Although not everyone has the luxury to reshoot as thoroughly as Woody Allen, it's important to recognize that even a director as skilled and experienced as he still has to feel his way through a project and make massive changes to reach his goal.

Editing for Style

The editing of feature films today has been strongly influenced by music videos, documentaries, and commercials. Fast cutting, visual effects, and jump cuts are the hallmark of "cool." Movies that fit this model include *Trainspotting, The Matrix,* and *Run Lola Run.* However, there's also a counter-trend in independent cinema that involves a no-frills style and lots of long shots where the action plays out with very little manipulation, such as the French documentary film *Trop Tot, Trop Tard* (Too Early, Too Late), or recent movies by Olivier Assayas (*Irma Vep; Late August, Early September*). Also popular is the handheld look borrowed from cinema verité and reality television, as seen in *Rachel Getting Married.* The choice is up to you, but a strong style can save an otherwise weak film.

Duration

Although it might sound trivial, one of the biggest jobs in editing is arriving at the proper duration for the project. Some projects have built-in durations: commercials are usually 10, 30, or 60 seconds long, and network TV shows are about 21 minutes or 42 minutes long. Trailers vary from short commercial spots to several minutes long. (Don't make the mistake of boring viewers with a trailer that tells the entire story.) Press kits usually include the full-length trailer(s) from the film, the 30- or 60-second teaser trailer(s), possibly a longer scene or featurette, and some selected takes, such as I.D. shots for each key cast member.

If your project doesn't fit neatly into a predetermined slot, it might be more challenging to arrive at the right duration. If you're editing a short film, keep in mind that it's rare for festivals to accept shorts that are longer than 10 minutes. The average length of the old Warner Brothers cartoons was six minutes, and most people seem to expect a short film to be about that length. If yours is a feature film, it will have to be at least 80 minutes long to qualify in most festivals. It used to be that a typical feature film was 90 minutes long, but lately, "serious" films tend to be at least 120 minutes and can often be as long as 180 minutes.

Remember, your story should dictate the duration of your film, not an arbitrary number that is the trend of the day.

The Big Picture

Russian filmmaker Andrei Tarkovsky aptly described filmmaking as "sculpting in time," and the longer your film, the more complex the "sculpture." As you try to get a final cut, here are some things to look at in terms of the structure of your film as a whole.

- **Rhythm and pacing:** If you start with a high-energy action scene and try to keep up that level of energy until the end, you'll probably fail. Action seems more intense when it follows a period of calm, and calmness seems more profound when it follows intense action or emotion. Good rhythm and pacing allow intensity to build over time, creating suspense and engaging the audience in the story.

- **Setups and payoffs:** Earlier, we talked about the concepts of setups and pay-offs within a scene or sequence of scenes. However, in a long film, there are also many setups that occur in the early part of the film and don't pay off until much later on. Make sure all the setups that play out over time are paid off later on.

- **Emotion:** Emotion is built into the script and the actors' performances, but editing plays a role as well. If scenes aren't allowed to develop or build, the emotion—whether happy, funny, angry, sad, and so forth—will fall flat. When you look at the film as a whole, make sure all the emotional beats that you intended are there.

- **Compressing and expanding time:** How long is the period of time covered in your story—a day, two weeks, five years? Does the structure of the film seem appropriate for the film's length? Would it benefit from rearranging the order and playing with the timeframe?

Last, but not least, you need to lock picture. Locking picture means that you have finished editing for story and will not make any further changes to the content of the film. You might still have some outstanding effects shots that need to be dropped in, but you won't be making any changes that affect the duration. Once picture is locked, it's time to take a more serious look at editing the sound.

15

Sound Editing

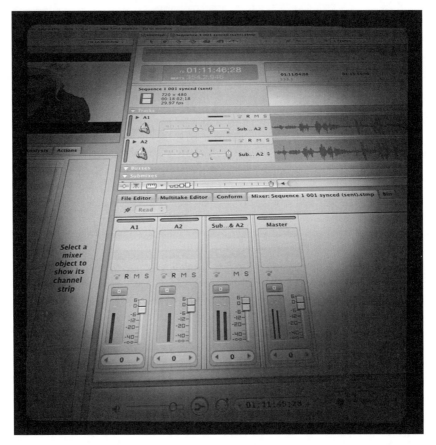

Photo credit: Sonja Schenk

Earlier in this book, we mentioned that sound is commonly considered to be 50 percent of a film. This may sound like an exaggeration to you, but once you start editing audio for your film, you'll quickly see that it's not. Sound can add emotional depth to a scene, clarify elements of the story, and make special effects and cheated shots pass the viewer's eye without raising any questions. Whether your project is a narrative feature film, a documentary, a corporate video, a commercial, or an animated short, sound editing is one of the most creative parts of the process of finishing a project.

In the course of editing your video, you've already done a lot of sound and dialogue editing, but as you probably discovered, things don't always go as planned when shooting. You might have encountered problem areas such as inaudible dialogue, unwanted extra sounds, dropouts, or inconsistent audio quality. And, of course, you probably didn't add any sound effects, unless they were essential to your picture editing (for example, matching action to a particular piece of music or sound effect).

Sound editing is the process of cleaning up all the mistakes and problems in the sound track, adding music, sound effects, and any re-recorded dialogue, and mixing and equalizing the whole thing so that it sounds as good as it possibly can.

Your editing software probably has pretty good sound editing tools, multi-track mixing capabilities, equalization, and a selection of special effects filters for altering the sound of your audio. These features often take the place of what once required huge rooms full of equipment and engineers. However, as with video editing, there are times when you still might need to use a professional audio suite to get higher fidelity sound, output a high-end master, or to enlist the services of a trained professional.

Sounding Off

If your video image is greatly degraded, it's possible that you can pass off such a flaw as an intentional style, but bad-sounding audio will quickly result in a frustrated, bored audience that most likely won't be able to follow your story.

Good sound editing strengthens the effect of each video edit. A few simple sound effects can ease the transition between pieces of audio shot at different times or at different locations.

Sound—whether sound effects, music, or sometimes *silence*—can add to, or completely create, the emotional impact in a scene. Can you imagine the shower scene in *Psycho* without the screeching violins? Or the shark in *Jaws* without the rumbling bass notes? And, of course, just try to imagine a sad scene of emotional confession without a sweet, heart-tugging swell of strings beneath it.

Music is often the most obvious sound effect, and we're all familiar with the experience of music providing important pieces of information. For example, a car drives up, a person we've never seen gets out, and the music suddenly becomes very ominous. Cut circus music into the same scene, and the audience will know this is a very different type of story.

Music is also used to set tone or atmosphere. If you had the opportunity to see one of the early director's cuts of *Blade Runner,* you saw a movie with an orchestral score, rather than Vangelis's synthesized score. As compelling as the visuals in *Blade Runner* are, laying orchestral music beneath them created an atmosphere that was not as effective.

Sometimes, the musical score carries all of the dramatic pacing in a scene. Try watching the last few minutes of *Jurassic Park* with the sound turned down. (This works especially well if you've never seen the movie.) You might be very surprised to realize the movie doesn't really have a strong ending without the musical score. If you don't remember the movie, the ending goes something like this: chased by a giant T-rex, the heroes race to get inside a building. The character played by Sam Neil tosses off a one-liner as they run inside, and the film cuts to a sweeping shot of the island as they escape by helicopter across the ocean. There's no giant explosion or climactic death of the T-rex—the actors simply run into a building and close the door. However, at the exact moment that they reach the door, the music swells to a crescendo, making it feel like a satisfying conclusion, and Sam Neil's little joke as icing on the cake.

When you think of sound effects, you often think of special effect types of sounds such as laser blasts or explosions. However, most of the time, your sound effects will be incredibly normal, everyday sounds. As with music, sound effects can often be used to increase the emotional intensity of a scene. Imagine a scene you've probably watched dozens of times: our hero is preoccupied as a villain sneaks into the room, slowly raises a gun, cocks the trigger, and prepares to fire. Next time you watch such a scene, pay attention to just how loud that trigger-cocking sound is. Would the scene carry as much impact without the help of this sound effect?

These types of augmented sounds can add a tremendous amount of drama to a scene, and they're a great way to guide the audience through a quieter, dialogue-free scene.

Finally, good sound editing can often be used to "dress" a set to make it more believable. If you cut to a shot like the one shown in Figure 5.11 and throw in echoing ambient sounds of Arabic crowd noise, a faraway steamship horn, and some Middle-Eastern music, your audience will believe that your location really is somewhere in the Middle East.

Like picture editing, the full importance of sound editing can be something that's very easy to overlook. In the rest of this chapter, we'll cover the types of equipment and software you'll need for good sound editing, provide tips for editing sound effects, ambience, dialogue, and music, and cover the basics of filters, equalization, and temporary mixes.

Setting Up

Before you begin any sound editing, you need to determine what types of sounds you'll need. Your sound editing process should begin with a screening of the final locked cut of your project. Ideally, you'll want to have your director, editor, sound editor, and music supervisor present at the screening. Your goal is to determine just what sound edits and effects will need to be created or acquired.

For every scene, you'll need to identify problems, necessary sound effects, and how and where your musical track (if any) will be edited into the scene. This process of watching, assessing, and listing your sound requirements is called *spotting*.

Next, your editor or sound editor will need to prepare your project file—the file you've been editing using your editing software—for sound editing. Presumably, you already have a few tracks from your original camera audio. You might have some additional tracks if you performed any preliminary audio editing or special effects work when you were editing for picture. You'll want an additional stereo pair for your music, and another track for special effects. Finally, you might want still another track for ambient rumble tracks that will be used to smooth the transitions between different sounds and locations. Typically, you'll have a minimum of eight tracks. For projects with simpler audio editing needs, such as those that rely heavily on narration, it's best to stick with eight tracks (or less). This is an easy number to manage and most editing applications are capable of real-time playback of eight tracks so you can avoid needless rendering.

By the time you're finished, you might have created many, many more tracks. Depending on how you will output your final project, these tracks will be mixed down to just a few tracks, a process we will detail in Chapter 18, "Finishing."

After the spotting session, you should have a better idea of what type of work lies ahead, and you can start thinking about what type of equipment and software you'll need to perform your audio edit.

Temp Mixes

It used to be that the "mix" was one of the last steps in the postproduction process, but nowadays mixing is something that starts during the editing of the video, gets built on during the editing of the sound, and then gets polished at the end in the final mix. The final mix is specific to the type of product you are creating—feature film, TV spot, Blu-ray release, and so on—and we discuss the varieties of final mixes in Chapter 18. But long before you get to that stage, you'll need to do a temp mix.

Mixing simply means setting the levels of the various sounds in your edited sequence and adding fades and equalization if necessary. Back when films were edited on film, the corresponding sound was edited on synchronized magnetic audiotape, or "mag." Film editing flatbeds typically only had room for two mag tracks and the volume could be controlled separately. Usually, one was used for dialogue and the other for music and effects. The sounds that accompanied many rough cuts prior to the late 1980s were very limited as a result.

Today, things are very different. Picture editors are expected to do a rough mix using their editing software in order to make their rough cuts better for screening purposes. They typically arrange the sounds across eight tracks and set the levels, add fades, and even basic equalization if needed. This process is called a "temp mix." By the time the sound editor gets to work on it, the mix should be decent. Since setting the levels for all of the sounds in your piece takes a long time, this saves the sound editor a lot of time. The sound editor continues to adjust levels to new sounds added to the piece as he works so that the mix continues to sound good. The goal of a temp mix is that at any time the project can be screened or output as a work-in-progress. By the time you get to the final mix, the mixer usually doesn't need to remix the entire project from scratch—instead, he will use the temp mix as a starting point and adjust levels on an as-needed basis.

Audio Levels Metering

The perception of audio is very subjective, and what sounds loud to one person might not sound loud to another. The loudness of audio is measured in decibels (dB), which represent a subjective scale: an audible increase in loudness means that the volume of the audio has increased 1dB. Software and hardware manufacturers put dB increments on the audio level meters that are a part of the equipment (see Figure 15.1), but 1dB on your video deck might sound louder than 1dB in your editing application. Unfortunately, this is a good introduction to the ambiguities you'll encounter when working with audio. Despite attempts to define it, sound is very subjective.

Digital audio meters place 0dB at the top of the scale (see Figure 15.1), and the midpoint is placed at –12, –14, or –20dB, depending on the manufacturer. Because it varies from one piece of equipment to another, this midpoint is also referred to as *unity*. The sounds louder and softer than unity might vary from one piece of equipment to another, but the sounds that fall exactly at unity should have the same volume on any piece of hardware or software.

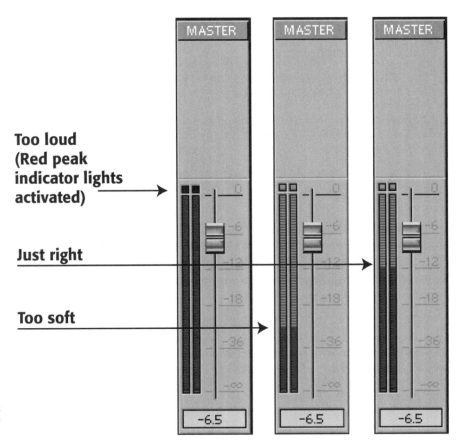

**Too loud
(Red peak
indicator lights
activated)**

Just right

Too soft

Figure 15.1

Digital audio meters provide a visual display to indicate the loudness of your sound.

Clipping and Distortion

You might be wondering what that red area on the audio level meter is. To simplify, it shows sounds that are very loud. Digital and analog audio levels differ when it comes to this portion of the dynamic range. Basically, it's perfectly natural that very loud sounds—a door slamming, for example—go to the top of the scale, or peak.

With digital audio, the red area should be avoided at all costs, because digital audio that is too loud gets clipped. Instead of distorting, the loud parts of the audio signal will simply get cut off. If, for example, the sound of a man yelling peaks, the high frequencies will get clipped, but the lower frequencies that aren't as loud will remain. The result will be a very strange sounding yell (see Figure 15.2).

Digital audio that goes above the peak level gets clipped...

Analog audio gets distorted - the signal remains intact but it surpasses the capability of the speakers

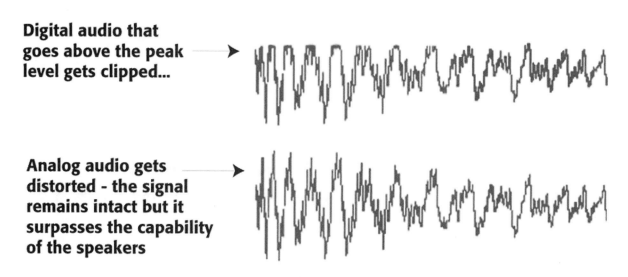

Figure 15.2

Digital audio that goes above the peak level gets clipped. The part of the signal that is too loud simply doesn't play.

Using Your Editing App for Sound

You will probably be able to perform most edits—audio cuts as well as cross-fades and simple effects—using the sound editing features of your editing software. Most editing packages provide a waveform display that makes it simple to zoom in on a sound to trim and cut, or to eliminate or replace problem areas (see Figure 15.3). As we said earlier, editing packages also usually include most of the audio filters you'll need for creating simple effects and for sweetening audio.

Figure 15.3

Audio editing tools and waveform display in the Adobe Premiere Pro timeline.

To determine if you'll need any additional sound editing software, you should examine your editing application to see if it has certain audio editing essentials. Consult your manual and do some tests with your software to determine if your NLE provides the following:

- **Multiple tracks and playback.** Most pro-level editing packages provide support for an unlimited number of audio tracks. Although your final master might only have four to eight tracks, being able to have extra tracks makes it easier to keep your project organized. At the very least, look for editing software that can play back eight tracks of audio in real-time.

- **Level controls for each track.** Any respectable, high-end editing package will have this feature, usually in the form of a simple line across the audio track that can be dragged up and down, and edited with control points. Play with your software's controls to see if you feel comfortable with this interface. You might decide you want to take your audio out to a program that provides a more traditional mixing interface. You might even want to take your audio out to a real mixing console. A hardware mixer, like the one shown in Chapter 11, "Editing Gear," is easy to connect to a computer and provides a good alternative to all that clicking and dragging.

■ **Can your editing app scrub audio?** For some edits, you absolutely have to be able to scrub through your audio very slowly. Scrubbing means that your audio plays at variable speeds as you drag your mouse through the clip. Ideally, you want an audio scrubber that slows the audio down when scrubbing, just like you'd hear if you played an analog tape at slow speed, as opposed to a scrubber that plays sampled bits at normal speed (the way an iPod does when you search forward or backward). Good scrubbing capabilities can be essential for making precise cuts or identifying individual words, sounds, and syllables.

■ **Sweetening and correcting filters.** There are a number of filters that you'll want to have to improve the quality of your audio and to correct problem areas. At the very least, you'll want an equalizer filter to adjust the various frequencies in your sound (see Figures 15.4 and 15.5). Ideally, you'll want to have a notch filter of some kind, a good selection of gates and compressors, specialized filters such as de-essers, and click-and-hum removers.

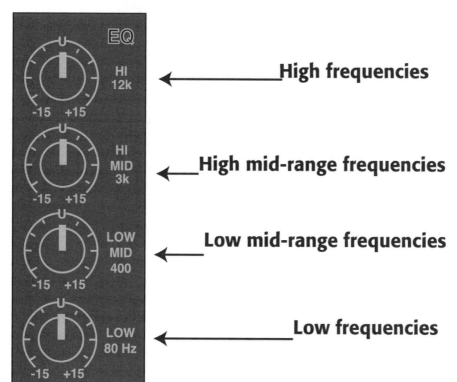

Figure 15.4

EQ controls let you adjust low, mid, and high frequencies for better sounding audio.

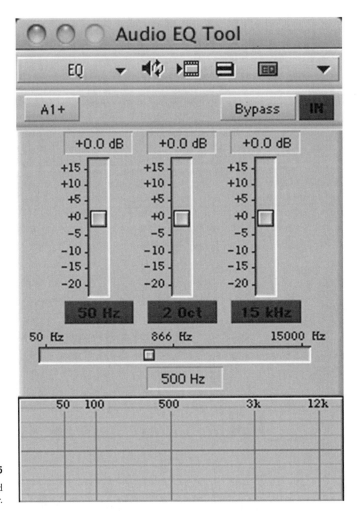

Figure 15.5

The EQ interface in Avid
Media Composer.

- **Special effects filters.** For added control, special effects filters such as echoes, reverbs, delays, and flangers can be used for everything from creating special sounds to creating ambient tone. Most higher-end editing applications will include a full complement of effects filters (see Figure 15.6).

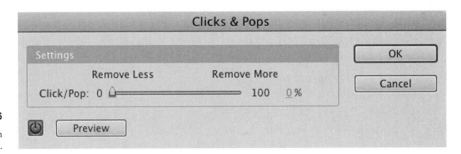

Figure 15.6

A simple click-removing plug-in
from Adobe Premiere Pro.

Dedicated Sound Editing Apps

If after looking at your editing software, you decide that you need more audio editing power, then you'll want to consider a dedicated audio editing application. There are several reasons why you might need more sound editing power.

Many editing apps only let you make cuts between individual frames, so if you need to make *very* precise edits, such as an edit at an interval that's smaller than a single frame, or 1/30th of a second, you'll need to move your audio out of your NLE and into a dedicated sound editing app.

As with picture editing, audio editing can be a very tactile process. Feeling where a cut should fall, or "riding" a level or EQ adjustment, are processes where you often want a fine level of hands-on control. If you prefer such controls to a mouse-driven audio editing interface, then you should consider moving your audio to an application that provides better on-screen controls (see Figure 15.7), or even hardware consoles that can be attached to your computer.

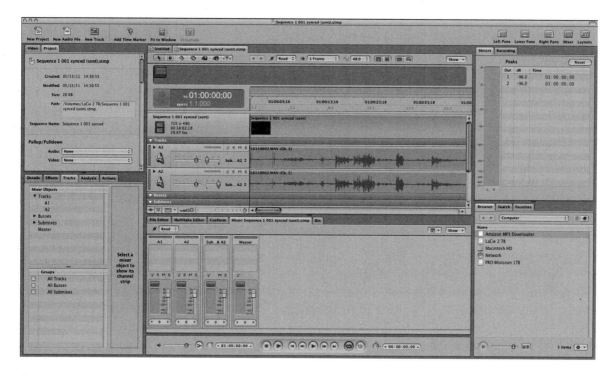

Figure 15.7

Apple SoundTrack Pro comes bundled with Final Cut Studio and provides robust audio editing controls.

Dedicated audio editors provide a number of other powerful features, such as the ability to define and label regions in an audio track. Regions allow you to label what each part of an audio waveform is, making it easier to spot locations for additional edits.

To select a digital audio application, you'll want to consider many of the same questions introduced earlier. In addition, look for the following:

- **How does the app play back video?** Many audio editing programs let you open a QuickTime movie for playback.

- **Does the app support the timecode you are using?** Although timecode is not essential for performing outboard edits on small pieces of your audio, you'll need it if you want to edit all your sound on a different software app or system (see the section "Moving Your Audio"). Many sound applications use timecode to synchronize their audio timeline to a QuickTime movie during the sound editing process.

- **Support for your editing app?** Many sound editing apps work hand in hand with a picture editing app: Apple Final Cut Pro and SoundTrack Pro, Avid Media Composer and ProTools, Adobe Premiere Pro and Soundbooth. If you're counting on exporting audio from your video editing app in the OMF format, make sure your sound editing app supports the same version of OMF. (For more about OMFs, see the section "Moving Your Audio.")

- **Are you editing in real-time?** For easier editing, you'll want an application that can apply effects in real-time. When making subtle EQ changes, for example, it's preferable to have your audio editor continuously loop and play the sound so that you can hear changes as you make adjustments. Many applications can perform simple stereo effects in real-time. For other effects, and for real-time processing of additional tracks, you'll need a system with special hardware.

- **Do you have room for more hardware?** If you opt for a system with special hardware, make sure that you have enough slots in your computer to support more expansion cards.

- **Do you need surround sound capabilities?** Some sound editing packages make it easy to create a five-channel surround sound mix that takes full advantage of the HD format. If you need surround sound, make sure that your software can handle it.

Obviously, if you're not going to be performing your audio edits yourself, then software might not be a concern. If you will be hiring a professional audio house to create your final audio edit, or if your sound editor has her own audio hardware, then you will simply need to find out how to deliver your audio. You should also plan to deliver copies of *all* of your original audio material. That is, all of your video files if you shot sync sound, and all of your original audio files if you shot double-system sound. There's no telling what your sound editor might need in the way of audio. Whether it's re-recording a sound, or building an entirely new sound from other material on your tapes, to do her job well, your sound editor will need all of your source material.

Just as there are many video editing applications on the market, there are also many sound editing applications. If you only need basic audio editing capabilities, though, you can stick with the tools in your editing application. However, if you need a more robust toolset, applications like Avid ProTools and Apple SoundTrack Pro, are of the caliber used by professional sound designers, dialogue editors, and mixers. All of them can handle synchronized playback of audio and video, support various types of timecode, import and export OMFs, real-time playback, and offer additional capabilities and performance through added hardware and software plug-ins.

Moving Your Audio

If you're going to edit your audio outside of your editing application, you'll need to move your audio—even if you're just moving it from one app to another on the same computer—and moving audio can be tricky.

Exporting an OMF file is often the easiest way to move sounds around. OMF files let you save the tracks you laid out in your editing software's timeline and can include audio levels settings, dissolves, and the audio media itself. However, OMF files come in a couple of different flavors: OMFs that only contain the timeline information, OMFs that contain the timeline and the level settings, OMFs that contain all of the aforementioned, and so on. Unfortunately, not all editing and sound editing apps are compatible with all the different types of OMFs, so be sure to check your software manufacturer's specs and do a little testing to be certain everything works right. Generally, once you export an OMF file from your editing software, you'll need to convert it to a project file that's compatible with ProTools or whatever sound app you're using.

If you need to perform a quick fix on a short, isolated piece of sound, then you can simply export your audio from your editing software in whatever format your sound app requires (AIFF, .WAV, SDII, and so on). Be sure to export at full quality so that the sound editor has a high-quality sound signal with which to work. In addition, no matter how you manipulate the piece of audio, you must take care to maintain the frame rate (usually 29.97fps, 24fps, or 23.978fps) and the audio sampling rate (usually 48kHz). This ensures that you'll be able to import the new treated audio back into your editing project without losing sync.

If you want to re-edit all of the sound in your entire project, the easiest way to take it out is by using OMF, but you can also output split audio tracks to any standard digital audio file format (WAV, AIFF, etc.). Assuming you have a locked cut of your picture, you'll have several tracks of sound that you edited along with the picture. By outputting each track to a separate file, and then importing each track separately in your sound editing app, you'll be able to start polishing the sound with a decent rough cut of the sound already in place. You'll need to make sure that the length of each track matches exactly the length of your final locked sequence in your editing project. Alternately, you can use sync marks, or 2-pops that match the countdown of your locked picture. 2-pops are a single frame of 60Hz audio reference tone cut into the countdown at the same frame that the two-second counter appears on-screen. Careful measures such as these to maintain sync are absolute necessities for this type of work—losing sync for an entire project is *one of the worst things that can happen in post!*

High-end sound editing apps such as ProTools work in tandem with a QuickTime video capture of the locked picture cut, so you'll also need to export a viewing copy of your locked picture sequence with a countdown, including a sync mark if applicable. When you're done editing the sound, you can reunite the polished audio in your video editing project. (You can find more about final mixes and audio outputs in Chapter 18.) As mentioned earlier, it's crucial that you maintain the same frame rate and audio sampling ratio that you used in your video editing project if you want your project to stay in sync.

Audio Editing Hardware

Sound editing applications are powerful tools, but even though you can get away with performing all of your audio edits using software alone, you might want special hardware to augment the process.

- **Mixing Boards.** If you're more comfortable with sliders and knobs than with a mouse, then you might want a mixing board for mixing and balancing your tracks. Although you might have used a simple mic mixer or four-track mixing board during your shoot, you'll probably want a beefier mixing board for your postproduction editing. FireWire-based mixing boards are the easiest to hook up because they don't require additional hardware.

- **Microphones.** Obviously, if you end up needing to re-record dialogue, or to record sound effects on location, you'll need microphones. For voice-overs and other dialogue recording, your best option will be a good handheld mic. Whether you choose to record directly into your computer or record into a tape deck, be sure you have the necessary cables and connectors to hook up your mic.

- **Speakers.** It almost goes without saying that all sound editing workstations need a good pair of speakers. See the section on audio hardware in Chapter 11 for more on speakers and other audio-related hardware.

- **Audio PCI Cards.** Many dedicated sound editing apps can be paired with special PCI cards designed to process audio in your computer. In addition, they add connectivity to other audio hardware devices. Check your software manufacturer for details.

Editing Sound

Once your equipment is in place, it's time to start working your way through the list of sound design elements that you created during your spotting session. In addition to the obvious sound effects—gunshots, screams, footsteps, howling wind, and so forth—and the questions of mood, atmosphere, and drama that we discussed earlier, there are a number of other sound edits that might be on your list. The following are all things you should look for when spotting and editing.

Unintelligible Dialogue

Remember that *you* already know what your actors are saying. Whether you wrote, directed, or edited (or did all three jobs), you've probably heard each line hundreds of times. Consequently, you might be more forgiving of a mumbled or quiet line of dialogue. Pay close attention to your character's speech, and make sure that it is clear and intelligible. If it's not, consider using EQ (more on this later), boosting the level, or using a different take (audio, or both audio and video). (Sometimes, you can sneak in a word from another take without any visible loss of sync, but be careful if you're going to end up projecting on a big screen.) As a last resort, you can always bring the actor in to re-record or "loop" his or her dialogue (more on ADR later in this chapter).

Changes in Tone

Does the overall audio quality change from one edit to another? Changes in tone can result from changes in microphone placement, changes in location, changes in ambient sound, or just weird "acts of God" that you might not be able to explain. Hopefully, you recorded some room tone at your locations.

A change in tone can often be masked by fading from one audio source to the next, to mask the change in sound quality. A bed of room tone, ambient sound, or music can further conceal this "edit" (see Figure 15.8).

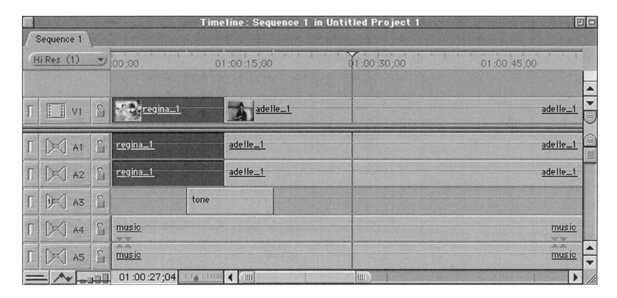

Figure 15.8

To improve sounds with mismatched tone, you can apply a bed of room tone. A cross-dissolve between the two bad tracks might further improve things.

Is There Extraneous Noise in the Shot?

When shooting on location, it can often be difficult to keep a quiet, controlled set. If there are extra, distracting noises—a loud conversation or music playing, for example—see if you can mask these sounds by placing sound or music effects that will keep your audience focused on your action.

Remember: The audience will pay attention to the things you lead them to. Just as you can brighten the foreground of your video to draw attention to your subject, you can "brighten" the foreground of your audio to ensure that your audience listens in the right "direction."

Are There Bad Video Edits That Can Be Reinforced with Audio?

Sometimes, a video edit with weak motivation can be reinforced with a good strong sound. The easiest way to reinforce an edit is to place a beat of music at that location. The rhythm of your music track will carry through to the audience's visual sense. If you're using pre-recorded, or "canned," music, consider adjusting the start of the music so that a strong beat falls on your weak edit. If you're working with an original score, perhaps your composer can suggest a change in music.

In addition to music, weak edits can be reinforced with an off-camera sound effect. A breaking window, for example, will provide plenty of motivation for a cut to another shot.

Is There Bad Audio?

There are many technical problems that can corrupt audio, from a boom operator bumping the mic, to a short in a cable, to interference with electrical fields. To eliminate thumps and bumps on the microphone, you can usually just bring the level of the audio down or cut it out. Hopefully, there's no dialogue or other important sounds during those moments. If there are, you might need to re-record those audio elements or try to do so. As we'll see later, other troubles can be corrected through EQ adjustments.

The clicks and pops that can result from a short in a cable are usually easy to fix because they're brief. Even if a click falls over dialogue, removing it usually won't affect the quality of your recording. Even if a click is in the middle of a word, sometimes just cutting it out sounds better than leaving it as is. Remember that, as with bumps, when you remove a click or pop, you don't want to delete it or use a "close gap" command, as this will shorten your sound and throw your sound and video out of sync. Instead, use a "lift" command, or select the area and use a silence command to reduce the selected area to nothing, or copy an appropriate length of room tone into the selected area.

If you have a hum in your audio, then your life might have just gotten very complicated. Some hums are easy to fix and can be removed with a simple notch filter. Fluorescent lights and some electrical sources sometimes create a 60Hz hum in your audio. Setting a notch filter to remove all the sounds at 60Hz can frequently eliminate or reduce a hum. Note that hums sometimes produce additional harmonic hums that also need to be removed. You can remove these with separate notch filters or use a special hum remover that automatically notches harmonics.

Some hums might be too "dirty" (that is, they fall over too much of the audio spectrum) to be removed. In most cases, living with it or re-recording your sound track is your only option.

If your hum is slight, you can often reduce or eliminate it with a simple EQ filter.

Are There Vocal Problems You Need to Correct?

While flubbed lines can often be fixed by re-recording, or pulling audio from alternate takes, other vocal problems might require special filtering. For example, if an actor's dialogue has loud, shushing "s" sounds, you can often correct these with a de-essing filter or with an EQ adjustment.

Dialogue Editing

When you edited your picture you, obviously, cut together your dialogue as well. However, you'll need to do a fair amount of editing to get your dialogue organized so that it can be easily adjusted and corrected, and to prepare it for the final mix.

Checkerboarding is the process of arranging your dialogue tracks so that one voice can be easily adjusted and corrected. Your goal is to separate different speakers onto different tracks so that you can manipulate and correct their dialogue with as few separate actions as possible. For example, if you've decided that all of your lead actor's dialogue needs a slight EQ adjustment, having all of that actor's dialogue on one track will make it simple to apply a single EQ filter to all of your actor's speech.

It's called *checkerboarding* (or *splitting tracks*) because, as you begin to separate different speakers, your audio tracks will begin to have a "checkerboard" appearance as can be seen in Figure 15.9.

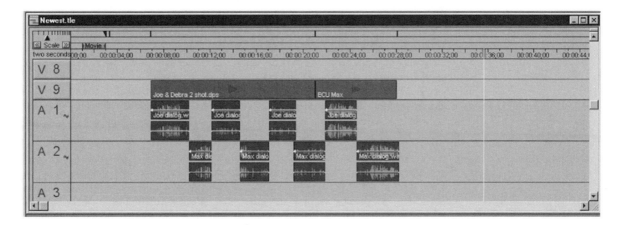

Figure 15.9

Checkerboard dialogue editing.

You won't necessarily separate out every single voice or even every occurrence of a particular speaker. Although you might be trying to split out a particular actor, splitting tracks during short lines or overlapping dialogue might not be worth the trouble. In addition to splitting up your dialogue, you'll also need to move all of the sound effects recorded during your production onto their own track.

In an editing application, the easiest way to split tracks is simply to select the relevant portions of the sound track and drag them to a new track. Remember to always make a backup of your sequence before you start any major reorganization of your project.

This is where the 30 to 60 seconds of room tone that you recorded during production will come into play. You'll use room tone to smooth the differences between different speakers, to fill silent areas, and to improve the sense of ambient space in your audio. If you didn't record room tone, then you can try to build up a sample of room tone by cutting and pasting together quiet moments from your original audio track.

ADR

ADR, or *automatic dialogue replacement,* is used to replace badly recorded dialogue, fix a muffed line, or insert dialogue that could not be recorded on location.

In a professional sound facility, a projector or monitor shows the scene to be re-recorded and then immediately replays the scene again without audio. The actors then record their lines while watching the scene. Sometimes, a continuous "loop" of the scene is shown; hence the term *looping.*

The actor is usually cued with a series of regular beeps that count down to the start of recording. The goal is to match the vocal performance to what they just saw on-screen.

Although you might be tempted to rely on re-recording dialogue—you might think it is easier than trying to get things correct on-set—be warned that getting good ADR is hard work. First, you'll need to try to match the tone and quality of the original recording. Everything from mic selection and mic placement to the qualities of the recording room will affect the tone of your recording. As if getting the actor to match his voice to the lip movements recorded on-screen isn't difficult enough, consider also that the actor's performance will probably be at a somewhat different energy and emotional level than what was originally shot. Outside of the scene, with no actors, build-up, or motivation, it can be difficult for an actor to achieve the same performance quality that he delivered on-set.

ADR is most difficult on close-ups because it's easier to see sync problems. An example of a scene that could benefit from ADR is a long shot of two people having a conversation near a freeway. The production sound will be very bad due to the noise from the freeway. Since the actors are far away, it will be difficult for the audience to see if the re-recorded dialogue is actually in sync with the actors' mouths. In addition, ADR that appears in sync on the small screen might seem "soft" on the big screen, so use ADR carefully if you're planning on a theatrical projection of your project.

If you have a sound editing product that supports TDM or AudioSuite plug-ins, then you can use Synchro Arts' VocAlign to automatically stretch or compress a re-recorded piece of dialogue to match the original production recording. If this sounds impossibly amazing, it is. But it works! If your project requires a lot of accurate ADR, VocAlign is worth the money.

Non-Dialogue Voice Recordings

Most other voice recording jobs will be simpler than ADR. Voice-overs (such as those used in a documentary or in a flashback scene in a dramatic feature), off-screen dialogue, as well as other vocal sound effects will require special recording sessions, but you won't need all the tools required for ADR recording. Rather, a good directional mic hooked up to your editing software will do.

For example, if you shot a restaurant scene with a silent background (to better record the voices of your actors), you might record the sound of the other restaurant patrons. (*Walla* is the term for the mumbling, unrecognizable din of a crowd of people.) However, if you can, try to get away with recording walla and other background sounds "wild" instead of paying for a studio recording session.

EQ Is Your Friend

If your home stereo has controls for adjusting bass and treble, then you're already familiar with a very simple form of equalizing (or *EQ*). An equalizer lets you control the loudness of different parts of the sound spectrum, called *frequencies*. For example, if you want to add some resonance to a voice, you might choose to use an EQ adjustment to boost the bass frequencies in the sound. In a sense, an equalizer is just a very refined volume control that allows you to make certain frequencies of sound louder or softer.

A graphic equalizer provides sliders for adjusting the volume of specific frequencies, as measured in Hertz (Hz). Move a slider up, and the sounds within that frequency will get louder; move it down, and they will get softer. It's important to remember that each slider represents a point on a curve. By moving the sliders, you are reshaping the curve. In other words, frequencies *around* the slider will be affected also (see Figure 15.10).

The best way to learn how to use EQ is to experiment, ideally with an editing system or mixing board that provides real-time filtering. Consider using an EQ filter in the following situations:

- **Sweetening or adding richness.** With a simple boost to the low or lower mid-range, you can add presence and richness to a voice. Don't add too much, though, or you'll end up with a muffled sound.

- **Making speech more intelligible.** Raising the mid-range frequencies (2000Hz, or *2kHz*) and reducing frequencies below 100Hz will frequently make for clearer dialogue.

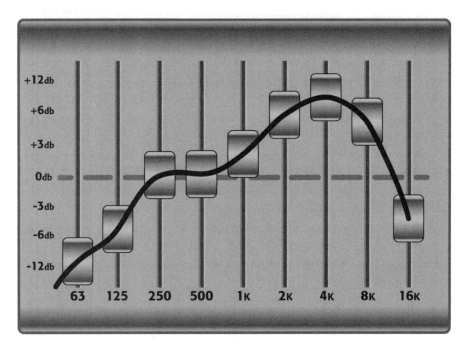

Figure 15.10

The frequencies between the slider controls on your equalizer are connected by a curve. Therefore, adjusting one frequency will shift the frequencies in-between. Don't expect to be able to adjust *only* the frequencies on each slider.

Too Much of a Good Thing

Because EQ is really just a refined way of adjusting volume, be aware that by increasing some of the frequencies, you can end up increasing the overall volume. Watch your level meter to make sure EQ'd sounds don't peak or distort.

- **Wind and mic bumps.** Wind and microphone noise (such as the low rumble noises caused by poor mic handling) can be minimized by reducing the low frequencies (60 to 120Hz).

- **Reducing hiss and other high-frequency sounds.** Just as you can eliminate low-frequency rumbles, you can also eliminate tape hiss and other high-frequency sounds by lowering frequencies above 5kHz.

- **Simulating audio sources.** You can use EQ to simulate the sound of a voice on a telephone or music from a car radio by rolling off the appropriate frequencies. For telephone voice, boost everything between 400 and 2000Hz and lower everything else. The same effect can be used to simulate a low-quality car radio, by using less extreme values. In other words, keep more of the high and low end than you would for a telephone effect (see Figures 15.11 and 15.12).

Note that to perform good EQ adjustments, you need to be sure you're listening to your audio on speakers with a wide dynamic range. If you're using speakers with a poor response at one end of the audio spectrum, you'll neither be able to hear or correct troubles.

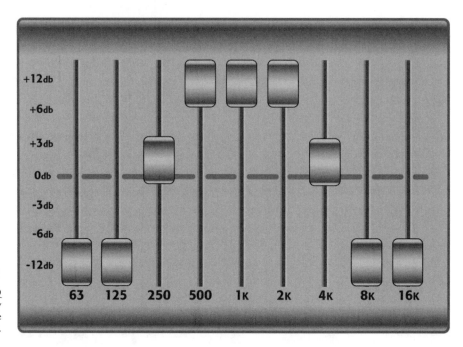

Figure 15.11

With some simple EQ adjustments, you can easily simulate the sound of a voice coming through a telephone.

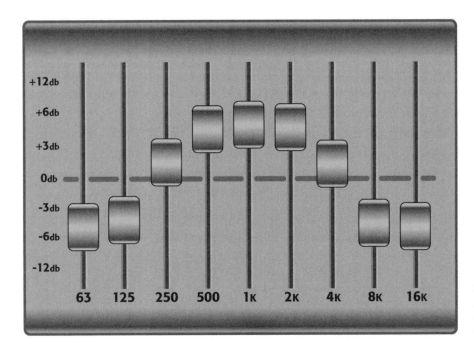

Figure 15.12

Or you can simulate the sound coming from a radio or car stereo.

Mixing Boards

If you're going to do a lot of equalizing, it might be faster to EQ your audio as you capture it by running it through a hardware mixing board.

Where's That Hum Coming From?

If you hear a hum when you play audio, it might have been recorded onto your original source tape; however, there's also a chance that it might be coming from your system itself. Faulty cables, loose connections, and power supply problems can all add a hum to your audio signal. Before you try to correct a hum with EQ, make sure that your system isn't the culprit.

Special Filters

There are tons of specialized applications and plug-ins to help you fix any number of problems, from within your editing application, within your sound editing app, or as a stand-alone application. For creating new sounds, embellishing old sounds, and creating special effects, there are a huge assortment of plug-ins that do everything from simulating Doppler effect to changing pitch and tone, to simulating the sounds of instruments and machinery.

Sound Effects

Your choice of what to use for a particular sound effect will weigh greatly on the overall impact of the scene. For example, if a scene needs the sound of a dog barking in the distance, you'll get a very different effect if you choose to use a Chihuahua or a Doberman. Depending on the tone of the scene, one might be a much better choice.

Going with the choice that is less obvious can often have very serendipitous results. Don't hesitate to try a number of different ideas, including ones that might initially sound strange. For example, consider the sound of the tornadoes in the movie *Twister*. Rather than sticking with simple sounds of storm and flying debris, the editors added guttural, snarling, sucking sounds that gave the twisters an almost conscious, animal-like menace.

Don't hesitate to create your own sound effects. A good mic and some simple field recording equipment can help you get good source material. In addition to getting sounds that exactly match the pacing and length of your video, you might come up with very original sounds. Consider the laser blasts from *Star Wars*. Originally created by banging on the tail ends of power lines, these sources were masterfully manipulated into high-tech, futuristic effects.

Sometimes one effect isn't enough. Layering two or more effects can add depth and impact to a sound event. The most famous example is the modern movie sound of a gunshot, which was developed by Sam Peckinpah in the early 1970s. Several layers of effects and reverb are combined to create a full, explosive sound, rather than the flat "pop" that's heard from a gunshot in real life.

When adding any type of effect, don't expect it to be perfect as soon as you drop it in. Most likely, you'll have to go through a lot of trial and error. There are no rules or numbers you can follow for these processes; instead, follow your ear.

To improve and blend in a sound effect, remember that you have all of the following with which to work:

- **Levels:** Make sure the level of the sound matches the intensity of what's on the screen—a small handgun shouldn't sound like a cannon.

- **EQ and effects:** You can use EQ to improve the quality of your sound effect and to try to separate the effect from the other sounds in your mix. Other effects can be added to match the sound effect to its surroundings. The sound of dropping a bowling ball in a cathedral, for example, should have a lot more reverb and echo than the sound of dropping a bowling ball in a convenience store.

- **The mix:** You might be able to improve your sound effect by adjusting other tracks in your mix. Maybe it's not that your airplane sound effect is too quiet; perhaps your dialogue is too loud. Play with your entire mix when editing in a sound effect.

Sound Effect Sources

Once you start editing, you'll need a number of different audio sources at your disposal. In addition to your original production audio files, you'll probably end up recording extra sounds on your own (called *wild* sounds). You might also want to invest in a sound effects library. Companies such as Sound Ideas provide vast, detailed collections of high-quality prerecorded sounds. These can be essential tools for adding effects and ambience to your audio tracks. If you're editing in a studio or postproduction facility, they might have a sound effects library you can use. More and more of these libraries are available online, as single track downloads, which is a great option if you just need a couple of effects and don't have the time or budget to invest in a full library.

Foley is the process of recording special ambient effects in real-time while watching your movie play on a screen. Door slams, footsteps, pouring water, clinking dinnerware, and all sorts of other "everyday" sounds that might not have been recorded during your shoot can be added by a foley artist. Foley work is usually done on a special stage equipped with props, cars, floor surfaces, and other materials.

Your mic might have picked up many ambient sounds while you were recording. Depending on the nature of your mic, though, these sounds can have varying degrees of quality, tone, and presence. If you used a directional mic to shoot footage of a woman getting out of a car, dropping her keys, picking them up, and closing the car door, some of the sounds might sound too far away or muffled since they were out of the primary field of the microphone. Foley sounds are an easy way to bring these sounds forward to increase the audience's involvement in the scene.

The advantage of adding sound effects with foley work (rather than editing sounds from a sound effects library) is that a good foley artist can often do all of the sounds for a shot (or even a scene) in a single take. In addition to being much faster than editing sounds separately, foley sounds will use fewer tracks in your mix.

With a good mic and a lot of care, you can do simple foley work on your own, although if a scene is very dependent on good foley sounds, you'll probably want to go to a professional foley studio. Experienced foley artists can do a decent pass on a feature film in one day.

Music

Music is one of the most powerful tools at your disposal. In films, music tells the audience how they should feel about a scene, and it can be used for everything from helping to establish a sense of location, to setting a mood, to embellishing an atmosphere. You'll probably spend a lot of time considering and tweaking the music in your production, and the nature of the tweaking will depend largely on the source of your music.

Typically, there are two types of music used in a feature: the music that underscores the action, and the source music that is meant to sound like it's coming from a source in your scene (radio, television, singer, and so on).

Many movies use a combination of original music composed specifically for the project, and prerecorded music that is licensed from an artist and publisher. Determining how much of each to use will depend on your project, budget, and the nature of the mood you are trying to create.

An original score can serve to bind themes and characters together throughout your feature. Through the use of repeating motifs and recurring melodies, a well-written score can provide a lot of narrative structure and continuity.

There are a number of reasons why you might choose to use prerecorded material. Your characters might be listening to a piece of music, for example, or perhaps you've found a song that simply serves the scene better than your original score does. Finally, certain songs, particularly music from a particular period, can do a great job of enhancing the authenticity of your scene.

Such prerecorded material can also be mixed and layered on top of your original score. In addition to creating an interesting "soundscape," pulling a song out of the scene and into the score can be an effective way to move a scene forward and join one character's action to something else in the movie.

For more about music for films, read the interview with a music supervisor on the companion Web site, in the Chapter 15 folder, "Interview with a MusicSuper.pdf."

WHAT TO WATCH

Easy A is a comedy that exclusively uses lyrics-driven pop songs as a musical score. This is a very unusual choice on the part of the filmmakers, but they somehow manage to make it work. When you watch the film, pay particular attention to how the music starts and stops and also how they mix the music to favor the in-scene dialogue.

Editing Music

Editing music can be a lot of fun, but it's a lot of hard work too, especially if you need your music to sound perfect. Feature films often hire a special music editor to edit all the music in the film. Why would you need a music editor if you already have a composer? Many projects do not have big enough budgets to hire a composer to score a project from start to finish. Instead, the composer will score key scenes and sequences, and then provide a selection of tracks for the editor to use as needed. Because these tracks are not composed to the timing of the video or film, someone needs to edit them to time. The same goes for prerecorded or library music.

At the most basic level, editing music means placing the tracks in the edited sequence and deciding where each cut of music needs to start and end. The start is easy—some songs have an introduction, or a "lead-in," to the main part of the song. Often, editors decide to cut out the "lead-in" and start with the main part of the song. Pop songs are usually structured with verses and choruses. Often, you'll decide to jump in with the chorus rather than the first verse.

Other songs have musical interludes, or "breaks." Since lyrics can be distracting under dialogue, starting with the "break" can be a good choice. No matter where you start the song, you can usually find a spot to make the first edit so that you don't need a dissolve to smooth it out. Each section of a song—the lead-in or intro, the verse, the chorus, the break, and the "outro" or ending—usually has a hard start. You can use the scrub tools in your editing software to find the first frame of that hard sound, whether it's a voice, a drum, or another musical instrument. As long as you avoid clipping the note, you'll be surprised to find that you can often start a piece of music in the middle of a song and the edit will sound good.

Editing the end of a piece of music is a little more challenging. The easiest way is to simply let the song end, but usually songs are too long for this to work. The next easiest way out is to put a long dissolve on the end to sneak the music out of your mix. A one-second dissolve is a really long dissolve for other types of sound, but for music it's very short. To successfully sneak a piece of music out so that no one really notices that it's gone, you'll need at minimum a three-second dissolve. Last, but not least, you can "pull up" the ending of the song by cutting the end of the song onto the middle of the song so that it "ends" where you want. This will take a little practice and an ear for music, but once you've done it successfully a few times, it will quickly become second nature and is an important skill in every editor's toolbox.

Can't Resolve It, Dissolve It?

This adage refers to the fact that dissolves are used as a bandage to solve every sort of problem in sound editing, from clipped dialogue to bad music edits to taking the edge off sound effects. But some people think they have to add a dissolve to every single edit that they make, no matter how it sounds. The fact is that if you can't hear a sound edit, it's "seamless," so you don't need to smooth it further by adding a dissolve. And often if an edit sounds bad, and you feel it needs a dissolve to improve it, it may simply mean that a small adjustment of the edit—a frame or two—will make it sound good without a dissolve. Dissolves are an extremely useful tool, but they shouldn't become a crutch.

Music Libraries

Just as there are tons of stock footage houses and sound effects libraries out there, there are many companies that specialize in selling music libraries. With some, you pay a large sum for access to the whole library and that purchase includes the license to use any tracks in the collection. Others charge per track and per minute. The quality and variety of music available on library collections has improved greatly over the last 10 years, and many tracks are available for purchase and download from the Internet.

License to Play

When licensing music for use in a film, you'll most likely have to pay a hefty fee. You'll also need to secure the rights, both to the music and to the particular recording that you want to use. Often, the cheapest solution is to acquire the "performing rights," which allows you to hire a band to replicate the song. Whatever your needs, it's really best to consult an entertainment lawyer before you decide to use a copyrighted song. Be sure to do so early on in your production; otherwise, you could very easily end up with a movie that can't be distributed.

Most movies have two people involved in selecting and arranging music. A composer writes the original music, while the music supervisor selects any prerecorded material. Often, the music supervisor will select a composer and help guide that person through the creation of the music.

When you've finished editing your picture, you'll want to sit down and have a screening with your music supervisor or composer to discuss any ideas that you might have about appropriate music. In some cases, you might simply discuss what type of feeling or emotion you're hoping to convey.

You might have already chosen some music to use as "scratch audio" during your editing process. You can use this to suggest music that you feel is appropriate. However, it's often better to simply give your music supervisor some direction and see what he can come up with. Your music supervisor might arrive at ideas that you had never considered but that work perfectly. One problem with using scratch audio is that it's very easy to get attached to it. Be careful not to get too enamored of a piece of music that you can't afford to license!

In addition, don't use scratch music that you would never be able to afford to produce. In other words, if you can't afford to pay for a full orchestra (or to license an orchestral recording), don't use orchestral music in your scratch audio.

In addition to ideas about mood and tone, you might need to give your music supervisor or composer a cue list showing exactly what pieces of music are needed and whether or not they have specific timings. If there are musical events that need to happen at particular times (a dramatic organ sting when the villain enters, for example), then these will be listed on your cue sheet.

Your music supervisor and composer will usually present you with a number of options for each section of music in your project. You can take these to your editor and see how they work. At this point, your editor or sound designer might have suggestions for how to mix different pieces of music together, or how to mix music with natural sound, or how to apply reverb or other atmospheric effects to better fit the music to the action and mood.

The Sound of Silence

Don't forget about the power of silence. Not only is silence sometimes more effective than music, but it often makes the preceding and following music more powerful. Don't feel pressured to fill every moment with sound and music. Do as much experimenting with no music as with music.

Finding a Composer

There are a number of resources for contacting and auditioning composers and music supervisors. You can see a list of these resources in the Chapter 15 folder on the companion Web site called "Finding a mus sup or compos.pdf."

Whoever does the work of choosing a composer might be tempted to select someone simply based on the composer's music. This might not be the best criterion. Certainly, you want to consider a composer's musical tastes and skill, but simply listening to a demo reel gives you no idea of how well the music served as a score. You will also get no idea of how well you can communicate with the composer, or how tuned in that person might be to the themes and ideas within your piece.

Before you make any decisions, you'll need to show your picture to the composer, discuss ideas, and see how well you can work together.

Today, composers are typically given about six weeks to write a score. While most big-budget films devote 1.5 to 2.5 percent of their budget to a score, low-budget films can often come in much lower. If the composer likes your work, she might be willing to work for much less.

In addition to paying your composer, you might need to pay the musicians required to record the piece, although sometimes the cost of musicians is included in the composer's fee. If you were imagining a full orchestral score, remember that you'll have to pay all the people in the orchestra. Many composers can cut production costs by using synthesized instruments or synthesizers augmented with a few acoustic instruments. You'll need to discuss production costs with your composer and try to determine what type of music you can afford to record.

Do It Yourself

If you're thinking that you might like to try your hand at composing your own score—or maybe you have some friends who you think could do a good job—remember that composing for the screen is not as simple as just sitting down and writing a song. Not only do you have to compose to achieve a particular narrative or emotional goal, but also, depending on the edits of your scene, you might need to compose with the intent of having certain movements, motifs, or beats occur at a particular time.

In addition, you'll need to compose with the understanding that your music will be competing with other sounds. Remember, your score is meant to complement and assist in the story-telling process. When composing, make sure that you are supporting the other audio in the scene. For example, a scene with many young children talking on a busy playground would not be well served by lyrical, high-pitched violin music, as the violins might be too close to the timbre of children's voices. When mixed with the natural sound, your music would only serve to muddle the sound and make the scene less intelligible.

Halfway between composing and canned music are programs like Apple's GarageBand and SonicFire Pro, which let you string together prerecorded loops to create original tunes (see Figure 15.13). Far superior to straight canned music, loop editors let you craft songs that exactly match the cuts in your movie. In addition, some of these applications also let you record live vocals or instruments over your sequenced loops.

Figure 15.13

Loop editors like SonicFire Pro let you easily create soundtracks that exactly match the timing of your edited picture and provide an interface to help you purchase and download library cues from the Internet.

Fix It in the Mix

As we'll discuss in Chapter 18, when you perform your final output to tape or film, you will also perform a final, finished mix. Although your final mix will give you the chance to balance your audio levels, and equalize your tracks, don't think that you can just wait and fix any audio problems then. It's best to try to get your audio as polished as possible during your sound editing. This will make it easier to identify any problems with your audio, and will make for a shorter (and possibly less-expensive) mixing session when you create your final output.

Color Plate 19

The four basic elements of color correction: brightness (aka lightness), contrast, saturation, and hue.

Color Plate 20

This image had a lot of red in it. After adjusting the luminance, we boosted the greens and diminished the reds to make the landscape stand out.

This image of a statue was over-exposed during the shoot. This problem can be reduced using the color correction filters in your editing application.

As you can see in waveform, the white levels are clipped in some areas, so "pulling down" the whites won't help much. But you can pull down the blacks, giving the image a better contrast ratio.

The vectorscope shows that the image consists mainly of cyan. Increasing the red gain helps make the hue more balanced.

Finally, decreasing the blue gain helps bring out more of the warm tones of the statue that are lacking in the original image. Note that the greens in the plant look more natural now. The image is still overexposed but it looks much better.

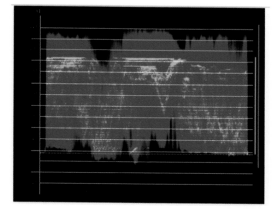

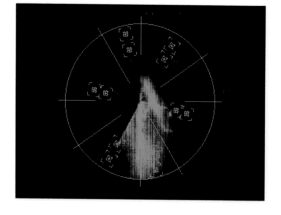

Color Plate 21

A very overexposed image and our steps for correcting it.

This image of two teapots is dull and muddy. The waveform in Figure 16.8 shows a lack of brightness and contrast.

Often the first reflex when trying to fix an image that seems too dark is to raise the black levels. But as this figure reveals, raising the blacks only results in an even more washed-out image.

By raising the white levels, the brightness of the entire image is pulled up. This appears to be on the right track but if you pull the whites up this much, you'll most likely see artifacting in the image when it plays.

In this figure, the whites have been pulled up but not quite as high. To compensate for this, the blacks have been pulled down, resulting in an image with better contrast. Now that the white and black levels are good, it's clear that the color balance doesn't need any adjusting.

Color Plate 22

A very underexposed image and the steps for correcting it.

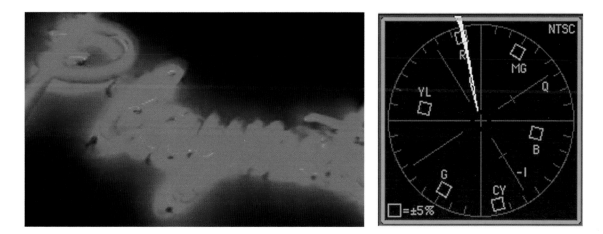

Color Plate 23

This red neon sign is oversaturated, which is a common problem with neon lights.

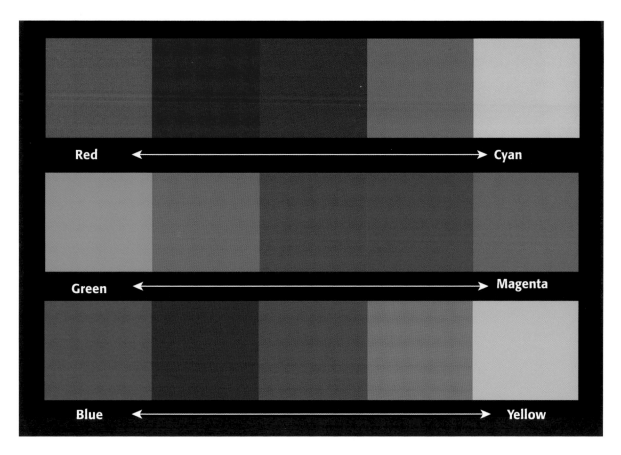

Color Plate 24

Complementary colors in the additive color system.

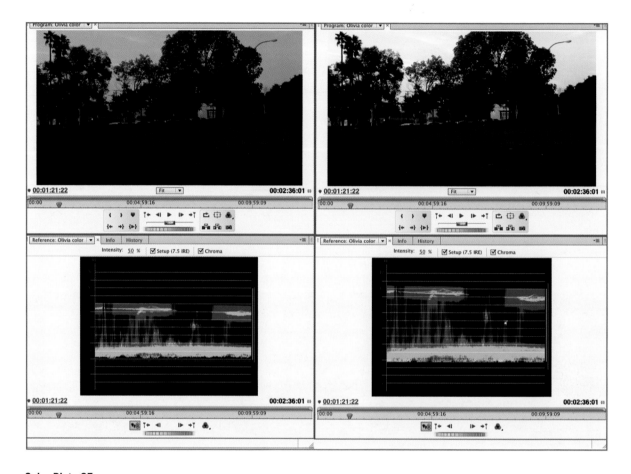

Color Plate 25

The waveform of the original image (left) shows that the luminance range is crushed. After the luminance is adjusted, the waveform of the image on the right shows a healthy range from black to white.

Color Plate 26

These shots don't match, due to quickly fading daylight conditions during the shoot.

Color Plate 27

The final color-corrected image matches the other shot surprisingly well. We increased the reds and greens and decreased the blues to create a more saturated image that favors the reddish-yellow sunset colors in the rest of the scene.

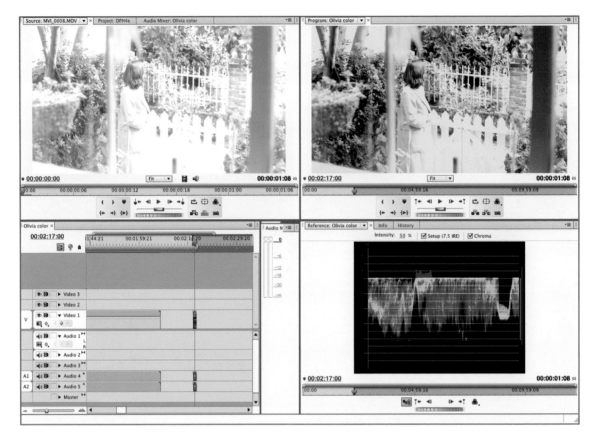

Color Plate 28

The original image (upper left) is severely overexposed. The corrected image (upper right) is much better looking, but some areas are not fixable. Note the area around the white picket fence near the bottom of the frame. The clipped whites are still visible in the waveform of the corrected image (lower right).

Color Plate 29

This image is overexposed (left) but correctable (right).

Color Plate 30

This shot from Chapter 16 has bad white balance. Note the overall blue cast to the image.

Color Plate 31

The final image with corrected white balance in Chapter 16.

The original foreground image (left) and background image (right)

The two original images blended together using different transfer modes.

Color Plate 32

Transfer modes can create unique color effects.

The original full color image (left) and fully desaturated (right)

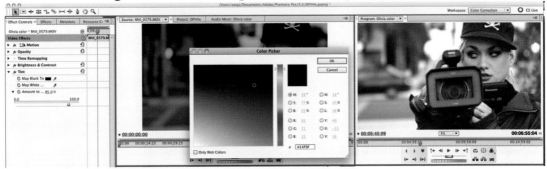

The image is tinted sepia by mapping to dark brown instead of black.

The image tinted blue.

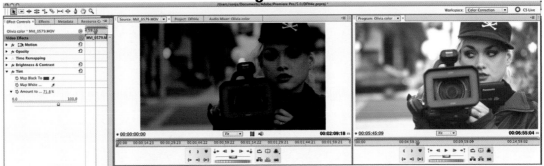

The amount of tinting is reduced to allow some color to show through. (Note the tail lights and other red/yellow highlights in the background.)

Color Plate 33

Tinting can produce a variety of monochrome looks.

Color Plate 34

Film look presets (left) in the Red Giant Magic Bullet Looks interface.

Color Plate 35

Another way to create a sunset: the sunset gradient in Magic Bullet Looks.

Color Plate 36

We chose to keep this title as separate from the background as possible by using brightly colored text, full opacity, and drop shadows. Shown here, the title tool in Adobe Premiere Pro.

Color Plate 37

Our original image (top) was compressed three times (middle) and then six times (bottom) to show the effects of too many rounds of compression with a lossy codec.

Color Plate 38

When compositing, you'll frequently need to apply color correction techniques to blend one layer into another. Here, we used Color Balance and Blur filters to better integrate the bullet holes into the door.

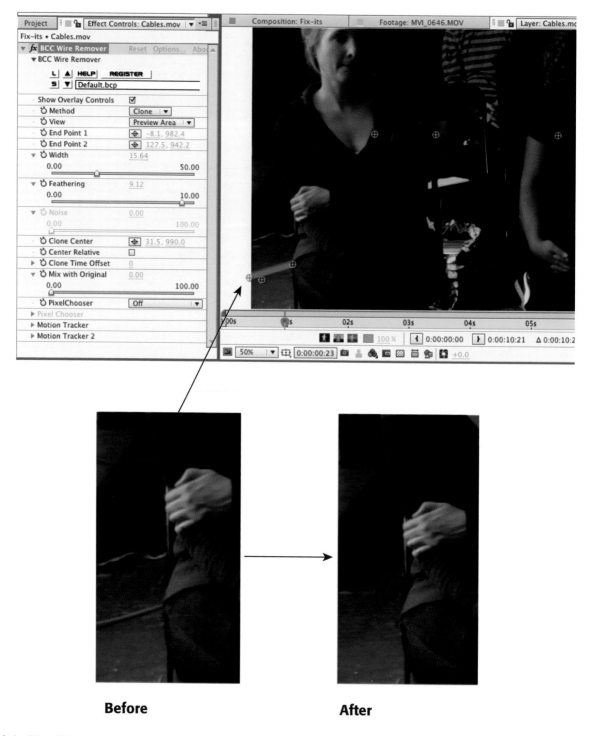

Before　　　　　　　　　　**After**

Color Plate 39

BorisFX Continuum Wire Removal plug-in lets you choose different ways to paint out a wire and also track motion within the shot (before and after inset).

16

Color Correction

Photo credit: Paquita Parks

Bright blue skies, rich green leaves, golden sunsets—color is one of the most basic components of our visual sense, and the enhancement and manipulation of color is perhaps the most basic way to refine and improve the visuals in your film. Some film-makers prefer a saturated, rich color palette, while others prefer muted, subtle hues. You decided on a color palette for your film when you began the process of art direction in pre-production and continued developing it as you decided on a lighting style and other visual elements during your shoot. Now you can continue that process by color correcting your footage in post.

Perhaps you are happy with your color choices that you made during the shoot and now you only want to enhance what you already have. More likely, perhaps, is that you are happy with some of your scenes but others have technical issues: cameras that don't match, bad white balance, exposure problems, lighting that doesn't match between your principle shoot and your day of pickups. All of these problems can be minimized or fixed entirely with color correction.

It might not always be bad news that sends you to the color controls of your editing application. Often, you'll want to perform color adjustments for more artistic reasons. Perhaps you want to amp up the reds or blues in an image to strike a certain emotional tone. Or maybe you simply like certain colors more than others. Whatever the reason, color-correction tools will be some of the most-used effects in your editing program.

Traditionally, movies shot on film go through a process called *color grading* when they are finished. Today with digital filmmaking technology, the term *color grading* is used to refer to the process of doing a final polish pass on your film to make the colors match across the length of the film and to fix any problems along the way. Color grading is a potentially complex process and hiring an expert colorist is usually recommended. But if that's beyond the budget or scale of your project, that doesn't mean you should skip this step in the finishing process altogether.

All the professional editing applications that we've mentioned so far provide sophisticated tools for correcting and changing the color in your video. In addition, there are software applications that are oriented especially toward image enhancement, such as Adobe After Effects, Apple Color, and special plug-in packages like Red Giant's Magic Bullet Suite.

Whether you use these tools for artistic reasons or for more practical concerns, an understanding of the color correction features of your software is invaluable. In this chapter, we'll show you how to use the basic tool set for correcting the color in your footage without putting your image quality at risk.

When to Color Correct

Typically, an overall color correction or color-grading pass is done at the end of the editing process, after the picture is "locked." However, you may want to spot-fix any distracting problems earlier.

Color Correction

At its most basic level, color correction consists of adjusting four elements of the image: brightness, contrast, saturation, and hue (see Figure 16.1) While each of these elements can be broken down further and the process can become quite detailed and complex, to give you a basic understanding of color correction, we'll start with these four components.

Figure 16.1

The four basic elements of color correction: brightness (aka lightness), contrast, saturation, and hue. See also Color Plate 19.

Brightness simply refers to how light or dark the image is (see Figure 16.2). Increasing the brightness in post is similar to increasing the exposure during the shoot: the whole image gets lighter. Typically, you can only adjust the brightness a little bit before the image starts to look noticeably "treated."

Contrast refers to the range from white to black in the image (see Figure 16.3). A high contrast image has bright whites and blacks that are truly black. Ironically, brightness and contrast filters do not actually control the color in an image but they are key to color correction, and you can fix many basic image quality problems simply by adjusting these two components and nothing more.

Saturation refers to the amount of color in the image. Increasing or decreasing the saturation is a way to refine the look of your color palette (Color plate 19). *Hue* refers to the overall color cast of your image. Shifting the hue can help correct bad white balance (see Color Plate 20).

Figure 16.2

Adjusting the brightness of an image makes everything in the image lighter (top) or darker (bottom). The blacks go gray in the brighter image and the whites go gray in the darker image.

Just to make things a little more complicated, these four components are related, because different hues have different brightness, so changing the brightness of an image might make colors appear slightly different.

Play with Your Software Filters

We recommend opening your editing application now and using the various color correction filters to adjust the brightness, contrast, saturation, and hue of some of your shots. Be aware that your editing application will probably offer several different ways to adjust color. Play around with them and see what looks better and what looks worse.

Figure 16.3

Adjusting the contrast changes the range from white to black. Shown here, a low contrast setting (top), a medium contrast setting (middle), and a very high contrast setting (bottom). Notice that the top image contains only shades of gray, while the bottom image is almost pure black and white.

Advanced Color Controls

Of the four basic components of color correction, probably the least useful is changing the overall hue because it doesn't allow for subtle control, and if you have people in your shots, you will be limited as to what you can change if you want to keep skin tones realistic. If your video needs color correction and adjusting the brightness, contrast, and saturation isn't enough, chances are you'll need to make adjustments to the individual RGB color channels that make up the hue of your image.

Back in Chapter 3, "Digital Video Primer," we talked about additive color and how digital video is comprised of three colors of light: red, green, and blue (see Color Plate 1). Added together, they form an image with a complete color spectrum (see Figure 16.4).

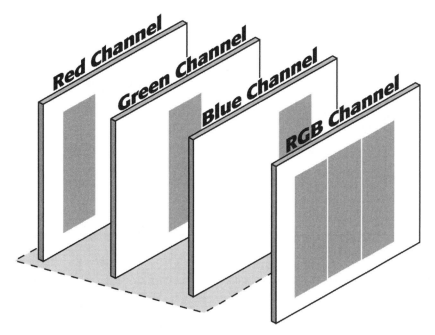

Figure 16.4

Each full color frame of video is made up of a red channel, a green channel, and a blue channel.

More sophisticated color-correction tools let you adjust each of these channels separately (see Figure 16.5). The level of control can get quite detailed here. You can adjust brightness, contrast, and saturation within each RGB channel. Some filters let you adjust each of these channels in certain areas of the luminance range: shadows, mid-tones, and highlights. By adjusting the hue in the shadows and highlights, you can avoid shifting the color in skin tones, which usually falls in the mid-tone range.

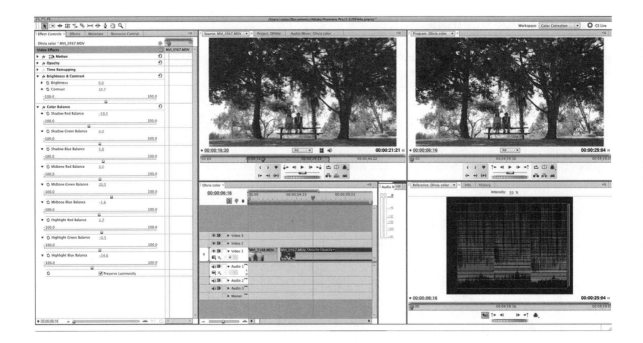

Figure 16.5

The Color Balance filter in Adobe Premiere Pro offers a complete set of controls for each color channel (red, green, and blue) and each part of the luminance range (shadows, mid-tones, and highlight).

Seeing Color

The appreciation of color is a highly subjective process, and it can be affected by the amount of light in the room, the type of monitor you are using, and the colors of the walls in the room itself.

To see color in the best possible way, using a good monitor is really important and so are the lighting conditions where you do your color work. Ambient light can cause you to misjudge colors and black levels. If your project is meant to be seen in a dark theater environment, you should be doing your color correction work in a similarly lit space. Most film and TV projects are intended to be viewed in dark conditions and that is why most editing rooms are dark and often the walls are painted a neutral gray.

Judging the color balance of a video image by eye can be a bit difficult at times, but there are tools available to help you "see" the video image better—waveforms and vectorscopes (see Figure 16.6).

Waveforms display the lights and darks, or luminance, of the video signal. At the left side of the waveform, there is a scale measuring brightness in units called *IRE*. Pure white is indicated by 100 IRE and black is set at either 0 or 7.5 IRE. By looking at the waveform display, you can see if the image is too bright (as shown in Figure 16.7) or too dark (see Figure 16.8). Later in this chapter, we'll show you how to set the white levels and black levels using a waveform display. Often, everything else will fall into place once you have these two key variables in place.

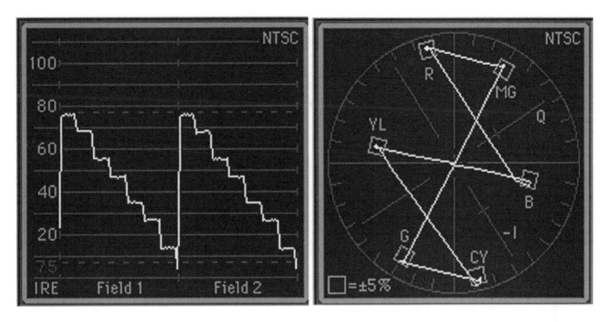

Waveform monitor   **Vectorscope**

Figure 16.6
A simplified waveform (left) and vectorscope (right) displaying the SMPTE color bars test pattern.

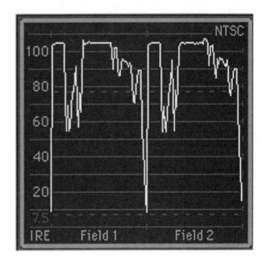

Figure 16.7
The waveform of this image shows that it's too bright. (See also Color Plate 21.)

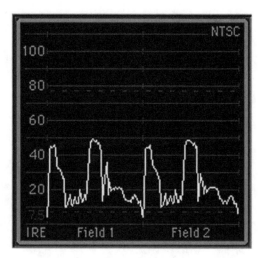

Figure 16.8

The waveform of this image shows that it's too dark. (See also Color Plate 22.)

Vectorscopes (see Figure 16.6) display the color information, or chrominance, in the video signal. Vectorscopes are similar to a color wheel: each area shows a different part of the color spectrum and within each section, there is a small box that shows the ideal positioning, or level, for each color. (YL is yellow, R is red, and so on.) Anything that goes beyond these boxes is highly saturated and anything that goes past the edge of the circle is so saturated that it will result in decreased image quality (see Figure 16.9).

After checking the black-and-white levels, you can use the vectorscope to make sure the color information is set correctly.

You can use either hardware- or software-based monitors to view waveforms and vectorscope in order to check the video levels. Professional colorists prefer hardware monitors, but most others find that the software-based monitors that are part of any professional editing application are sufficient for their needs. Be aware that waveform monitors and vectorscopes do not do anything to the video signal itself—they simply display it, just like regular video monitors. To adjust the video signal, you'll have to use color correction filters in your editing application.

Waveforms and vectorscopes serve one really important function and that is they let you know when color correction goes too far and actually makes the quality of your image worse. Whites that go above 100 IRE, blacks that are not even close to the black line on the waveform (7.5 IRE), and colors that stretch to the outer edge of the circle in the vectorscope are all signs that your image quality is in serious trouble.

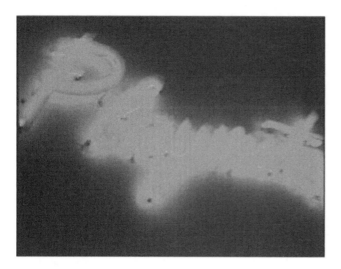 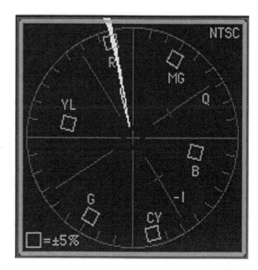

Figure 16.9

The vectorscope of this image shows that the red is oversaturated, a common problem with neon light. (See also Color Plate 23.)

Safe Colors

NTSC and PAL video have much smaller color gamuts than your computer monitor does. This means that colors that look fine on your computer screen might not display correctly—in fact, they might look plain awful—when displayed on an NTSC monitor. Very saturated colors will tend to bleed and fringe, with reds suffering worst of all. Most editing and effects applications provide an NTSC Colors filter that will convert your graphics to NTSC-safe colors.

A Less Scientific Approach

Using waveforms and vectorscopes can help you avoid making color correction choices that accidentally degrade your image. But within the guidelines that they provide, there is a lot of room for interpretation, and there is no replacement for developing a good eye and learning to trust your own opinion. After all, that is what the best colorists do: they make sure the film or video will pass a basic quality control test and then they work their magic.

Knowing a little more about how color works with video will definitely help. When you were a kid, you were shown the color wheel and taught about colors and how they mix together. The primary colors are red, blue, and yellow, and the opposite of red is green, the opposite of blue is orange, and the opposite of yellow is purple. These opposite colors are known as the *secondary colors*. The color mixing system you were taught in elementary school is subtractive color, and it works with paint, crayons, ink, and so on.

Video, like film, is made up of light, and light follows the rules of additive color. The primary colors for video are red, green, and blue, and the secondary colors are cyan, magenta, and yellow (see Color Plate 24). For video, the opposite of red is cyan, the opposite of green is magenta, and the opposite of blue is yellow.

RGB color balance filters like the one shown in Figure 16.5 give you control over the Red, Green, and Blue channels of the video signal. They work on a sliding scale, and if you decrease the blue, you will increase its opposite color, yellow. Decreasing the red will increase the cyan, and decreasing the green will increase the magenta.

And last, but not least, remember that enhancing skin tones is one of the primary concerns when manipulating the color of your film. It might look amazing to have the sky turn bright green but not if it renders your actress' skin blue. If you are unsure about your color correction choices, keeping an eye on the skin tones of your cast is the easiest way to feel confident that you aren't going too far.

Save Your Presets

As you work with color correction filters, save the ones you like along the way. You may find that you can use them to correct a number of shots.

Too Much of a Good Thing

If you've been trying out the color correction filters in your editing app, you've probably noticed that it doesn't take much to make a wildly dramatic change to the look of your image. It might be fun to look at, but it's rare that you are going to use such extremes in your final product. It's important to recognize that it *is* possible to apply too much color correction.

Here's what happens when you go overboard with color correction filters.

A digital image is composed of numbers that represent the color of each pixel. Color-correction tools simply manipulate these numbers using complex transformations. Unfortunately, a digital image has a finite amount of color data in it. You can manipulate this information, but eventually you'll find that there simply isn't enough data to take a correction as far as you might like. At this point, you'll introduce artifacts and aberrations into your image.

When you apply color correction operations to a digital image, the computer will often have to discard image data. The result of these operations will be the same: with less image data, some tones in your image will posterize, resulting in areas of flat color in your picture. These artifacts probably won't be as dramatic as our example, but they'll still be there, and they can be very noticeable, particularly in the darker, shadowy areas of your image (see Figure 16.10).

Also, sometimes these artifacts are not that noticeable when you are only looking at a single frame, but when you play back your video at full motion, they can be very noticeable.

Choosing what type of correction to make is a subjective, aesthetic choice. Knowing when you've corrected too far, though, is a technical skill that separates good correction from bad. In the following examples, practice looking for posterization and reduction of tones as you perform your corrections. This is a habit that you will need to develop for all of your personal correction chores.

Figure 16.10

This image has suffered a little too much correction, resulting in the posterization of some of its tones.

Brightening Dark Video

Good lighting is often all it takes to make the difference between bad lighting and good lighting. Unfortunately, good lighting isn't always naturally available, and good artificial lighting is very expensive and requires a skilled crew. For either of these reasons, you will, at times, find yourself shooting in low light. Whether it's a concert venue, a night shot, or simply a budgetary reality, low-light footage is something you might need to correct when you start editing.

Fortunately, HD cameras are pretty exceptional at shooting in low light. Because digital image sensors are incredibly light sensitive, your camera can capture details that even your eye might not be able to see. However, you might have to coax this detail out of your footage.

We shot the footage in Figure 16.11 at sunset. The shot on the left was shot during the golden hour, and we liked the look, but the shot on the right was shot after sunset and the light was fading fast. Not only is it dark, but it also doesn't match the other shots in the scene.

Figure 16.11

These shots don't match due to quickly fading daylight conditions during the shoot. (See also Color Plate 25.)

Most image editing applications come with several different luminance control filters. In Adobe Premiere Pro, the Fast Color Corrector filter has an Input Levels slider that works very similarly to the Levels controls in Photoshop. The center (gray) slider adjusts the gamma. The great thing about a gamma control is that it lets you brighten the mid-tones of your image without lightening the blacks. This is ideal for dark footage, as it allows you to brighten the image without washing out the shadow tones. The black slider lets you set the black level, and the white slider lets you set the white level (see Figure 16.12).

Use the Waveform Display

Look at the waveform display as you adjust the black-and-white levels. The black levels should fall around 7.5 IRE, and the white levels should max out at 100 IRE.

Another way to achieve a similar effect is to use the Brightness/Contrast filter. Increasing the Brightness is similar to increasing the exposure—it makes the whole image lighter. You can then adjust the Contrast to get better black-and-white levels.

You can see our original image in Figure 16.13 on the left and the image corrected this way on the right. As you can see, the waveform on the corrected images shows a much healthier range from black to white.

If you look at the Color Plates, however, you'll see that the image is brighter, but it's not that great looking (Color Plate 26). The colors are dull, and it doesn't match the other shots from the scene. We added the Color Balance filter and increased the reds and greens and decreased the blues to create a more saturated image that favors the reddish-yellow sunset colors in the other shots (see Color Plate 27).

The original shot was quite dark, and it doesn't appear to have much color in it, so this image also serves as a good example of how well HD footage can respond to color correction even though it's underexposed.

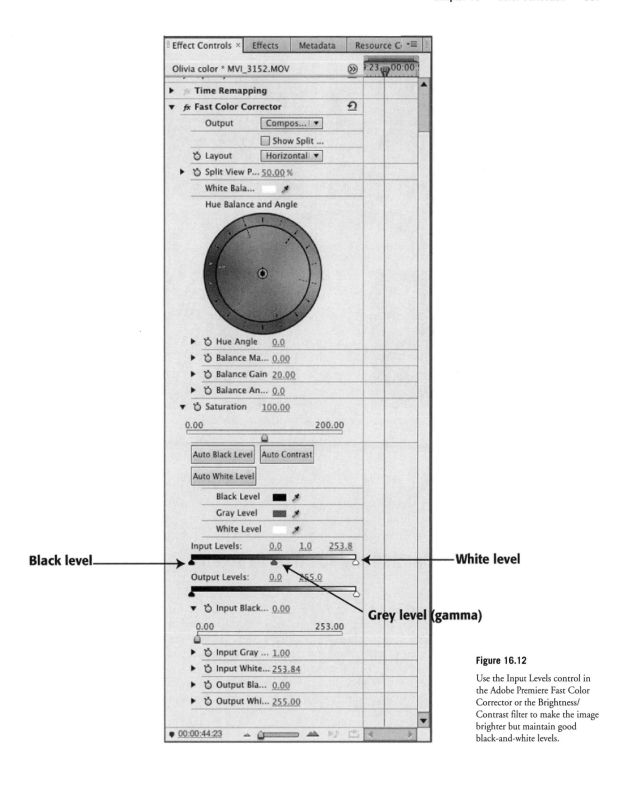

Black level

White level

Grey level (gamma)

Figure 16.12

Use the Input Levels control in the Adobe Premiere Fast Color Corrector or the Brightness/Contrast filter to make the image brighter but maintain good black-and-white levels.

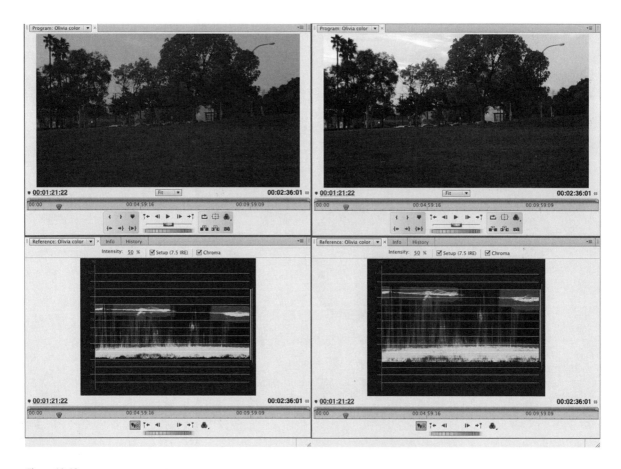

Figure 16.13

The waveform of the corrected image on the lower right shows a healthy range from black to white (see Color Plate 26).

Compensating for Overexposure

Digital video is very good at handling low-light situations, and it can hold a lot of information in dark areas—information that isn't visible to the eye but can be pulled out during color correction. Unfortunately, the opposite is true with overexposed digital video. Areas of overexposure that show a loss of detail suffer from a problem that isn't fixable—clipping. Just as digital audio that goes above a certain level gets clipped, digital video that goes above a certain white level also gets clipped. So the white overexposed areas you see in an image like the one in Figure 16.14 simply contain no information. You can pull down the brightness and make other corrections, and they will improve other parts of the image, but the clipped areas will stay the same—white.

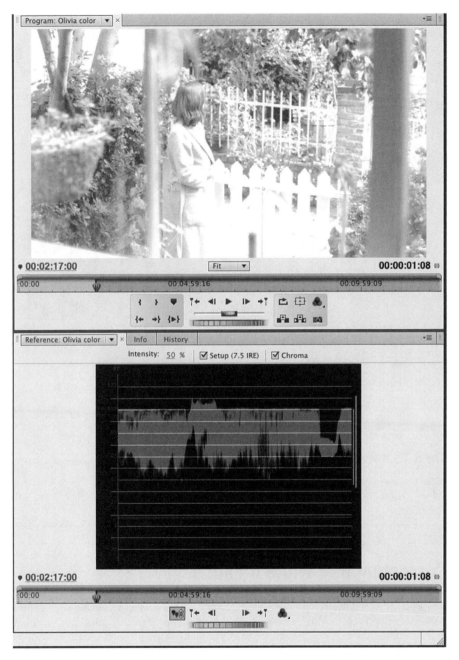

Figure 16.14

This image is very overexposed. Notice the lack of detail in the area near the white picket fence in the lower center of the image. The waveform indicates serious clipping. (See Color Plate 28.)

Color Plate 28 shows that although the video in Figure 16.14 can be greatly improved, the overexposure is impossible to fix. The blown-out area of the white picket fence has not improved. However, it was possible to correct the exposure in the areas that are not so severely overexposed, such as the woman's hair. And because we humans tend to be drawn to the faces and heads of other humans, having her hair properly exposed helps a lot to mask the problems in the rest of the frame. On the other hand, the image in Figure 16.15 is also overexposed but not so severely. You can see the corrected color in Color Plate 29.

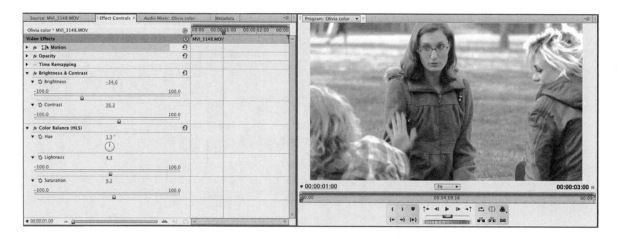

Figure 16.15

This image is overexposed but still correctable. (See Color Plate 29.)

Try It Yourself

We've provided short clips of the video files shown in this chapter so that you can try your hand at correcting the color yourself. They can be found at *www.thedigitalfilmmakinghandbook.com/chapter16*.

Correcting Bad White Balance

As we discussed in Chapter 7, "Using the Camera," properly white balancing your camera before shooting is essential to getting good color. However, there's no guarantee that your camera's white-balance function will always work properly. A bad auto-white-balance function can often perform inaccurate—or outright bad—white balancing, and can sometimes change white balance in the middle of a shot. Even if you're manually white balancing, mixed lighting situations—tungsten lights in a sun-filled room, for example—can yield troublesome results.

Bad white balance can lead to everything from a simple green tinge in highlight areas to an extreme blue cast throughout the entire image. Color Plate 30 shows a *very* poorly white-balanced shot of a woman sitting on a couch. Before we shot this scene, we had been shooting outside on a very cloudy day. Although we had white balanced the camera outside, after quickly moving inside, we forgot to adjust the white-balance settings for the new lighting conditions. As you can see, the bad white balance resulted in an extreme blue cast throughout the image. Color Plate 31 shows the image after it was corrected.

Most editing apps and many effects packages include filters for the white balance of an image. Filters such as the 3-Way Color Corrector in Apple Final Cut Pro let you use an Eyedropper tool to select an area that should be white and correct the rest of the image accordingly. If that doesn't work, making subtle hue adjustments can also go a long way toward correcting bad white balance.

Check Out the Tutorials on the Web Site

The companion Web site to this book contains several great tutorials that will help you understand the basics of color correction, compositing, and other postproduction effects. Also, we've provided the video footage that is shown in this chapter so that you can try your own hand at color correcting some problematic shots. All can be found at *www.thedigitalfilmmakinghandbook.com/chapter16*.

Matching Footage from Different Cameras and Shoots

Even if you have set the white balance, exposure (or f-stop), and other variables, if you are using different cameras, odds are high that your footage won't match perfectly. For example, some manufacturers consistently produce cameras that shoot "warmer" images than cameras from other manufacturers. If you end up shooting with multiple cameras—either simultaneously, or at different times during your shoot—you could very easily end up with different shots in the same scene that don't have quite the same color quality or sharpness.

Low-budget filmmakers who are borrowing equipment are especially susceptible to this problem, as they might not always be able to borrow the same gear. If your principal shoot is over and you're now trying to get some "pickup" shots, you might find yourself shooting with a different brand or model of camera, or with the same camera but during a different time of year when the light is slightly different.

Matching footage from different cameras can be difficult because it's often a combination of factors that make footage from one camera look different from another camera. When performing such adjustments, consider the following:

- **Use the same approach that we used earlier.** Identify the main problem, correct it with a filter, and then use additional filters to remove lingering color troubles.

- **Note that some cameras have different levels of sharpness and detail.** Differences in detail can often be perceived as slight differences in tone or color. Just as a pattern of black-and-white dots in a newspaper photo can appear gray to the eye, more or less detail in an image can make color appear different. Higher sharpness can also increase the level of contrast in an image. Experiment with subtly using image-sharpening filters to sharpen details from softer cameras. Be very careful, though! When sharpening, you run the risk of increasing aliasing and other artifacts in your image.

■ **Be careful of flesh tones.** In the previous example, the blue cast in the image appears mainly in the bright whites of the walls and couch. It's easy to focus on these areas when applying correction. However, it's important to ensure that, while correcting the background of the image, you don't corrupt any skin tones in the foreground. The human eye is very discerning about skin tones and can easily recognize incorrect, or "bad," color.

Correcting Part of an Image

Through the use of masks, stencils, alpha channels, or layers, you can selectively apply color corrections to part of an image, rather than to the entire image. You can even apply different color corrections—one to the foreground, another to the background. We'll discuss this more in Chapter 17, "Titles and Effects."

Using Tracks and Layers to Adjust Color

If you're using Adobe After Effects or another effects program that provides control over transfer modes, then you can perform color adjustments by layering different video tracks on top of each other. Although not so useful for fixing color problems, stacking tracks (or layers in a compositing program) is an easy way to increase contrast, pump up color, and create unique color effects.

Usually, when two video tracks occupy the same space in the timeline, the track that is higher in the stacking order is the only one that's visible—lower tracks are simply covered up. However, if your editing application provides control over the transfer mode of a layer, then you can set upper tracks to mix and blend with lower tracks. (If you've ever changed the transfer mode of a layer in Photoshop, then you've seen such effects in action.)

If you change the transfer mode of a layer, the pixels in that layer will be mathematically combined with pixels in the lower layer (that layer, in turn, can be combined with the layer below it, and so on). The pixels that result from the combination can often be very different from either of the original pixels (see Color Plate 32).

You Say "Track," I Say "Layer"

When we speak of putting a video clip on a layer, this is synonymous with putting a video clip on a track. No matter what terminology your editing or effects package uses, the concept is the same.

Black-and-White Effects

Monochrome, or "black-and-white," video is one of the easiest and most common color effects out there. It can add a sense of historical significance, make disparate elements match, and it can often look very elegant or cool. Old film and video was truly black-and-white, but when colorists change full color video to monochrome, they usually leave some element of color intact (see Color Plate 33).

The easiest way to make your footage monochrome is to use a simple Tint effect. You can choose to go with a true black-and-white image, or you can map black to a different color, such as dark blue or brown for a subtly tinted image. You can also select how much you want to tint the original image. Using 100% means a fully monochrome image; less than that, and you can get subtle color effects, such as in the tail lights of the passing car in Color Plate 33.

Correcting Color for Film

If your project will eventually be transferred to film, color correction in the computer will be a bit of a problem. If you've ever tried to print images on a color printer, you've probably discovered that what's on your screen doesn't always correspond to what comes out of your printer. The same is true for transferring images to film. The reasons for the disparity are many, and they range from differences in color gamut between video and film to differences in transfer processes to differences in how the film is exposed during the transfer.

Professional editing and effects houses try to deal with this problem through expensive, complicated procedures for calibrating monitors and other digital equipment. In the end, such systems still give little assurance of what the final color will look like. If your final destination is film and you want to do a lot of color correction and color effects, it's a good idea to talk to your film transfer facility. Tell them you're concerned about color control and ask their advice on how to proceed. You can also give single frames to your film lab and have them shot and tested.

Making Your Video Look Like Film

No matter how great your digital video looks, many filmmakers still covet the look of 35mm film. With its softer contrast and focus, different color gamut, grain, and slower frame rate, images shot on film look very different from video.

Before you get dead set on a "film look," though, spend some time and look at what you already have. Film might be pretty, but high-resolution HD or digital cinema video is nothing to sneeze at either. Rather than trying to force it to be something it's not, consider what digital video can do that film can't, and try playing to those strengths.

If you're dead set on a film look, there are a number of things you can do in postproduction.

Before you go filtering all of your video, be aware that there are different concerns for different types of output. If your final output will be film, then you don't need to worry about most of what is covered here. The transfer to actual film stock will be all you need to make your video look like film. Don't add extra grain, gamut enhancement, temporal changes, or special filters. (We cover film transfers in detail in Chapter 18, "Finishing.")

You can create a "film look" effect on your own using the color effects and filters we've discussed in this chapter, but there are a number of good plug-ins that can create a film look for you, such as Red Giant's Magic Bullet Looks (see Figure 16.16 and Color Plate 34). If you're serious about matching particular film stocks, creating a complicated effect such as old film, or having a high degree of control, the extra expense of these filters might be worth it. In Color Plate 35, we used a Magic Bullet Looks preset to add a gradient sunset effect on the same shot we color corrected in Color Plates 25–27.

Figure 16.16

Here we used Magic Bullet Looks to add vignetting for a more film-like look. (See also Color Plates 34–35.)

"Film look" effects are really for people who are mastering for digital distribution. Your goal is to make your footage look as it if were shot on film and transferred to a digital format. When creating a film look, there are several characteristics that you'll need to modify:

- **Film Grain:** A piece of motion picture film consists of a layer of photo-sensitive silver halide particles suspended in an emulsion that is bonded to a strip of celluloid. The texture of these particles results in what is known as *film grain.* The more light sensitive the film stock, the bigger the silver halide particles, and the more visible the grain. Instead of grain, video has electronic noise that looks very different—it's bigger, moves around more, is more colorful, and is generally considered to be more distracting.

- **Film Color:** Film typically has a very different color quality than video does. What's more, different types of film yield very different types of color. We've all seen the bright, Technicolor pastels of 1950s cinema, and we've also seen the hip, overexposed colors of modern music videos that use a bleach by-pass process.

- **Film diffusion:** Film typically has a lower contrast ratio than video, and most film-look plug-ins offer several different ways to add diffusion so that you get a more film-like contrast ratio.

- **Frame rates:** If you didn't shoot 24fps footage, you can use an effect in your editing software to change the frame rate. Also, if you didn't shoot progressive scan, you can use a filter to de-interlace your video footage.

- **Blurring:** Film also has a very characteristic motion blur that results in images that are a little softer and blurrier than the sharp contrast of video. Hopefully, when shooting, you kept your shutter speed to something reasonable like 1/60th of a second, so you've already got some motion blur in your image. Film-look plug-ins offer tools to add motion blur for a more film-like look.

One More Thing

Finally, we recommend color-correcting your footage before you composite any other elements on top of it. Your composited layers might have color issues of their own, so it's better to separate the color troubles that your layers might have. Once you've corrected each layer, you can composite them together and then apply touch-up corrections to smooth the "seams" of your composites. If you're not sure what we mean about composites, don't worry, because a thorough discussion of compositing is coming up next.

Developing an eye for color correction takes practice. In particular, dig in to your software's manual and try to learn about the different color-correction tools at your disposal. No matter what the nature of the tool, or the specifics of its controls, you'll still need to be careful not to overcorrect and to stay on the lookout for troublesome artifacts. There is always something new to learn about color, and the more you practice, the better you will become.

By now you should be comfortable with the basics of color correction using your chosen editing application. If you're still not comfortable using levels, curves, color balance, or the other color-correction tools provided in your editing program, then you'll need to get some more practice. The best way to practice is to simply shoot some bad footage (just choose an incorrect white-balance setting) and start correcting. Color correction is a staple effect that's well worth learning.

17

Titles and Effects

Photo credit: Sonja Schenk

E very summer, theatres across the country are filled with big blockbuster movies and part of the draw is the parade of mind-blowing special effects. Also mind-blowing, perhaps, are the budgets of these movies.

These kinds of special effects involve scores of technical specialists and a laborious process that is well beyond the scope of most lower budget or indie film projects. But that doesn't mean motion graphics and special effects will be absent entirely from your project. Almost every film has titles and, at the very least, uses basic special effects technology to enhance selected shots or to fix problems.

If you've taken a look at the effects available to you in your editing software, you'll probably find an alarmingly large list. But many of these effects are very specific and won't be that useful to you. In this chapter, we'll cover the visual effects tools that you'll use the most: titling, motion effects, and basic compositing (mattes and keys). We'll also show you how to integrate still images into your project, how to handle mixing SD and HD footage, and how to fix basic image problems using the special effects tools available in your editing application.

Titles

Although your production might not need fancy special effects such as 3D-rendered dinosaurs or complicated composites and morphs, it probably will need a title sequence at the beginning and a credit roll at the end. If you're shooting a documentary, you might also need to use titles to identify interviewees and locations.

Most editing packages include titling functions that let you superimpose simple text titles over your images. Some packages include more advanced functions such as rolls and animated text. Your editing program's manual should cover everything you need to know to use the built-in title tools. No matter what software you use, there are several things to keep in mind when building your titles.

Title Titles

As with everything else related to filmmaking, there are a whole bunch of terms related to titling. Whether you use these terms or not is up to you.

- **Title card:** A non-moving title.

- **Main title:** The title card featuring the name of the film.

- **Opening credits (or head credits):** The typical series of title cards that fade in and out at the beginning of a movie. Typically, opening credits follow (roughly) this order: studio or production company, sometimes a producer, main title, lead actors, casting, music, music supervisor, costumes and makeup, designer, director of photography, editor, executive producer(s), producer(s), writer, director.

- **End credits (or tail credits):** The credits at the end of a movie. Typically, if a movie skipped opening credits, it will present the opening credit information in reverse order as end credits, before going on to a normal end credit roll.

Title Titles (continued)

- **Title roll:** A long list of titles that scrolls from the bottom of the screen to the top. Usually used for end credits. A very efficient way of presenting titles, as every name is on-screen for the same duration.

- **Title crawl:** A line of titles that moves horizontally across the screen, usually at the bottom. Used more in television.

- **Supers (or super'd):** Titles that are superimposed over other video.

- **Lower thirds:** Titles that fit into the lower third of the frame. Usually credits identifying a speaker, such as you might use in a documentary. Also called "Chyrons."

- **Pad:** A colored background or stripe behind a lower-third title. Pads improve a title's legibility.

- **Textless version:** A version of your project with no titles. These are almost always necessary for foreign distribution.

Choosing Your Typeface and Size

You'll need to consider the final goal of your project when choosing the typeface (or font) and the size of the text for your titles. These days, there are so many typefaces available that choosing the typeface is an art in and of itself. Experienced title designers often mix and match different typefaces, for example, if they prefer the question mark symbol from a different typeface or a different capital letter. Having the knowledge of the many different typefaces out there is a huge asset, and if you don't have that knowledge, plan on some time doing research.

If it's meant to be projected, you can choose a smaller size, but always keep in mind that many people will watch your project on a video monitor or as streaming video on the Web, which means you'll need to make sure the titles are large enough to read on a small screen or if they are highly compressed.

When creating titles that will play over video, be certain that the typeface you choose is readable throughout the clip. Fast-moving images with lots of clutter will make smaller, finer-lined typefaces more difficult to read.

When choosing a type size, legibility should be your first concern. At small sizes, some typefaces will be more legible than others, but in general, anything below 20 points will be too small (see Figure 17.1).

Installing Fonts

If you find a typeface you like but don't own, you'll have to install it on your computer before you launch your editing software.

Figure 17.1

Be sure to consider both legibility and composition when creating titles.

Ordering Your Titles

If you're working with union actors, their contract might specify where their name must appear in the title sequence. Similarly, credit position might have been stipulated from a "producer" when you talked him (or her) out of some funding. Be sure to consider all of these agreements and obligations when ordering and creating your titles.

Start with a Text File

If you have a long list of titles, such as lower thirds for a feature-length documentary, subtitles for an entire film (or even just a scene or two), or a long credit list, use a word processing program to create the list of titles, and be sure they are proofread and error-free before you start creating graphic titles. You can easily cut and paste them into your title tool when you're ready to create your graphics.

Coloring Your Titles

The simplest choice is to put white text over a black screen, but if you want to do something more colorful than that, or if you are planning to superimpose your titles over moving images, text color choice is critical. First, finding a color that contrasts enough with your background can be difficult. If the video you're superimposing over is changing a lot, then finding a color will be even more difficult.

Your first impulse will be to go for really saturated colors, but remember that heavily saturated colors might bleed. It's safest to stick with a Web safe color. If your project is intended for broadcast television, it's still best to stick with NTSC safe colors even though your footage might be HD. (We discussed safe colors in Chapter 16, "Color Correction.")

If you've got a really busy or really colorful background, your best way of making your text more visible is to add a drop shadow or an edge. A drop shadow will place a light border behind the text to separate it from the background, while an edge will simply stroke all of the edges of your text with a specific color. Both of these techniques make text much more readable (refer to Figure 17.1).

Be certain to watch the entire clip that your title is superimposed over, and make certain that the text is legible throughout the entire clip. Although a blue title might look great at the beginning of a clip, make sure there are no blue, title-obscuring objects moving through the frame later in the clip.

Placing Your Titles

If you're planning on superimposing your titles over video, you'll want to give some thought to their placement, not just for the sake of readability, but for good composition as well. Hopefully, you shot the underlying videos with titles in mind. Although titles might sit on top of an image, they should not be thought of as separate. Be sure to consider the composition of the entire image—titles and video—when placing your graphics. If your titles are going to move about the screen, make sure they are readable across all action over which they are superimposed.

Legible titles don't really do any good if the viewer doesn't have time to read them. A good rule of thumb is to leave the title up long enough for you to read it two times aloud. Usually, this means two to four seconds for each page, not including fades in or out. Even if you read fast, the title will probably be up long enough for most people to read it.

In general, pay close attention to the pacing of your opening title sequence. Remember: this is the beginning of your presentation and it is a chance for you to set an initial tone for your story. If you have already presented a "prelude" before the credits, your title sequence can function as a dramatic beat to prolong what has come before. Although you don't want to bore the audience with a long title sequence, if the beginning of your story is somewhat somber, a slower title sequence might be just the thing to bring your audience down to a more receptive pace. Titles can serve as another beat in your storytelling process, so give them some thought.

Safe Titles

Digital television doesn't have the same limits that old school analog (aka NTSC or PAL) television does, but not everyone has a widescreen HD monitor and that means that most broadcasters, VOD distributors, and even Web sites still rely on the standard analog rules for safe titles and safe colors.

Action safe and title safe (see Figure 17.2) are guidelines for making sure that titles and action are visible on analog video monitors that are known for overscanning, or cropping, the image.

Because widescreen footage could get cropped to 4:3 on display, it is considered safest to keep your titles within the standard 4:3 title safe area (Figure 17.2). If you are positive that your project won't be subject to the delivery requirements of a television network or video-on-demand distributor, you can safely go beyond the boundary of the 4:3 analog image; however, be aware that cropping at the edge of the image can occur on many HD monitors so it's best to avoid positioning anything important too close to the edge of the screen.

Most editing applications provide an overlay of title safe and action safe guidelines to help you while you are building your titles.

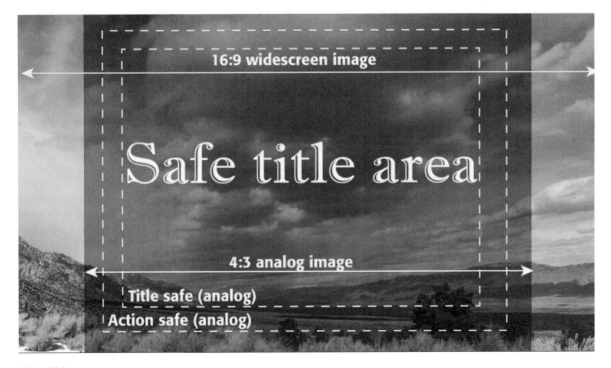

Figure 17.2

Because there is always a chance that your widescreen image might get cropped on display, it's best to keep your titles within the boundaries of a standard 4:3 analog image.

WHAT TO WATCH

Be sure to watch *other people's titles.* The next time you're at the movies, consider how the director has used the title sequence. Many action movies, for example, skip titles altogether and "cut right to the chase," so to speak. James Bond movies are famous for their elaborate title sequences that occur *after* an initial high-energy sequence. These sequences serve to bring the audience down from the chase-scene high to the typically more sedate "first" scene.

Some movies choose to superimpose their titles over initial, expository action. *Jerry Maguire* is a good example of this technique. Be careful, though. You don't want to distract the audience from your exposition, and you don't want to give short shrift to your titles.

At the opposite extreme from these approaches are the title sequences used by Woody Allen in most of his movies. Simple slates on a black background, these titles sequences are completely separate from the "main" presentation.

Although you might think we're making rather a big deal out of something that can be very simple, don't forget that every frame that you show the audience can—and usually does—carry some type of information about your story.

 ## Create Your Main Title

No matter how minimal your project, you will want a main title at the beginning. In this tutorial, we'll walk you through the basic steps of creating a main title card in your editing application. We used Adobe Premiere Pro, but you can use the software of your choice.

STEP 1: CREATE A PROJECT
Create a new project in Premiere with the DSLR 1080p24 preset (see Figure 17.3). Import the clip called "sundial.mov" from the Ch 17 folder on the Web site and drag it onto the timeline. From the title menu, select New > Default Still, and the title tool window will open up.

STEP 2: TYPE IN THE NAME OF YOUR MOVIE
Click on the Text tool icon (upper left) and type in the name of your movie. You can either use the preset title styles in the menu below or you can set the typeface, font size, alignment, and other variables in the typeface settings at the top of the window (see Figure 17.4).

STEP 3: POSITION THE TYPE
With the arrow tool selected, you can position this outline by dragging it around the screen. (As a shortcut, you can hold down the Cmd key [Mac] or Ctrl key [Win] to temporarily change your cursor to the Move tool. When you let go, it will revert back.)

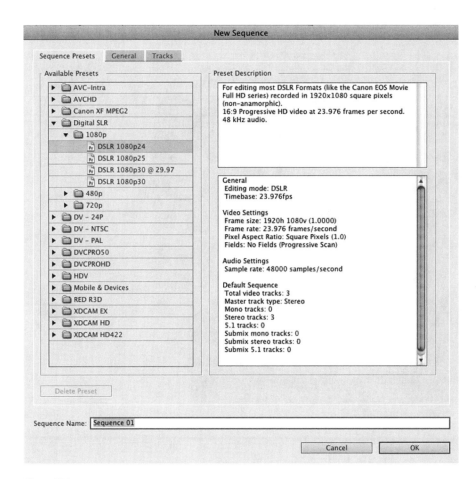

Figure 17.3

Select the preset for "DSLR 1080p24" when you set up the project for this tutorial.

STEP 4: ADD SOME STYLE

Use the Title Properties window (refer to Figure 17.4) to select a fill color and add outlines or drop shadows. You can also make your text slightly transparent to have it blend in a little more with the background image. We chose to leave it at full opacity since the background image has a lot going on visually. We also enhanced the drop shadow and chose a brightly colored fill with a thin outline to further help the type stand out from the background (see Color Plate 36).

Text alignment   **Title Properties**

Text tool

Presets

Figure 17.4

The Adobe Premiere title tool window.

STEP 5: EDIT THE TITLE INTO YOUR TIMELINE

Close the title tool. You'll now see the clip "Main title" in your Project window. Drag it onto Video track 2 in the timeline and position it over the video clip you added in step 1 (see Figure 17.5). You can use the Move tool to reposition it more precisely in the timeline. Just select the arrow in the tool bar and then go to the Program window and click and drag the title around until you are happy with the placement.

STEP 6: RENDER THE TITLE

Go to the sequence menu and select Render. That's it—you're done. You can add some dissolves if you want it to fade in and out.

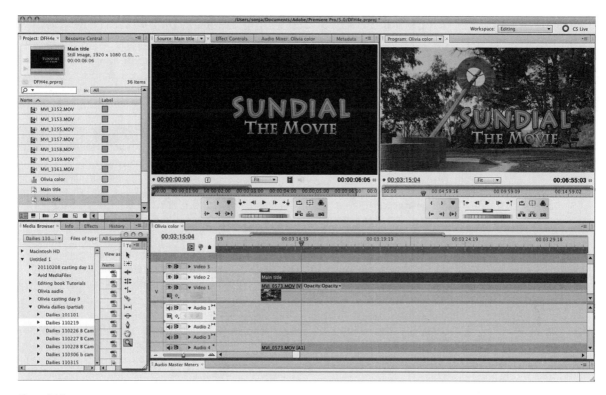

Figure 17.5

Position the title on the second video track in the timeline.

Making Titles for Film

If your final destination will be a film output, you will need to have your titles recorded from the digital files directly onto film, a process called *film printing*. You'll need to create your titles at the proper aspect ratio, usually 1920 × 1080. Until the recent advent of HD, the standard film resolution for digital files was 2K per frame, or about 2020 × 1092 pixels for 1.85 theatrical release format 35mm. 2020 × 1092 seems bigger than 1920 × 1080, but it includes space for an optical sound track—about 200 pixels of the width—so the image resolution of 2020 × 1092 is actually about 1820 × 1090, a little less than 1920 × 1080. 2K still exists, but its usage is less and less common. There is another standard for film resolution, 4K, which is double the size of 2K and almost double the size of 1920 × 1080 HD. 4K is usually reserved for projects and formats that require a very high resolution, such as the IMAX film format.

Be sure to keep your titles within the TV safe guidelines, even though you'll be creating files with a wider aspect ratio because it's very likely that they'll end up on a Standard Definition TV screen eventually. In some cases, you'll have to create one set of titles for film and another for Standard Definition TV.

Check Out the Advanced Titling Tutorials on the Web Site ▬▬▬

We have several great tutorials on the Web site from previous editions of this book. If you're serious about visual effects, be sure to work through them. They can be found at *www.thedigitalfilmmakinghandbook. com/chapter17*.

Motion Graphics Software

If special effects and compositing are central to your project, then you may want to consider using a third-party motion graphics application or a collection of plug-ins that's compatible with your editing system. Titling and motion graphics applications run the gamut from simple character generators to full-blown animation apps that let you create 3D flying logos with photo-realistic lighting. If you need more visual effects power, consider one of these stand-alone software options:

- **Adobe After Effects:** After Effects is a full-blown, exceptional compositing program suitable for feature film effects work and advanced titling. With scores of third-party plug-ins available, After Effects is usually the application of choice for 2D visual effects artists and designers.

- **Apple Motion:** Apple bundles a program called Motion with Final Cut Studio. It's an excellent titling and motion graphics package. Offering easy-to-use titling, really cool particle effects, and excellent 3D motion control, Motion is particularly impressive for its ability to perform all of these tasks in real-time, making for a much simpler workflow when it comes time to tweak and refine your titles. Motion is even suitable for simple compositing tasks (see Figure 17.6).

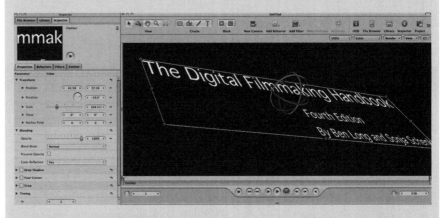

Figure 17.6

Apple's Motion provides an excellent motion graphics/titling application that gives you real-time control over your motion graphics.

In addition to these stand-alone apps, there are some truly great plug-ins out there, designed to work inside your favorite editing or motion graphics software, and the best thing about plug-ins is that they are often available individually for purchase, which means you don't necessarily have to spend the money for a whole package that you won't use much. What's also great is that many plug-ins are compatible with standard editing applications so you can use them without having to change applications or workstations.

Motion Graphics Software (continued)

Here are some of our favorites:

- **BorisFX:** Boris makes a number of excellent titling applications and plug-ins. Boris Graffiti and Boris Red are plug-ins that are compatible with over 20 different editing and compositing applications. Both plug-ins provide most of the titling functionality you'll ever need. From simple rolls to text on a path to cool shattering effects, Boris' plug-ins provide a tremendous amount of power and can create both 2D and 3D text. Because they plug directly into your editing application, Red and Graffiti are incredibly convenient and Boris Continuum provides a great palette of effects filters.

- **Red Giant:** Red Giant is most famous for Magic Bullet—the plug-in that lets you create truly great-looking film-look effects. Magic Bullet Looks offers specialized film stock presets and a range of controls to re-create things that used to be only available if shot in-camera. Magic Bullet Colorista is a sophisticated color correction plug-in, and Red Giant also offers the Primatte keyer plug-in.

- **GenArts:** GenArts makes the Sapphire plug-ins, famous for their ability to create sophisticated lighting effects and also the Tinder family of plugs-ins, both very popular among visual effects professionals.

- **DigiEffects**: DigiEffects makes two great sets of plug-ins: Damage and Delirium. The plug-ins in Damage help you degrade your image by adding aged film looks, video interference, camera shake, and other "bad" effects. Delirium offers an array of color and compositing tools along with glows, fog effects, and many others. Buena Depth Cue lets you adjust depth of field in post.

Motion Effects

Motion effects are possibly the most basic and commonly used effects in postproduction. When we speak of the motion features in a motion graphics or editing package, we're not talking about features that let you control the motion of objects *within a shot*. In other words, you're not going to be able to take a video clip of a basketball game and control the motion of the ball. Instead, motion control is limited to specifying the movement of an entire image. In addition to position, you can control other properties such as opacity, scale, cropping, and rotation.

Keyframes and Interpolating

In traditional hand-drawn cel animation, a director draws certain frames that indicate where a character should be at a particular time. These keyframes might occur every 10 frames, or every two minutes, depending on the amount and nature of the action in a scene. Once the keyframes are defined, a group of animators draw all of the intervening frames that are required to get from one keyframe to the next. This process is usually called *in-betweening* or *'tweening*. It can also be referred to as *interpolation,* as the animators must figure out, or interpolate, which frames are required to get from one state to the next.

This same keyframe/in-betweening approach is used in editing and effects programs to animate the properties of a clip or image. By properties, we mean the parameters and characteristics that define how a clip looks, such as position, scale, and rotation. Some packages add control over additional properties, such as distortion, opacity, cropping, or 3D rotation. Many programs also let you animate the parameters of any filters you might have applied to a layer, letting you change the amount of, say, Gaussian blur or color balance that you've applied to a video clip. The ability to animate all of the properties of a clip is an easy way to create complex effects (see Figure 17.7).

Most keyframe interfaces work roughly the same way:

1. Go to a particular point on the timeline.

2. Adjust the parameter you want to animate.

3. The computer will either automatically set a keyframe at that point, or you'll have to manually tell it to set a keyframe. During playback, the computer will automatically interpolate all of the frames between your keyframes.

4. Repeat the preceding steps until your entire animation has been defined.

5. Render and play the video to see the full animation, including all of the in-between frames that the computer has interpolated.

Figure 17.7

The Timeline window from Adobe After Effects. Notice that there are many animatable properties ranging from position and opacity to parameters of filters that have been applied to the layers. In addition, you can also adjust the acceleration and velocity of an animated change.

Some programs also give you control over the velocity of an animated element. Such controls let you make an object slowly accelerate and decelerate as it moves, and they make it possible to sync the animation of a property to another element in your composition.

A discussion of the specifics of the animation controls is beyond the scope of this book. If you are not familiar with the features of your package, consult your manual. Look for topics such as animation, keyframes, and velocity.

Slow-Mo and Speed Ramps

A very popular effect is to slow down or speed up the timing of a shot. Most editing applications are very good at handling these sorts of effects. You can pick a speed, pick a duration, or set key frames for a variable speed shot, also known as a *speed ramp*. A classic speed ramp is a shot that starts out at normal speed and then gradually ramps up into ultra fast motion (see Figure 17.8)

Figure 17.8

Changing the speed of a clip in your editing application is easy.

True Slo-Mo

True slow motion footage is shot at a very high frame rate so that a great amount of detail in motion is preserved—think shot of a hummingbird where you can see each beat of its wings. Only a few special cameras can shoot high frame rate video, so if ultra-smooth slow motion video is important to you, you'll have to shoot with the right camera to get it.

Integrating Still Images and Video

One of the most common effects is adding motion to still images. Using a basic "Resize" or "Motion" effect, you can pan across the image, zoom in, or reframe to create a dynamic sequence. Once upon a time, you actually had to reshoot the images with a video camera, a process called *motion control,* but happily those days are long gone, and you can do anything you need with the simple effects available in your editing application.

Here are a few basic tips when working with still images:

- Use the highest resolution images that your editing application can support. That way, you'll have lots of room to zoom in without degrading the image quality (see Figure 17.9). Premiere, for example, can accept an image that is 10,000 × 8,000 pixels. That's about five times bigger than the resolution of 1920 × 1080 HD video.

- If your editing application doesn't let you import still images that are larger than your current video resolution, and you need to zoom in or otherwise enlarge an image, use a dedicated motion graphics program like Adobe After Effects to create your moving still image shots.

- Remember that dissolving between static still images can also create a sense of motion.

- Try to choose images that will work well when framed to fit the aspect ratio of your video. Vertically-oriented photos can be hard to work with.

Figure 17.9

Using a high-resolution source image means that you have lots of room to enlarge the still photograph when adding motion effects.

Special Effects Workflow

Before we start talking about manipulating the image, it's important to consider some workflow issues. If you're using the internal effects tools in your editing application, you won't need to worry about workflow much, but if you are farming your compositing out to a visual effects specialist or to a dedicated special effects application such as Adobe After Effects, you'll benefit by taking workflow into consideration.

Think about the following scenario: You're editing a low-budget sci-fi epic about extraterrestrial book authors who invade Earth and begin boring everyone to death by reading detailed digital video specifications at them. You have a 45-second-long edited sequence of the Grand Canyon. At 10 seconds into this segment, you want to composite an animation of a flying saucer over the edited footage of the Grand Canyon. The saucer will take about 10 seconds to majestically descend into the Grand Canyon and will be out of sight by 20 seconds into the clip (see Figure 17.10).

Although you're editing in Adobe Premiere, you plan on performing the composite of the spaceship using Adobe After Effects. Therefore, you'll need to export footage from Premiere, import it into After Effects, perform the composite, and then bring the composited final footage back into Premiere.

Figure 17.10

With good storyboards, we can better determine which parts of a clip are required for an effect.

Although our Grand Canyon sequence in the preceding example lasts 45 seconds, the section where the spaceship will be seen is only 10 seconds long. Therefore, rather than move the whole 45 seconds into our compositing program, it's better to move only the 10 seconds that matter. In general, most effects shots are very short—a couple of seconds here, a few frames there—so you'll be able to get away with moving very short clips between your effects and editing packages.

In the preceding example, our compositing work will proceed as follows:

1. First, we will find the 10 seconds of footage that we need for our composite.

2. This footage will be marked for output. In most editing programs, you do this by setting special in- and out-points in your timeline that denote which section of a sequence will be rendered and output.

3. Next, we will output the selected video. In our output settings, we'll select the QuickTime Animation codec as our compressor. The Animation codec is lossless, but creates substantially larger files than most other codecs (see Figure 17.11).

Figure 17.11

No matter what application you're exporting video from, at some point you will be given a choice of which QuickTime codec to use for compression. When moving between applications, use a lossless codec such as Animation.

4. The resulting 10-second clip will be imported into After Effects. There, we will perform our composite.

5. In After Effects, we'll render our finished composite. Again, we'll choose the Animation codec when saving, to ensure the highest quality.

6. Now, we'll import the new, composited, animation-compressed clip into Premiere and edit it into our sequence, replacing the footage that was there before. When we create our final output, this new clip will be compressed with the same codec as the rest of our footage.

In the interest of staying organized, when naming new files—such as composites and other effect clips—use the same naming conventions that you used when you digitized your footage, and be sure to back up the new files on a hard drive.

Moving Media

When moving files between apps, you'll also want to be sure that you always use the same frame size and frame rate. Note that some applications will default to 30fps rather than 29.97. The only time you should render to a different size or time base is when you are intentionally trying to shrink your movie for output to the Web or other low-bandwidth medium.

Compositing 101

In theory, compositing sounds like a very basic effect: put one layer of video on top of another to create a composite. In practice, though, compositing is one of the most powerful tools at your disposal. At the simplest level, you can use compositing tools to superimpose custom titles and graphics over video, or stack clips on top of each other to create a video collage. More sophisticated compositing tools allow you to do everything from mixing computer-generated elements with live video to placing your actors inside virtual sets. Although good compositing tools are the foundation of all special effects work, they can also be used for more everyday concerns, such as fixing bad pixels or letterboxing to mix SD and HD footage.

In most non-linear editing packages, you can create a simple composite by creating multiple video tracks, each containing a different clip or image (see Figure 17.12). For every-day compositing, your editing software will provide a set of tools that will suffice for all but the most specialized tasks.

Dedicated compositing programs such as Adobe After Effects provide more compositing power by letting you stack many layers of video and stills, and they provide more robust control over how those layers interact. After Effects also lets you animate the properties of layers to create sophisticated, animated effects.

No matter which program you use, the process of compositing is fairly simple. First, you import your video clips and stack them in the appropriate order. Obviously, if you put one piece of video on top of another, the upper clip will simply obscure the lower clip. Therefore, after creating your stack of video, you must define the method by which each layer will reveal the contents of the underlying layers. The method you choose will depend on the type of footage with which you are working.

Compositing methods fall into two categories: keys and mattes.

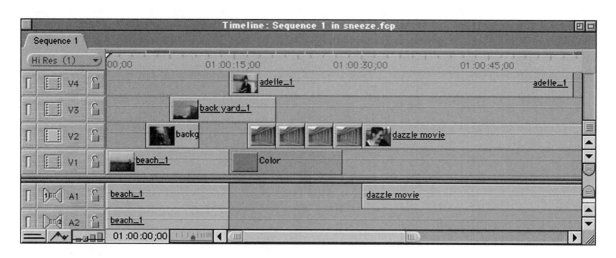

Figure 17.12

Composites are made by stacking tracks or layers on top of each other and then specifying how those layers will combine.

Keys

If you've ever seen a local TV weatherman standing in front of a weather-filled map of the country, then you've seen an example of keying. The weatherman is not really standing in front of a map, of course. Rather, he's standing in front of a blue or green screen that is electronically keyed out and replaced with the image of the map, as shown in Figure 17.13.

Figure 17.13

The upper image was shot in front of a blue screen, which can easily be "keyed out" and replaced with another image, such as this billowing smoke.

Most editing apps provide keying functions that let you superimpose footage shot in front of a colored screen over another video clip, animation, or still image. In these programs, you import both your blue-screen footage and your underlying layers, stack them up, and then tell the program to apply a chroma key (sometimes called a *color key*) to the uppermost layer. The chroma key feature will provide controls to let you select which color you want to key out.

When the image is rendered, the computer will look for every occurrence of the specified key color and make it transparent, allowing the underlying layer to show through.

A luminance key functions the same way, but rather than keying out pixels of a certain color, a luma key keys out pixels of a certain brightness. Many programs offer variations of these keys, such as screen, multiply, or difference. Consult your manual for details.

Because you must shoot in front of a specially colored screen and perform very precise lighting, chroma key effects are not ideal for every compositing task. (The screens are blue or green because there is rarely any blue or green in the skin tone of a healthy human.) Chroma keys are usually used for situations where you want to superimpose a person in front of another video clip or still. Luminance keys can be used for situations where you can't put a blue screen behind your foreground element. For example, you could use a luma key to key out a bright sky behind a building. Luminance keys can also be used to touch up parts of a chroma key composite that have not keyed out properly.

Shooting blue- or green-screen footage requires a great deal of care and expertise.

 ## Creating a Luminance Key

A luminance key lets you superimpose one layer over another by knocking out either the very bright or very dark parts of a layer to expose underlying layers. In this tutorial, we'll use a luminance key to superimpose a flash of gunfire over another video clip (see Figure 17.14).

For this tutorial, you'll need an editing or effects package that provides luminance keys (for example, Adobe Premiere, Apple's Final Cut Pro, Adobe After Effects, Sony Vegas, Avid Media Composer). This tutorial assumes that you understand how to add clips to a project, search through them using a "source monitor," add clips to a timeline, and add luminance keys to a clip. If you're unclear on any of these, check your editing software's manual.

STEP 1: SET UP YOUR PROJECT

In your editing package, create a project. Import the files hand-gun.mov and GS125.mov from the Chapter 17 page on the companion Web site at *www.thedigitalfilmmakinghandbook. com/chapter17*. Hand-gun.mov is a short clip showing a hand "firing" bullets. It was shot with a Canon GL-1. GS125.mov is from the ArtBeats Gun Stock Digital Film Library and is a short movie showing a number of muzzle flashes shot in near darkness.

Place the hand-gun.mov clip on the first video track in your timeline. Create a second video track above this one. Place the GS125.mov in the upper video track.

STEP 2: FIND THE FIRST MUZZLE FLASH

Load the GS125.mov clip in your timeline into your source monitor. Scrub through the clip to find a muzzle flash you like. Position the playback head on the first frame of one of the muzzle flashes and set an in-point. Scrub forward one or two frames to be sure the flash has ended and set an out-point.

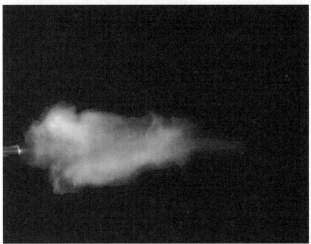

Figure 17.14

In this tutorial, we're going to superimpose the footage of a muzzle flash over footage of a hand to create a final composite that will show a hand firing bullets.

Finding the Muzzle Flashes

Note that most of these flashes are only one frame. Depending on your computer's performance, you might not see each frame during playback. Consequently, you'll probably have to scrub to find the single frames. Look for places in the clip where the hand recoils. This is a good way to zero in on the flash.

STEP 3: POSITION THE FLASH IN THE TIMELINE

In the timeline, scrub through your footage and watch the program monitor to find the frame where the finger seems to fire. This is where you want the muzzle flash to appear (see Figure 17.15). Position the GS125.mov clip in a higher track so that it begins at the point in time where the finger fires. Note that the program monitor will now be filled with the muzzle flash on the black image of the GS125.mov clip. Your background plate that shows the finger will be completely obscured, but not for long.

Figure 17.15

Your muzzle flash footage should start right when the finger begins to recoil.

STEP 4: DEFINE YOUR LUMINANCE KEY

Add a luminance key to the GS125.mov clip. If you're unsure of how to add a key, consult your manual for details. Some luminance keys allow you to choose between keying out light areas or dark areas. Others default to keying out darker areas. If your luma key provides an option, set it to key out darker areas.

Most luminance keys provide at least two sliders for adjusting the key effect: one that specifies which values will be keyed out, and another that controls how transparent those areas will become. Adjust the sliders in your luminance key filter until the black areas are gone and only the flash remains. Your goal is to find a balance of settings that eliminates the background without reducing the luminance of the flash too much. Pay particular attention to the edges of the flash. Even though it's only one frame, a hard edge or a black fringe will be noticeable to the viewer (see Figure 17.16).

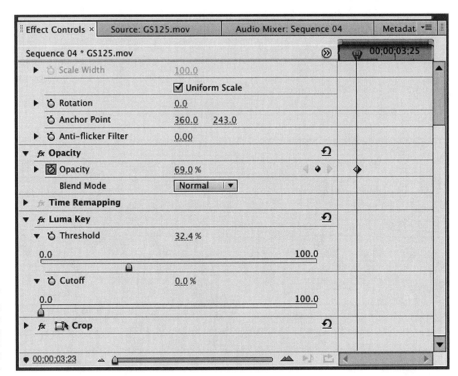

Figure 17.16

Experiment to find luminance key settings that eliminate the background, without dulling the intensity of the flash and without creating a hard, distinct edge on the flash.

STEP 5: POSITION THE FLASH IN THE FRAME

With your key defined, you should be able to see the background beneath the muzzle flash. Unfortunately, the flash is probably over at the left side of the screen. Obviously, we want it to look like it's coming out of the finger. Using your software's motion controls, reposition the flash so that it sits just off the tip of the finger. You might also want to try scaling it down so that it doesn't overwhelm the composition.

Finally, many of the flashes in the GS125.mov clip have a visible gun barrel on the left side of the frame. Your editing software should provide a motion control tool that allows you to crop the frame so that the barrel is removed from view without affecting the flash (see Figure 17.17). (See your user documentation if you don't know how to do this.)

Figure 17.17

Move the muzzle flash to the end of the "barrel" and scale it down to be more appropriate to the "caliber" of this finger.

STEP 6: NOW, DO THE REST

Render your footage and take a look. Pay close attention to the timing of the flash; it might need to be moved forward or backward a frame or two to match the recoil of the finger. You might also see that you need to adjust the settings of your luminance key. When you're satisfied, choose another four muzzle flashes and edit them into the appropriate locations, as shown in Figure 17.18. ◄◀

Filtered Footage

If you don't have or don't want to use clip footage of a muzzle flash, consider using a computer-generated one. DigiEffects' Delirium collection of After Effects plug-ins includes an excellent Muzzle Flash filter that can generate muzzle flashes for you.

That's it! With the simple application of some stock footage and a luminance key we've created . . . well . . . a kind of silly special effect. However, you can see that, in a more practical situation, such effects would save you the danger and expense of using a real gun. In the next chapter, we'll increase the realism of the shot through the use of a little rotoscoping, but first, let's see if we hit anything during our little target practice.

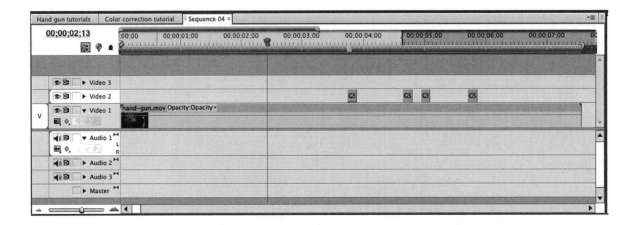

Figure 17.18

When you've placed all of your muzzle flashes, your timeline should have five clips on it.

   **Using a Chroma Key**

In the last tutorial, we used a luminance key to knock out dark areas of a layer. However, not all footage is suited to luminance keying. With chroma keying, we can knock out a specific color to reveal underlying layers.

A chroma key is usually used to knock out a background to superimpose an element over other footage. That's what we're going to do here to create footage of gunshots hitting a door. (The results of this footage can be edited onto the end of our previous tutorial to create a finished shot of a hand firing bullets that hit a door.)

For this tutorial, you'll need an editing or compositing package that supports chroma keying.

STEP 1: SET UP YOUR PROJECT

Create a project and load the following media from the Chroma Key Tutorial folder: door still.psd, bullethole still.psd, bullethole.mov. Place door still.psd in your timeline. If your editing program does not support Photoshop files, you can try the TIFF version of the documents. (Note that, in the interest of saving space on the Web site, we have chosen to use a still of the door, rather than a movie. In practice, it's a better idea to use a video of the door, even though there's no movement in the image. A movie will show changes in noise and grain, while a still will have a slightly different quality that will be recognizable to your viewers.)

STEP 2: ADD A BULLET HOLE

Add the bullet hole still to a layer or track above the door's layer. (This bullet hole is a still from the same ArtBeats Gun Stock collection that provided the muzzle flashes.) The door will be completely obscured by the blue surrounding the bullet hole.

STEP 3: ADD A CHROMA KEY

Add a chroma key to the bullet hole still. Next, you need to specify the color you want to "key out" or eliminate. Many chroma key functions provide an Eyedropper tool that you can use to sample the key color directly from the image in your program monitor. Other programs require you to specify the color numerically or with a slider.

Don't be surprised if you don't see any changes after selecting the color. Most blue screens have a degree of variation in them, so selecting one single color isn't going to eliminate an entire field of slightly varying hue. Fortunately, most chroma keys also have some type of tolerance control that lets you specify a degree of variation from your chosen color. Adjust the tolerance control until your background is removed.

Your chroma key function also probably provides controls for thinning and blurring (or feathering) the edges of the keyed areas. Adjust these to eliminate any remaining blue fringes around the bullet holes, and to soften the edges to better blend them into the door (see Figure 17.19).

Figure 17.19

By feathering the edge of our chroma key, we can blend the bullet hole into the underlying video.

STEP 4: POSITION AND SCALE THE BULLET HOLE

At its normal size, this bullet hole is rather large (after all, it was plainly a small-caliber finger). Scale down the bullet hole to something more appropriate and then position the hole somewhere on the door. In After Effects, we can scale the bullet hole layer by dragging one of its corners to resize. We can then reposition by dragging the image to another location. Other programs might require the use of a dialog box or special motion command.

STEP 5: TINT THE HOLE

At this point, the bullet hole plainly looks like it's floating over the door layer. But why? What's not quite right? As we've discussed throughout this book, video is composed of luminance and chrominance information (lightness and color). It's good to think in those terms when trying to match two pieces of video, either when editing shots into each other or compositing them on top of each other. Is there a chrominance difference between the bullet hole and the door? Unfortunately, because the door footage was underlit, it has a very slight greenish hue to it. This is in fairly sharp contrast to the strong reddish tones of the splinters in the bullet hole layer. Using the color correction facilities in your package, apply a slight green tint to the bullet hole.

Next, look at the luminance of the hole. It's a little bright compared to the duller tones of the door. Again, using the color correction tools at your disposal, adjust the luminance to darken the bullet hole a little bit. Because the bullet hole has few highlights, and because its blacks are very black, you can probably concentrate your luminance adjustments to the mid-tones. See Color Plate 38 for before and after examples of this color correction.

STEP 6: STILL NOT QUITE RIGHT

It still looks like a decal, doesn't it? Consider the overall image quality of the two layers. Is there any difference? The bullet hole looks sharper and more detailed than the door. This makes sense, since the bullet hole was shot using 35mm film and digitized at high-resolution. Apply a slight blur to the bullet hole layer (see Figure 17.20).

STEP 7: ADD THE REST

When you're satisfied with your first bullet hole, make two more copies of it and stack them on separate layers. Drag each copy to a different location on the door. You should also apply different scale amounts and a little rotation to each bullet hole to hide the fact that they're really all the same image. Separate them by a few frames or seconds in the timeline to correspond with the timing of the bullet hits. There were four shots fired from our "handgun." For the last one, let's see it actually impact the door.

STEP 8: ADD THE LAST HIT

Bullethole.mov (*www.thedigitalfilmmakinghandbook.com/chapter17*) actually shows a whole bullet hit. Drag it into yet another layer and apply the same chroma key, color balance, and blur filters that you applied to the still images. Position, scale, and rotate the layer appropriately. ◄▌

That's it! Now, you can render out a final shot and edit it into your footage of the handgun firing. If you cut to the door shot right before the impact of the last bullet, you'll have a somewhat dynamic little scene.

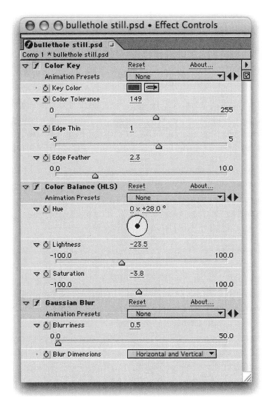

Figure 17.20

Our final composite looks good, but as you can see, it takes a good number of filters to get it there.

Non-Special Special Effects

Often, when you think of special effects, you think of giant dinosaurs or horribly "be-weaponed" space cruisers. However, you will probably find that most of your special effects needs fall into the simple, non-special realm such as the muzzle flashes and bullet holes we just created. As special effects hardware has grown less expensive, it has become reasonable to create digital effects for many tasks that used to be achieved practically.

Even relatively "simple" practical effects—such as gunfire—can quickly become expensive, even for a high-budget feature. Paul Verhoeven's *Starship Troopers*, for example, used over 300,000 rounds of blank ammunition! With the effects power of the average desktop computer, it's worth spending some time assessing whether some of your "normal" shots and effects might be cheaper to produce using computer-generated imagery.

Keying Tips

Getting a good key—no matter what type you're using—has more to do with shooting good footage than postproduction tinkering. However, there are some things you can do to get better results from key footage. Consider the following when defining your keys:

- **It might take more than one.** It's okay to apply more than one key to an image. Because it can be difficult to light a blue-screen background evenly—particularly a large one—you'll often find that the blue screen is darker around the edges than in the middle. In other words, the edges are a different shade of blue. Rather than adjusting the tolerance of a single key to include all the blue—a process that will most likely eliminate some of your foreground—use one key for the lighter blue around your subject and another key to eliminate the darker blue.

- **Try mixing keys.** There are some instances where you can use a chroma key to knock out a background and a very slight luma key to eliminate some of the leftover fringy weirdness. Because it's easy to overlight the foreground when lighting your blue screen, an additional luma key can help remove halos around your subject.

- **Use garbage mattes.** Don't worry about trying to key out areas that don't contain a foreground element. Instead, mask those areas with a garbage matte. Most editing packages include a cropping tool or masking tool that lets you crop out unwanted sections of the frame easily (see Figure 17.21). For more complex garbage mattes, consider using an alpha channel (which we'll get to shortly).

- **Use better software.** If the keying function in your editing or effects package isn't doing a good enough job, or if your production depends on a lot of key effects, consider investing in some higher-quality keying software, such as Primatte Keyer by Red Giant Software. No matter what keying program you use, Red Giant's Composite Wizard provides extraordinary filters for improving your composites. In addition to helping you remove fringes around your foreground elements, Composite Wizard can automatically match the overall color tones of your foreground and background. Composite Wizard can also add light to the edges of your foreground to make it look like your foreground element is affected by the lighting in your background plate.

Some chroma keying plug-ins and apps can use screen correction to improve the quality of their mattes. For screen correction to work, you'll need to shoot an additional plate of your blue-screen set with full lighting but no foreground elements. The keying package can use this plate as a reference to pull a cleaner matte.

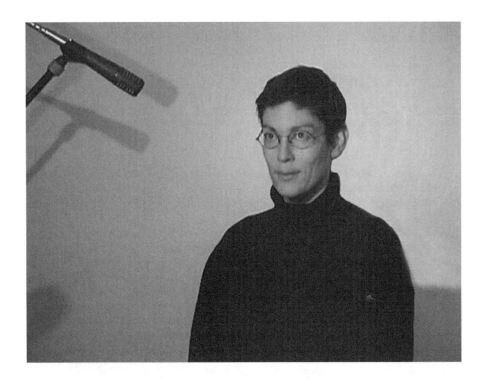

Figure 17.21

You'll have an easier time keying out the background in this shot, if you first use a "garbage matte" to cut away the unwanted stuff around the edges of the frame.

Mattes

Because it's difficult to get a good composite using a key, and because it's not always possible to hang a colored screen behind something during the shoot, you can also perform composites using a special type of mask called a *matte*. Akin to a stencil, a matte makes it possible for you to cut areas out of one layer of video (or a still) to reveal the layers below. For example, say you want to create a composite showing a giant tuna flying behind a building. Because you can't hang a giant blue screen behind the building, you'll need to use a matte inside your compositing program to knock out the background behind the building layer to reveal the giant flying tuna in the underlying layer.

In the old-fashioned film world, mattes used to be drawn by hand. Their purpose was to act as a stencil when inserted into a stack of film. For example, if you wanted to composite a shot of a model spaceship into a background that was shot on location, you would photograph film of the model spaceship against a blue background. Matte cutters would then go in and, by hand, black out the background of each frame of the model spaceship footage. Through a photographic process, a negative, or inverse, of the matte would be created. Next, the background and inverse matte plates would be stuck into a special machine called an *optical printer*. The optical printer would project the footage of the background onto a new piece of film, but the inverse matte would leave a perfect, spaceship-sized hole in the image. Before developing the piece of film, you would place the spaceship footage and the positive matte into the optical printer and project that onto the new piece of film. The spaceship would project into the hole left from the previous shot, while the matte would keep the background from being overexposed. Through this sandwich of film clips, you would have your final composite.

If that doesn't sound complicated enough, consider what happens to color when it's diffused through several layers of celluloid. Although that bright-red spaceship model might look great on your original film, after projecting light through it *and* several other pieces of film, its color will definitely change.

As a digital filmmaker, you don't have to worry about such problems and, in most cases, you can have your software create a matte for you automatically. Best of all, your digital mattes can have varying degrees of opacity, rather than the simple stencil-like opacity of a practical matte.

Alpha Channels

Most of the time, color is stored in a digital still image or movie by splitting it into its component red, green, and blue parts, and storing each component in a separate channel. (For some print applications, color is stored using four channels: cyan, magenta, yellow, and black.) When viewed individually, each channel appears as an 8-bit grayscale image. When combined, these separate channels mix together to create a full-color, 24-bit image.

A fourth 8-bit grayscale channel, the alpha channel, can be added to an image or movie. Each pixel in the alpha channel specifies the level of transparency that will be used when compositing the image or video with something else. In other words, the alpha channel is like a stencil, but with the advantage that some areas can be defined as semitransparent.

In Figure 17.22 (top), you can see how the different channels combine to create an image. The red, green, and blue channels are mixed together to create a full-color image. In Figure 17.22 (bottom), you can see how the alpha channel is then used to determine which parts of this full-color image will be opaque, and which will be transparent. If an area is transparent, underlying video or image layers will show through.

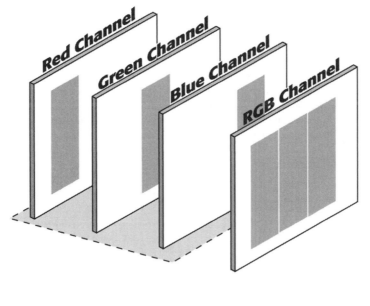

Figure 17.22

In a normal color image, the red, green, and blue channels are combined to create a full-color image (top). If you add a fourth, "alpha" channel, then you can specify which full-color pixels will actually be seen and how opaque they will be (bottom).

Because each frame of your video includes its own alpha channel information, you can create animated alpha channels (also known as *travelling mattes*) that correspond to the action in your clip. Therefore, in the preceding example, our alpha channel would be animated to follow the movement of the spaceship.

Most of the time, the alpha channel will be stored in your movie document. You won't have to think about where it is or go through an extra step to import it into your project. However, there might be times when you want to create a separate alpha channel movie for use in more complicated special effects.

There are a number of ways to create an alpha channel. Many programs—such as 3D rendering and animation programs—can create alpha channels automatically when they generate an image. Some editing and effects programs let you generate alpha channels from a key. For example, you could use a chroma key to pull an alpha channel matte from blue-screen footage. For certain effects, working with an alpha channel is easier than working with a key, and alpha channel mattes are fully editable—that is, you can go in and reshape them if you need to, unlike key effects.

Mixing SD and HD Footage

One of the most basic uses of mattes is letterboxing. Letterboxing is simply a black matte that covers part of the frame so that a widescreen 16:9 image fits onto an SD 4:3 monitor.

But combining SD & HD footage in the same project can be a little more complicated than just adding a matte. For starters, SD video is *much* smaller than HD video. The primary effect you'll use to convert SD to HD or vice versa is the Resize effect (Avid) or the Motion effect (Premiere and Final Cut).

You have two choices: make the SD video bigger or make the HD video smaller. Most editors will opt for the first choice, but it really depends on how you shot your video. If your project is mostly HD, you should enlarge the SD video. If your project is mostly SD, you should scale down the HD video.

Sometimes, your editing software will make this choice for you. If you set up your project for widescreen HD video (like the Adobe Premiere project settings in Figure 17.3), when you import SD footage, it will retain its true size and appear very small in the monitor.

You have two choices for enlarging SD video (see Figure 17.23):

- Enlarge it so that the height fills the frame, leaving two black bars on the right and left of the frame. (Some choose to fill these empty parts of the screen with a background plate or graphic.)

- Enlarge it so that the width fills the frame, which means the top and bottom of the image is cropped. This might be less distracting but the SD image may not be well suited to widescreen framing and also you'll have to enlarge it even more, resulting in an even more degraded image.

If you decide to scale down your HD video, you also have two options (see Figure 17.24):

- Add a matte to letterbox it so that the whole HD image fits into the width of the SD frame.

- Crop the HD image so that it fills the full SD frame. Sometimes a technique called *pan and scan* is used to make sure that the most important parts of the image are visible.

None of these choices is ideal, but because so much of the media created in the last century has a 4:3 aspect ratio, the need to mix the two is not going away in the near future.

SD image at full size within a frame of 1080 HD video

SD image enlarged to fit the height of the HD frame

↕ **Cropped area**

↕ **Cropped area**

SD video enlarged to fit the width of the HD frame

Figure 17.23

A frame of SD video is much smaller than a frame of HD video (top). You can either enlarge it to fill the height (middle) or enlarge it to fit the width and crop it (bottom). Note that both options will induce video artifacts due to the extreme amount of size increase.

HD image sized to fit within a frame of SD video

HD image sized and cropped to fill the entire SD frame

Figure 17.24

A frame of HD video can be reduced to fit the width of the SD frame, aka letterboxing (top), or to fit the height of the SD frame and cropped (bottom).

In addition to resizing your video, you may need to change the frame rate and de-interlace your video.

Modifier Keys

Adobe Systems does a great job of creating identical keyboard commands and interfaces for their separate Mac and Windows products. However, to better understand the following tutorial, note that Cmd on the Mac is synonymous with Ctrl on a Windows computer, and Option on the Mac is synonymous with Alt on a Windows computer.

Adding Camera Shake

In Chapter 4, "Choosing a Camera," we told you to buy a camera with good optical image stabilization. Then we nagged you to use a tripod during your shoot. Now we're going to risk sounding hypocritical and show you how to *add* a shaky camera effect to your footage. Why on earth would we want to do this?

Next time you see a big action/adventure movie, pay attention to how much the camera shakes when something explodes or when cars crash into each other. Adding a camera shake can greatly increase the sense of impact in a special effect or stunt shot.

Earlier in this chapter, we created a video of a finger firing a gunshot. We're going to return to this clip now and add a tiny bit of camera shake to make the image more compelling. We'll do this by animating the position of the clip to make it jitter up and down.

We recommend using Adobe After Effects for these types of effects, as its motion features are much easier to use, as well as more powerful, than many editing programs. A demo version of After Effects is available for download at the Adobe Web site. However, although After Effects is the ideal tool, you can use any editor or effects package that allows you to change and animate the position of a layer (see Figure 17.25).

STEP 1: CREATE A PROJECT
In After Effects, create a project, and import the hand-gun.mov file from the Camera Shake Tutorial folder located on the Chapter 17 page on the companion Web site. Create a new composition with the same size and duration as the movie. Place the movie in the composition.

STEP 2: ENABLE ANIMATION OF MOTION
In many programs, you must specify that you want to animate a particular property before you can set any keyframes for that property. This ensures that you don't accidentally set keyframes for things that you don't want to animate. In the After Effects Time Layout window, open the arrow next to the hand-gun.mov file. Now, open the Transform arrow. Next to each property is a small Stopwatch icon. Click the Stopwatch icon next to the Position property to tell After Effects that you will be setting keyframes for the position of this layer.

STEP 3: SET THE FIRST KEYFRAME
In the Time Layout window, scrub forward until you find the frame where the first muzzle flash occurs. When we clicked the Stopwatch icon in Step 2, After Effects automatically set a position keyframe at frame one. The current time marker is now at the first frame of muzzle flash. If we reposition the frame here, After Effects will automatically interpolate between the first frame and the current frame, creating a very slow movement of the image between those two frames. That's not what we want. We want a sharp jolt from the first position to a new position.

Back up one frame and set a new keyframe by clicking in the check box at the extreme left of the Time Layout window, in the same row as the Position property. This will set a keyframe at our current position—one frame before the muzzle flash—and serve to "lock down" the position of the image until we want it to move.

Figure 17.25

By setting keyframes for the "hand-gun" layer's position, you can make it jitter up and down, resulting in the appearance of a shaky camera.

STEP 4: SET THE NEXT KEYFRAME

Now, move forward one frame. You should be back on the first frame of the first muzzle flash. Click on the image in the Comp window. You should see a bounding box and handles appear over the image. Press the Up arrow key three times to move the image up three pixels. Now click the Left arrow key twice to move the image two pixels to the left. Notice that After Effects automatically sets a keyframe for you—be sure to thank it.

STEP 5: BRING THE IMAGE BACK DOWN

Think about how you might shake a camera when you are startled. The initial movement will be sharp and extreme. Going back to your original position will be slower. We don't want a huge shake in this case because the gunfire is not a huge event. However, we still want a slower return to our original position.

Move forward one frame. Press the Down arrow twice and the *Right* arrow once. This will move your image most of the way back to its original position.

Now, move forward one more frame. Press the Down arrow once and the Right arrow once. This will return your image to its original location.

STEP 6: NOW DO THE REST OF THE FLASHES

Use the same technique to shake the camera during the rest of the flashes. The flashes have different intensities, so not all of the shakes need to be the same. In addition, move the frame in different directions and in different amounts so that each flash doesn't look identical. You might also find that you want to put a second, smaller movement immediately after your first one. This will create a "bounce" as the camera returns to its original position.

When you're done, render your movie and look at it. You might find that some shakes are too quick and need to be slowed down. You can click on a particular keyframe and reposition your image to adjust the degree of shake, and slide the keyframes around to adjust the timing of your camera shakes.

You'll probably also notice that when we moved the frame, we exposed the empty black space that's lying beneath it. If your final destination is video, this is not a problem, as we only moved the frame a few pixels. These black areas are at the far extreme of the action-safe area, so any monitor will crop out these areas.

If you're going out to film, or distributing this movie on the Web, DVD, or film, then you'll have a couple of options:

- **Place another copy of the original footage beneath the shaking copy.** When the top copy moves, it will reveal the lower copy. Although the pixels aren't necessarily accurate, they're close enough that no one will notice.

- **Shrink your image size or enlarge your footage.** Instead of the previous option, you can always just crop your frame to eliminate the black areas. If you're going to the Web, you're probably going to be reducing the size of your image anyway (usually to something like 320 × 240 or smaller). Therefore, even if you crop your image now, you'll have plenty of pixels left to do a good resizing later. We'll discuss resizing for Web output in detail in Chapter 18, "Finishing." The other option is to enlarge your footage. For the small screen, you can probably get away with enlarging it 90–95% without noticeably degrading the image. For the big screen, enlarging more than a tiny amount is not recommended. For the Web, you can get away with enlarging it by 80% or more, depending on your material. ◄

Automatic Camera Shake

In addition to superior keying functions, After Effects comes with a number of powerful extra plug-ins, including special motion controls such as motion tracking (which lets you match the position of one layer to the movement of an image inside another layer). DigiEffects Damage also includes a special Destabilizer plug-in that can greatly ease the creation of camera shake effects.

Using Effects to Fix Problems

Compositing explosions is pretty fun, but the most common use of special effects isn't special at all: correcting problems in your footage. Whether it's a shaky camera, wire removal, or the dreaded "rolling shutter" effect in DSLR footage, special effects can help solve many problems in your footage.

Eliminating Camera Shake

Don't worry, we're not going to tell you to take out all of that camera movement that you just put in. However, you can use similar techniques to stabilize footage shot with a shaky camera. *This process is hard, time-consuming work! Don't use it as a substitute for good shooting!*

Just as we animated the movement of an image to make it shake, we can animate the movement of an image to make it stand still. The easiest way to script such an animation is to pick a reference point on your image and animate the position of your image so as to keep that reference point in the same place. Here are some guidelines:

- **Work at high magnification.** Remember, you're concerned about tracking an individual pixel. So pick an area of high contrast and zoom in close!

- **Use guides.** If your program allows you to set *guides* on an image (as in After Effects), set guides along the top and side of the pixel you are going to use as your reference. This will make it easier to tell if your reference point is in the right position.

- **Remember to think backward.** Zoomed in close, it can be difficult to remember which direction you need to move. You might have to switch back and forth between frames to figure out which direction the camera is moving. (You might also have to stop for a moment to figure out which frame you're looking at.) Once you've figured that out, move the camera in the opposite direction.

- **Don't expect your reference to always look the same.** Unfortunately, as the camera moves and the light on the object you're tracking changes, the pixel colors and patterns will change slightly. Although your reference point might have been a nice solid black pixel in the first frame, it might be a 60-percent gray pixel in the second. Depending on your camera, it might even change color as it moves! Consequently, when trying to decide how and where to move the frame, you might need to look at several frames before and after your current location to get an idea of how the pattern you are tracking is changing in appearance.

- **Don't use motion blur!** If your program can blur motion to smooth animation, be sure this feature is off!

- **Watch those subpixels.** Some programs actually calculate movement by using distances smaller than a pixel. When zoomed in close, if you press the arrow key to move the image, you might not see anything happen. This is because the program has performed a subpixel movement. You might have to zoom out to test your footage, or zoom out a few steps and try again. You can probably find a zoom level that will let you move in single pixels.

- **Aim for a reasonable amount of correction.** If your image is moving a lot, you'll have to settle for merely calming it down, as opposed to making it completely static.

- **Don't bother trying to stabilize blurry footage.** If your camera was shaky enough that its motion caused your image to blur slightly, then you're not going to be able to stabilize your footage. The results will be too blurry and weird looking. Image stabilization is really just for evening out slight vibrations and shakes.

- **Use a plug-in.** There are several specialized image stabilization plug-ins out there, such as After Effects Warp Stabilizer.

As in the previous example, as you move the frame, you'll be exposing the empty space around the edge of the layer. You can fix this problem with the same steps described in the preceding tutorial.

Getting Rid of Things

There are many things you might want to remove from your footage: bad pixels or dropouts, cables, and other equipment from the set, wires used for puppeteering, camera artifacts such as the infamous rolling shutter effect, flicker from fluorescent lights, naked people with foul mouths—the list goes on.

Here are some tips on how to get rid of unwanted things that somehow ended up in your shots.

Bad Pixels and Dropouts

Sometimes a pixel in your camera goes bad and sometimes a dropout occurs when the magnetic particles in a particular part of the tape get scrambled. Either way, in digital video, dead pixels and dropouts appear in your image as a square of gray (see Figure 17.26). Often, your best course of action is to repair the problem digitally. Fortunately, most dropouts only last for one or two frames, so digital fixes are fairly simple. There are several approaches to take.

- **Edit the previous frame over the frame with the dropout.** This is the least favorable alternative, as it will create a brief, possibly perceptible stutter in your motion. If you're in a hurry, though, this will be the quickest fix.

- **Paint over the dropout.** Take the individual frames into an image editor and fix the bad areas with a Paint Brush or Clone tool. If you have a copy of After Effects, use the Clone tool to clone the same area from a good frame.

- **Mask and composite over the dropout.** Take a still of a frame that isn't bad and composite it over the bad frame. Using Cropping or Masking tools, matte the upper layer to create a small patch that covers the dropout in the lower layer.

- **Enlarge the image.** If the dropout is near the edge of the frame, you can enlarge your image and get rid of it.

Figure 17.26

An example of a digital video dropout.

Wire Removal

If your film had any sort of puppeteering, you'll have some wires to remove. It's also common that light stands, cables, and other gear on the set accidentally end up in some of your shots. Often, they are difficult to see until you are in the editing room when suddenly you realize there's a bright orange cable in a dark corner. Luckily, wires and light stands are thin and don't take up a lot of screen real estate so usually you can get rid of them pretty easily.

- **Paint out the wire.** Take the individual frames into an image editor and fix the bad areas with a Paint Brush or Clone tool. If you have a copy of After Effects, use the Clone tool to clone a clean part of the image over the wires.

- **Mask and composite over the dropout.** Take a still of a clean frame and composite it over the bad area in the frame with the wire. Using Cropping or Masking tools, matte the upper layer to create a small patch that covers the problem area in the lower layer.

- **Enlarge the image.** If the wire or light stand is near the edge of the frame, you can enlarge your image and get rid of it.

- **Use a plug-in.** If your shot has camera movement, painting or masking will be much more difficult. Plug-ins such as Boris Continuum Wire Removal offer a couple different ways to get rid of wires and also offer sophisticated motion tracking tools (see Figure 17.27 and Color Plate 39).

Figure 17.27

BorisFX Continuum Wire Removal plug-in lets you choose different ways to paint out a wire and also track motion within the shot.

Flickering Lights

Sometimes you don't notice the flicker in a bad fluorescent bulb until it is too late or maybe your footage was shot in a foreign country with a different electrical cycle. Either way, flickering lights are distracting to the viewer, but luckily they can be minimized. The most popular solution is to use the Stabilize Color Effect in After Effects. It can also be used to correct iris flares and other shifts in exposure.

Rolling Shutter Problems

DSLR cameras and other cameras with CMOS sensors are notoriously prone to the "rolling shutter effect," which causes footage to look wobbly or diagonally distorted. The Foundry Rolling Shutter plug-in works with Premiere, Final Cut Pro, and Media Composer to help you straighten out image distortion due to rolling shutter problems (see Figure 17.28).

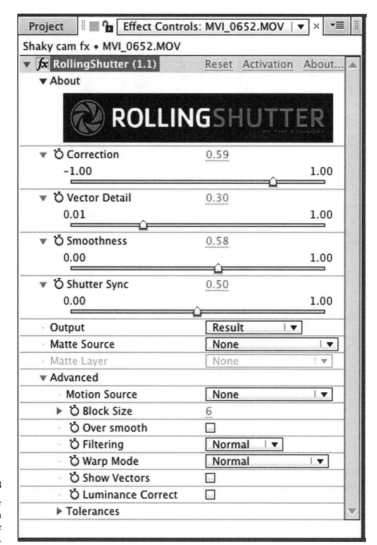

Figure 17.28

The Foundry's Rolling Shutter plug-in helps correct camera artifacts common in footage shot with DSLRs.

Not Ready for Primetime Material

Nudity and bad language might seem harmless to some but highly offensive to others. Some distributors would rather not take any chances. If your project is a feature film, you may have to cut out certain material in order to get the MPAA rating you want for your film. If your project is destined for television or the Web, the tendency is to leave the offending material in the cut but to blur the footage so that you can't see it. Some networks go so far as to require blurring mouths when foul language is used. Here are a few ways to obscure potentially offensive material:

- **Blur it.** You can do a DIY blur using the effects tools in your editing software or you can use a specialized plug-in such as the Boris Witness Protection effect.

- **Put a black bar over it.** Using a simple matte effect, you can create a black bar to cover the offending area and use key frames to make sure it follows any movement.

- **Paint some clothes on it.** We've seen TV shows paint over footage to make bikinis less revealing and so on. It's time-consuming, but it can be done.

For audio, the standard TV choice is to add a bleep to cover the soundtrack, but if you don't want to call that much attention to it, you can simply drop the audio out. Some movies also record inoffensive words such as "frick" to replace bad words in ADR.

Moving On

Perhaps the most important thing to know about effects work is that there's rarely ever a "best" way to do something. Every effects shot is a puzzle with many different solutions. In the end, if you get the look you want, then it doesn't really matter how you pulled it off. Don't be afraid to experiment and explore, and be prepared to try different approaches to your effects troubles. As long as you keep your original files backed up, and you are diligent about not compressing video through your workflow, then there's nothing to risk by experimenting.

18

Finishing

Photo credit: Sonja Schenk

At the beginning of this book, we talked about how much has changed in the 10 years since we wrote the first edition. Digital filmmaking has indeed become better, cheaper, and easier. In fact, it's also become more digital.

Thankfully, the film finishing process has finally started to see the benefits of digital technology. Nowadays, postproduction stays digital *and* file-based until the very last step of the finishing process, whether you are finishing on 35mm film, HDCAM, or a highly compressed QuickTime movie intended to play on smart phones. And digital image quality standards continue to improve. A few years ago, 4K was the terrain of highly specialized CGI animations, today we have cameras that shoot 4K, digital cinema projectors that can display it, and there is talk of 6K on the horizon.

That said, many films that are released theatrically at the time of this writing are still screened as 35mm film prints. And most projects broadcast on television or distributed through video-on-demand services are still delivered on digital videotape. DVDs are still the most popular distribution format for viewing copies of your film and also for individual sales. File-based delivery is still primarily the territory of streaming or downloadable media on the Web.

But what about digital cinema projection? Many films that are projected digitally in theaters are still printed on 35mm film or mastered to HDCAM-SR videotape before they are converted to the DCI format used in file-based digital projection. And if a film is to be screened outside of major U.S. cities, the odds are high that a 35mm film print will be required since many smaller cities and towns do not have theaters with digital projection yet. So even though many big studio films are delivered digitally to certain theaters in major cities, they still need 35mm prints to screen everywhere else.

If this all sounds a bit awkward, it is because we are still in a transitional period, technologically speaking. But digital cinema projection and file-based delivery of feature films to theaters is becoming increasingly more common. DVD may still dominate as the household player of choice, but Blu-ray offers a much higher quality alternative, and it's pretty safe to assume that both will become obsolete as streaming technologies and cloud storage options improve. In the near future, file-based delivery will be the norm for all types of media.

At the high end of finishing (file-based digital cinema, 35mm film prints, HD digital videotape masters), you'll need to enlist the help of a postproduction facility, and they will handle some of the harder, technical tasks for you. At the mid to low end of finishing, you'll have the option of doing it yourself—creating Blu-ray Discs, DVDs, and video for the Web, whether for streaming or to download. Of course, there are postproduction facilities that will be happy to do this work for you as well, if your budget allows.

Navigating the film finishing process is tricky, and there are two questions to answer. What type of masters do you need and how will you go about getting them? These are not simple questions, but in this chapter we'll do our best to teach you how to answer them.

What Do You Need?

If your project is a feature film, you will need to know about all the different types of outputs covered in this chapter because you will probably create more than one master, as well as many supplemental materials (see Figure 18.1).

You'll need DVD viewing copies to send to film festivals and distributors (page 427). You'll need Internet-ready outputs to post trailers and promos of your film on the Web (page 432), and you'll probably need a Web site for the film. If your film is accepted to a festival, you'll either need a 35mm film print or an HDCAM videotape master or a DCI-compliant Digital Cinema Package (DCP) for projection in a theater. You'll need to have mixed stereo or surround sound audio tracks on your film print, videotape master, or DCP (page 418). You'll need to keep an archive of your edited project files, uncompressed copies of your video and audio files (page 426), and also you should save a basic split track mix of your audio so that you can easily remix it at a later date if necessary (page 420).

Imagine that you screen your film at Sundance, find a distributor who wants to release it in theaters, and later broadcast the film on the Independent Film Channel and on European TV. You'll take your textless master (page 420) and the basic split track mix of your audio that you saved and use it to remix according to the different broadcast specifications of the Independent Film Channel, European broadcasters, and others. For Europe, you'll need a split-track dialogue, music, and effects (M&E) mix, in addition to a stereo mix so that they can dub your film into other languages (page 419). If you hate dubbed films, you'll probably have to add subtitles yourself, with the help of a postproduction facility that specializes in subtitling. Finally, you'll need to create the Blu-ray Disc and DVD for home video distribution, including any supplementary materials, and also create the various files you will need to distribute the film over the Internet (page 432).

Start Early

Though we've put this output discussion at the end of the book, finishing is often something you need to think about early in your production process. Keeping an eye on your final delivery goals will affect decisions ranging from equipment choices to shooting and audio recording techniques. If you're just starting your production, make a list of all of the different formats that you think you'll need (for example: Web, DVD, 35mm transfer, and so on). Once you've listed all of your finishing formats, take note of the requirements of the one that has the highest quality. You'll need to maintain these specs throughout your production workflow.

For example, if you're going to create files to embed in a Web page, then you know that you don't need a high resolution. Now you can double-check your equipment choices to ensure that you have what you need, and you can avoid spending extra money on higher-quality gear when you know it won't be necessary for your final delivery format.

You can also review your shooting plans, production design, effects pipeline, and all of the other aspects of your production with an eye toward evaluating whether you've got the requisite level of quality for your intended output. You might not need to worry about refined design and effects work if your final output is going to be very small. On the other hand, if your final output will be digital cinema or 35mm film projection, then you'll need to keep a close eye on even the smallest details in your frame.

File-based finishing workflow

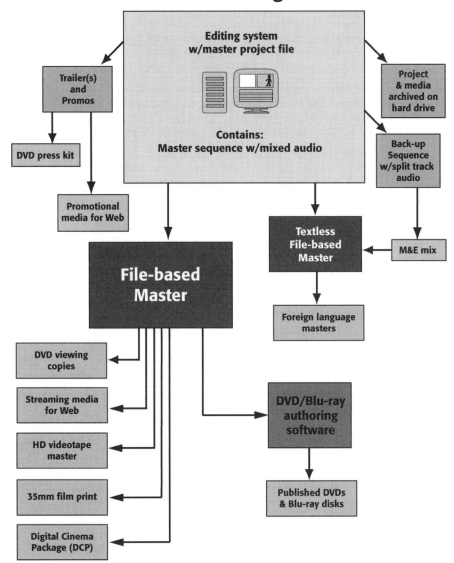

Figure 18.1

File-based finishing workflow.

What Is Mastering?

A master is the final output (whether film, tape, or file) from which all copies of your movie are made. Masters are a necessity when dealing with expensive formats such as 35mm film prints and HD videotapes. With file-based media, copies can be made at the click of a mouse so file-based masters are not a necessity, but they will make your life much easier.

Everyone has had the experience of creating a text file and then making some backup copies and then getting confused as to which file is the most recent and sending out the wrong version to your professor or boss.

File-based digital media of all types runs the same risk. The simplest way to avoid any confusion is to create a final version of your film and store it on digital videotape, optical disk (DVD or Blu-ray), or a special hard drive and make any copies off that version, the master.

With digital file-based workflow, you will need to keep two masters. One is the master project file from your editing application that contains the final edited sequence of your film and the other is an uncompressed output of your film saved in a digital file format such as QuickTime, XMF, or DPX. (We'll talk more about digital file formats for finishing your film later.)

If you need simple copies, you'll use the digital file master as a source to transcode your project into various digital delivery formats. If you need something more complicated, such as a different audio mix, you'll use the master project file to create secondary digital master files as needed.

What to Do Now

Most likely, you have no idea what will happen to your film once you've finished postproduction. Will you need a digital projection print or simply a DVD? The most cautious choice is to start small but keep your options open: create a "do-it-yourself" file-based master with the best color grading and audio mix that you can afford; put your trailer or clips up on the Web; and make some DVDs and Blu-ray Discs as viewing copies to pass around and send to festivals. Be sure to back up your media and your project in case you want to go back and re-edit or re-master it and eventually finish it on film, videotape, or digital cinema. We recommend that you read this entire chapter before proceeding.

Preparing for Film Festivals

If you're planning to put your film on the festival circuit, your first step will be to create a polished cut to send out with your festival applications. Most film festivals prefer to get DVDs for the initial submission or that you use a Web-based submission service, such as Withoutabox. Some festivals are more lenient than others when it comes to submitting "rough cuts" or works in progress, but bear in mind that there is a lot of competition out there, and that it's always better to show a finished product if possible.

If your film is accepted to a festival, you will then have to make a festival print of your film, according to their technical guidelines. Most film festivals will screen 35mm film prints or digital videotape masters, usually HDCAM. A few of the bigger festivals, such as Cannes, can screen file-based digital cinema. The rules are usually pretty strict and very specific.

Many filmmakers choose to create a festival print that is not necessarily the final version of the film. This print may have temporary elements, such as music that is only licensed for festival screenings. Temporary elements are often borne of financial necessity, and the idea is that if the film is sold to a distributor at the festival, the distributor will cover the costs of properly finishing the film.

Many of the big film festivals (Sundance, Toronto, and so on) are known as "first look" festivals, and they will not screen your film if it has been screened elsewhere in the country. Private screenings, such as focus group tests and cast/crew screenings, are fine, but if you have charged admission to the public for a screening or made your film available to download off the Internet, you may not qualify for these top flight festivals.

Take the time to visit the various festival Web sites and look at their submission policies and delivery requirements before you start the finishing process.

DIY File-Based Masters

By now you should have a locked cut of your project, you should have done a pass on the sound design, you should have fixed any basic problems using color correction and visual effects, and your film should have whatever titles and graphics it requires. If that's the case, you are done with the hard creative part of making your project. Now you just need to make it available for others to see it.

Back in Chapter 11, "Editing Gear," we talked about how editing workstations are pretty much plug-and-play these days, thanks to digital acquisition formats. That makes it a lot easier to get started editing, but it also limits what you'll be able to do on your own without adding hardware.

You can easily make an uncompressed file-based master of your film and then create file-based submasters using codecs suited to different digital delivery standards. You can also pretty easily create a video DVD because odds are high that your computer has a recordable DVD drive. If you need to make Blu-ray Discs or output to digital videotape, things start to get a little more complicated because you'll need some extra hardware added to your system. For Blu-ray, you'll need to add the appropriate kind of disk burning hardware.

If you are outputting to FireWire-based digital video (DV and HDV), it's not too hard—you'll need a computer with a FireWire connector and a deck (or camcorder) that records in that format. But it's not that likely that you'll be delivering anything on HDV (or DV) because the quality isn't that great. If it's just a viewing copy and quality isn't a concern, stick to DVDs or other optical disk formats. If quality is a concern (and it's likely that whoever you are creating the videotape for will tell you *exactly* what they require in terms of quality), it's more likely that you will need to deliver on HDCAM-SR. HDCAM-SR decks are *very* expensive, and you'll need HD-SDI coming out of your editing workstation to guarantee that the quality remains intact. To get HD-SDI out of your editing workstation, you'll need some sort of video card or breakout box. If this is only an occasional need, you'll be better off going to a postproduction facility and letting them take care of this process for you. More on that later.

Even if you are planning to finish on 35mm film or HDCAM, it is likely you'll want to create file-based masters to use as a source for Web distribution.

Preparing Your Sequence

Before you output your video, you need to prepare your sequence. Make sure that you've replaced all temporary footage and proxies with the real thing. Next, you need to clean up your sequence. All normal video should be dragged down so that it's all on one video track in your sequence. The only things that should remain on the other video tracks are composites such as superimposed titles, luma/chroma keys, and so on (see Figure 18.2). Technically, it is safer to take your composites and export them individually to an uncompressed QuickTime format and then bring them back into your project as new shots and cut them into the sequence to replace the mulit-track composites. However, if you are doing a DIY file-based master, you don't necessarily have to do this. Put your titles and other texted graphics on a separate track, at the top level of your sequence. This makes it easy to remove them or turn off their display.

Figure 18.2

Clean up your sequence (top) by minimizing the number of video tracks (bottom) before you export.

The first frame of your movie should start at 01:00:00:00. Some editing applications have a default start time of 00:00:00:00, but this is not the industry standard, so if you are going to be working with a post facility, you should change it. If you're going to stay DIY all the way, it doesn't matter.

If you are going out to videotape, add two minutes to the head of your sequence. This is a part of the tape that is most prone to physical damage. Instead, start your sequence with bars and tone followed by a head slate and a countdown. Most videotapes are a minute or two longer than their stated length, so don't worry about wasting a little tape. Remember that these two minutes come before 01:00:00:00 so start your sequence time at 00:58:00:00 to accommodate them.

If your goal is a file-based master, we don't recommend adding a head slate. You probably just want your project itself and the opening credits to be the first thing that viewers see. Instead, add a tail slate at the end of your sequence, which is simply a title card that lists information such as the name of the project, the name of the producer/director, the name of the editor, the production company, the date of the output, the type of output (master, rough cut, audio-only, textless, and so on), the total running time (TRT), and, possibly, contact and copyright information. This is not technically a part of your film, but it's a safe way to keep relevant information available to anyone who needs it. You should also add this information to the metadata of your file if you have an application that lets you edit metadata, like Adobe Bridge (see Figure 18.3).

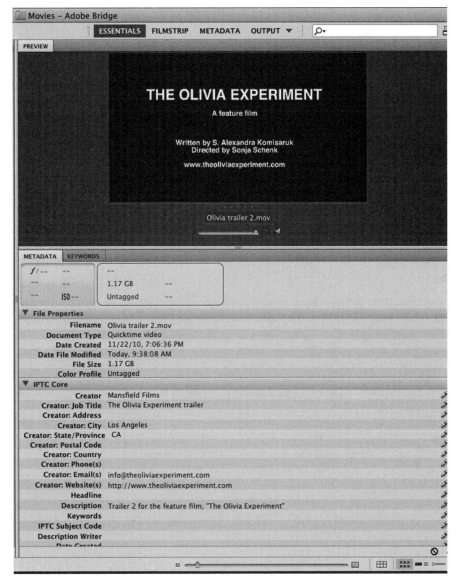

Figure 18.3

A tail slate and metadata in Adobe Bridge.

Save your sequence in a special bin and give it a name that indicates that this is the master. You may want to lock the tracks on your sequence and lock the bin if your software allows, for added security.

Sync Pops

If you are doing a professional mix or finishing on 35mm, you need to be extra careful about sync. To be safe, put a 10-second countdown at the start of your sequence with a sync pop at the frame with the number 2 in the countdown. A sync pop is simply one frame of "tone," which your editing application should be able to generate for you.

Color Grading

At this point, it's common to spend half a day doing an additional color correction pass. Presumably, your earlier color correction was aimed at fixing problems. Now you'll need to take a look at the film as a whole and try to match the color and create a consistent "look." Some people find this incredibly intimidating, but it's not beyond the scope of what you can do yourself. Of course, a professional colorist will have a practiced eye, top of the line equipment, and loads of experience to back it up. In other words, that person will be faster and better than you. But if the choice is between no color grading at all and DIY color grading, we say you should take your chances with doing it yourself. It's common that the DP is present for the color grading session. If so, he should be able to offer some technical advice about black levels, white levels, and gamma, along with his creative opinion.

DIY Beware

Don't make any editing changes when you are color grading or mixing. Be sure that your cut is "locked" before you start.

The Final Audio Mix

Your final cut might have 20 or more tracks of sound if it's a complicated feature. To do an output, you'll need to mix those tracks into a more manageable number, usually between two and eight tracks. High-end professional videotape formats usually only have four tracks of audio, while low-end professional and consumer videotape formats usually only have two tracks. Audio for films often has five or more tracks to accommodate the surround sound that's used in theaters. Films that have been transferred to DVD/Blu-ray for home video release offer both a stereo mix and a surround sound mix so that viewers can choose according to their hardware setup.

Mixing the audio consists of setting the levels for each piece of sound in the project and then combining the tracks into a final mix. There are several standard types of mixes:

- **Mono:** Mixing all your audio down to one track is called a *mono mix*. While mono mixes are sufficient for work-in-progress viewing copies and radio broadcasts, for any other final output, you should at least do a stereo mix.

The Final Audio Mix (continued)

- **Stereo:** We're all familiar with stereo mixes because that's how music is mixed. The tracks in your project are mixed down to two channels, left (track 1) and right (track 2). For true stereo, these tracks should be slightly panned to the left and right, respectively, but often, only the music is true stereo. Some stereo mixes feature specific sounds that move from the left to the right channel.

- **Dialogue, music, and effects (M&E):** In a four-channel M&E mix, the sync dialogue is mixed down to one channel, while the stereo music is placed on the second and third channels. The fourth channel is used for sound effects. By keeping these three elements separate, an M&E mix allows you to keep your remixing options open. The dialogue is there as a guide and can be replaced easily for foreign language dubbing.

- **5.1 surround sound:** The most popular type of surround sound is 5.1, which uses six channels to "surround" the viewer. Dolby Digital 5.1 (or AC-3) and DTS (Digital Theater System) are the two formats that deliver 5.1 surround sound and of the two, Dolby Digital 5.1 is the most popular choice for encoding. Dolby Digital and DTS use 5.1 channels: left, center, and right speakers in the front of the theater, left and right surround speakers in the rear, and an LFE (Low Frequency Effects) subwoofer channel. (The subwoofer only uses a tenth of the dynamic range of a normal channel; hence, you get a total of 5.1 channels.) Surround mixes are generally balanced toward the front channels, with the rear channels used for occasional effects or ambience.

- **7.1 surround sound:** SDDS (Sony Dynamic Digital Sound) uses 7.1 channels, adding center-left and center-right speakers in the front to the standard 5.1 speaker layout. In addition to theatrical support, SDDS is also supported by Blu-ray but is less commonly used than 5.1.

Create a Mix

Doing the audio mix yourself using your editing software or dedicated sound software, such as ProTools, gives you the luxury of time, but it's unlikely that you'll be able to do anything more complicated than a stereo or M&E mix. Luckily, most editing applications can take your stereo mix and turn it into a 5.1 surround sound mix automatically. With this approach, you won't be paying expensive hourly fees, so you'll have the freedom to get your mix exactly right. Most likely, you were mixing your tracks as you worked, so you'll probably only need a final pass to set the levels across the entire project.

When it comes to mixing, dialogue is usually king. Watch the level meters in your application as you mix; if you have audio hardware, such as a mixing board, watch the level meters on your hardware. The dialogue should tend toward a consistent range throughout your project. Music and effects should fall at a significantly lower level, except in special circumstances when they need to be intentionally louder. Mixing is a very subjective art, and many people think their way of mixing is the only way to do it right. If you're not confident about your "ear," get a professional sound editor to come in for a day and do a quick and dirty mix for your film.

No matter how many audio tracks you have, you'll want to start by mixing them down to eight tracks. Since you're doing it yourself, you can use as many tracks as you want, but its ultimately simpler to use fewer. A typical eight-track configuration includes two tracks of checkerboarded sync production dialogue, including voice-over if applicable, two tracks of sound effects and ambience, a track of stereo left music, and a track of stereo right music.

Remember to work on copies of your sequence as you mix down your tracks, in case you need to go back and remix. Refer to your editing software documentation for directions on how to mix down tracks of audio.

Make a copy of your eight-channel split track sequence for each different type of mix you want to create.

- To create an M&E mix, mix the sync production dialogue down to one track, and the effects and ambience tracks down to another track. Leave the stereo music as is on the last two tracks.

- To create a stereo mix, you need to mix the dialogue, effects, and stereo music left to channel one, and the dialogue, effects, and stereo music right to channel two. Be sure to balance your levels, since this different configuration can easily result in the dialogue and effects overpowering the music.

- To create a surround sound mix, use the preset offered by your editing or DVD/Blu-ray authoring application to create standard 5.1 surround sound mix. If you want to customize the balance of audio across the six speakers, things get a lot more complicated. You'll need extra hardware to monitor it correctly—surround sound speakers and a mixing board to send each audio track out to a separate speaker. If you need a specialized surround sound mix, we recommend hiring a professional mixer.

Make a Textless Master

Earlier, we suggested putting your titles and other text-based elements on a separate video track in your timeline. This makes it easier to create a textless master. The textless master will be used for foreign dubbed and subtitled versions. It's also good for using as source material for publicity clips and so on. The only text-based element in a textless master is the end credit roll. Typically, this will stay as is for the textless master, and any additional credits for foreign versions will be subtitled over later on. For foreign language versions, take your M&E mix and add it to your textless master.

Export Your Masters

So now you should have two master sequences—a texted master sequence and a textless master sequence. Be sure to render everything before you export.

When you export, you have to choose a codec, and that is a very important decision. The bottom line is that you can't improve the quality of your original footage, but you can degrade it. So if you shot in a 4:2:2 HD format, then used a 4:2:2 intermediary codec to edit, you will not improve the quality of your film by exporting the final file-based master to a 4:4:4 format. However, if you export it to, say, a 4:2:0 format, you will lose some image quality. So whatever codec you choose, it should be the same as what you started with or better (see Figure 18.4). Higher quality codecs create larger files, but it's better to have a large file than to accidentally downgrade your image quality.

The good news is that it is digital and if you don't like the results, you can always do it again.

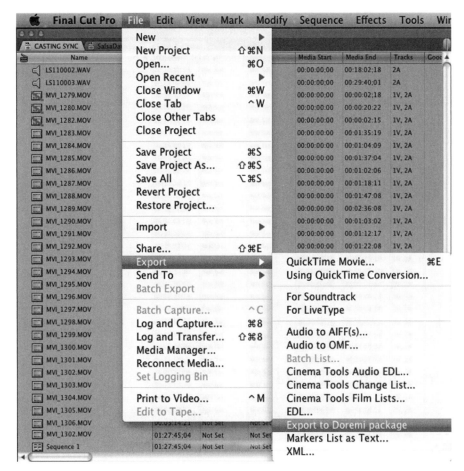

Figure 18.4

Export options in Apple Final Cut Pro.

Watch Your Export

It might sound silly, but many people don't watch their final exported file. By the time you get to the point of making your master, you've probably watched your project hundreds of times and so are hesitant to sit through it again. This time, forget about story, pacing, and other concerns, and just watch the images and listen to the sound. Look for any problems and if you find them, go back into your editing software, fix them, and export again until it is perfect.

Make More

Now that you have a file-based master, you can transcode it into different formats for different viewing needs. For more on creating Web video, DVDs, and Blu-ray Discs, read on.

Web Video and Video-on-Demand

Digital distribution has become the viewing method of choice for both filmmakers and viewers alike. It's a boon for independent filmmakers who might have trouble getting their films shown on television or in theaters. There are many different distributors out there, but they break down into three categories:

- Self-distribution through your own Web site.
- Free streaming media sites such as Vimeo and YouTube.
- Paid video-on-demand services such as Netflix.

The last two are easy—sort of. Typically, the host Web site will either compress your video for you or tell you exactly how it needs to be compressed.

As for your own Web site, you have some choices to make. Streaming or download?

A lot of your Web output decisions are dependent upon how you will host your file. Different Web hosting services provide support for different video formats. If you have a preference for a very particular video technology, then you'll want to find a host that supports that. If you already have a host, then you might need to determine what technologies they're capable of serving before you commit to a particular approach.

The good news is that basic movie delivery is something that pretty much every Web host is capable of. Things only get trickier if you are interested in streaming.

Streaming or Download?

Streaming is similar to on-demand broadcasting. When a user decides to view a streaming movie, the host server begins sending a data stream to the user's computer. That stream is decompressed by the user's computer and displayed, but no copy of the movie is kept on the user's machine. When the stream is over, the user has to re-stream if she wants to view the stream again.

Streaming is ideal for live events and for content that you don't want the user to be able to save a copy of (although, this is not foolproof, as there are ways for the user to capture the stream and save it in a reusable format).

If you want to use a streaming technology, you first have to ensure that your host supports your chosen streaming server. Most services charge money for hosting streaming media, so you'll probably have to pay an extra fee for streaming hosting. In addition, you'll need to compress your final movie using special software provided by the makers of your chosen streaming system.

Most users will simply want to make a movie file available on demand, without the hassles of streaming, and without concern for whether or not the user can save it at the other end. Just as you can create a link to a graphic or a file in an HTML page, you can create a link to a movie. When users click that link, their computer will automatically download and play that movie, either using some sort of playback software, such as the QuickTime or Windows Media Player, or as a video embedded in the Web page using the video playback architecture of your Web browser.

These days, most video architectures and Web browsers are smart enough not to download the entire movie before starting playback. Instead, they employ a progressive download scheme. The downloading begins, and the computer calculates how long the entire download will take, based on the current download throughput. When enough content has downloaded that the computer can play back the entire movie without outrunning the download speed, then the movie will start playing. This greatly reduces the delay that the user experiences before the movie begins playback. (Nearly instant playback startup is another advantage of streaming video. Progressive downloads, though, can be very quick to start, depending on the user's connection speed, your hosting speed, and the duration of your movie.)

Compressing for the Web

As you've probably already guessed, your final video must be compressed before it can be served from the Web. In fact, it has to be compressed *a lot*. Fortunately, there are a number of high-quality compressors now that allow you to deliver first-rate quality from a Web download. Luckily, software compressors like Sorenson Squeeze (see Figure 18.5) make this very easy for you.

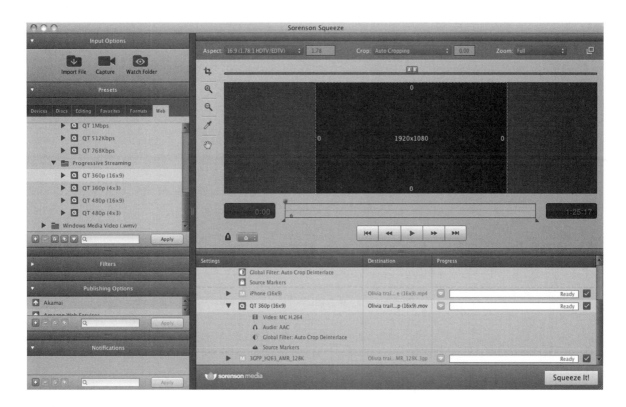

Figure 18.5

Stand-alone batch encoding apps like Sorensen Squeeze make it easy to encode your file-based master in multiple delivery formats.

Compressing

No matter what codec you choose, compressing can take a long time. You'll want to make sure that you have everything right before you start compressing, and you'll probably want to perform your compression overnight.

Ultimately, you might want to compress your video using several different options to support the greatest number of users.

QuickTime is the most popular architecture for online video. With a free player available for both Mac and Windows, you can be pretty certain that just about anyone will have the capability to play back your movie if you post it in QuickTime format. If you decide to do a multi-format posting, then you'll need to recompress your file-based master using the appropriate software for each format that you want. Converting from one compressed format to another is not always possible, and when it is, will always produce severely degraded video so it is better to create each version off your file-based master.

The standard QuickTime export box provides access to all of the standard QuickTime codecs. Anyone who has installed the latest version of QuickTime will have these codecs, so feel free to select any one.

QuickTime Components

For Mac users, you can go to the QuickTime folder in the Library to see which codecs and components you have installed for QuickTime.

For Web delivery, your best codec choices are MPEG-4 or H.264 and 30p (30 frames per second progressive scan) is the standard. These codecs all yield exceptional results and produce very small files.

Some compressors provide lots of settings and customization options, allowing you to finely balance final movie size with image quality. Knowing how to optimize these settings can make for dramatically better-looking footage. Often, the best way to determine good settings is just through trial and error. Because compression can take a long time, perform your tests on a small clip of your final movie, ideally one with representative lighting and color.

In addition to setting compression options, you'll also need to resize your movie. In general, Web-based QuickTime movies are usually 50% or 25% of the original size, though if you know your server and intended audience can handle it, you can go full screen.

Note that there is no overscanning when exporting for the Web—in other words, the viewer will see the entire frame. If you want to conceal action outside of the action-safe area of your screen, you'll need to crop your frame before exporting.

Also note that some older video formats, such as VHS, typically have an area of jittery garbage at the bottom of the frame. This garbage is usually obscured by your monitor's overscan, but it will be visible in your Web outputs, so it's a good idea to crop the image a little to eliminate this area.

Similarly, some cameras produce a black edge or border within the overscan boundary. You'll definitely want to crop this out.

Choosing a Data Rate

Some codecs let you limit your movies to a specific data rate. Choosing a data rate is one of the ways that you can choose to balance file size and image quality. A higher data rate will yield better image quality, but much larger files. Though you will usually want to strike a balance of these, to deliver good-looking video in a reasonable file size, there might be times when you need to opt for a larger, higher-quality file—perhaps to post a file for a "private" screening by an investor—or a very small file for users with slow connections.

Choosing a Keyframe Interval

One of the techniques that a codec employs to compress video is to only store pixels that change from one frame to another. In compression terms, a keyframe is an entire frame that has been compressed spatially; that is, its color information has undergone some compression (see Figure 18.6). The next frame is called an *intermediary frame,* or *i-frame,* and it contains only the pixels that have changed since the previous frame. (They're called intermediary frames, because they're the frames that come between keyframes.) Each successive i-frame contains only the pixels that have changed from the previous i-frame. The next keyframe contains a complete frame, which corrects for any errors or artifacts introduced in the intermediary frames. This is often referred to as *temporal compression.*

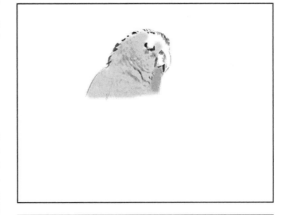

Figure 18.6

Movies are partially compressed by storing only the pixels in the intermediary frames between key frames.

Obviously, the more keyframes you have in a movie, the higher the quality will be, but the lower your compression ratio will be. In other words, your file will be bigger. Video with a lot of action will benefit from more keyframes, while clips that are more static can get away with very few keyframes.

DVD and Blu-Ray Discs

DVD and Blu-ray Discs are great ways to watch movies. They're small, portable, and in the case of Blu-ray, offer full HD quality if your television monitor is up to snuff. Streaming and downloaded video-on-demand is poised to take over the market, but DVDs and Blu-ray Discs are still an important part of the delivery spectrum, and it's hard to beat the Blu-ray format when it comes to quickly accessible high quality playback.

There are two types of DVD and Blu-ray production: the small batches that you can make at home using your computer's DVD or Blu-ray disc burner, and larger batches that you can have created by a professional duplication house. No matter how your final disks will be made, you'll still need to prepare the content that will go onto them.

DVD-V

While most people use the term "DVD" to refer to a DVD disk containing video, it's important to remember that there are different DVD specifications. There are the DVD-ROM formats that your computer can read data from (these, in turn, break down into subcategories by format and operating system) and there's DVD-Video (or DVD-V), which is a complex specification for presenting standard definition video onto a DVD disk. You'll use DVD-ROMs for backing up your project and other data, but you'll use DVD-V when you want to give someone a copy of your video that can be played in a normal DVD player. For Blu-ray Discs, there are also three types: BD-ROM is the counterpart to DVD-V, a complex specification for presenting high-definition video on a Blu-ray Disc. BD-R is the Blu-ray data disc format, and BD-RE is the rewritable Blu-ray data disc format. For this discussion, we'll be concerning ourselves with DVD-V and BD-ROM.

Technically speaking, DVDs and Blu-ray video discs are simply optical discs, a type of file storage media that will contain a file-based master of your film. But making DVDs and Blu-ray Discs is a little more complicated than simple file-based mastering. In addition to having to compress your final video into the MPEG-2 or H.264 format that these optical disc formats demand, you'll need to author the menu system of the disk. If you've ever watched a commercial DVD video, you know that they can have complex interactive menus that allow the viewer to select specific scenes, configure special audio options such as commentary tracks, activate and deactivate subtitles, and view slide shows of still images.

Even if you don't want a menu, if you want a disk that simply plays your movie when you hit play, then you'll need to do a tiny bit of authoring to set up the disk so that it works this way. All of these tasks are accomplished using a DVD authoring program.

Making DVD Viewing Copies of Your Film

The best way to make viewing copies of your film is on DVD. Almost everyone has a DVD player or computer with a DVD drive. But rather than dragging an exported QuickTime movie of your film onto a DVD data disc, you should use a simple DVD authoring app like Roxio Toast Titanium to create a DVD video disc that will open in any DVD player and start playing (see Figure 18.7). This will ensure that pretty much anyone will be able to watch it without technical problems.

Figure 18.7

Use a simple DVD/Blu-ray Disc authoring app like Roxio Toast Titanium to create viewing copies for works-in-progress and festival submissions.

The biggest selling point for DVDs and Blu-ray Discs is the supplemental content beyond the feature film itself. Outtakes, gag reels, featurettes, original storyboards, rough special effects shots, director commentaries, and interviews with cast and crew members are all part of what makes DVDs and Blu-ray Discs worth owning. The latest trends include Web links and hidden bonus tracks. The production of some of these materials will require time during your regular production schedule—on-the-set interviews, making-of segments, and so on. Other features, such as audio commentaries, can be produced after you've finished your final cut.

The commercial DVDs and Blu-ray Discs that you rent come in several different formats. Although they all conform to the DVD-V or Blu-ray Disc specification, they might have very different capacities, depending on whether or not they have information on both sides or on separate layers within the disk. Table 18.1 shows standard DVD-V and BD-ROM formats:

Table 18.1 Standard Optical Disc Video Formats

Name	Type	Capacity
DVD-5	Single-sided, single-layer	4.7GB
DVD-9	Single-sided, dual layer	8.54GB
DVD-10	Dual-sided, both sides single-layer	9.4GB
DVD-14	Dual-sided, one side dual-layer	13.24GB
DVD-18	Dual-sided, both sides dual-layer	17.08GB
BD-ROM	Single layer	25GB
BD-ROM	Double layer	50GB

(Note that in terms of actual storage capacity, these formats all have slightly less capacity than what's listed here. A DVD-5 disk only holds 4.37GB, as far as your computer is concerned. This is because computer manufacturers consider a GB to be 1,024MB, while DVD manufacturers consider a GB to be 1,000MB. The figures listed here are the numbers you'll see preferred by DVD manufacturers. They are the numbers you'll most commonly see.)

Most computer-based DVD burners write in the DVD-5 format. Although this is the lowest capacity, it's still enough room to easily hold a two-hour movie while maintaining very good image quality.

What format you need depends largely on your project. If you simply want to create viewable DVDs as a way to give copies of your movie to people, then a single-layer DVD burner will be fine. Similarly, if you're creating a final master for delivering to a DVD/Blu-ray Disc duplication facility, and you've authored some simple menus and added a couple of audio commentary tracks, then a single-layer DVD or Blu-ray Disc will still probably be plenty of capacity. (We'll talk more about preparing for mastering at a duplication facility later in this chapter.)

If you've got a more complex project that requires more storage—a movie with lots of menus, lots of extra video, several commentary tracks, or different audio mixes—then you may not be able to fit all of that into a 4.7GB DVD or 25GB Blu-ray Disc, so you will need to consider moving to a higher capacity.

You probably won't ever need to worry about DVD-14 and 18. These are generally used for distributing entire seasons of TV shows or extremely long documentary productions.

Your first step in outputting to optical disk begins with encoding your file-based master.

DVD and Blu-Ray Compression

Video for DVDs and Blu-ray Discs gets compressed using MPEG-2 or H.264 (a type of MPEG-4) compression. After your video is completely finished and you've locked picture and audio, you can consider your compression options.

There are several different ways to go about encoding for optical disks:

- Most authoring packages include built-in encoders. In most cases, you can take your file-based master and import it into your authoring program, and it will perform the necessary encoding for you.

- You can install a software-based encoder and compress the video yourself, such as Apple Compressor. In addition to stand-alone software encoders, you can export MPEG-2 or H.264 video directly from your editing program.

To encode a DVD or Blu-ray Disc, whether you're using an editing application or authoring software, you'll need to give careful consideration to your compression settings. Choosing compression settings is a process of balancing disk capacity, image quality, and the throughput capability of the DVD and/or Blu-ray specification. If you're trying to cram a lot of extra material onto a disk, you might have to sacrifice some image quality.

DVD and Blu-ray audio come in five flavors: PCM, Dolby AC-3, MPEG, DTS, and SDDS. PCM audio is the same as the audio that's recorded on audio CDs, and you can use any WAV or AIFF file as the source for PCM audio in a DVD project. Dolby AC-3 is 5.1 channel Dolby Digital Surround Sound that has been compressed using a special codec. Typically, the 5.1 channels are designed to create a surround environment in a movie theater, so the channels are laid out as left, center, right, left surround, right surround. The .1 channel is an optional subwoofer track for low-frequency sounds. However, if surround sound is out of your league, don't worry. Dolby AC-3 doesn't require that your sound tracks be arranged this way—you can also have just a normal stereo mix. MPEG audio is not used in North America. DTS and SDDS audio are other forms of surround sound used for feature films—we discussed them a little in the section on audio mixes earlier in this chapter. You'll need a professional mixer to get DTS or SDDS sound, and that person will be able to give you the mix in the properly encoded format for inclusion on a DVD or Blu-ray Disc. DVDs and Blu-ray Discs can also have multiple streams of sound, each containing a full mix for different language versions or extras such as director commentaries. Though you might often err on the side of PCM audio, since it's uncompressed, if you have a lot of audio or alternate audio tracks, then you might need to compress some or all of them using Dolby AC-3, simply to fit them all onto your disk.

Finally, DVDs and Blu-ray Discs have up to 32 special built-in subtitle tracks, again for distribution in many languages.

All of these details and concerns will be further explained in the documentation for your DVD/Blu-ray authoring package.

Presentation Values

If you make your own DVDs or Blu-ray Discs be sure to create professional looking labels. 3M and Avery create blank laser printable optical disk labels, or you can enlist one of several online self-publishing services such as *www.createspace.com*. Labels should include the following information: production company, producer/director's name and contact info, project title, date, total running time (TRT), and format.

DVD and Blu-Ray Disc Authoring

Once you've compressed your files, you're ready to author the menus and interactivity that will form the interface for your DVD or Blu-ray Disc. Through special authoring software, you'll use still images and short video clips to create the menus and interface for your disc, as well as establish how the user will navigate using their player's remote control.

Many packages such as Apple's DVD Studio Pro (Figure 18.8) include software MPEG-2 encoders, allowing you to buy a complete DVD authoring system for under $500. If you're a Windows user, Adobe's Encore is an excellent professional-level authoring tool. If you have the Apple Final Cut Studio or Adobe CS5 bundles, you already own DVD Studio Pro or Adobe Encore.

Figure 18.8

Apple's DVD Studio Pro lets you author professional-quality DVD and Blu-ray videos, complete with menus and interactivity.

When creating your DVD or Blu-ray Disc, here are some technical tips to keep in mind:

- Optical discs are designed to play on both video and computer monitors. This means that they are susceptible to all the limitations of video. Unless you're absolutely certain that your DVD or Blu-ray Disc will only play on a computer monitor (perhaps because it's a corporate or industrial presentation that will be shown under controlled conditions), you'll need to make sure your DVD interface uses only NTSC-safe colors, and that the buttons and text all fall within the standard title-safe area. Test your DVD or Blu-ray Disc on a video monitor before you publish it.

- Pretty much all DVD or Blu-ray Disc players have a handheld remote control device, while computer-based DVD players include an equivalent virtual remote. Don't forget to program interactivity for the remote as well as the on-screen menus.

- Whatever the size of your DVD or Blu-ray Disc, you'll need to double that in computer storage space in order to create the disc. If your DVD is 4GB, you'll need 4GB for the source materials for your compressed MPEG-2 video and 4GB for the rendered DVD files.

- Blu-ray Disc graphics should be created at 72dpi, with a pixel resolution of either 1920 × 1080 or 1280 × 720, depending on which type of HD you prefer.

- DVD graphics should be created at 72dpi, with a pixel resolution of 720 × 480 (for NTSC video). Remember that if you create menus and buttons in a square-pixel environment, like Photoshop, you should work with files that are 720 × 540, and then resize them to 720 × 480 when you're ready to import them into your DVD authoring application.

If you plan on burning the disk yourself using a recordable DVD or Blu-ray Disc drive, then you'll want to be sure that you buy the right type of media for authoring. Check the packaging and your disc burner's manual to be certain.

If you plan to have your DVD or Blu-ray Disc mass produced by a professional replication house, then you should consult with them about the different capacities (and prices) that are available. If your final DVD or Blu-ray Disc will be a higher-capacity disk and you only have a single-layer burner (or no burner at all), you can still author the disk yourself. You'll just have to write the final files to your hard drive and move the resulting files to the replication house when you're ready to make the disk. Most authoring programs allow you to output to a disk image or to a hard drive. Check with your replicator to find out what media they can accept.

Pass the Buck

If all of this sounds too complicated, there are companies that will take your final video master and create a DVD or Blu-ray Disc for you. Services provided by these companies vary from simple MPEG compression to full mastering, including interface authoring.

Deliverables

If you sell your film to a distributor, they are likely to have a long list of things you'll have to provide, so here's a typical list:

- DCP, 35mm, or HDCAM-SR master
- Dubs of the master with various mixes
- Key art (graphics, still photos for use in publicity materials)
- DVD/Blu-ray Disc cover
- Press kit
- Sound spotting list
- Production notes (including crew list, contact list, deal memos, shooting schedule, time cards, location agreements, camera and sound reports, final shooting script, call sheets, releases for talent and extras, and pretty much any other documents you generated during the shoot)
- Music cue sheet
- Composer agreement
- Copy of musical score
- Chain of title documents (proving that you and your production company own the rights to the film and the rights to the screenplay)
- E & O (Errors and Omissions) insurance certificate to cover any liability over legal/ contractual things you didn't do right (errors) or at all (omissions).

Be aware that the deliverables can vary greatly from one distributor to another and also depending on what you are delivering (VOD, theatrical feature, etc).

High-End Finishing

In a perfect world, you made your DIY file-based master, distributed it via optical disk or the Web, the right people saw it and liked it, and now you need to make a high-end videotape master, 35mm film print, or file-based Digital Cinema Package (DCP). You've now officially left behind the world of DIY.

Reel Changes

If you're heading for a 35mm film print, you'll most likely have to break your project into 20-minute segments to accommodate reel changes. This is due to physical limitations on the length of a reel of 35mm film. Even if you're mastering to videotape, there is a chance that your project won't fit on a single tape. The longest HDCAM-SR tapes are 124 minutes. Even for digital cinema delivery, reels are still the norm.

Earlier we mentioned that most films that deliver DCP still also deliver on 35mm as well. For that reason, films are still broken down into reels. Also, shorter reels allow you to spread work-flow across multiple workstations when color correcting or rendering, which is especially useful for large, uncompressed format projects such as 4K Red footage.

Talk to your post facility about this as early as possible. Be sure to make these breaks at a hard cut, not at a dissolve. In addition, make sure they're at a natural lull in the soundtrack, not in the middle of a line of dialogue or music—the transition from one reel to another might not be seamless. As a rule, make sure there isn't any important dialogue in the one to two seconds leading up to and following a reel change. For this reason, reels can vary in length and can be as short as 15 minutes or even less. Sometimes, it's hard to find a place to make a reel change.

Preparing for a Professional Audio Mix

If your edited sequence has 48kHz audio, you can use the tracks directly from your editing project as sources for your mix. To do this, you'll need to create a split-track audio export from your edited sequence. How many tracks you choose to export can vary, depending on your project, but it helps if your audio is somewhat organized with dialogue on one group of tracks, effects and ambience on another group, and music on a third. If your audio tracks are a mess, they'll clean it up for you, but you'll be paying by the hour. You'll also need to provide a guide for the video in your project, usually a QuickTime movie.

The most popular sound editing application for mixes is Avid ProTools, but there are several others. Most of them can accept OMF files. When you export the OMF files, you'll need to make a couple choices (see Figure 18.9):

- Choose an audio sampling rate (usually 48kHz).

- Choose a bit rate (usually 16 bit).

- Choose between an encapsulated OMF (contains all of your sequence info from your project) or separate audio track OMF (each track of your project gets its own separate file).

Ask your mixer and/or post facility what works best for them.

Figure 18.9

Export options for OMF audio files.

Before you go to the mix, you should have a sound spotting session to make notes of things you'd like to fix or change. A basic professional mix starts with a short sweetening, or sound editing, session. If you know of special effects you want to add, it's a good idea to let the sound effects editor know about them in advance so that he'll have some options loaded up and ready to go at the beginning of your sweetening session. Your sound effects editor will probably be working on a ProTools or other high-end sound editing system. Unless you have lots of time and money, the amount of sound editing you do in the sweetening session will be limited to things you couldn't do on your editing software.

After you've tweaked your sound, it's time to mix. Your tracks will be sent through a large mixing board, and the mixer will set the levels as your video master plays and continue to tweak things until it sounds good. You'll probably want more than one type of mix—for example, a stereo mix, a 5.1 surround sound mix, and an M&E mix. If you're creating a Dolby surround sound mix for a film print, a technician will record the mix using specialized hardware. If you're mastering to HDCAM-SR, which has 12 audio tracks, the typical choice is to use two tracks for the stereo mix, two tracks for the M&E mix, and six tracks for the 5.1 surround mix. That leaves two extra channels, which are sometimes used for Dolby E encoding.

Preparing for Professional Color Grading

Always talk to your colorist or postproduction facility before you prepare your media for color grading. Typically, you will be asked to provide a DPX export of your film for the color grading session. DPX is sequential still image file format that is the current standard for digital cinema finishing, although other uncompressed sequential still image formats, such as sequential TIFF files, will often work as well. In some cases, your colorist may be able to work directly with your project's master sequence; for example, if you are editing in Avid Media Composer and your colorist is using Avid Symphony or any other software-compatible combination. You'll be able to give her a copy of your project and drives containing your media, and she can import your sequence directly into her app and do her magic.

You'll want to clean up your sequence by doing the following:

- Make a copy of your project and sequence and add "for color" or similar to the name of both the sequence and the project.

- Remove the titles. Unless you want them color corrected as well, which isn't the norm.

- Remove any color filters that you added as temporary fixes while editing. Make notes of these problem areas and send the list to your colorist.

- If you have composites, motion effects or other special effects shot, it is considered best to export these shots to an uncompressed file format and reimport them as new shots and replace the composites in your sequence. Talk to your post facility about what they can best work with.

- Collapse all of your video onto one track.

- Create a drive with copies of all your original media files (that are in the cut) on it. Most films will fit on a 1TB drive. It is best to always have people work on copies of your media, because that way you still have the originals and can keep your editing workstation functional.

- They might not require it, but give them a mixed down track of your audio as a guide track. When you watch your project at the color grading session, you may want to hear the audio.

As a director or editor supervising a color-grading session, your goal is to make sure your final master looks as you intended it to look. For example, you might have a scene that was intentionally shot with unnatural blue levels. Unless you are there to tell her otherwise, the colorist will probably try to correct this "problem" by taking down the blue. Most projects will include situations such as this so it's important that you sit in on the session.

Putting Audio and Video Back Together

Your audio is off at the sound mixer's workstation and your video is over at the colorist's; that means that when they are done, the audio and video will have to be put back together before you create the final master.

If you are finishing in a file-based format, you'll simply import the uncompressed color graded video and the uncompressed mixed audio tracks back into your editing software and put them together in a new sequence. You'll want to make sure nothing has gone wrong with the sync and watch the new version from beginning to end.

If you are finishing on videotape, you can choose to marry the sound and picture together in your editing application, the same as for file-based finishing, or your post facility will lay the color graded picture off to videotape and then separately lay back the audio. For 35mm film prints, the picture and audio will stay separate until the very end when the audio will get converted to an optical soundtrack and printed on the final release print, along with the picture.

Digital Videotape Masters

There is no good reason to make a videotape master unless someone requires it of you, but if your film does well, odds are high that you'll have to deliver it to someone on digital videotape. Digital videotape is still a viable way to master your final product, and HDCAM-SR mastering is a commonly required delivery format for television networks, VOD distributors, and film festivals.

If you need to make an HDCAM-SR master, you need to decide whether you want to do it yourself using your editing system and a rented video deck or go to a postproduction facility.

If you shot on a digital format, you can save a lot of money by creating a master yourself. The quality of your master is entirely dependent on how well your footage was shot and how much care you took with your finishing and color grading.

You'll also need to add some hardware to your system. First, you'll need a video card or breakout box that adds HD-SDI outputs to your system (see Figure 18.10). Second, you'll need to rent an HDCAM-SR deck (Figure 18.11). To really do things properly and to ensure the best quality, you should also have a mixing board for audio and a hardware waveform monitor and vectorscope. In Chapter 16, "Color Correction," we talked about how to read waveforms and vectorscopes. In addition, there is a more detailed discussion on the Web site at *www.thedigitalfilmmakinghandbook.com/chapter13*.

Head Room

Avoid using the first minute or two of the videotape for your project. This is the part of the tape that is most prone to physical damage. Instead, cover the head of the tape with bars and tone followed by a head slate and a countdown. Most videotapes are a minute or two longer than their stated length, so don't worry about wasting a little tape.

Figure 18.10

If you plan to output full-quality HD 2K or 4K video to HDCAM-SR, you'll need a video card that has HD-SDI outputs like this DeckLink HD Extreme 3D card from BlackMagic Design.

Figure 18.11

You'll also need to buy or rent an HDCAM-SR VTR.

Keep Your Crew Involved

Your director of photography and your editor probably know a lot about film and video image quality. Keep them involved throughout the entire process, from digital image enhancement to mastering your videotape to film transfer.

35mm Film Prints

High-quality video footage is the key to a successful tape-to-film transfer. Everything that looks bad on video is going to look worse on film, especially when projected. The resolution of 35mm film is much, much greater than that of video, and any overexposed whites will read as large expanses of white nothingness, without the detail you would normally expect to see in film. In addition, any artifacts, noise, focus problems, and other image flaws will be enlarged as much as 25 times. If you shot your video properly—that is, if you took the time to light it like film, and set your video black-and-white levels properly when you created your videotape master—then you'll be giving your film recordist the best possible image containing the most information. Avoid any type of image processing that removes information, such as de-interlacing. In addition, avoid any image processing that adds artifacts or noise, like boosting the video gain. The company that does your video-to-film transfer will take care of these things. If you're careful, well-shot HD footage transferred to film can look surprisingly good.

There are two ways to deliver your footage to the film recordist: digital files or videotape. We've already discussed how to best create a textless videotape master via a professional online session or by doing it yourself. This is the easiest and most practical way to deliver your film to the film recordist. The other option is to deliver digital video files, usually DPX, QuickTime, Targa, or sequential PICT formats, on a hard drive. Talk to your film recordist before assuming that she can work with digital files.

The primary reason to deliver digital files is if you've done some effects work, such as color correcting or compositing, and do not want to recompress those shots by going back out to tape. Titles should also be delivered digitally as high-resolution 2K files, or else they should originate on film via optical printing. (See the section on titles for film in Chapter 17, "Titles and Effects.") Ask your film recordist how she prefers to have titles and effects shots delivered.

Reel Changes

If you're heading for a film transfer, you'll most likely have to break your project into 20-minute segments to accommodate reel changes. Talk to your film recordist about this as early as possible. Be sure to make these breaks at a hard cut, not at a dissolve. In addition, make sure they're at a natural lull in the soundtrack, not in the middle of a line of dialogue or music—the transition from one reel to another might not be seamless. As a rule, make sure there isn't any important dialogue in the one to two seconds leading up to and following a reel change.

The Film Printing Process

Modern 35mm motion picture finishing has changed a lot, thanks to digital technologies. Whether you shot on HD video, a digital cinema format, or 35mm, the postproduction process is pretty much the same: high-resolution media is brought into an editing system where it gets edited, color graded, and mixed before printing to 35mm film. This simplifies the film printing process greatly. The final color graded cut of the film is exported to a digital file format that works well for film printing, usually DPX, QuickTime, Targa, or sequential PICT or TIFF formats on a hard drive.

Transferring your digital video project to 35mm film can dramatically improve the look of your final product. If you're planning to make a film print of your digital media, it's important to understand the traditional film printing process (see Figure 18.12). For example, 16mm and 35mm motion picture films are very similar to 35mm still film: the negative is exposed in the camera, and the film is taken to a lab where it is processed and used to create a print of the film. If you've ever compared a bad "one-hour photo" print to a professional print of the same image, then you know how different two prints from the same negative can look. Good film printing is all about controlling the look of the final film print. Some film transfer companies have their own labs, others work closely with a nearby lab, or others will work with the lab of your choice. Once you have a negative, you'll follow the same process as traditional film printing.

It's important to choose a lab for your film print fairly early in the editing process. Each lab has a different, usually proprietary, method for transferring digital media to film, and they will have specific instructions for you—how long each reel should be, how the white levels and black levels should be set, how to deal with text on-screen, and so on.

They will probably suggest that you let them handle the entire finishing process, rather than a do-it-yourself file-based output from your own system. This will cost more money, but the resulting quality might be worth it. However, if you're really on a shoestring budget, you should shop around for a lab that thinks they can work with your DIY file-based master. Technically, this shouldn't result in any significant image problems if you have good image quality.

Printing from a Negative

The film recordist takes the digital file and prints each frame in the file to a frame of 35mm motion picture film negative (see Figure 18.12). The negative is then used to strike a positive film print. In traditional filmmaking, several trial prints are made at this stage. The final, successful print is called the *answer print*.

Once an answer print is made, an intermediate is created using the answer print. The intermediate will either be a color internegative (IN) or an interpositive (IP). The IN or IP is then used to strike the release prints. Because these intermediate prints are used to strike release prints, you can store your original negative away for safekeeping. If your intermediate print gets damaged, you can create a new one from your original negative.

Direct-to-Print

If you aren't going to need too many copies of your film, you can also choose to go "direct-to-print" and bypass the negative process. Special film recording machines can take your digital files and create a positive print frame by frame. It works in a way that's very similar to traditional Polaroid film, using special reversal film stocks that do not need a negative in order to make a print. However, like old Polaroids, it's a one-time process. If you will need more than one or two copies of your film print, it's better to go with the traditional negative film printing process. This is a great option for saving money when creating a 35mm festival screener.

Optical Soundtracks

Once you have a release print, a stripe of photoactive chemicals is added to the print next to the picture. A sound facility specializing in optical soundtracks will then take your audio master, either an MO (magneto-optical disk), videotape, or file, and record it onto the optical stripe on the film.

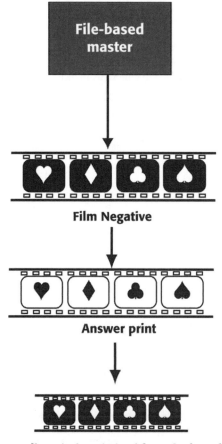

File-based master

Film Negative

Answer print

Intermediate (IN) or (IP) with optical track audio

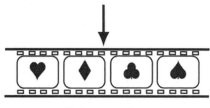

Release prints

Figure 18.12

Printing a final 35mm print from a negative is a complex process.

Film Math

Film is measured in frames and feet (hence the term *footage*). 35mm film shot at 24 frames per second has 16 frames per foot. Typical film lengths are 50' (about 30 seconds), 100' (about a minute), 400' (about 4.5 minutes), 1000' (about 11 minutes), and 2000' (around 22 minutes). 16mm film shot at 24 frames per second has 40 frames per foot. When companies quote prices for film, they might quote by the frame, by the foot, or by the minute.

Digital Cinema Masters

A DCP is a set of files stored on a hard drive that can be projected in a theater using a digital projection system. As with all other things video, there is a set of standards for digital cinema delivery, known as the Digital Cinema Initiatives, or DCI.

The rules for DCI-compliant DCPs are pretty straightforward:

- JPEG2000 compression (JP2K)
- 2K or 4K resolution with 12-bit color in an XYZ color space
- 24 bits per sample, 48 or 96kHz PCM audio (usually .WAV format)
- .MXF file format with XML wrapper
- Optional encryption with security keys (KDMs)

Typically, the files are saved and delivered on hard drives, and similar to DVDs and Blu-ray Discs, they consist of a group of files without subfolders.

Creating a digital cinema file-based master is cheaper, easier, and better than 35mm film or videotape. At the time of this writing, software apps for creating digital cinema file-based masters are just starting to become available on the market (see Figure 18.13). Probably the most challenging issue is quality control because the DCP files need to be tested on a digital projection system, which involves renting a theater or using a postproduction facility. For that reason, most filmmakers prefer to have a postproduction facility handle the creation of their digital cinema master.

Expect lots of changes as this technology evolves.

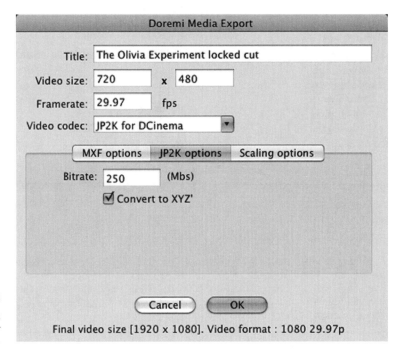

Figure 18.13

The Doremi CineAsset plug-in lets you export a DCP directly from Final Cut Pro.

Archiving Your Project

The final step in the entire digital filmmaking process is to archive your project. The best way is to simply dedicate a drive (or set of drives) and save your project and all your uncompressed media files on it. Disconnect it from your computer and store it somewhere safe. To be truly secure, you should make a second backup and store it at another location.

It's also a good idea to store a full version of your file-based master somewhere on the Internet. Many Web hosts let you have unlimited storage via FTP, so we recommend storing a full copy of your film on your film's Web site in a secure folder that is not accessible to the public. This will take a while, but you'll always be able to access it if needed.

Believe it or not, over these last 18 chapters, we've been covering the *easy* part of film production. Now the hard part begins: selling your product. Hopefully, you have some idea of who might be interested in your final product. Or perhaps you have backers who are already committed to moving your project forward.

Odds are, though, that you have no idea what will become of your piece. Now is the time to make something happen. With new delivery technologies on the Web, and inexpensive DVD/Blu-ray self-publishing, there are any number of avenues you can pursue to sell your feature or documentary.

No matter what, remember that getting feedback from a live audience, other directors, and actors can be an invaluable and fun experience for improving your current project or starting your next one.

Glossary

1080i High-definition (HD) video with a resolution of 1920 × 1080 pixels where each frame consists of two interlaced fields.

24p A digital video frame rate that consists of 24 progressively scanned frames per second and is akin to the frame rate of 35mm film.

2K A digital cinema video format with a resolution of 2048 × 1556 pixels. *See also* 4K.

2-pop In a traditional eight-second countdown before a film starts, there is a short pop that occurs at the first frame of the "2" (as in "8, 7, 6, 5, 4, 3, 2"); the last two seconds before the first frame of the film are black. The "2-pop" makes it easier to tell that the film is in sync before it starts.

3:2 pulldown A method for transferring 24fps film to 29.97fps NTSC video. The film is slowed by .1%, and the first film frame is recorded on the first two fields of video, the second frame is recorded on the next three fields of video, and so on.

3-act structure A type of story structure based on the idea that each story has a beginning, middle and end. *See also* three-act structure.

3D A type of digital media that combines two stereoscopic video streams to create an illustration of enhanced depth perception.

3-point editing *See* three-point editing.

4K A digital cinema video format with a resolution of 4096 × 2160 pixels. *See also* 2K.

720p High-definition (HD) video with a resolution of 1280 × 270 pixels where each image consists of a single progressively scanned frame.

A/B rolling *See* checkerboard.

A/V An acronym for "Audio-Video."

accelerator cards Custom hardware that can accelerate certain features such as 3D rendering, rendering of plug-in filters, or compositing.

acquisition format The digital format with which a piece of digital media was created. Because digital media can originate from sources other than cameras, it is common to say that it is *acquired*, rather than *shot*.

action safe The area of your image that will most likely be visible on any video monitor. Essential action should be kept within the action safe area, because action that falls outside this area might be lost due to overscan on older TV monitors.

additive color The color mixing system for light and digital video. The primary colors are red, green, and blue. If you mix them together, they get lighter and all of the colors mixed together yield white.

address A frame of video, as identified by timecode information.

AES/EBU An acronym for the Audio Engineering Society and the European Broadcaster's Union; also a standard for professional digital audio that specifies the transmission of audio data in a stream that encodes stereo audio signals along with optional information.

aliasing The "jaggies" or stair-stepping patterns that occur on diagonal or curved line on a computer or video display. Can be smoothed or corrected through anti-aliasing processes.

alpha channel An 8-bit color channel (*see* channels) that is used to specify the transparency of each pixel in an image. An alpha channel works like a sophisticated stencil, and it is the digital equivalent of a matte.

alternate data rates When streaming QuickTime files from a Web site, it is possible to specify several copies of the same movie, each optimized for a different data rate. The server can then decide which movie is best for the speed of the user's connection.

A-mode EDL An EDL sorted in order of master record in timecode (*see* EDL).

amp Short for ampere, a unit that measures the voltage of an electrical source.

analog Information represented electronically as a continuous, varying signal. (*See also* digital.)

anamorphic lenses Special lenses that shoot a wide-screen 16:9 image, but optically compress the image to a normal 4:3 aspect ratio for storage on 4:3 film or video. The widescreen image can be uncompressed by a projector fitted with a similar anamorphic lens, by a monitor that displays 16:9 video or by software that knows to stretch the image.

Animation compressor A lossless QuickTime codec.

answer print The final print of a film after color-timing.

anti-aliasing The process of eliminating "jagged" edges on computer-generated text and graphics. Anti-aliased graphics have their edges slightly blurred and mixed with background colors to eliminate the jagged, stair-stepping patterns that can occur on diagonal or curved lines.

aperture In any type of camera, light is focused by the lens, through an aperture and onto the focal plane. The size of the aperture controls how much light passes through to the focal plane. In addition to controlling the brightness of the exposure, the aperture controls the depth of field in the image. By balancing the size of the aperture (as measured in f-stops) with the shutter speed, you can trade off between varying depth of field and the ability to better resolve fast motion.

Apple ProRes A set of codecs designed for use in digital video editing applications, particularly Apple Final Cut Pro.

array *See* RAID.

ARRIRAW A high-end, uncompressed digital cinema codec created by the Arri Group for use in its line of digital cinema cameras.

art director The person in charge of the execution of the production designer's vision. The art director manages set construction, set dressing, props, and scenic painting.

aspect ratio The ratio of the width of an image to its height. Aspect ratios can be expressed as ratios, such as 4:3, or as numbers, such as 1.33.

assemble edit When editing onto videotape, an edit that records over the entire tape, including the video track, the audio tracks, and the control track.

ATA A type of hard drive interface. Not as fast as SCSI, but fast enough for DV.

ATSC Advanced Television Systems Committee—established to set the technical standards for DTV, including HDTV.

attenuator A circuit that lowers the strength of an electronic signal.

audio compressor A filter (or piece of hardware) that reduces the dynamic range of a sound to accommodate loud peaks.

audio guide track A mixed audio track generated from the final cut. The guide track is placed onto one of the audio tracks of the online master for reference during the online editing session.

audio mixing board A piece of hardware that takes several audio signals and mixes them together, allowing for the combining of different sources. Mixers usually include some type of equalization control.

audio sampling rate The number of samples per second that are used to digitize a particular sound. Most DV cameras can record at several audio sampling rates. Higher rates yield better results. Measured in kilohertz, 44.1kHz is considered audio CD quality, and 48kHz is considered DAT quality.

AVCHD A high-definition acquisition and mastering codec developed by Sony and Panasonic and compatible with Blu-ray Discs.

AVC-Intra A high-definition acquisition codec developed by Panasonic for use with their P2 line of cameras.

Avid DNxHD A set of codecs designed for use in digital video editing applications, particularly Avid Media Composer.

AVR Avid Video Resolution, a series of low- and high-resolution codecs included with older Avid editing systems.

Axial One of several linear, hardware-based online editing systems.

balanced audio A type of microphone connector that provides extra power. Sometimes needed if you want to have microphone cable lengths of 25 feet or longer.

balancing light sources In a lighting setup with several different light sources, the process of making the color temperature of all the lights the same, either to match daylight or tungsten light. Usually, this is done with CTO or CTB lighting gels.

bandwidth The amount of digital information that can be passed through a connection at a given time. High bandwidth is needed for high-quality image transfer.

barndoors A set of hinged door-like flaps that attach to the front of a light and serve to control where the light falls.

bars and tone A combination of color bars and 60Hz audio reference tone, usually recorded onto the head of each videotape. Used for calibrating video and audio levels.

bin A film-editing term that refers to the place where the shots for a scene are stored. In software editing systems, bins can also be referred to as *folders*, *galleries*, or *libraries*.

binary A system for encoding digital information using two components: 0 and 1.

bit-depth The number of bits used to represent the color of a single pixel in a frame of digital media. HD video typically has 8- or 10-bit color.

black and coded tape A "blank" videotape that has been striped with a combination of a black video signal and timecode.

black burst A composite video signal with a totally black picture. Used to synchronize older professional video equipment. Black burst supplies analog video equipment with vertical sync, horizontal sync, and chroma burst timing.

black burst generator A piece of video hardware that generates a black composite video signal, or *black burst*. Used to sync older analog professional video equipment to black and code tapes.

black level The black level defines how dark a video image is allowed to get. Improperly set black levels can result in dull, grayish blacks. Also known as *pedestal*.

black wrap A heavy-duty aluminum foil with a matte black coating on one side used to block light. Can be wrapped around light sources to make them more directional.

Blu-ray Disc An optical disc format that can deliver high-definition video.

blue screen A special screen, usually composed of blue cloth or backdrops painted with special blue paint, that is placed behind a foreground element. Blue-screen shots are those shots that you intend to later composite with other elements through the use of a chroma key function. Sometimes, blue elements are used in the foreground to facilitate later compositing.

blue spill In blue-screen shooting, a bluish light that is cast onto the back of a foreground subject due to reflection from the blue screen.

BNC connector A connector used to carry SDI, SDI-HD, composite video, component video, timecode, and AES/EBU audio signals.

boom A long (sometimes up to 100 feet) pole with a microphone at the end. Technically, a boom is a large, sometimes hydraulically controlled device, as opposed to a fishpole, a smaller, handheld pole. Increasingly, the term *boom* is used to refer to any stick with a mic on the end.

bounce card A piece of white material, like foam core, used to create soft, indirect lighting.

breakout box A box that has connectors and ports for attaching video and audio peripherals. The box can be fitted to some video cards to provide easier access to the input and outputs provided by the card.

broadcast quality A somewhat vague term, referring to the minimum quality considered acceptable for broadcast television. Until the 1980s, 3/4" Umatic tape was considered broadcast quality; then Betacam SP was introduced and became the standard for broadcast quality. Thanks to HD video, broadcast quality is not a big issue today.

broadcast safe colors Your computer monitor can display many more colors than an NTSC or PAL analog video monitor. Broadcast colors are those colors that are safe—that is, they will display properly—on an analog television set. Many programs, such as Adobe Photoshop and Adobe After Effects, include special filters that will convert the colors in an image to their nearest broadcast safe equivalent. (*See also* NTSC legal.)

BT. 601 A document that defines the specifications for professional, interlaced video standards as the following: 720 × 480 (59.94Hz), 960 × 480 (59.94Hz), 720 × 576 (50Hz), and 960 × 576 (50Hz) 4:2:2 YCbCr. Also called *CCIR 601* and *ITU-R 601*.

bumping up The process of transferring a videotape from a lower-quality format to a higher-quality format; for example, bumping up HDV tapes to HDCAM SR.

byte A unit of computer storage. How much one byte equates to depends on what you are storing. If you're just storing text, then a single byte can hold one character. For video or audio, what a byte holds depends on how your video is compressed and stored.

camera negative After film stock is exposed in the camera and is processed, the result is the negative, also called the *camera negative*, which is usually transferred to video using a telecine process and then, after editing, is used to strike the final print.

candelas A measurement of the intensity of light.

capturing The process of moving videotape data from a camera or deck into a computer.

cardioid The roughly heart-shaped pattern that certain mics can "hear."

CCD *See also* charge-coupled device.

CCIR 601 *See also* BT. 601.

CDR (CD Recordable) A special type of compact disc that can be recorded by the end user using a special drive. Standard audio or data formats are supported by most recording programs, along with Video CD, a special format that can store 70 minutes of full-screen, full-motion MPEG1-compressed video, and the DVD video format, which can store about 18 minutes of full-screen, full-motion MPEG2-compressed video.

Century stand *See also* C-stand.

CG (character-generator) A special machine for creating titles and other text characters for inclusion in a video. Most editing packages include CG features.

CGI (computer generated imagery) Used to refer to any effect that is created digitally, be it a composite, or a fully digital image such as a walking dinosaur. CGI is often used as a noun: "We'll fill that spot with some CGI of a duck."

channel The color in an RGB image is divided into channels, one each for the red, green, and blue information in the image. When these channels are combined, a full-color image results. Certain effects are easier to achieve by manipulating individual color channels. Additional alpha channels can also be added for specifying transparency and selections. *See also* alpha channel.

charge-coupled device (CCD) A special type of chip that can convert light into electronic signals. A modern video camera focuses light through a lens and onto a CCD where it is converted into electronic signals that can be stored on tape.

checkerboard A way to arrange each piece of sound across a group of audio tracks so that no piece of sound is directly "touching" any other piece of sound, resulting in a checkerboard-like appearance. Also called *A/B rolling*.

chroma The part of the video signal that contains the color information.

chroma key A function that will render a specific color in a layer transparent. For example, if you shoot someone in front of an evenly lit blue screen, you can use a chroma key function to render the blue completely transparent, thus revealing underlying video layers.

chromatic aberration Color shifts and color artifacts in an image caused by faults in a lens, or by the camera's inability to register all three channels of color information. Single-chip video cameras are especially prone to chromatic aberration.

chrominance The saturation and hue of a video signal. Although slightly different in meaning, this term is often used interchangeably with the term *chroma* to refer to color.

Chyron A title identifying a speaker in a documentary that runs along the bottom of the screen. The name derives from the Chyron character-generator once popular in many post facilities. These I.D. titles are also known as *lower thirds*.

cinematographer *See* director of photography.

Cinepak A QuickTime codec; very lossy.

clipping In digital media, an electronic limit that is imposed on the audio and/or video portion of the signal in order to avoid audio that is too loud and video that is too bright, too saturated, or too dark. Clipped blacks are any blacks in an image that are darker than the set black level, or 7.5 IRE. Clipped whites are any whites that are brighter than the set white level, or 100 IRE. Clipped audio is any sound that goes into the red area on an audio level meter. Clipped media is indicated by a flat line in a waveform view of the signal.

close-up A shot where the subject fills the majority of the frame. If the subject is a person, the shot will consist primarily of the person's head and shoulders.

C-mode EDL An EDL sorted nonsequentially by source tape number and ascending source timecode (*see also* EDL).

CMOS (complementary metal-oxide semiconductors) A type of image sensor used in digital video cameras and digital SLR cameras.

CMX A hardware-based linear online editing system. CMX-3600-format EDLs are the default for many other editing systems.

codec COmpressor/DECompressor, an algorithm for compressing and decompressing video and audio.

color bars A test pattern used to check whether a video system is calibrated correctly. A waveform monitor and vectorscope are used, in conjunction with color bars, to check the brightness, hue, and saturation.

color correction A postproduction process to correct the overall color of a video master in order to get the best quality image, with an emphasis on enhancing skin tones. Also referred to as *color grading*.

color depth The number of colors that a given video system can display. The more bits-per-pixel that are used to store color, the higher the color depth.

color sampling ratio In component digital video, the ratio of luminance (Y) to each color difference component (Cb and Cr). 4:2:2 means that for every four samples of luminance, there are two samples of chroma minus blue and chroma minus red. 4:2:2:4 indicates an additional four samples of the alpha channel or keying information.

color spectrum The range of visible light that extends from violet to red.

color temperature Light sources have different color temperatures, which are measured in degrees Kelvin. The color temperature of tungsten light is 3200°K, and the color temperature of daylight is about 5600°K.

Color Temperature Blue (CTB) A special color of lighting gel or camera lens filter that changes tungsten light to daylight.

Color Temperature Orange (CTO) A special color of lighting gel or camera lens filter that changes daylight to tungsten light.

color timing The process of setting the red, green, and blue lights when creating a film print. Usually, the color settings are timed to change with each significant scene or lighting change in the film. *See also* color grading.

component video An analog video signal consisting of three separate color signals (or components), usually RGB (red, green, blue), YCbCr (luminance, chroma minus blue, and chroma minus red), or Y, R-Y, B-Y (luminance, red minus luminance, blue minus luminance).

composite video An analog video signal that contains all the luminance, chroma, and timing (or sync) information in one composite signal.

compositing The process of layering media on top of each other to create collages or special effects.

compression The process of encoding information in a digital format and discarding information to reduce file size.

condensor A type of mic that records sounds through a "capacitance" mechanism. Condensor mics require a power supply (usually in the form of a small battery). Because of the nature of their pickup mechanism, condensor mics can be made very small.

conforming The process of meticulously re-creating an edit using, usually, higher quality footage.

container file A type of digital media file that can hold more than one type of data and more than one data stream. For example, a QuickTime movie is a container file that can include video streams, audio streams, meta data, and others.

continuity During a shoot, the process of keeping track of dialogue changes, actors' positions, wardrobe, and props so that the footage from shot to shot, and day to day, will cut together. Usually, the person in charge of continuity—the script supervisor—makes notes on a copy of the script and takes photos of the set.

control track A part of the analog videotape signal that contains the timing, or synchronization, information used to regulate the motion of the tape itself as it plays through a VTR.

co-processors Extra processors that are used to speed up a computer, or to perform special functions. *See also* accelerator cards.

coverage Shooting all of the footage that will be needed to cover an event or scene properly.

CPU (central processing unit) In a computer system, the box that contains the motherboard, peripheral cards, and some storage drives. Also used to refer to the main processing chip that the system uses.

cross-platform Programs or hardware that come in different versions for different platforms. Ideally, the program's interface and features are identical from one platform to the next.

CRT monitor Older computer monitors that use a cathode ray tube (as opposed to LCD displays).

C-stand A heavy-duty collapsible metal stand designed to hold lighting accessories, such as flags and nets.

CTB *See* Color Temperature Blue.

CTO *See* Color Temperature Orange.

cutaway In a scene, a shot of something other than the main action or dialogue. Used to build the story and smooth rough edits.

daisy chain A group of storage devices that have been chained together. Although cabled in series, each can be accessed independently.

DAT (digital audio tape) An audio tape format developed by Sony that records audio using a sampling rate of 48kHz and is capable of recording SMPTE timecode information.

data rate The amount of data that a particular connection can sustain over time; usually measured in megabytes per second.

DaVinci A professional digital color-correction system.

daylight Daylight is the combination of sunlight and skylight.

dBm *See* decibel milliwatt.

dBSPL *See* decibel sound pressure loudness.

decibel The standard unit for measuring sound. A subjective scale where one unit equals one increment of "loudness."

decibel milliwatt A unit for measuring sound as electrical power.

decibel sound pressure loudness A measure of the acoustic power of a sound.

degauss To completely erase all the information on a magnetic video or audio tape, using a demagnetizing device.

depth of field A measure of how much, and what depth, of the image is in focus.

destination monitor The monitor or window that displays an edited sequence as it plays, as opposed to the source monitor, which plays unedited source footage. Also called the *record monitor*.

destructive editing Any form of editing (either video or audio) that physically alters your original source material.

device control The ability of a piece of hardware, such as an edit controller or a CPU, to control a peripheral device, such as a VTR, via a remote control cable.

diffuse light Light from a soft, undirected source, such as a typical household light bulb.

diffusion gel A semi-transparent piece of white plastic used to make a light softer.

digital Information recorded electronically as a series of discrete pulses, or samples, usually encoded using a binary system.

digital cinema A phrase used to describe very high-quality digital video that is intended to compete against traditional 35mm film as an acquisition and distribution medium. Digital cinema formats have a resolution of 2K or higher.

Digital Cinema Package (DCP) A set of digital files used to deliver digital cinema media for digital projection in a theater. DCP video uses the MXF format with the JP2K (JPEG 2000) codec and follows a set of specifications set out by the Digital Cinema Initiatives (DCI).

digital intermediate File-based media created by transferring 35mm film to a digital format for editing and mastering.

digital zoom A "fake" zoom that creates a zooming effect by enlarging the image digitally. Unfortunately, the process of enlarging usually severely degrades the image.

digitizing The process of taking analog video or audio information from a camera or deck and turning it into digital information that can be used by a computer.

diopter An adjustment on the eyepiece of a camera that allows you to correct the focus of the eyepiece to match your vision.

director of photography (DP) The film lighting and camera specialist responsible for the look of the photography, and the person in charge of the camera and lighting crews.

dissolve A transition in which the first shot is partially or completely replaced by a gradual superimposition of the next shot.

distressing A process of making objects on a set look aged or weathered.

DLT An optical tape backup system, DLT tapes typically hold about 40GB of media.

DM&E *See* M&E.

DP *See* director of photography.

drag-and-drop editing A two-step editing method where the user selects a shot and drags it from one position and drops it in another position; for example, from a bin to the timeline or from one position in the timeline to another.

drive chassis A box, mount, or rack for holding hard drives; usually separate from the CPU.

drop-outs A weak portion of the video signal that results in a problem in playback. Hits are small dropouts that are only one or two horizontal lines in size, glitches are larger, where five percent or more of the image drops out. Large analog dropouts can result in a few rolling video frames, and large digital dropouts can result in random "holes" across the screen for several frames.

DSLR Acronym for *digital single lens reflex* still photography cameras. Commonly used to describe digital still cameras that are capable of shooting full-resolution HD video.

DTV Acronym for *digital television*, the digital television broadcast standard, DTV is an umbrella term that includes several subgroups, including HDTV and SDTV.

dual-stream processing The ability to handle up to two video signals at a time.

dub A copy of a videotape, also known as a *dupe*.

Duvetine A black felt-like cloth used to block unwanted light sources, such as windows.

DV An early standard definition digital video format.

DVD (digital video disc—sometimes called "digital versatile disc") An optical storage medium that is the same physical size as a compact disc. There are several different DVD standards and formats ranging from DVD-R (a rewritable format) and DVD-ROM (a read-only format) to DVD-video (the format that is used for video releases).

DVD-R (recordable DVD) Similar to CD-R, recordable DVDs can store 4.7GB of data on an inexpensive DVD disk, using a special drive attached to a computer. DVD-Rs can also be used for creating DVD videos.

DVD-RAM A rewritable DVD format that uses special DVD cartridges for storage.

DVD-RW (rewritable DVD) DVD-RWs work just like a DVD-R, but you can erase them and re-use them later. Note that most DVD-Rs can only be read using the same drive that created them.

DVE An acronym for *digital video effects*. The term comes from the professional analog linear video editing world and applies to what has become a fairly standard set of effects: wipes, dissolves, picture-in-picture, barn doors, and split screen, to name a few. Based on a trade name for a system sold by NEC.

dynamic microphone A mic that derives its power from the pressure of the sound that is being recorded. Handheld mics are usually dynamic.

dynamic range In video, the range from the darkest shadows to the brightest highlights, also referred to as "latitude." In audio, the range from silence (or 0dB) to the loudest sound that can be heard without distortion.

edit controller A piece of hardware used in linear editing systems to control and synchronize multiple video decks.

Edit Decision List A list of all of the edits in a project, identified by a chronological event number, source name, source in-point, source out-point, master in-point, and master out-point. Used for analog video online mastering and other types of conforming.

EDL *See* Edit Decision List.

egg crate A sectioned metal frame that attaches to soft light sources to make them more directional.

EIDE A type of hard drive interface. Not as fast as SCSI, but fast enough for DV.

EIS *See* electronic image stabilization.

EISA slots A type of expansion slot used in Windows-based computers.

electret condensor A cheaper, lower-quality version of the condensor mechanism.

electronic image stabilization Special circuitry in a camera that attempts to eliminate or reduce camera shake by electronically shifting the image. Electronic image stabilization frequently results in a slightly blurred image.

electronic zoom Electronic controls that are used to zoom the lens in and out. These are the only zoom controls found on most prosumer camcorders.

EQ *See* equalization.

equalization The process of adjusting the volume of individual frequency ranges within a sound. Equalization can be used to correct problems in a sound, or to "sweeten" or enhance the sound to bring out particular qualities.

eSATA Serial ATA drives that offer the high data transfer rate needed for HD video bandwidth.

ethernet A standard networking protocol for connecting computers together through one of several types of networking cable.

exabyte A digital, optical tape-based storage system used for backing up projects with large amounts of data.

exposure The process of allowing light to enter the camera and expose the film or video stock to produce a recorded image.

fade out A dissolve from full video to black video or from audio to silence.

field Each frame of interlaced video consists of two fields: one field contains the odd-numbered scan lines, and the other field contains the even-numbered scan lines. In analog NTSC video, each field has 262.5 horizontal lines.

field dominance The order in which the two fields in a frame of interlaced video is displayed. Hardware and software that play the field of video containing the odd-numbered scan lines first are known as *upper field dominant*. Those that play the field of video containing the even-numbered scan lines first are known as *lower field dominant*. *See also* field.

film grain Images are recorded on film by exposing the film's light-sensitive emulsion. Composed of chemical particles, the film's emulsion has a visible grain when projected. Many video producers try to mimic this grainy look to produce an image that appears more filmlike.

film recorder *See* film recordist.

film recordist The person responsible for transferring (or recording) video to film.

filters Special glass attachments that can be added to a camera lens to change the optical properties of the lens. Or special pieces of software that can be added to a host application to perform image processing functions.

FireWire Apple's name for the IEEE-1394 specification.

flag A black cloth held by a metal frame, used to block light.

flash memory A memory chip that employs solid-state technology to create a very stable digital storage medium. Used by newer digital cameras and camcorders to record digital video to memory cards.

flats Large wooden "walls," used on a soundstage to construct the set.

fluid head tripod A special type of tripod head that is filled with hydraulic fluid that smoothes the motion of the camera head.

focal length The size of the angle of view of the lens, measured in millimeters. The smaller the number, the wider the lens. Zoom lenses have a range of focal lengths.

focal plane The area in a camera onto which light is focused. In a film camera, the film rests on the focal plane; in a digital video camera, the CCD rests on the focal plane.

focus ring A rotatable ring on the lens of a camera that allows for manual focusing. Ideally, a focus ring should have distance markings so that you can perform more complicated manual focus effects such as pulling or racking focus.

foley The process of creating and recording ambient sound effects in real-time while the video or film plays. Foley work is usually performed by two or more foley artists on a foley stage equipped with special surfaces and props (named for Jack Foley, the originator of the technique).

footcandles A measurement of the amount of illumination falling on a subject, using the English measuring system. *See also* lux.

fps Fps, or frames per second, is used to describe the speed at which film and video play. Film plays at 24fps, PAL video at 25fps, and NTSC video at 29.97fps.

frame One complete film or video image. Moving images need at least 18 frames per second to appear as full-motion and 24fps to allow for sync sound. NTSC video plays at 29.97fps and PAL video at 25fps.

frame accuracy The ability of a device, particularly a VTR, to accurately perform edits on a specific frame. Non-frame accurate VTRs might miss the mark by one or more frames.

frame rate When speaking of video or film recording, the number of frames per second that are recorded (and then played back).

frequency An audio signal is made up of different frequencies, or wavelengths, that yield the high (or treble), mid, and low (or bass) tones. The human voice resides mostly in the mid-tones. Light is also composed of different frequencies, which appear to the human eye as different colors.

fresnel lens A lens attached to a light that allows for focusing the beam of light.

f-stop A measure of the size of a camera's aperture. The higher the f-stop, the smaller the aperture.

gain The strength (or amplitude) of an audio or video signal.

gain boost A method of electronically increasing the strength, or amplitude, of an audio or video signal. In video, the image gets brighter but has more visible noise.

garbage matte A special matte used to knock out extraneous objects in a compositing shot. Garbage mattes are usually applied to a blue-screen shot before chroma-keying. They can be used to eliminate props, mic booms, and other objects that can't be eliminated through keying.

gate A special type of audio filter that only allows a specific range of frequencies to pass. Also, the mechanism that holds a frame of film in place behind the camera or projector's lens.

gel frame A metal frame that holds lighting gels in front of the light.

Glidecam A camera-stabilizing mechanism similar to a Steadicam.

globes The professional term for *lightbulb*.

green screen Same as blue screen, but used for those occasions where you need to have blue elements in your foreground.

green spill The same as blue spill, except that it occurs with a green screen as a backdrop, rather than a blue screen.

h.264 A high-quality HD codec that is popular as both an acquisition format and a delivery format for the Web and Blu-ray Discs.

handheld microphone The typical handheld mic used by rock stars, comedians, and wandering talk show hosts. Usually an omnidirectional, dynamic microphone.

handles Extra footage at the head and tail of each shot that allow the editor room to add dissolves and manipulate the pacing of a scene.

hard cut An edit from one shot to another without any type of transition in between, such as a dissolve.

hard light Light from a direct, focused light source.

HD Acronym for high-definition video, a type of digital video defined as having a resolution that is greater than that of standard-definition (SD) video, or 720 $\times$ 480 pixels.

HDCAM A high-definition digital video format developed by Sony as an upgrade of the popular Digital Betacam format. HDCAM-SR is currently the most popular delivery format for digital videotape.

HDTV High-definition television, a subgroup of the DTV digital television broadcast standard that has a 16:9 aspect ratio, a resolution of either 1280 $\times$ 720 or 1920 $\times$ 1080, a frame rate of 23.96, 24, 29.97, 30, 59.95, or 60fps and either interlaced or progressive scanning.

HDV A video format that can record high-definition video on standard DV tapes. HDV was designed as an affordable interim format for producers who are trying to make the transition from SD to HD.

HMI lights High-powered arc lights used to simulate daylight. The lights at a baseball stadium are HMI lights.

horizontal blanking interval The part of the analog composite video signal between the end of the image information on one horizontal scan line and the start of the image information on the next horizontal scan line.

horizontal delay A display feature available on professional video monitors that shows the video signal offset horizontally, so as to allow the editor to see and analyze the horizontal sync pulses. *See also* vertical delay.

horizontal line resolution The number of lines in the visible portion of the video signal.

horizontal sync The sync pulses in the video signal that regulate the movement and position of the electron beam as it draws each horizontal scan line across the video monitor.

hot-swapping Replacing a peripheral without shutting off the computer's power. Note: Not all peripherals are hot-swappable!

HSB Just as colors can be defined by specifying RGB (red, green, and blue) values, colors can also be defined by specifying hue, saturation, and brightness. Many color pickers allow you to switch to an HSB mode. For some operations, selecting a color is easier in one mode than in another.

hue The shade of a color.

IDE drives Hard drives that adhere to the IDE interface specification.

IE1394 *See* FireWire.

IEEE-1394 A high-speed serial interface that can be used to attach DV cameras, storage devices, printers, or networks to a computer.

I-frame A video compression term. An intermediate frame between two keyframes. I-frames store only the data that has changed from the previous frame.

iLink Sony's name for the IEEE-1394 specification.

illumination The amount of light cast on a subject.

in-betweening The process of calculation (or interpolation) that is required to generate all of the frames between two keyframes in an animation.

incidental light Light that comes from a direct source, such as the sun, a light, and so forth.

infrared The area beyond red, outside of the visible part of the color spectrum.

in-point The starting point of an edit.

insert edit An edit onto analog videotape that does not replace the control track and allows for the separate editing of video, audio, and timecode. *See also* assemble edit.

insert mode In most NLEs, a method of editing in the timeline that allows the placement of a shot between two shots without covering up what's already there. Instead, the second shot (and all the shots following it) are pushed down the timeline to accommodate the new clip. *See also* overwrite mode.

intensity (of light) The strength of a light source, measured in candelas.

interface The controls and windows that you use to operate a program.

interframe compression A sophisticated type of digital video compression algorithm that uses keyframes to reduce file sizes while maintaining image quality.

interlace scan The process of scanning a frame of video in which one field containing half the horizontal lines is scanned, followed by another field that contains the other half of the horizontal lines, adding up to a complete frame of video.

interlaced *See* interlace scan.

interleaving The process of alternating data across multiple discs, as in an array.

intermediate codecs Codecs used primarily for editing, as opposed to acquisition or distribution.

internegative An intermediary step sometimes necessary in film processing. The camera negative is printed and a new negative, the internegative, is made (or struck) from that print. The internegative (or IN) is then used to create more prints.

interpositive An intermediary step sometimes necessary in film processing. The camera negative is printed and this print, called the interpositive (IP), is used to create a new negative. The release prints are then struck from that negative.

intraframe compression A type of digital video compression algorithm that compresses each frame individually.

iris Synonymous with *aperture*. The iris is the physical mechanism that can be opened or closed to change the size of the aperture. "Irising down," for example, means to close down the iris (go to a higher f-stop).

IRQ Special addressing information used by peripherals attached to a Windows-based computer. Each peripheral must have its own IRQ.

ISA slot A type of expansion slot used in Windows-based computers.

ISO-9660 A format for writing CD-ROMs. Can be read by either Mac or Windows-based computers.

ITU-R 601 *See* BT. 601.

JKL A way of editing using the J, K, and L keys on the computer keyboard. Allows for fast shuttling through clips in an NLE.

JP2K *See* JPEG 2000.

JPEG 2000 A newer codec intended to replace MJPEG and used in digital cinema delivery.

Kelvin scale A temperature scale used by scientists. The color temperature of light is described in degrees Kelvin.

key effect Different types of "keys" can be used to render parts of a video clip transparent, thus exposing any underlying video. *See* chroma key and luminance key.

keyframe In animation, keyframes allow you to explicitly define the parameters of each property of each element in the animation (motion, position, transparency, etc.). The computer will automatically calculate the changes that occur between each keyframe. *See* in-betweening. In video compression, a keyframe is a non-interpolated, spatially compressed frame.

keyframe interval When compressing video, the frequency at which a keyframe will occur.

kinescope A method of making a film copy of a videotape by recording the image off a video monitor.

Kino-Flo lights Color-corrected fluorescent light tubes used to replace normal fluorescent light tubes when shooting at a location that will have fluorescent lights visible in the shot.

LANC (or Ctrl-L) A device control protocol most commonly found on consumer equipment and incapable of frame accuracy. (*See also* RS-422 and RS-232).

latitude The size of the gray scale ranging from darkest black to brightest white. The human eye sees more latitude than can be recorded on film or video.

lavalier A small, clip-on mic; usually an omnidirectional, condensor microphone.

layback The process of recording the finished audio back onto the master videotape after sweetening. With the digital formats, the process of reuniting audio and video tracks after separate editing of each.

LCD (liquid crystal display) The type of display used as a viewfinder on most cameras. In terms of cameras, LCD usually refers to a small, flip-out screen, as opposed to the optical viewfinder.

LED (light emitting diode) A type of light source based on semiconductors that requires very little power and emits very little heat. LED lights for film and video consist of hundreds of tiny bulbs that fit into an electrical circuit.

lens Usually a series of separate glass lenses, the lens on a camera focuses light onto the focal plane to create an image.

letterboxing The process of putting black bars at the top and bottom of the screen to change a 4:3 aspect ratio image to a wider aspect ratio image.

light kit A set of professional lights, light stands, and lighting accessories, usually contained in a heavy-duty carrying case.

light meter A small, handheld device used to measure the illumination at a particular location; usually measured in footcandles or lux, which can then be translated to f-stops.

lighting gel Translucent pieces of special colored plastic used to change the brightness and color of a light source.

linear editing Editing using linear media—tape to tape—as opposed to using random access media stored on a computer hard drive. All tape is linear, so linear media can be either digital or analog.

locking picture The process of formally finalizing the editing of a film for story, so that the sound editors can start working without have to deal with any changes in timing.

logging The process of recording the contents of each field tape using timecode, shot names, and descriptions; the first step in the editing process.

long shot A shot that plays out over a long period of time.

looping The process of re-recording dialogue in a studio. Called "looping" because the actor sometimes watches a continuous loop of the scene that is being re-recorded. Also known as *ADR*, for *automatic dialogue replacement*.

lossless Used to denote a form of compression that does not degrade the quality of the image being compressed.

lossy Used to denote a form of compression that degrades the quality of the image being compressed.

lower thirds *See* Chryon.

LTC An acronym for *longitudinal timecode*, a type of timecode that is recorded onto the audio track of a videotape.

luma clamping *See* luminance clamping.

luma key *See* luminance key.

luminance The strength (or amplitude) of the grayscale (or brightness) portion of a video signal.

luminance clamping The process of clamping (or clipping, or scaling) the luminance value in a video signal. In video that has been luma clamped, luminance values over 235 are eliminated, frequently resulting in video with bright areas that look like solid blobs of white.

luminance key A special key function that will use the luminance values in a layer to determine the transparency of that layer. For example, a luminance key could be set to render the darkest areas of the layer transparent.

lux A metric measurement of the amount of illumination on a subject. *See also* footcandles.

M&E Acronym for *music, and effects*, a four-channel, split audio mix that allows for easy remixing in case the audio needs to be dubbed in a foreign language.

Master shot A wide shot that contains all of the action in particular scene, which is used as the basis for building the scene.

micro four-thirds A system of lenses and image sensors that results in smaller, lighter cameras (and lenses).

mix The way that several audio tracks or streams are combined. Stereo mixes are balanced to the right and left, while surround sound mixes are designed to replicate the 3D sound that we hear in real life.

M-JPEG *See* MJPEG.

MJPEG An older lossy, high-quality codec that can deliver full-motion, full-frame video.

mono sound A single channel or stream of audio.

montage In editing, the process of juxtaposing two shots against each other to arrive at an effect different from what each shot would imply on its own.

motherboard The main circuit board inside a computer.

motion blur When an object moves quickly, it will look blurrier. Individual frames of video or film should show a certain amount of blur around moving objects. Motion blur is usually the result of average shutter speeds (1/60th to 1/125th of a second). Faster shutter speeds will result in less motion blur; slower shutter speeds will result in more. A lack of motion blur will result in stuttery, stroboscopic motion.

MPEG A lossy, high-quality family of codecs. MPEG-1 is used for the VCD format; MPEG-2 is used for DVD format video. MPEG-4 comes in two flavors: highly compressed Web video (MPEG-4 part 2) and high-quality HD video (MPEG-4 part 10).

ND *See* neutral density.

negative cutter The person who physically cuts the film negative to conform to the final cut.

neon light A light consisting of a glass tube filled with neon gas, which varies in color.

net A large screen used to decrease the strength of the light falling on the subject; usually used for exterior shoots.

neutral density A lens filter or lighting gel that tones down brightness without changing the color temperature.

NLE *See* non-linear editing system.

noise Unwanted data in a video or audio signal, often an artifact of signal processing such as gain boosting. Video noise looks like rapidly moving pixels, or snow, and audio noise sounds like a hiss or hum.

non-destructive editing Any form of editing (video or audio) that leaves your original source material unaltered.

non-linear editing system A digital editing system that uses a software interface and digitized audio and video stored on a hard drive. An NLE allows for random access, non-linearity, and non-destructive editing.

notch A special type of audio filter that can eliminate a specific, defined frequency of sound.

NTSC An acronym for *National Television Standards Committee*, NTSC is the oldest analog broadcast video standard for North America and Japan, with a frame rate of 29.97fps and 525 horizontal scan lines.

NTSC legal Refers to colors that fit within the NTSC guidelines for broadcast television. A vectorscope is used to determine if an image is within the NTSC legal color boundaries.

NTSC monitor *See* NTSC/PAL monitor.

NTSC/PAL monitor Analog video monitors and television sets that were popular prior to the advent of HDTV.

off-line clip An off-line clip is one that has been logged but does not have any audio or video media attached to it, whether that is because it hasn't been captured yet or because the media has been deleted.

off-line editing Off-line editing means working in a draft mode with the intention of eventually taking the project to a better resolution and possibly better videotape format in order to do a final pass that will improve its look, quality, and polish.

omnidirectional microphone A mic that picks up sounds from all directions.

OIS *See* optical image stabilization.

one-light print A one-light print is a film print created from the film negative. A single, constant, optimized light setting (for example, one light) is used for the red, green, and blue lights used to create the print.

onion-skinning Some animation programs can display semi-opaque overlays of previous frames. These "onion-skin" frames can be used as a reference for drawing or retouching the current frame.

online editing Creation of the final master, whatever the means or format involved, usually conformed from the original production footage using an EDL.

operating system The low-level program that controls the communication between all of the subsystems (storage, memory, video, peripherals, etc.) in your computer.

optical disc A type of digital storage media that uses lasers to read data. Variations include CDs, DVDs, Blu-ray Discs, and the Sony Professional Disc format.

optical image stabilization A special optical apparatus in a camera that attempts to compensate for shaking and vibrating by altering the camera's optical properties on-the-fly to compensate for camera movement. Because OIS doesn't alter your image data, there is no image degradation.

optical viewfinder On a camera, the eyepiece that you look through to frame a shot, as opposed to the flip-out LCD viewfinder present on some cameras.

opticals Special effects that are traditionally added by an "optical" department; usually, these are effects that are added through a separate optical printing pass. Lightning bolts, light flares, glows, and halos are all traditional optical effects that can now be performed through roto-scoping or with the application of custom filters.

out-point The end point of an edit.

overexposure Refers to video or film that was shot with too much light, or the wrong camera settings, resulting in a whitish, washed-out, faded-looking image.

overlapping edit An edit where the picture ends before or after the sound ends. Also called an *L-cut* or a *split-edit.*

overscan All video formats scan more image than they need to compensate for the fact that not all monitors and televisions display images at exactly the same size. Overscan is a big problem with older analog NTSC monitors, but also still a problem, although to a lesser degree, with HD monitors.

overwrite mode In most NLEs, a method of editing that allows the placement of a shot that covers up anything that was previously occupying that space in the timeline. *See also* insert mode.

P2 card A proprietary solid-state storage card used in certain Panasonic cameras.

PAL An acronym for *Phase Alternate by Line,* an analog television standard used in most of Europe and Asia, with a frame rate of 25fps and 625 horizontal scan lines, resulting in somewhat higher quality video than NTSC.

PAL Monitor *See* NTSC/PAL monitor.

pan To rotate the camera left and right around the camera's vertical axis.

parabolic A special type of mic that can be used to record sounds from great distances.

patch bay A rack of video and audio input and output connectors that make it easier to reconfigure the hardware in an editing system.

PCM (Pulse Code Modulation) A process for encoding lossless digital audio, used by high-end digital audio file formats such as WAVE and AIFF.

pedestal To raise the camera up or down; it's also a setup for black levels.

phono connector A medium-sized, single-prong connector used primarily for analog audio, especially headphones. Also known as *1/4" connector.*

pistol grip tripod A tripod with a head that is controlled by a single pistol-grip mechanism. Such heads can be freely rotated around all axes simultaneously, making it very difficult to perform a smooth motion along a single axis.

pixel Short for *picture element.* A single point on your screen.

pixel dimensions The size of a digital image or frame of video, as measured in pixels and described as width × height. Also referred to as *resolution.*

platform The computer hardware/OS combination that you have chosen to work on.

plug-ins Special effects and add-ons that can be added to a host application. *See* filters.

polarizer A lens filter that polarizes the light coming into the lens. Can be used to increase saturation and to eliminate reflections in glass or water.

post house *See* postproduction facility.

postproduction facility A service bureau that provides editing and other postproduction facilities and services.

practical light A light source that is both part of the scenery and a source of light for the camera.

preroll The process of rewinding the videotape to a cue point several seconds prior to the in-point, so that playback of the tape is stabilized and up to full speed when the tape reaches the in-point.

prime lens A lens with fixed focal length.

prism A special optical construct (usually a single piece of glass) that can split light into its component parts.

production board A hard-backed set of spreadsheets designed specifically for organizing film production.

production designer The designer who is responsible for the look of the entire production. Supervises the set decorators, costumes, and other visual artists.

production strip A removable color-coded paper strip that fits into the spreadsheet layout of the production board and allows for easy reorganization.

progressive scan A type of video display where each horizontal line is scanned consecutively from top to bottom, resulting in a full frame of video without the need for fields. (Compare to interlaced scan.)

prop Short for *property*, a prop is any object on the set that is used by the actors, such as a knife, as opposed to set dressing and scenery, which provides a backdrop for the action.

proxy A placeholder; usually used in editing programs to take the place of video that has yet to be shot, or that has yet to be ingested at the highest quality.

pull focus Pull (or pulling) focus is a technique used to change focal lengths during a large camera or subject move, such as a dolly. The camera assistant literally moves the lens to compensate for the camera/subject movement so that the subject remains in focus throughout the shot.

QuickTime A software architecture for displaying and manipulating time-based data (such as video and audio) on a computer.

R3D *See* REDCODE RAW.

rack focus A shot where the focus is set on an object in the background and then the focus is pulled, or racked, to an object in the foreground (or vice versa).

radio cut An edit of a scene based on dialogue only, disregarding whether the picture works or not. The idea being that the result should play like an old-fashioned radio show.

RAID (redundant array of independent discs) A group of hard drives that have been arranged to act like a single, very fast storage device.

RAM (random access memory) The electronic memory inside your computer used to hold programs and data when working.

RCA connector A small, single-prong connector most commonly used to carry analog composite video and unbalanced audio signals.

reaction A shot of a person reacting to the dialogue or action in the scene.

Real Media A special streaming video and audio architecture created by Real, Inc.

real-time A function, such as playback or recording, that occurs immediately without the need for rendering and without any speeding up of the process, such as 4x (quadruple speed) recording.

real-time editing Editing that can happen in real-time. That is, effects and edits do not have to be calculated or rendered before they can be seen.

REDCODE RAW A digital cinema codec developed for the Red Digital Cinema Camera Company and capable of recording 4K digital video. Also known as *R3D*.

reflective light Light that comes from an indirect source, such as a bounce card, the sky (but not the sun), and so forth. *See also* incidental light.

reflector A shiny board or fabric used to redirect a bright light source, such as the sun.

RGB color space The range of colors that can be displayed and recorded by your computer.

rolling shutter effect A type of digital image artifact common to cameras with CMOS image sensors (such as DSLR cameras).

room tone The sound of the room in which a scene was recorded. During a shoot, the sound recorder will record roughly one minute's worth of the quieted location to create an "empty" sound with the right atmosphere. This sound will be used by the dialogue editor to fill spaces between edits.

rotoscoping The process of painting over existing frames of video or film. Used for everything from painting in special effects to painting custom-made mattes for compositing.

rough cut An early edit of a project, as opposed to the final cut.

route An electronic patching system for audio and video equipment.

RS-232 A serial device control protocol that allows for computers to control video decks and other hardware. RS-232 is most commonly used for low-end professional and consumer equipment.

RS-422 A serial device control protocol that allows for computers to control video decks and other hardware. RS-422 is the standard for professional equipment. It carries the SMPTE timecode signal and is capable of frame accuracy.

RT11 A floppy disk format used by older high-end linear online editing equipment to store EDLs.

SAG Acronym for the *Screen Actors' Guild*, a union representing actors and other performers.

saturated colors The technical term for bright, bold colors is saturated. For example, a pure red is saturated, while pink and maroon are desaturated reds.

saturation The amount of color in the video signal.

screen correction shot A shot of a blue-screen or green-screen stage that has no actors in it. Screen correction shots are used by compositing software to help create a more accurate key effect.

scrim A lighting accessory used to tone down the brightness of a light. Single scrims dim the light by 1/2 f-stop, and double scrims dim the light by a full f-stop. Half scrims are a half-moon shape, to allow for further manipulation of the light.

SCSI (small computer systems interface) An interface standard for connecting hard drives and other peripherals. Comes in many different flavors, including SCSI-2, Ultra-SCSI, and Ultrawide-SCSI.

SCSI IDs When using SCSI devices, each device on the SCSI chain must have its own, unique SCSI ID. A SCSI port can support up to seven devices.

SD (secure digital) card A small solid-state memory card used in small digital still cameras and camcorders.

SD video Digital video with a resolution of 720 × 480 pixels or less.

SDI An acronym for *Serial Digital Interface*, SDI is the professional digital video standard I/O protocol with a data rate of either 270Mbps or 360Mbps. (*See also* FireWire.) SDI-HD has a data rate of 1.458Gbps or higher and supports the transfer of full HD video I/O.

SDTV An acronym for *Standard Definition Television*, a subgroup of the DTV broadcast standard designed as a digital update of the current NTSC standard.

seamless edit A style of editing where the edits appear natural and do not call attention to themselves. A traditional Hollywood movie dialogue scene is usually seamlessly edited.

SECAM An acronym for *Sequence Colour à Memoire*, SECAM is an analog broadcast television standard for France, Russia, and much of Eastern Europe.

sequence An assembly of shots edited together.

sharpening In a video camera, a special algorithm that is applied to the video image to make it sharper.

shooting ratio The ratio of the length of footage shot to the length of the final film. For example, a project with a 5:1 ratio would have shot five hours of footage for a one-hour long final project.

shot list A list of the shots a director plans to shoot on a particular day of filming or taping; usually, a shot list is derived by carefully going over the script, the storyboard, and blocking the scene with the actors in rehearsals.

shotgun A very directional mic that is often affixed to the front of the camera or to a boom or fishpole.

shutter In a camera, a rotating plate that opens and closes to control how long the focal plane is exposed to light. There is no physical shutter in a digital video camera; instead, the camera's CCD samples light for an appropriate length of time, and then shuts off.

shutter speed The speed of the rotation of the shutter inside the lens, measured in rotations per second.

sides A dialogue-only version of a script, used to make readings easier for actors.

signal Electronic information (video or audio) that is passed from one device to another.

single-chip A camera that uses a single CCD to gather all three (red, green, and blue) of the signals that will be used to create a full-color image.

single-field resolution Some low-resolution codecs cut down the size of the captured video files by discarding one field for each frame of video. The resulting single-field video plays fairly well, but contains half the information of two-field video.

sixty-cycle tone (60Hz) Sixty-cycle tone, or 60Hz tone, is used as an audio reference to calibrate the audio levels on editing equipment and speakers. Typically, the 60Hz tone should fall at 0dB on a VU meter.

skylight The ambient light from the sky, which consists of the reflected light of the sun. On a cloudy day, there is no sunlight, but there is still skylight.

slating When recording the sound separately from the video or film, the process of holding a slate in front of the camera. On the slate are written the scene and take numbers. The top of the slate can be clapped to produce a distinct sound that will be used for syncing the audio and video.

slow reveal A moving shot, often a pan or dolly, that reveals something slowly, such as a slow pan of a bathroom that reveals a dead person in the bathtub.

slow-motion A shot that plays at a slower speed than full-motion film or video; usually described as a percentage of full motion.

SLR camera A single lens reflex camera. Unlike a camera with a separate viewfinder, in an SLR camera, you actually look through the lens at your subject. A 35mm still camera with removable lenses is typically an SLR.

slugline In a screenplay, the first line of a scene. Identifies whether the scene is interior or exterior, the location, and the time of day, all in uppercase letters.

SMPTE The Society of Motion Picture and Television Engineers, an organization that has developed many of the technical standards for film and video in the United States, including the specifications for timecode, SMPTE timecode.

snow The image that results from a video signal that lacks a control track. Also known as *noise*.

soft light Light from a diffuse, often indirect light source.

Sorenson compressor A lossy but very high quality QuickTime codec.

source monitor The monitor or window that displays the unedited source footage, as opposed to the destination (or record) monitor, which plays the edited sequence.

SP-DIF Short for *Sony/Phillips Digital Interface*, a digital audio format used for consumer equipment.

spec A screenplay or teleplay written on speculation, or with the hope of eventually selling it, as opposed to writing a work for hire.

spin rate Measured in revolutions per minute, the speed at which a hard drive spins.

split-track dialog Dialogue that is spread across several separate tracks, rather than mixed onto a single track. Usually, split-track dialogue has one track dedicated to each actor, or if the dialogue is checkerboarded, two tracks dedicated to each actor.

spot meter A type of light meter that measures reflective light rather than incidental light.

spotting Watching a locked-picture edit of your project with the intent of identifying all of the sound effect and music cues that will be needed.

steadicam A special camera mount that provides hydraulic, gimbaled support for a camera. Allows steady, fluid motion of the camera.

stereo Audio with two channels or streams, balanced to the right and left to mimic the way humans hear sound in real life.

stereoscopic *See* 3D.

storage Non-volatile storage that is used for long-term holding of programs and data; usually magnetic or optical.

streaming video Video that is downloaded, on-demand, interactively, to the viewer's computer.

striped drives Hard drives that have been indexed with special information so that they can be used as an array.

strobing The odd, stuttery motion caused by fast shutter speeds. Strobing appears because of a lack of motion blur.

subtractive color A color mixing system used by ink and paint where the more colors you mix together, the darker they get until you get black. The primary colors of paint are red, yellow, and blue. The primary colors of modern printing inks are cyan, yellow, and magenta.

sunlight The light from the sun.

super To superimpose; usually used to refer to the process of superimposing a title over an image.

supercardioid A very narrow cardioid pattern that indicates that a mic is very directional.

surround sound 6- or 8-channel audio that mimics the sound of a 3D environment, used for theatrical projection and also in home theaters.

S-video connector A proprietary cable used to carry the Y/C video signal.

sweetening The process of polishing the audio on a project by adding effects, equalizing, and fine-tuning edits.

sync Short for *synchronization*, the electronic pulses used to coordinate the operation of several interconnected pieces of video hardware. Also, the electronic pulses used to regulate the playback of the videotape in the VTR. *See also* sync sound.

sync sound Recorded sound and video that are synchronized together, whether onto the same tape or by two or more separate recording devices.

Tb *See* terabyte.

TBC Acronym for *time base corrector*, an electronic device used to correct video signal instability during videotape playback. Most modern professional VTRs have internal TBCs.

telecine The process of transferring film to videotape.

telephoto lens A lens with a very narrow field of view (and, therefore, a long focal length). Telephoto lenses magnify objects in their field of view. Typically, lenses with focal lengths greater than 70mm (equivalent to a 35mm film camera) are considered wide angle.

terabyte 1,000 gigabytes.

termination A connector used at the end of a SCSI chain. The last device in a SCSI chain must have a terminator. Bad termination can result in the entire SCSI chain malfunctioning.

textless master A videotape master that has no titles or any other text in it. Used for foreign language versions.

three-act structure A type of story structure based on the idea that each story has a beginning, middle, and end. *See also* 3-act structure.

three-chip A camera that uses three separate CCDs to gather separate red, green, and blue data.

three-point editing A method of editing where each edit is performed using an in- and an out-point on both the source footage and the edited sequence. Once the editor enters three of the four in- and out-points, the NLE or edit controller will automatically calculate the fourth in- and out-point.

three-point lighting The standard way to light a person using a strong directed key light, a diffuse, less intense fill light, and a strong backlight.

throughput A measure of the speed at which data can be moved through a computer or storage system.

Thunderbolt A high-speed data transfer protocol capable of moving media at the rate of 10Gbps in two directions (in and out).

tilt To rotate the camera up and down around its horizontal axis.

timecode Timecode is a numbering system encoded in the video signal itself. It measures time in the following format: hh:mm:ss:ff, where h = hours, m = minutes, s = seconds, and f = frames.

timeline A chronological display of an edited sequence in a non-linear editing system.

title safe Another guide similar to the action-safe area, the title-safe area is slightly smaller. To ensure that your titles are visible on any monitor, always make certain that they fall within the title-safe area.

transcoder A device or piece of software that changes the video signal from one format to another, such as from component to composite or from analog to digital or from one codec to another.

transcoding The process of taking a digital media file and re-encoding it with a different codec.

transfer mode The type of calculation that will be used to determine how layers that are stacked on top of one another will combine.

traveling matte A matte that changes over time to follow the action of a moving element. Traveling mattes are used to composite a moving element into a scene. In the digital world, an animated alpha channel serves the same function as a traveling matte.

trim mode The process of adjusting, or fine-tuning an existing edit in an NLE.

TRS connector The small audio interface used in earbuds and other small audio devices. A scaled-down version of 1/4" phono connectors. Also known as *mini connectors*.

t-stop Similar to f-stops, t-stops are used to calibrate motion picture lenses and are specially designed to account for the amount of light absorbed by the lens itself. For practical purposes, this means that cinema lenses can be changed and the t-stop setting can remain unchanged.

tungsten light Light from an incandescent source, such as a household light bulb. Tungsten light is weaker than daylight, and tends to have a warm cast.

turnkey system A video editing system that is preconfigured and assembled.

tweening *See* in-betweening.

UltraATA A type of hard drive interface. Not as fast as SCSI, but fast enough for DV.

ultraviolet The area beyond violet on the color spectrum, beyond the range of visible light.

uncompressed video Video that has not had any compression applied to it, either by the camera or by a computer.

underscan A display feature available on professional video monitors that allows the viewer to see the complete video signal, including the sync pulses.

unidirectional A mic that picks up sounds from a particular direction.

USB (Universal Serial Bus) A standard for attaching serial devices such as keyboards, disk drives, and some types of storage. USB devices can also be used to digitize Web-resolution video clips.

UV filter A filter that can be attached to the front of the lens. Filters out excess ultraviolet light and serves to protect the lens from scratching and breaking.

vacuum tubes Before the invention of the CCD, video cameras used vacuum tubes to convert light into electronic signals.

VCD (video compact disc) A format for storing 70 minutes of full-frame, full-motion, MPEG1 compressed video on a normal compact disc or recordable compact disc.

vectorscope A special monitor or software display for calibrating the hue, or color information, in a video signal.

vertical banding Bright vertical smears that can occur in some video cameras when the camera is pointed at a very bright source.

vertical blanking interval The period during which the video image goes blank as the electron beam returns from scanning one field of analog interlaced video to start scanning the next field. This "empty" space in the analog video signal is sometimes used to store VITC timecode, closed captioning, and other information.

vertical delay A display feature available on professional video monitors that shows the video signal offset vertically so as to allow the editor to see and analyze the vertical sync pulses. *See also* horizontal delay.

vertical line resolution The number of horizontal lines in a frame of video.

vertical sync The sync pulses in the video signal that control the field by field scanning of each frame of interlaced video.

VGA monitor The monitor attached to your computer.

Video for Windows A software architecture for displaying and manipulating time-based data (such as video and audio) on a computer.

virtual memory A process by which disk space can be used as a substitute for RAM.

VITC (vertical interleave timecode) Timecode that is encoded in the vertical blanking interval of the video signal.

VTR Video tape recorder, the professional term for VCR.

VU meter Volume unit meter. The volume meters on a sound recording device. VU meters help you gauge whether you are recording acceptable audio levels.

wattage A measurement of the amount of electrical power used by a light, which determines the light's intensity.

waveform monitor A special monitor or software display for calibrating the brightness, or luminance, of a video signal. Waveform monitors are used to set the proper white and black levels.

white balance When a camera has been calibrated to correctly display white, then the camera is white balanced. Once it is calibrated for white, other colors should display properly.

white level The peak level of the luminance (or gray scale) of the video signal; in other words, the brightest part of the image, usually set at 100 IRE.

wide angle lens A lens with a very wide field of view (and, therefore, a short focal length). Typically, the smaller the focal length of the lens (measured in millimeters), the wider the angle.

widescreen Footage that's shot with a 16:9 aspect ratio (or wider). Most film features are shot in a wide-screen aspect ratio.

wild sound Non-sync sound recorded by hand "in the wild" using a portable recording system.

wipe A type of transition effect where one image is wiped over another.

XDCAM An HD acquisition format that is recorded on optical discs or memory cards.

XLR cable *See* XLR connector.

XLR connectors Three-pronged, balanced audio connectors for connecting mics and other recording equipment.

Index

Numbers

1:1 compression ratio, 49
1.33:1 aspect ratio, 43
1.6:1-10:1 compression ratio, 49
1.85:1 aspect ratio, 40
2K
    resolution, 39
    video recording, 35–36
2-shot, storyboarding, 100
3D cameras, 74–75
3D effects, 265
4:1:1 color sampling rate, 49
4:2:0 color sampling rate, 49
4:2:2 color sampling ratio, 48–49
4:3 aspect ratio, 40, 43
4:4:4 color sampling ratio, 48
16:9 aspect ratio, 40
24P
    considering, 59
    digital video, 37
29.97fps color signal, 45
35mm film prints
    answer print, 438–439
    direct-to-print, 439
    film math, 439
    film transfers, 437
    optical soundtracks, 439
    printing from negatives, 438
    printing process, 438

180° axis, crossing, 169
640 × 480 resolution, 43
720 resolution, 35–36
720 × 480 resolution, 43
720/24p HD video, 41
1080 resolution, 35–36, 59
1080/60i HD video, 41
1080p HD video, pixels in, 46
1280 × 720 resolution, 35–36
1920 × 1080 resolution, 35–36
2001 A Space Odyssey, 41
2048 × 1080 resolution, 39

A

AC (first assistant camera), role of, 204
Acme Studios script, 20
acquisition formats
    Apple ProRes, 58
    ArriRAW, 58
    AVCHD, 57
    AVC-Intra, 57
    Avid DNxHD, 58
    DV, 57
    DVCPRO-HD, 57
    HDCAM, 57
    HDV, 57
    intermediate, 58
    MPEG-IMX, 57

acquisition formats *(continued)*
  Red R3D, 58
  XDCAM HD, 57
"Action!," calling, 205
action, matching, 306
actors
  creating sides for, 21
  lighting, 132–135
  respecting, 205–207
Acts I-III, three-act structure, 15–16, 18
Adobe After Effects software, 376
Adobe Premiere codecs, 50, 52
Adobe Premiere Pro editing program, 268
ADR (automatic dialogue replacement),
  332
aerials, 223
Allen, Woody, 314, 372
alpha channels, compositing, 396–398
Amelie, 125
American Beauty, 112
analog NTSC video, frame rate of, 45
analog sound wave, 43
analog video
  versus DV video, 246
  frame rate, 44
  interlaced, 44
analog/SD footage
  aspect ratio, 43
  resolution, 43
animatics, using in effects, 118
answer print, 438–439
aperture
  controls, 76, 79
  f-stop markings, 154
  size of, 153
Apocalypse Now, 112
Apple Final Cut Pro editing program, 268
Apple Motion software, 376
Apple Pro Res acquisition format, 58
archiving projects, 441
Arri Alexa digital camera, 66
ArriRAW acquisition format, 58
art directing, 113–114

aspect ratio
  considering, 162
  digital video, 40
audience, knowing, 26
audio
  5.1 surround sound, 419
  7.1 surround sound, 419
  creating final mix, 418–419
  dialogue, 419
  effects, 419
  exporting OMF files, 327
  importing, 282–283
  M&E mix, 419
  mono mix, 418
  moving, 327–328
  music, 419
  perception of, 320
  stereo, 419
  See also sound editing
audio container files, using codecs with, 55
audio editing, 266
  audio effects and filters, 267
  audio plug-in formats, 267
  equalization, 267
  mixing, 267
  OMF export, 268
audio editing hardware
  microphones, 328
  mixing boards, 328
  PCI cards, 328
  speakers, 328
audio equipment
  checklist, 199
  external speakers, 249
  surround sound interface, 249
audio hum, dealing with, 330, 335
audio interfaces, 251
audio levels metering, 320–321
audio media workflow, 237
audio mixing board, 249
audio recording
  camera mic, 228
  crew of one, 199

dialogue, 177
double-system, 227–230
implementing, 197
inputs, 186
overlapping, 309
quality, 178–179
room tone, 198
run-and-gun, 198
to separate devices, 227–228
See also recordings versus mixes; sound editing
audio sampling, 42–43
audio scrubbing, using in editing apps, 260
audio tracks
mono sound, 42
recordings versus mixes, 42
stereo sound, 41
surround sound, 42
auto-focus, using, 145
auto-iris function, 154
automatic dialogue replacement (ADR), 332
A/V screenplay format, 20
AVCHD acquisition format, 57
AVC-Intra acquisition format, 57
Avid DNxHD acquisition format, 58
Avid Media Composer editing program, 268

B

back light, three-point lighting, 123–124, 133
backup systems, including in editing workstations, 246–247
Baghead, 16
Barry Lyndon, 121
base plate, 221
battery backup, using with editing systems, 248
The Battleship Potemkin, 291
beginning/middle/end structure, 15–16
best boy, role of, 205
Birth of a Nation, 291

bit depth, digital image quality, 48
black-and-white effects, 362–363
Blade Runner, 318
The Blair Witch Project, 171–172
blue screen
lighting for, 140–141
shooting effects, 237–238
blur, applying to images, 157
Blu-ray authoring software, 275. *See also* DVD and Blu-ray Discs
blurring, modifying for film look, 365
Bond, James, 95
boom kit, using with mics, 192
boom operators
in multi-cam shooting, 232
responsibility of, 193
BorisFX software, 377
bounce cards, 129
bracketing, defined, 154
Brazil, 112
breakdown sheet, 28
brightness
defined, 346
increasing, 356–357
Brightness/Contrast filter, using, 356
broadcast network TV, 36
budget planning exercise, 117
budgeting articles, downloading, 11
Burden of Dreams, 30, 112

C

camcorders, 73
entry level, 143
shoulder-mount, 144
camera crew
AC (first assistant camera), 204
best boy, 205
camera department, 205
camera operator, 204
cinematographer, 204
dolly grip, 205
DP (directory of photography), 204
electricians, 205

camera crew *(continued)*
    gaffer, 205
    key grip, 205
    PA (production assistant), 205
    second AC, 205
camera department, role of, 205
camera diagrams, 104–107
camera equipment checklist, 158
camera mic audio, recording, 228
camera movement
    considering, 173
    dolly shots, 171
    handholding, 171–172
    panning, 170–171
    tilting, 170–171
    tracking shots, 171
    zooms, 171
camera operator, role of, 204
camera rigging and supports
    aerials, 223
    base plate, 221
    car mounts, 223
    cranes, 223
    dollies, 223
    Glidecams, 223
    jibs, 223
    matte boxes, 221
    riggings, 221–222
    rods, 221
    shotmakers, 223
    sliders, 223
    steadicams, 223
camera settings, double-checking, 205
camera shake
    adding, 401–404
    automatic, 403
    eliminating, 404–405
cameras
    3D, 73–75
    AC adaptors, 86
    aperture control, 79
    audio, 84–85
    auto gain control, 84
    auto limiter, 84

autofocus mechanism, 77
batteries, 86
body types, 73–74
choosing, 91
cost of, 216
depth of field, 65
digital cinema, 74
digital zoom, 72
DP (director of photography), 88
DSLR accessories, 90
DSLRs (digital single lens reflex), 87–88
evaluating, 61
field monitors, 90
filters, 90
focus, 76–77
frame rates, 79
f-stops versus t-stops, 70
with hard drives, 85–86
headphone jack for audio, 84
image quality, 62–68
image stabilization, 81–82
in-camera effects, 83
lighting situations, 64
manual controls, 76
media type, 85
menu interface, 83
microphones, 90
mount lights, 126
prices of, 4
professional shoulder-mount, 74, 76
progressive scan, 79
remote controls, 90
renting versus buying, 75
SD cards, 86
shutter speed, 77–78
single-chip, 63
slow motion, 79
specialty, 74
synchronizing on sets, 231
testing before shooting, 79
three-chip, 63
tripods, 89
video noise, 64
viewfinder, 82

widescreen, 80

wireless, 86

zebra stripes, 82–83

See also DSLR (digital single lens reflex) cameras; multi-cam shooting; still cameras

camera-top monitors, using on sets, 225

Canon Rebel T2i DSLR camera, 5

car interiors, lighting, 139

car mounts, 223

cardioid patterns for mic, 180

Casablanca, 18

cast. *See* actors

Catfish **documentary,** 24

Cave of Forgotten Dreams, 75

Cb and Cr, role in color sampling, 48

CCDs (charge-coupled devices), 62–64

Celtz **software,** 21

characters, developing, 18

charge-coupled devices (CCDs), 62–64

checkerboarding dialogue tracks, 331

checklists

    audio equipment, 199

    camera equipment, 158

    editing software, 269

    editing systems, 252

    lighting equipment, 137–138

    shooting, 174–175

chroma keys, compositing, 390–394

chromatic aberration, 70

cinema lenses, 71

cinematographer, role of, 204

Citizen Kane, 291

clapping slate board, using, 230

clipping and distortion, 321

close-up (CU), storyboarding, 100

cloud storage, 248

cloud-based filesharing, 275

CMOS (complementary metal-oxide semiconductors), 62, 64

codec data, displaying from QuickTime, 50–51

codecs (COmpressor/DECompressors), 46–47

    asymmetrical, 54

    audio container files, 55

    converting media from, 55–57

    DCT-based, 54

    DV, 54

    interframe, 52–53

    intraframe, 52–53

    JPEG 2000, 54

    lossy and lossless, 52

    MJPEG, 54

    MPEG-1, 54

    MPEG-2, 54

    MPEG-4, 54

    using with uncompressed video, 54

    VC-3 based, 54

    See also compression

color controls, RGB channels, 349

color correction

    applying, 354

    black-and-white effects, 362–363

    brightness, 346–347

    considering, 345

    contrast, 346, 348

    for film, 363

    filters, 347, 354

    footage, 365

    hue, 346–347

    layers, 362

    process of, 346

    saturation, 346

    tracks, 362

    tutorial, 361

    waveforms, 350

color grading, 345

color sampling, 47–49

color temperature, 125

colors

    additive, 353

    creation of, 47

colors *(continued)*
    safe, 353
    seeing, 350–355
    for video, 353
    waveforms, 356
company move, making, 29
complementary metal-oxide semiconductors (CMOS), 62, 64
Composer. *See* **Media Composer**
composers, finding for music, 340–341
compositing, 382
    alpha channels, 396–398
    camera shake, 401–404
    chroma keys, 390–394
    filtered footage, 389
    keying tips, 394–395
    keys, 384–385
    luminance keys, 385–390
    mattes, 396
    muzzle flashes, 387
    non-special special effects, 394
    SD and HD footage, 398–400
    tools, 265
composition, 162–164
    axis of action, 169
    breaking rules, 170
    clearing frames, 169
    defined, 162
    dramatic framing, 167–168
    eyelines, 168
    following versus anticipating, 167
    framing, 164–165
    getting close, 167–168
    headroom, 164
    leading subjects, 164, 166
    listening, 168
    setup shot, 163
    stage line, 169
    tight framing, 167–168
    tutorial, 361
    TV framing, 169
compression, 46–49, 65. *See also* codecs (COmpressor/DECompressors)

compressors, third-party, 275
condenser mics, 182–183
Consumer Electronics **script, structure,** 17
container files, using with digital video, 50
continuity, process of, 208
contrast, defined, 346
controllers, including in editing workstations, 246
conversations, shooting, 168
corporate projects, 9, 25–26
CPU, including in editing workstation, 242
cranes
    features of, 223
    storyboarding, 101
creative writing exercises, 17–18
credits
    end, 367
    opening, 367
Crimes and Misdemeanors, 314
C-stands, 129
CU (close-up), storyboarding, 100
cutaways, 305, 309

D

data rate, digital image quality, 49
database software, 275
day-for-night, lighting, 139
daylight
    enhancing, 137
    mixing with interior light, 135
DCP (Digital Camera Package), 440
DCT-based codecs, 54
Demme, Jonathan, 121, 177
depth of field
    considering, 174
    and exposure, 157–158
    shallow, 65, 157, 218–219
dialogue
    cleaning up transition to, 309–310
    formatting in scripts, 19
    recording, 177
    refining, 307

dialogue editing, 328, 331
    ADR (automatic dialogue replacement), 332
    non-dialogue voice recordings, 332
    See also sound editing
dialogue tracks, checkerboarding, 331
diffusion lens filters, 162
diffusion of light, 131
DigiEffects software, 377
digital, terminology, 48
digital audio. *See* audio
digital camera masters, 438–439
Digital Camera Package (DCP), 440
digital cameras
    2K video, 35–36
    format, 35–36
digital cinema
    cameras, price of, 4, 73
    format, 39
digital files, delivering, 437
digital filmmaking
    big picture, 315
    considerations, 11
    emotion, 315
    rhythm and pacing, 315
    setups and payoffs, 315
    time compression and expansion, 315
digital image quality, 45
    bit depth, 48
    camera, 46
    color sampling, 47–48
    compression, 46–47, 49
    data rate, 49
    display, 46
    editing software, 46
    image sensors, 46
    lens quality, 46
    subject, 46
    See also image quality
digital image stabilization (DIS), 81
digital media files
    audio container files and codecs, 55
    codecs, 50, 52–54
    digital video container files, 50–52

digital rights management (DRM) data, 50
digital single lens reflex (DSLR) cameras.
    See **DSLR** (digital single lens reflex) cameras
digital stills. *See* still images
digital video
    24P, 37
    aspect ratio, 40
    audio tracks, 41
    container files, 50
    film resolution, 39
    frames, 36–37
    horizontal resolution, 39
    mono sound, 42
    pixel shape, 40
    pixels, 38
    recordings versus mixes, 42
    scan lines, 37–38
    stereo sound, 41
    surround sound, 42
    tracks, 36
    uncompressed, 54
    vertical resolution, 38
digital video masters, 435–437
digital zoom, 72
directing, job of, 202–203
Directing Actors, 203
director of photography (DP)
    consulting, 88
    role of, 204
DIS (digital image stabilization), 81
dissolves, 311, 339
distortion and clipping, 321
Do the Right Thing, 109, 112
documentaries, 10
    Catfish, 24
    deductive approach, 24
    field notes, 208
    inductive approach, 24
    interviews, 116
    Lost in La Mancha, 30
    outlining, 25
    previsualizing, 25
    scheduling tasks, 32

documentaries, *(continued)*
    versus scripted features, 32
    scripting, 25
    terminology, 32
    visual planning for, 116–117
Dogtown and Z-boys, 116
Dolby AC-3 audio, 55
dollies, 100–101, 223
dolly grip, role of, 205
dolly shots and zooms, 171
DP (director of photography)
    consulting, 88
    role of, 204
Dr. Strangelove, 41, 174
DRM (digital rights management) data, 50
drop frame timecode, 45
dropouts and pixels, getting rid of, 405
DSLR (digital single lens reflex) cameras, 74,
    87–88
    accessories, 213
    advantages, 212
    apertures, 212
    body of, 88
    Canon Rebel T2i DSLR camera, 5
    changing lenses, 212
    cost of, 4, 87
    and HD format, 5
    lenses, 216–218
    limitations of, 87–88
    making ergonomic, 211
    overheating, 213
    shooting HD video, 213
    versus still cameras, 211–212
    See also cameras
DSLR settings for HD video, 214–215
DV acquisition format, 57
DV codecs, 54
DV Expo trade show, 7
DV format versus HD, 3–4
DV versus analog video, 246
DVCPRO-HD
    acquisition format, 57
    data rate, 49
DVD and Blu-ray Discs
    authoring, 430–431
    compression, 428–429
    deliverables, 432
    DVD-V, 426
    formats, 427–428
    labels, 429
    making viewing copies, 427
    presentation values, 429
    selling point, 427
    See also Blu-ray authoring software
DVD authoring software, 275
dynamic mics, 182

E

Easy A, 338
ECU (extreme close-up), storyboarding, 100
editing
    building rough cuts, 293–294
    development of, 291
    drag-and-drop editing, 293
    fine cutting, 314–315
    multi-cam, 313–314
    project duration, 315
    solving technical problems, 312–313
    for style, 314
    three-act structure, 293
    transitions between scenes, 311–312
    tutorials, 295
    See also rough cut; sound editing
editing app, using for sound, 321–324
editing preparation
    capturing tape-based media, 280–282
    checking components, 288–289
    file-based media, 271–272
    importing and transcoding, 276–280
    importing audio, 282–283
    importing still images, 283–284
    moving media, 284–285
    organizing media, 272–276
    preparing multi-camera media, 288
    sorting media after ingest, 285–286
    synchronizing sound and picture,
        286–287
    troubleshooting, 288–289
editing projects, setting up, 272, 274–276.
    See also projects

editing software
Adobe Premiere Pro, 268
Apple Final Cut Pro, 268
assembling shots, 255–256
Avid Media Composer, 268
checklist, 269
effects, 264–265
finishing tools, 268
importing media, 262–263
interface, 255–256
organizational tools, 261
recommendations, 268
record viewer, 255–256
Sony Vegas, 268
timeline window, 255–256
titles, 266

editing systems
audio equipment, 249
audio interfaces, 251
battery backup, 248
checklist, 252
digital video cables and connectors,
250–252
Fibre Channel, 251
FireWire, 250
HDMI (high-definition multimedia
interface), 250
HD-SDI, 250
networking, 247–249
non-linear, 261
RS-422, 251
SDI (Serial Digital Interface), 250
technical specs, 252
Thunderbolt I/O protocol, 251
See also non-linear systems

editing techniques
avoiding overcutting, 305
cutaways, 305
matching action, 306
matching emotion and tone, 308
matching screen position, 307
overlapping edits, 307–308
pauses and pull-ups, 308–309
reaction shots, 305
sound effects and music, 309

editing tools
audio scrubbing, 260
drag-and-drop editing, 256
insert and overwrite editing, 257
JKL editing, 247
lockable tracks, 261
match frame, 260
multi-camera editing, 259
network editing, 261
ripple and roll, 258
slip and slide, 259
three-point editing, 256–257
trimming, 258

editing troubleshooting
audio and video syncing, 289
audio distortion, 289
audio speed, 289
batch imports, 289
cables, 289
computer, 289
dropped frames, 289
hardware, 289
software settings, 288
stuttery playback, 289
video appearance, 289
video corruption, 289

editing workstation
backing up, 246–247
components, 241, 245
controllers, 246
CPU, 242
keyboards, 246
monitors, 243–244
RAM, 242
storage, 242–243
videotape interface, 244

edits, overlapping, 307
effects
3D, 265
compositing, 265
image enhancement, 265
motion, 265
planning, 117–119
transitions, 264
workflow, 380–382
See also non-special special effects

effects shots, creating, 119

Eisenstein, Sergei, 291

El Mariachi, 305

electret condenser mics, 183

electricians, role of, 205

electronic equipment, grounding, 249

elevator pitch, 22

emotion and tone, 308, 315

EQ (equalizing) filter
    avoiding overuse, 334
    enhancing speech, 333
    reducing hiss, 334
    simulating audio sources, 334
    sweetening, 333
    wind and mic bumps, 334

equipment, considering, 11

establishing shots, placing, 311–312.
    See also shot lists

exposure, 152–153
    aperture, 153–154
    auto-exposure setting, 153
    controlling manually, 153
    defined, 76, 152
    and depth of field, 157–158
    double-checking, 175
    gain, 156
    judging by eye, 152
    shutter speed, 154
    See also overexposure; underexposure

exterior lighting, 137
    enhancing daylight, 137
    golden hour, 137
    See also interior lighting; lighting

EXTerior scene, indicating in script, 19

extreme close-up (ECU), storyboarding, 100

eyelines, matching in close-ups, 168

Eyes Wide Shut, 115

F

fades, 311

feature films
    scripted, 10
    structure, 16

Fibre Channel protocol, 251

field monitors
    using, 146
    using for blue-screen effects, components
    using on sets, 226
    See also monitors

fields
    in frames, 37
    in interlaced video, 38

file naming conventions, 273–274

file-based acquisition, explained, 49

file-based finishing workflow, 413

file-based masters
    color grading, 418
    creating mixes, 419–420
    DIY (do it yourself), 415
    final audio mix, 418–419
    preparing sequences, 415–418
    sync props, 418
    See also mastering

file-based media, 271–272

files
    moving between apps, 382
    naming, 236
    placing in folders, 235–236
    renaming in batches, 273
    See also large-sized files

fill light, three-point lighting, 123–124, 134

film
    color correcting for, 363
    measurement of, 439
    shooting video for, 140

film color, modifying for film look, 364

film diffusion, modifying for film look, 364

film festivals, preparing for, 414–415

film finishing process. *See* finishing process

film grain, modifying for film look, 364

film look
    achieving with video, 363–365
    basis of, 59

film math, 439

film noir classics, 122

film printing, 375, 438

film resolution, digital video, 39

film scheduling software, 31
film-based master, 439
film-like projects, making, 59
filmmaking
    big picture, 315
    emotion, 315
    rhythm and pacing, 315
    setups and payoffs, 315
    time compression and expansion, 315
filtered footage, compositing, 389
filters
    diffusion, 162
    neutral density, 161
    polarizing, 160
    UV, 160
Final Draft software, 21–22
finishing process
    35mm film prints, 437–439
    archiving projects, 441
    assembling audio and video, 435
    audio mixing, 433–434
    Blu-ray Discs, 426–431
    color grading, 434–435
    digital camera masters, 440
    digital video masters, 435–436
    DIY file-based masters, 415–420
    DVD discs, 426–431
    film festivals, 414–415
    high-end, 432–435
    mastering, 413–414
    reel changes, 432–433
    requirements, 412–414
    starting early, 412–413
    textless masters, 420–421
    video on demand, 422–426
    Web video, 422–426
    workflow, 413
firelight, lighting, 139
FireWire, 250
first assistant camera (AC), role of, 204
The Fisher King, 112
Fitzcarraldo, 112
fluorescent lights, 126

focal length
    comparing, 150
    considering, 175
    defined, 148
    lenses, 151
    multiplier, 147
focus
    adjusting viewfinder, 144
    controls, 76–77
    measuring, 219–220
    plane of, 145–146
    pulling, 220
    setting, 144–146
folders, placing files in, 235–236
foley, process of, 337
follow focus, 221
footage
    making monochrome, 362–363
    matching, 361–362
    See also media; video footage
Ford Copolla, Francis, 112
frame rates, modifying for film look, 364
FrameForge 3D Studio storyboarding app,
    103
frames, digital video, 36–37
framing. *See* composition
Friday Night Lights, season 1, 23
f-stops
    versus t-stops, 70
    using for aperture, 154

G

gaffer, role of, 205
gain boost feature, 156. *See also* low-light
    shooting
garbage mattes, using with keys, 394
gels, 129, 131
    CTB (color temperature blue), 131
    CTO (color temperature orange), 131
    neutral density, 131
GenArts software, 377
generators, battery-operated, 139

Gilliam, Terry, 112
Glidecams, 223
The Godfather, 122
golden hour, 137
The Great Train Robbery, 291
green screen, lighting for, 140–141
Griffith, D.W., 291

H

handheld mics, 183, 189
handheld shots, 171–172
hard cuts, 311
HD (high-definition) video, aspect ratio, 40
HD and SD footage, mixing, 398–400
HD format
    720, 35
    1080, 35
    describing, 41
    digital cinema, 35
    versus DV, 3–4
    frame rates, 37
    showing with DSLRs, 5
    transferring analog video to, 44
HD video, DSLR settings for, 214–215
HDCAM acquisition format, 57
HDMI (high-definition multimedia interface), 250
HDMI cables, using on sets, 226
HD-SDI and SDI, 250
HDV acquisition format, 49, 57
HDV camera versus Sony SDCAM, 46
Hearts of Darkness, 30, 112
Herzog, Werner, 112
high-definition multimedia interface (HDMI), 250
hi-res HD, warning about, 313
Hitchcock, Alfred, 93
HMI lights, 126–127
"holding" day, 30
horizontal resolution, digital video, 39
hue, defined, 346
hum, dealing with, 330, 335

I

i (interlaced scanning), 37
image enhancement effects, 265
image quality
    compression, 65
    improvements in, 3–4
    sensors, 62–65
    sharpening, 66–68
    tweaking, 68
    white balance, 68
    See also digital image quality
image stabilization
    digital, 81
    optical, 81–82
importing
    audio, 282–283
    still images, 283–284
    and transcoding media, 276–280
in-betweening, defined, 377
Incredible Adventures of Wallace and Gromit, 118
industrial projects, 9
insert edits, 257
interior lighting
    doing test shoot, 136
    household lights, 136
    mixing daylight with, 135
    power supply, 135
    See also exterior lighting; lighting
INTerior scene, indicating in script, 19
interlaced HD video, describing, 41
interlaced scanning (i), 37
intermediate acquisition format, 58
interpolation, defined, 377
IRE scale, using in color correction, 350, 352
iris, explained, 76

J

Jerry Maguire, 372
jibs, 223
JKL editing controls, 257
JPEG 2000 codecs, 54

Jurassic Park, 318
JVC GY-HM100 handheld camcorder, 73
JVC GY-HM790U, 76

K

°K (degrees Kelvin), 125, 159
key code Web site, 45
key grip, role of, 205
key light, three-point lighting, 122, 132
keyboard editing, 257
keyboards, including in editing
    workstations, 246
keyframes and interpolating, 377–378
keying tips, 394–395
keys
    compositing, 384–385
    mixing, 394
    using garbage mattes with, 394
Kubrick, Stanley, 115, 121, 174

L

large-sized files, transferring, 275. *See also*
    files
lavalier mics, 184, 189–190
Lawrence of Arabia, 41
L-cuts, 307
LED lights, 126–127
Lee, Spike, 109
lens filters
    diffusion, 162
    neutral density, 161
    polarizing, 160
    UV, 160
lens flares, 70
lenses
    accessories, 71
    aperture control, 70
    caring for, 150
    choosing, 216–218
    cinema, 71
    features, 70–71

f-stop rating, 70
    interchangeable, 71, 216–218
    manual focus, 70
    minimum objective distance, 70
    prime, 71, 147
    quality, 69–70
    zoom, 70–71, 147
light
    camera mount, 126
    color temperature, 125
    fluorescents, 126
    hard key, 129–130
    HMI, 126–127
    LED, 126–127
    measuring, 129
    neon, 126
    primary colors of, 47
    sodium, 126
    soft key, 129–130
    tungsten, 126
    wattage, 126
light kit for video, 128
light quality
    bounce cards, 129
    controlling, 129
    C-stands, 129
    diffusion, 131
    lighting gels, 129, 131
lighting
    for 360° shooting, 140
    actors, 132–135
    bad versus good, 355
    for blue and green screen, 140–141
    for darker skin tones, 135
    equipment checklist, 137–138
    film-style, 121–122
    low-light shooting, 139
    three-point, 122–124
    video, 138
    for video-to-film transfers, 140
    See also exterior lighting; interior lighting

lighting gels, 129, 131
  CTB (color temperature blue), 131
  CTO (color temperature orange), 131
  neutral density, 131
lighting plot, making, 129
lighting situations
  car interiors, 139
  day-for-night, 139
  firelight, 139
  illusional spaces, 139
lighting technology, improvements in, 6–7
lights
  battery operated, 139
  fire hazards, 133
  flickering, 407
  household, 136
  tungsten, 131
locations
  changing for shooting, 29
  scouting, 108–112
  See also shooting projects
lockable tracks, using in editing apps, 261
Lost in La Mancha, 30, 112
"lower third" title, using, 170
low-light shooting, 139. See also gain boost
  feature
Lumière brothers, 291
luminance, representing, 48, 350
luminance keys, compositing, 385–390

M

Magic Lantern, using with Canon cameras,
  215
main title, creating, 372–375
The Maltese Falcon, 122
Man with a Movie Camera, 291
master shot, storyboarding, 100
mastering, process of, 413–414. See also
  file-based masters; textless masters
match frame, using in editing apps, 260
matching
  action, 306
  emotion and tone, 308
  screen position, 307

Matewan, 111
matte boxes, 221
mattes, compositing, 396
MCU (medium close-up), storyboarding,
  100
media
  backing up originals, 273
  cataloguing software, 275–276
  creating naming systems, 273–274
  importing, 262–263, 276–280
  moving, 284–285
  multi-camera, 288
  organizing, 272–276
  renaming files, 273
  sorting after ingest, 285–286
  storing, 275
  transcoding, 276–280
  See also footage; tape-based media; video
    footage
Media Composer
  adding splices, 304
  dragging shots in Timeline, 301
  "Salsa Dancing" project, 295–304
  Track Selector, 300
medium close-up (MCU), storyboarding,
  100
medium shot (MS), storyboarding, 100
Meliès, Georges, 291
mic fishpole, operating, 191
microphone placement
  handheld, 189
  lavalier, 189–190
  multiple, 194
  shotgun, 191–194
  windscreens, 189
microphones, 328
  adjusting echo, 193
  attaching, 180
  balanced connectors, 186
  batteries, 194
  cardioid patterns, 180
  choosing position for, 192
  clip-on, 184
  condenser, 182–183
  connectors, 186–187

consulting cinematographers, 193
consulting directors, 193
coverage charts, 181
directional, 192
directional characteristics, 179–181
dynamic, 182
electret condenser, 183
function of, 182–183
handheld, 183
hanging, 194
headphones, 186
holding poles, 193
hypercardioid, 181
lavaliers, 184
managing set, 196
mixers, 185, 194
mounting, 192
mounting poles for, 192
omnidirectional, 180
on-camera, 178
polar chart, 182
positioning, 193
sensitivity of, 180
shotgun, 185
supercardioid, 180
unbalanced connectors, 186
unidirectional, 180–182
watching grips, 193
wireless, 187–188
missing elements, dealing with, 312
mixing, defined, 319
mixing boards, 328
MJPEG codecs, 54
monitors
    improvements in, 4
    including in editing workstations, 243–244
    See also field monitors
mono mix, creating, 418
mono sound, digital video, 42
monochrome footage, making, 362–363
motion effects, 265
    keyframes and interpolating, 377–378
    slow-mo and speed ramps, 379

motion graphics software
    Adobe After Effects, 376
    Apple Motion, 376
    BorisFX, 377
    DigiEffects, 377
    GenArts, 377
    Red Giant, 377
MP3 compressed audio format, 55
MPEG-1 codecs, 54
MPEG-2 codecs, 54
MPEG-4 codecs, 54–55
MPEG-IMX acquisition format, 57
MS (medium shot), storyboarding, 100
multi-cam editing, 259–260, 313–314
multi-cam shooting
    framing shots, 232
    lighting shots, 232
    matching cameras, 232
    positioning boom operators, 232
    synchronizing cameras, 231
    See also cameras
multi-camera media, preparing, 288
music
    DIY (do it yourself), 341
    editing, 338–339
    finding composers, 340–341
    libraries, 339
    licensing, 339–340
    and sound effects, 309–310
    using in features, 337–338
muzzle flashes, compositing, 387

N

Narc, 113
NAS (network-attached storage), 247–248
native support, explained, 57
negatives, printing from, 438
neon lights, 126
network editing, using in editing apps, 261
networked editing systems
    battery backup, 248
    cloud storage, 248

networked editing systems *(continued)*
NAS (network-attached storage),
247–248
render farms, 248
SANs (storage area networks), 247–248
neutral density lens filters, 161
non-linear systems, 261
correcting filters, 323
EQ controls, 323–324
level controls for tracks, 322–323
multiple tracks and playback, 322
scrubbing audio, 323
special effects filters, 323–324
sweetening filters, 323
See also editing systems
non-special special effects, compositing,
394. *See also* effects
North By Northwest, 18
NTSC monitor, colors displayed on, 353
NTSC video (analog), frame rate of, 45

O

offensive material, obscuring, 408–409
OIS (optical image stabilization), 81–82
OMF files, exporting, 268, 327
omnidirectional mics, 180
opening credits, 367
optical discs
limitations of, 431
video formats, 428
OS (over-the-shoulder), storyboarding, 100
overexposure, compensating for, 358–360.
See also exposure
overwrite edits, 257

P

p (progressive scanning), 37
PA (production assistant), role of, 204
pan, storyboarding, 101
Panasonic AG-AF100 HD camcorder, 69
panning and tilting, 170–171
Paranormal Activity, 45
pauses and pull-ups, 308–309

PCM audio formats, 55
pedestal, storyboarding, 101
pickups, planning for, 32
picture and sound, synchronizing, 286–288
pilots, 10
pitch reel, 10
pitches, 22
pixel shape, digital video, 40
pixels, digital video, 38
pixels and dropouts, getting rid of, 405
pocket cameras, 73
point of view (POV), storyboarding, 100
polarizing lens filters, 160
Porter, Edwin S., 291
POV (point of view), storyboarding, 100
power supplies, using on sets, 226
PowerProduction's storyboarding apps, 102
preproduction, scheduling, 29. *See also*
production schedule
prime lenses, 71, 147
producers, types of, 27
producing, 27
production assistant (P.A.), role of, 204
production boards, 30–31
production design, 112
art directing, 113
building sets, 113
DIY art direction, 114–115
goal of, 112
planning exercise, 117
set dressing and props, 114
production schedule, creating, 26–27.
See also **preproduction**
progressive scanning (p), 37, 79
project files, storing, 275
project management applications, 275
Project Runway, season 8, 25
projects
archiving, 441
corporate, 9
documentaries, 10
industrial, 9
scripted feature films, 10
short films, 9

television pilots, 10
video shorts for Web, 9
webisodes, 9
See editing projects; shooting projects
props and set dressing, 114
pull-ups and pauses, 308–309

Q

quantization, defined, 48

R

Rachel Getting Married, 121, 177
radio cuts, creating, 294
Raiders of the Lost Ark, 16–17
RAM (random access memory), including in editing workstation, 242
reaction shots, 305
Reality TV, 25
recordings versus mixes, 42. *See also* audio recording
Red, 112
red, green, blue (RGB). *See* RGB (red, green, blue)
Red Giant software, 377
RED One camera
figure, 6
price of, 4
use in feature films, 39
Red R3D acquisition format, 58
rehearsals
conducting, 203
staging table readings, 204
releases, getting on sets, 205
render farms, 248
resolution
640 × 480, 43
720 × 480, 43
film, 39
horizontal, 39
of SD video, 43
vertical, 38

resolution, 720 and 1080, 35–36
reverse, storyboarding, 100
RGB (red, green, blue), 47
RGB channels, 349
RGB color
filters, 354
sampling ratio of, 48
rhythm and pacing, 315
Richard III, 17, 28
ripple and roll editing, 258–259
rods, 221
"Roll sound," calling, 205
rolling shutter problems, fixing, 407–408
rough cut
adding shots, 299–301
adjusting shots, 301
auto backup, 304
auto save, 304
bringing in media, 296
building, 293–294
cleaning up audio, 302–304
collapsing video tracks, 301–302
cutaways, 309
foundation for cut, 299
master shot, 294
music, 309–310
overlapping audio, 309
project setup, 295
radio cuts, 294
refining, 309–310
style coverage, 294
transition to dialogue, 309–310
watching footage, 296–298
See also editing
RS-422 cable, 251

S

safe titles, 371
SAG (Screen Actor's Guild) agreement, 30
"Salsa Dancing" project, naming, 295
sampling, process of, 47–48

San Joaquin Valley Swiss Club, 292
SANs (storage area networks), 247–248
saturation, defined, 346
Sayles, John, 111
scan lines, digital video, 37–38
scenes
    adding visual symbolism to, 113
    continuing in scripts, 20
    transitions between, 311–312
scheduling, 26–27
    importance of, 30
    for unscripted projects, 32
Screen Actor's Guild (SAG) agreement, 30
screen position, matching, 307
screenplays. *See* scripts
screenwriting, 11
    adding goals to stories, 14
    alternative structures, 18
    audience, 26
    cutting scripts, 17
    deciding on stories, 14
    developing characters, 18
    finding stories, 14
    Reality TV, 25
    "show, don't tell," 17
    software, 21
    structure, 14–15
    teases, 23
    for television, 23
    three-act structure, 15–16, 18
    treatments, 15
    for "unscripted," 24–25
    writing silents, 17
    writing visually, 16–17
    See also stories; writing
scripted feature films, 10
scripted projects, script supervising,
    208–209
scripts
    A/V format, 20
    breakdown sheet, 27–28
    changing locations, 29
    continuing scenes in, 20

    conventions, 20
    creating sides for talent, 21
    cutting, 17
    determining length and pacing of, 18–19
    formatting, 18–20
    multi-column formats, 20
    sample, 20
    shooting by page, 29
    shooting order, 29
    sluglines, 19
    See also shooting script; unscripted proj-
      ects
SD and HD footage, mixing, 398–400
SD cards, using, 86, 235
SD video, resolution of, 43
SDI (Serial Digital Interface) and HD-SDI,
    250
SDI cables, using on sets, 226
second AC, role of, 205
sensors, size of, 64
set dressing and props, 114
sets
    building, 113
    continuity, 208
    documentary field notes, 209
    getting releases on, 205
    managing, 204–205
    script supervising, 208–209
    upgrading, 114–115
    viewing video on, 224–227
setups and payoffs, 315
sharpening, applying, 66–68
The Shining, 174
shooting
    low-light, 139
    multi-cam, 230–233
    planning by day, 29
    protocol of, 205
    using production boards, 30–31
    video for film, 140
shooting checklist
    depth of field, 174
    exposure, 175

focal length, 175

shutter speed, 175

white balance, 175

shooting order, choosing for scripts, 29

shooting projects

advice about, 58–59

budget, 117

legal legwork, 106–107

production design, 117

shot lists, 117

storyboarding, 117

video for film, 140

See also locations; projects

shooting script

changing, 202

creating shot list from, 207

preparing for, 201

updating, 202

See also scripts

short films, 9

shot lists, 104–107

making, 207

planning exercise, 117

See also establishing shots

shotgun mics, 185, 191

shotmakers, 223

"show, don't tell," 17

shutter

"electronic," 154

rolling, 407–408

shutter speed, 77–78

double-checking, 175

fast versus slow, 154, 158

sides, creating for talent, 21

silence, power of, 340

SketchUp Film & Stage storyboarding app, 103

slate board, using, 230

sliders, 223

slip-and-slide editing, 259

slow reveal, storyboarding, 101

slow-mo and speed ramps, 379

sluglines, including in scripts, 19

Slumdog Millionaire, 40

smart phone, shooting with, 58

SMTPE timecode, 45

The Social Network, 75

sodium lights, 126

software

for producers, 27

screenwriting, 21

Sony SDCAM versus HDV camera, 46

Sony Vegas editing program, 268

sound

dialogue, 177

getting right, 194–195

reference tone, 196

testing, 195–196

sound and picture, synchronizing, 286–288

sound editing, 317–318

apps, 325–327

audio, 330

audio levels metering, 320–321

changes in tone, 329

editing app, 321–324

EQ (equalizing), 333–335

filters for fixing problems, 335

fixing in mix, 342

hardware, 328

mixing, 319

moving audio, 327

music, 317–318, 337–342

noise, 329

setting up, 318–319

sound effects, 336–337

temp mixes, 319

unintelligible dialogue, 328

video edits, 330

vocal problems, 330

See also audio recording; dialogue editing; editing

sound effects

blending in, 336

considering, 336

improving, 336

and music, 309–310

sources, 337

speakers, considering, 249, 328
special effects
    3D, 265
    compositing, 265
    image enhancement, 265
    motion, 265
    transitions, 264
    workflow, 380–382
    See also non-special special effects
splices, adding, 304
split edits, 307
splitters, using on sets, 226
stage line, crossing, 169
steadicams, 223
stereo sound, digital video, 41
still cameras, 211–212. *See also* cameras
still images
    editing applications, 275
    importing, 283–284
    integrating with video, 379–380
storage, including in editing workstation,
    242–243
storage area networks (SANs), 247–248
storage drives, improvements in, 4
stories
    adding goals to, 14
    beginning/middle/end structure, 15–16
    deciding on, 14
    finding, 14
    structure, 14–15
    See also screenwriting; writing
storyboarding, 93–95
    2-shot, 100
    camera angles, 97–101
    computer-generated, 101–103
    crane, 101
    CU (close-up), 100
    dolly, 100
    dolly counter zoom, 101
    ECU (extreme close-up), 100
    example, 106
    FrameForge 3D Studio, 103
    master shot, 100

    MCU (medium close-up), 100
    MS (medium shot), 100
    OS (over-the-shoulder), 100
    pan, 101
    pedestal, 101
    planning exercise, 117
    POV (point of view), 100
    PowerProduction apps, 102
    reverse, 100
    shots and coverage, 93–97
    SketchUp Film & Stage, 103
    slow reveal, 101
    tilt, 101
    tracking, 100
    WS (wide shot), 100
    zoom, 101
surround sound, digital video, 42
surround sound interface, 249
Survivor, 232
sync props, using with file-based masters,
    418
sync sound, invention of, 291
synchronizing software, 275

T

table readings, staging, 204
talent
    creating sides for, 21
    lighting, 132–135
    respecting, 205–207
tape, shooting on, 6
tape-based media
    capturing, 282
    logging, 280–281
    See also media
tapeless
    audio media workflow, 237
    editing workflow, 6
    file naming conventions, 236
    going, 233–234
    media cards, 234–235
    on-set media workstations, 234

organizing media on sets, 235–236

SD cards, 235

workflow, 234–235, 237

Tarkovsky, Andrei, 315

teases, writing, 23

telephoto lenses, versus zoom lenses, 148

teleplays, scripted, 23

television

black-and-white versus color, 45

broadcast network, 36

pilots, 10

writing for, 23

textless masters, 420–421. *See also* mastering

three-act structure, 15–16, 18, 293

three-point lighting

back light, 123–124, 133

fill light, 123–124, 134

key light, 122, 124, 132

Thunderbolt I/O protocol, 251

tilt, storyboarding, 101

tilting and panning, 170–171

time, compressing and expanding, 315

Time Bandits, 112

timecode

drop frame, 45

time-of-day, 45–46

time-of-day timecode, 45

Tiny Furniture, 75

title card, defined, 367

title crawl, defined, 368

title roll, defined, 368

titles

coloring, 370

creating, 266

end credits, 367

installing fonts, 368

lower-third, 170, 368

main, 367, 372–375

making for films, 375

motion graphics software, 376–377

opening credits, 367

ordering, 369

pad, 368

placing, 370

safe, 371

supers, 368

textless version, 368

typeface and size, 368

watching, 372

Tomorrow Never Dies, 95–97

tone and emotion, 308, 315

tracking, storyboarding, 100

tracking shots, 171

tracks, digital video, 36

trade shows, attending, 7

Trainspotting, 112

transcoding, 55–57

transcoding and importing, 276–280

transition effects, 264

treatment, writing, 15

trimming interface, 258

tripods, features of, 89

t-stops versus f-stops, 70

tungsten lights, 126, 131

TV

black-and-white versus color, 45

broadcast network, 36

pilots, 10

writing for, 23

TV framing, 169

TV projects, making in U.S., 59

tweening, defined, 377

U

underexposure, occurrence of, 152. *See also* exposure

unidirectional mics, 180–182

unscripted projects, scheduling for, 32. *See also* scripts

UV lens filters, 160

V

VC-3 based codecs, 54

vectorscopes, using for color correction, 350–352

vertical resolution, digital video, 38

Vertigo, 93

Vertov, Dziga, 291

video

analog versus DV, 246

brightening, 355–358

color opposites, 353

compressed versus uncompressed, 49

integrating with still images, 379–380

making look like film, 363–365

primary colors for, 353

video cameras. *See* cameras

video edits, reinforcing with audio, 330

video footage, high-quality, 437. *See also* footage

video for film, shooting, 140

video lighting, 138

video streams, capture of, 48

video viewing on sets, 224–225

camera-top monitors, 225

enhanced viewfinders, 225

field monitors, 226

HDMI cables, 226

power supplies, 226

SDI cables, 226

splitters, 226

video village, setting up, 224–225

video-on-demand. *See* Web video and video-on-demand

videotape interface, including in editing workstation, 244–245

viewfinders

adjusting, 144

enhanced, 225

eyepiece, 82

flip-out LCD, 82

vocal problems, correcting, 330

voice recordings, non-dialogue, 332

W

wattage, considering for lights, 126

waveforms, using for color correction, 350–351, 356

Web

shooting for, 173

video shorts for, 9

Web sites

analog video, 44, 246

aspect ratios, 40

budgeting articles, screenwriting

color correction tutorial, 361

compositing tutorial, 361

DV Primer, 246

feature film structure, 16

key code, 45

pitches, 22

pixel aspect ratios, 40

postproduction effects tutorial, 361

Richard III, 17, 28

scheduling articles, 11

timecode, 45

titling tutorials, 376

writing silents, 17

Web video and video-on-demand

compression, 423–424

data rate, 425

downloading, 422–423

keyframe interval, 425–426

streaming, 422–423

Web-based design tools, 275

webisodes, 9

Welles, Orson, 291

Weston, Judith, 203

white balance, 68, 158–159

in °K, 159

alternative, 158–159

aspect ratios, 162

considering, 175

correcting, 360–361

manual, 159

process of, 159

widescreen images, 80
windscreens, using with mics, 189
wipes, 311
wire removal, 406
Workers Leaving the Lumière Factory, 291
wrappers, container files as, 50
Writers Guild, 25
writing
    for corporate projects, 25–26
    exercises, 17–18
    silents, 17
    teases, writing, 23
    warm-up, 17
    See also screenwriting; stories
WS (wide shot), storyboarding, 100

X

XDCAM HD acquisition format, 57

Z

zebra stripes, 82–83
Zeiss Compact Prime cinema lens, 72
zoom lenses, 71
    controlling, 151
    features of, 147
    focusing, 145
    versus telephoto lenses, 148
    using, 147–151
zooms
    and dolly shots, 171
    storyboarding, 101